Lands of New World Neighbors

HANS CHRISTIAN ADAMSON

LANDS OF

NEW WORLD

NEIGHBORS

New York *Whittlesey House* London
McGRAW-HILL BOOK COMPANY, INC.

LANDS OF NEW WORLD NEIGHBORS

Copyright, 1941, *by the* McGraw-Hill Book Company, Inc.

PUBLISHED BY WHITTLESEY HOUSE
A division of the McGraw-Hill Book Company, Inc.

Printed in the United States of America by The Maple Press Co., York, Pa.

To

HERBERT JOHANSEN

whose fine Italian hand, like those of
Columbus, Cabot, and Vespucci, had much
to do in creating this book

and to

ALMA COOK and JEAN WIEDEMER
who typed and toiled

Introduction

❦

IN *Lands of New World Neighbors*, Hans Christian Adamson
has brought between the covers of one book the exciting,
instructive and inspiring adventure story created by the
conquerors, explorers, and pioneers who carved a New World
out of the wilderness of the Americas.

First of all, *Lands of New World Neighbors* is a factual book
of American history and geography, but in his treatment of
this theme, Hans Adamson has made the facts read like
thrilling fiction. The book is a review of the men and events
that made America from the very beginning of New World
history. It is a record of the hopes and fears, failures and
accomplishments of men, who lived dangerously and often
died with their eyes fixed on new horizons.

If you have a thirst for knowledge, a zest for travel, a hunger
to go armchair adventuring for new horizons, then *Lands of
New World Neighbors* is your book. I can think of no one, young
or old, whatever his interest or outlook, who can read this
glorious tale of human adventure without having the blood
course faster in his veins and feeling a deeper appreciation of
the kinship and unity of purpose of all Americans in all the
Americas.

I can wholeheartedly promise the reader of *Lands of New
World Neighbors* that when he has finished the last page of this
book, he will be the richer for having relived within its pages
the stirring and heroic drama of the making of the lands of
New World neighbors.

ROY CHAPMAN ANDREWS.

Contents

꧁꧂

ix

Lands of New World Neighbors

CHAPTER 1

Dawn of a New World

Highlights of the Americas

Discovered: From 10,000 to 15,000 years ago by Asiatics reaching
North America by way of Bering Strait.

Population: 268,137,000 including Hawaii, the West Indies, and
Greenland.

Area: 17,000,000 square miles, including Hawaii, the West Indies,
and Greenland.

Languages: English, Spanish, Portuguese, French, Dutch, and
various native dialects.

Countries: Twenty-one independent republics, one self-governing
dominion, twenty territories and colonies, and the Canal
Zone.

NO one knows when man first came to America. But it
has been fairly well established that he found foothold
in the Western Hemisphere as an immigrant and not
through evolution. Scientists base this belief on the fact that, so
far, no trace has been found anywhere in the New World of
apes or similar types of animals that are regarded as being the
ancestor of Homo sapiens—man.

It is generally believed that the first settlers in America
were slant-eyed Mongols who came here by way of Siberia,
Bering Strait, and Alaska. These early immigrants have left
no clues of their coming and going. The oldest human skeleton
found to date in this part of the world is probably not more
than five thousand years old. The oldest stone tools found in

the Americas may not be more than fifteen thousand years old.

Having established that little is known concerning the arrival of man in America the next question is: How did he get here? The answer to that is twofold. He may have come by foot across a land bridge which, in ancient times, connected eastern Siberia with western Alaska over the 50-mile gap of shallow island-dotted water which we today call Bering Strait. As well as walking across this bridge, soon after the last glacial period, man may have come to North America on the choppy waters of the Bering Strait in tiny but seaworthy canoes.

These Asiatic wanderers did not come to America in great numbers at any one time. Nor did they come in steady waves, but in slow and broken dribbles over the centuries. They probably arrived in family groups or small tribal units. Little by little, this broken stream of humanity traveled southward from Alaska and branched out. In time these people made the long journey from Canada to Chile, from the Pacific Ocean to the Atlantic shores.

The face and form and way of life of the early American are hidden by the mist of time. We know that he was a hunter rather than a tiller of the soil. As a matter of fact, it was not until rather recent times, as history is measured, that his descendants, the American Indians, learned how to grow foods. It is generally believed that their first cultivated food was Indian corn. This discovery, the knowledge that seeds planted in the soil by man would grow and provide a rich harvest, was the first great American invention. It revolutionized the Indian way of living. Where families and tribes had been kept continually on the move to hunt, they could now settle down, have permanent homes, and cultivate fields.

As we look down the long trail of human wandering and progress in the Americas, we see a wide variety of customs and cultures branch out from the main trunk line of migrating traffic. We see different tribes and different types of people develop, bloom, and fade. We see the New World become populated from the barren fringe of the Arctic Ocean to the jungle wilderness of the tropics; from the lofty plateaus on the crest of the Andes Mountains to the wind-swept solitudes above Cape Horn near the tip of South America.

We see, although not at the same time, the migrants of Mongolia transformed into different types of American Indians. The Woodland Indians, the Plains Indians, the Cliff Dwellers, and other Indian tribes develop in North America. In Mexico and Central America the empires of the Mayas, Toltecs, and Aztecs rise, dominate, and crumble. In South America, the Incas hold sway from Ecuador to Chile. The Chibchas rule the highlands in the interior of Colombia. In brief, all along the 7,500-mile stretch from the top to the bottom of America, from the core of the continent to the islands off its shores, we see man establish himself. The languages, customs, and the cultural progress of these Indians are widely different.

In trying to trace the times and travels of man in North America, scientists have dug into the graves of ancient Americans and probed into the refuse heaps they left behind them. Through human bones, arrow and spear points, pottery, and other implements, scientists have tried to reconstruct the early calendar of man in America. Up to now, the progress in that direction has been slow and uncertain.

Among the most interesting monuments or milestones along the road marched by man in the misty past are the mounds built in the Ohio and Mississippi Valleys by a people that vanished long ago. These mound builders constructed tens of thousands of man-made molehills in different shapes and sizes. Some were large and stretched across the ground like snakes, others were small and shapeless hummocks. Many of these mounds were burial places.

Better known to the general public than the Mound Builders

are the ancient Cliff Dwellers of the Southwest. These people built their strange community dwellings in caves in the steep sides of cliffs in the deep canyons in the desert country of southern Colorado, southern Utah, New Mexico, and Arizona. These ancient homes were usually built of flat pieces of sandstone neatly fitted and held together by mortar. The Cliff Dwellers got up to and down from their homes by means of ladders or handholds and toe holds in the sides of the cliffs. The Cliff Dwellers lived as they did mainly to escape their enemies. To protect themselves and their stores of food, they built their fortress homes high up in the rock of steep canyon walls. The caves in which they made their homes ranged from small caves that held only a dozen rooms or so, to large caves like the famous Cliff Palace Cave. This cave was about 425 feet long, 80 feet wide, and 80 feet high. It contained more than a hundred rooms and must have housed about 500 persons. Not all the ancient people lived in caves in the cliffs. Some of them built their homes on the table tops of low, flat mountains or mesas near streams or rivers. They were good engineers as well as excellent farmers. They had, for one thing, learned the art of irrigation.

Explorers who recently investigated the ruins at Los Muertos near Tempe, Arizona, found a canal that was 9 miles long. It ran from the Salt River to Los Muertos. Not only that, but this canal had enough side branches to irrigate about 200,000 acres of land. Some of those old canals have been cleaned out and are being used for irrigation purposes once more.

No one knows for sure how long ago these Cliff Dwellers lived. Their immediate predecessors were basketmakers who lived in caves some two thousand years ago, and it is believed they took to the cliffs about a thousand years later. But what happened to them? Chances are that most of them moved southward to the localities now occupied by the Pueblo Indians, their descendants.

Today there are only about 12,000 to 15,000 Pueblo Indians left. They are concentrated in some twenty-eight apartment villages. These Pueblos have virtually the same type of existence as that of their forefathers. Most of them live in New Mexico, although there are nine Hopi villages in Arizona.

The Pueblo Indians were not only among the first apartment dwellers in this country, but they also led in the recognition of women's rights. The woman was the senior partner in the household. She was the owner of the house. She built it and furnished it with the utensils of daily use. The man of the house was a mere provider. His wife had the right to send him back to his mother, bag and baggage, when she got tired of him. The woman's duties were purely domestic. The men did all the work in the field. But that does not mean that the women were idle. There could be no idle hands in a civilization that had to fight as hard for survival as these people did. Their culture developed despite the terrific handicaps of a hostile environment. The Pueblos grew corn and beans and other kinds of crops. They were skillful craftsmen, for they made beautiful pottery and baskets, wove excellent cloth for garments, and made beads of turquoise.

One of the largest North American families was the Woodland Indians, all members of the great Algonquian family. They made their homes in the great forests that stretched down the Atlantic coast from the Saint Lawrence to the Chesapeake, from Maine overland to the Mississippi. The Woodland Indians were hunters and fishermen. Deer was their main source of food. They were masters of woodcraft and could move through the forests as silently as shadows. Nearly all the Algonquins lived in more or less permanent villages, and their bark-covered houses were often surrounded by gardens where they grew various kinds of vegetables such as corn, squash, and beans.

Of all the Woodland Indians, the Iroquois tribe was not only the most powerful but also the most interesting. Owing to the fact that their domiciles usually consisted of long spacious buildings, these red men of northeastern America were known as the People of the Long Houses. The Iroquois were intelligent and industrious and they had made quite a place for themselves on America's map before the whites came. About five hundred years ago they set up the Union of the People of the Long Houses, ruled by a council of fifty sachems.

As among the Pueblos, the woman was the real head of the Iroquois household. She owned all the property, and if she died, her children belonged to her clan and the widower went back to his mother's family. Even the bloodthirstiest Iroquois warrior dared not go on the warpath unless his wife gave her permission.

The tribes that formed the Union of the People of the Long Houses lived mainly in New York, between the Hudson River and Lake Erie. They were the Mohawks, Onondagas, Oneidas, Cayugas, and Senecas. These Iroquois tribes were everlastingly on the warpath until they were united under the wise and powerful leadership of Hiawatha. He directed the great native intelligence of his people toward peace instead of battle. Many people believe that Hiawatha is just a character in Longfellow's famous poem. As a matter of fact, he was the real leader of the People of the Long Houses.

Another great group of North American red men were the Indians of the Plains. For the major part they were nomads and hunters. The now-extinct herds of American bison were the staff of life of these people of the prairies. Their territory was the grazing lands of the vast buffalo herds which, in those days, moved across the green grasslands of the plains like enormous floating islands. The range of the bison was from the Illinois River to the Rockies; from Lake Winnipeg to Texas. By means of the bison, the Indians of the Plains met all their needs. From its beef they got food, from its skin they made garments for their bodies and coverings for their tents.

From its tendons they got strings for their bows. Some of the Plains Indians had permanent villages and cultivated fields, but most of them followed the buffalo.

Most of us associate the horse with the Indian of the Plains. But until the Spaniards arrived, there were no horses in America. As a matter of fact, the coming of the horse to North America with Spanish expeditions such as those of Narváez, de Soto, and Coronado, completely changed the life of the Plains Indians. Prior to that, they had followed the buffalo on foot. Before the horse, their beasts of burden were dogs that carried a strange assortment of loads ranging from babies to tent poles.

For a man on foot, armed with only spear or bow and arrow, to kill a bison, was a major accomplishment. It took craft as well as courage. To get close to the herds, the Indians would often try to disguise themselves by crawling up to the herds under the skins of buffalo, wolves, or coyotes.

The Plains Indians spoke in many different tongues, but they had two common means of communication. One was the sign language, the other consisted of a series of smoke signals.

Aside from the tribes already mentioned, there were the Indians to the south, from Florida along the Gulf of Mexico. These were mainly fishermen and tillers of the soil. The tribes along the California coast, later known as the Mission Indians, were unimportant and had a low culture. The Indians along the northwest Pacific coast were principally fishermen, seal and whale hunters. These Indians were master woodcraftsmen. They invented the unique totem pole which is at once a family record and a coat of arms. Totem poles usually stood in front of the large well-built wooden houses that were the homes of these people.

Lastly, there were the Eskimos, hunters of polar bears and seals, as well as great fishermen. When they traveled on land many of them used sleds drawn by dogs. On the water, they had kayaks, small skin-covered boats. In the summer, the

Eskimos lived in tents made of skin. In the winter, they piled snow around their skin tents or built igloos out of blocks of ice.

All the Indians and Eskimos of North America lived the primitive lives of Stone Age people. They had no beasts of burden, except the dog, and they knew little about the value and use of metals. Nevertheless, they had a decided and distinctive culture. Also, they had a highly developed society wherein a strong tribal spirit extended from small family groups or clans up to large confederations.

The Indians who lived in the Americas knew nothing beyond the world they lived in. They did not know that, to the east, beyond the horizon of the morning light, there were countries inhabited by people that were hungry for expansion and thirsting for conquest. To get the picture of that situation, we must go to Europe as it was in the middle of the fifteenth century when Spain and Portugal cast envious eyes on the trade monopoly in Oriental luxuries enjoyed by the rich Italian merchant cities of Venice, Genoa, and Florence. This wealth came to the warehouses of the Italian merchants over the great caravan routes through the deserts from the fabulous East. There were many items in the Oriental trade, but the most valued of all was spice.

Spices are taken for granted today. On every kitchen shelf, pepper holds a humble and ordinary place. But in the days of Columbus, pepper was the king of spices. Pepper was worth its weight in gold, (1) because of the great demand for it as a food flavoring and as a preservative, and (2) because it was scarce. The reason for its scarcity was that in the fifteenth century the Turks had gained the upper hand over the trade routes through Asia Minor. Through their control of the trade routes, the Turks imposed high taxes on caravan goods which, in turn, created high prices.

When the price of pepper and other spices went so high that only the rich could afford them, merchants and navigators began to wonder if some new route could not be found to the Orient; a route free from grafting Turks, ruthless bandits, and the deadly dangers of the deserts—an all-water route.

One of the prime leaders in this search for a short and safe route to the Indies was Prince Henry the Navigator, of Portugal. He earned that title because he created the first maritime research bureau ever established. To his great stone tower on the Atlantic shores of Portugal, he called all the famous pilots and navigators of his day. He summoned geographers, astronomers, and map makers. With their combined knowledge, he set out to reconstruct the map of the world as it was then known. His idea was to find a waterway to the Indies— a waterway around the southern tip of Africa. When Prince Henry died in 1463, about one-fourth of the west coast of Africa had been explored by navigators sailing under the flag of Portugal.

While the Portuguese were probing southward along the African coast looking for an eastward passage to the Indies, a young Italian startled the learned men of his day by boldly claiming that the way to the Indies did not lie to the east around Africa, but to the west across the Atlantic. This young man was Christopher Columbus.

When, where, and how Columbus got this idea, no one knows for certain, but when he settled in Portugal in 1477 he was thoroughly convinced that his plan was practical. Although Columbus was only twenty-five years old at that time, he was a thoroughly trained and experienced navigator. If Prince Henry the Navigator had still been alive, he would no doubt have given this eager young man an opportunity to prove his theory. Unfortunately for Columbus, and for Portugal, King John II of Portugal refused to finance Columbus in a transatlantic voyage.

It may seem strange that Portugal, with its great maritime ambitions, should have ignored Columbus so completely. But there are several good reasons: (1) Portugal was definitely committed to the idea of finding an eastward passage to the Indies around Africa; (2) superstition and ignorance had given the Atlantic Ocean, then called the Sea of Darkness, an evil reputation; (3) the prevailing idea was that the earth was flat. In line with this, it was believed that anyone who sailed westward on the Atlantic would sail over the rim of the earth into space and be forever lost.

Another factor that worked against Columbus was that outside the Mediterranean nearly all ships clung closely to the coasts. In fact, it took exceptionally bold sailors to strike across the open sea to the Azores, Madeira, and the Canary Islands.

After many years in Portugal, Columbus realized that he was wasting his time trying to get Portuguese support. He went to Spain where, year after year, he tried to get King Ferdinand and Queen Isabella to finance him. But they were too busy with their wars against the Moors, wars that had drained the Spanish treasury close to the bottom. Then, too, Columbus was looked upon as a visionary dreamer.

Columbus appeared twice before the Spanish court. His first appearance was in 1486, when his project was referred to a royal commission. Four years later, this commission reported that the plan was impractical. On learning this, Columbus decided to leave for France. When he reached the seaport of Palos, he visited the Monastery of La Rabida. The prior, Father Juan Pérez, had been confessor to Queen Isabella and he still had great influence with the queen. Father Pérez was so impressed by the story Columbus told that he sent word to the queen, asking her to give Columbus another audience. This request was granted in the winter of 1491. Again Columbus presented his case before the court; again he was put off.

One of the great turning points in human affairs happened on a blustery January day in the year 1492. A tall thin man, astride a small but sturdy mule, was riding over the narrow and muddy highway that ran westward from Santa Fe to the coast through southern Spain. He was on his way to the Port of Palos. There he hoped to find a ship that would take him to France.

When he reached the timeworn Bridge of Pines, the solitary traveler stopped. He swung his feet to the ground to give his mule a rest and drew the animal close to the low stone wall that lined the bridge, for traffic was heavy. The road was crowded with soldiers and nobles. The soldiers plodded their weary way on foot through ankle-deep mud. The nobles rode on horseback or in stately carriages. All were coming home from the wars! Happy! Victorious! Under the leadership of King Ferdinand and Queen Isabella, the Spaniards had at long last defeated their archenemies, the Moors.

The tall man on the bridge gazed moodily into the cold, dark waters that flowed swiftly beneath him. He was about forty years old, but stooping shoulders and deep lines in his face made him look older than his years. His face was long and narrow. His brow was broad. His nose was sharp and straight. His long unkempt hair was reddish, streaked with gray. Under bushy brows were deep-set blue-gray eyes.

As he stood on the Bridge of Pines lost in thought, a royal messenger, dressed in the brilliant uniform of the court, galloped down the road. He spurred his horse through the slowly moving traffic and kept a sharp eye on everyone he passed. When he saw the tall man leaning over the edge of the bridge, the messenger reined his horse to a swift halt, and cried out: "Christopher Columbus! I have an order from the court! The King and Queen demand that you return to Santa Fe."

"I am not taking orders from anyone in Spain," replied Columbus as he turned to look at the messenger. "Tell King Ferdinand and Queen Isabella that I am tired of pleading. Weary of delays. I am going to the King of France. I believe he will give me money for an expedition westward to the Indies."

Saying this, Columbus made ready to swing astride his mule. But the rider took the reins and held him back.

"Wait. Wait a bit, Columbus," urged the messenger. "Talks and delays are over. Their Majesties will give you ships and men. They will make you Grand Admiral of Spain; make you viceroy of the lands you discover, and give you all the things you have asked for your expedition."

Columbus stared silently into the eyes of the messenger. Then he said: "Is it really true what you say?"

"Yes," answered the court messenger.

"Very well," replied Columbus after another pause. "I will return to Santa Fe."

As Columbus spoke, the stoop went out of his shoulders, his head lifted proud and high. In his eyes flashed the fire of renewed hope. He laughed softly as he turned his mule around and headed the animal along the road that eventually was to lead him on one of the greatest adventures of discovery in all history and one of the most tragic.

During the spring and summer of 1492, Columbus prepared for his great voyage in the port of Palos. Here lived Martín and Vicente Pinzón, two rich shipowners with a zest for adventure. They helped Columbus obtain his three ships, the *Santa Maria*, the *Pinta*, and the *Niña*. The Pinzóns also helped gather a crew of eighty-eight men. It has been said that most of them were thugs and ruffians who feared the hangman's noose more than the dangers of the Sea of Darkness. Other historians say, however, that no criminals sailed with Columbus as he lifted anchor on August 3, 1492, and began his first voyage.

As the three small ships plowed westward, the wind blew from the east day after day. This gave the sailors cause for alarm. For, they argued, if the wind always blew from the east on this unknown ocean, how could they ever sail back to Spain?

The peculiar behavior of the needle in the compass came

close to starting a mutiny aboard the *Santa Maria* on the night of September 13. When the stars came out, the helmsman discovered that the magnetic needle of the compass no longer pointed toward the North Star, but had swung 5 degrees to the west. Thinking quickly, Columbus quieted the fears of his crew by explaining that the real North Pole is fixed, but not the North Star. On the part of Columbus, this was a piece of very straight and quick thinking. He did not know, as we know today, that the compass needle points neither to the North Star nor to the north geographic pole, but to the north magnetic pole. These two poles are about 1,200 miles apart.

About 2 o'clock in the morning of October 12, one of the lookouts shouted: "Light ahead!" No one knew what the light was, but Columbus concluded that where there was light there must be land and living men. Everyone cheered. Cannons boomed in joyous salutes. All offered prayers of thanksgiving. A few hours later, dawn disclosed a cluster of small islands rimmed with white sand and crowned with verdant palm trees. Columbus solemnly told his crew that these were the long-sought Spice Islands along the coast of Asia.

Shortly after sunup Columbus landed on the nearest island and took possession in the name of Spain; he named the island San Salvador after the Holy Savior. The natives called it Guanahani. Today this small island in the Bahamas is called Watling Island.

Thus in 70 days, Columbus had completed the first transatlantic voyage and begun the series of discoveries that led to the mapping and making of the New World.

On Watling Island Columbus found no spices, only a few natives, shy but friendly. Nothing daunted, Columbus sailed on looking for the porcelain towers of China, the golden roofs of Japan, and the fragrant Spice Islands of the Indies. All in vain. Columbus discovered a world of blue water and green islands—hundreds of islands ranging from mountainous land masses such as Cuba and Haiti to tiny specks of coral reefs or rock. On these islands Columbus found men, and because he thought he had reached the Indies, he called these red-skinned people Indians.

About five weeks after their first landfall, Columbus and Martín Pinzón, who commanded the *Pinta*, quarreled about the course. The result was that Pinzón sailed off in a huff, leaving Columbus with only two ships, the *Santa Maria* and the tiny *Niña*. On Christmas Eve, 1492, along the coast of Hispaniola (Haiti) Columbus lost his flagship, the *Santa Maria*. The vessel was wrecked when one of the ship's boys, a lad of twelve, ran it aground shortly before midnight. Unable to get the ship afloat, Columbus with the help of Guacanagari, chief of a tribe of friendly Indians, got the *Santa Maria's* cargo ashore. With the timbers of the wrecked ship, Columbus built a fort and called it La Navidad. This was the first white settlement in the New World.

Columbus had not planned to establish a colony, but the loss of the *Pinta* and the wreck of the *Santa Maria* left him no other choice. A Spanish noble, Diego de Arana, was placed in charge of the little colony which numbered only thirty-eight men. After commanding the colonists to remain on good terms with Guacanagari, Columbus set sail for Spain. He reached Palos on March 15, after weathering severe storms. Close behind him came the *Pinta*, as Martín Pinzón had rejoined Columbus before he left the Americas.

All the honors worthy of a conqueror were heaped upon the great discoverer on his return to Spain. He sat side by side with the king and queen. In streets and squares, wherever he went, shouting, cheering crowds acclaimed Columbus. As for that next voyage he was talking about! Admiral Columbus could have what he wanted. He wanted seventeen ships. He got them. Columbus wanted 1,500 soldiers and colonists. He got them. Columbus wanted grass and plants and seeds for the new colony, horses, cows, hogs, plows, spades, and axes. He got them. He wanted titles and honors and guarantees of wealth for himself and his sons. He got them.

Spain was aglow with the fever of the Indies. True, Columbus had not brought back silks or spices. But give him time. The all-water route to the Asiatic mainland behind the islands he had discovered would surely be found on the next voyage.

The only thing wrong with this reasoning was that Columbus had not reached the Orient as he believed. No one disputed him because in those days navigators had no means of knowing longitude. They had a fairly good idea as to latitude. They could establish their north or south position by means of astrolabe and quadrant. Knowing latitude is very important in sailing north or south. To know his east or west position, a navigator must be able to determine longitude. That determination is based upon the keeping of accurate time. In the days of Columbus there were no chronometers or accurate timepieces. It is strange to realize that Christopher Columbus, the greatest of all discoverers, did not know where he was going when he sailed; that he did not know where he was when he reached the West Indies; and that, when he returned to Spain, he did not know where he had been. Columbus thought he had reached islands off the coast of Asia; he was wrong by a matter of some 10,000 miles. One reason for this mistake was that Columbus thought the earth was smaller than it is.

On a bright September day in 1493, Columbus, with a fleet of seventeen ships and 1,500 sailors, soldiers, and colonizers, including many adventurers of noble birth, again left Spain for the Indies. His first landfall was the island of Dominica. Then came Guadaloupe. Sailing northward, Columbus put new islands on the map every day, including Puerto Rico. But these islands were not the Spice Islands. As a matter of fact, the most important discovery Columbus made on this part of his second voyage was a disturbing one. He learned about the warlike and bloodthirsty Carib Indians who terrorized the peaceful natives of the islands Columbus discovered on his first visit.

An even more unpleasant surprise awaited Columbus when he reached Haiti and found Fort La Navidad in ruins. Not a single Spaniard was left alive. Chief Guacanagari told Columbus that the colonists had brought this fate upon themselves by robbing, torturing, and enslaving the Indians in their insane greed for gold.

A lesser man might have been discouraged by the destruction of his first colony. But Columbus, for all his ability to dream, was a realist at heart. He established a new settlement and named it Isabella. Here he had the 1,500 colonists build crude houses. Here he unloaded the seeds and cattle and farming implements he had brought from Spain. Having done that, Columbus left his brother Bartholemew in charge, and set out to find China and Japan. When Columbus returned to the colony several months later, he had found only more spiceless islands, including Jamaica.

On this occasion, Columbus may have realized that, in his quest for the Indies, he was pursuing a will-o'-the-wisp. At any rate, he made all members of his expedition swear that they had seen the mainland of Asia. Having their tongues slit and receiving a hundred strokes of the lash was the penalty for breaking this oath.

During his absence from Haiti, things had gone from bad to worse in the colony. The Indians had attacked the settlers. The crops had failed. Most of the stores of food brought from Spain were rotted and inedible. Boxes, barrels, and bags that should have contained food were filled with worthless trash. Instead of peace in Isabella, there was discord; instead of prosperity, there was starvation. To top it all, the site on which the colony stood was swampy and unhealthful.

Among the colonists were men of all kinds. Many of them had gone to the Indies with a genuine desire to work, but a large number were adventurers. They had come to carve their fortunes with their swords. When Columbus forced these soldiers of fortune to work, they rebelled. In punishment, Columbus put them on short rations. Scores of them returned to Spain. The tales they told back home undermined the popularity of Columbus with the people but not with the king and queen.

When Columbus returned to Spain in the summer of 1496 there were no cheering crowds to greet him, although his reception at court was friendly enough. But when Columbus, in the fall of 1496, tried to recruit men for his third expedition, he ran into trouble.

The dauntless discoverer asked for eight ships. The king and queen were willing to supply them. But when it came to getting crews, hardly a man was to be had. Months of idle waiting went by. Delay followed delay. During this time, Columbus sent a message to his brother Bartholomew at Isabella, ordering him to abandon the colony and build a new one on a more healthful site on the south coast of Haiti. This was done and the new colony was named Santo Domingo. At last, in May, 1498, Columbus sailed for the third time. To man his ships, the king and queen had found it necessary to open the jails. Indeed it was a motley crew that sailed with Columbus on this third voyage.

One might think that Columbus would have set his course for the new colony on Haiti. Instead, he steered a southerly course that brought him to Trinidad, and to the delta of the Orinoco River. This was the first time Columbus cast eyes on the mainland of America, but he barely took time to look at it. Next he reached the pearl islands of Margarita and Cubagua. There Columbus got more than 3 pounds of fine pearls in exchange for a handful of beads and copper bells.

While in the Pearl Islands, Columbus found that his eyes were failing him. Since he was the only one who knew how to navigate the ships, Columbus set sail for Santo Domingo as fast as the winds could carry him. It might have been better for Columbus, had he steered clear of the new colony and gone home to Spain.

The flicker of rebellion that flared forth in Santo Domingo before Columbus left in 1496, swept the settlement like a prairie fire on his return. Intrigue was the order of the day. Lies and libel were the chief products of poison pens and wagging tongues. This state of affairs may have been news to Columbus on his arrival in Santo Domingo in August, 1498, but the deplorable state of affairs in the Indies was no longer news in Spain.

This time the king and queen could not ignore the accusations against Columbus. Columbus did not improve his standing with the king and queen when he offered to send 500 Indians to Spain as slaves in return for much-needed food and supplies. This was a serious mistake and the enemies of Columbus at court took quick advantage of it. They knew Isabella disapproved of slavery, and they used Columbus' offer to substantiate the charges of cruelty, disloyalty, and dishonesty against him.

The enemies of Columbus also claimed that his two brothers, Bartholomew and Diego, both at Santo Domingo, were working against the interest of Spain. The result was that Don Francisco de Bobadilla, was given power to take absolute charge at Santo Domingo, even to the extent of placing the three Columbus brothers under arrest and sending them back to Spain if he wanted to.

Don Francisco arrived in Santo Domingo on August 23, 1500. He wasted no time in using his powers. He moved into the house occupied by Columbus, and assumed all the powers of the governor. Within a month, he arrested Columbus and his brothers. He placed them in irons as if they were common criminals, and when a ship was ready, he sent them back to Spain.

Columbus arrived in Spain with chains on hand and foot, but these badges of dishonor did not remain on him long. When Columbus told the king and queen his side of the story, his rank and titles were quickly restored and he was given a handsome money award. The only stipulation was that he should not return to Santo Domingo.

Columbus wanted to make a fourth voyage to find the Indies. Although a Portuguese, Vasco da Gama, had reached the Indies by sailing eastward around the southern tip of Africa and had returned to Lisbon in 1599 with a cargo of spices, Columbus still did not realize that a vast continent and another ocean stood between the Atlantic Ocean and China.

Columbus sailed for the fourth and last time in May, 1502, with four ships and 150 men. In the face of royal orders not to put in at Santo Domingo, Columbus and his four ships arrived outside that harbor toward the end of June after a stormy passage. He asked the governor for permission to enter the harbor to make repairs. It was denied. When Columbus learned that a treasure fleet was about to sail from Santo Domingo for Spain, he warned the captains of the fleet that a hurricane was brewing. They laughed at him. While Columbus took his four tiny ships into a sheltered cove, the treasure fleet sailed—sailed to its doom. Most of the vessels were wrecked in the hurricane. The flagship went down with all hands and among them was Don Francisco de Bobadilla.

From 1502 on, the life of Columbus draws toward a tragic and pathetic close. On his last journey, he searched in vain for Cathay and Cipango along the coast of Central America until his two remaining ships were driven ashore on the coast of Jamaica. Here half his men deserted him after months of futile waiting for rescue. His food supplies ran out and the natives refused to give the Spaniards food. It was in these dire straits that Columbus used his knowledge of astronomy to make the natives come to terms with him. In fact, his life and those of his men was saved by an eclipse of the moon which he accurately predicted.

At long last, Columbus got away from Jamaica. He returned to Spain in 1504, just about the time of the death of his friend and patron, Queen Isabella. With the queen's death, the sun of Columbus quickly set. He died poor and forgotten on May 20, 1506. But even to the very moment when the light of life went out of his feeble eyes, Columbus thought that in the waters of the West Indies was the waterway to the porcelain towers of Cathay and the golden roofs of Cipango.

Highlights of Bahamas

Discovered: By Christopher Columbus for Spain in 1492.

Population: Some twenty islands have a total population of 60.000.

Area: 4,404 square miles, comprising 3,077 islands.

Language: English.   *Capital:* Nassau.

Government: British crown colony.

In the course of his journeys, Columbus placed nearly all the islands of the Caribbean on the map, starting with the Bahama group. The more than 4,000 islands in this cluster are all the product of coral formations. Only one of them, Andros, can boast of fresh-water streams. All the other islands have to depend upon rain for moisture and wells for drinking water. Although these islands were the first to be discovered, they were not settled by white men for a long time. Their Indian population was virtually wiped out in the days of the conquistadors. The natives either succumbed to diseases brought overseas by the Spaniards, or else died in slavery in the mines or on the plantations of New Spain.

Highlights of Bermuda

Discovered: By Juan Bermúdez for Spain in 1515.

Population: A close cluster of small and large islands have a population of 32,000.

Area: 19 square miles, comprising 360 small islands.

Language: English.   *Capital:* Hamilton.

Government: British crown colony.

The Bermuda Islands were discovered in 1515 by Juan Bermúdez. The discovery was an accident. Bermúdez was bound from Spain to Cuba with a cargo of hogs. His ship ran into a heavy storm and was swept upon the beach of one of the Bermuda Islands, which he named after himself. For years, the Bermudas were avoided by sailors because the islands were believed to be inhabited by devils and evil spirits. They were rediscovered by Sir Thomas Gates and Sir George Somers in 1609 when their ships were wrecked there while en route to the Jamestown colony. The Bermudas remained virtually unsettled until the time of the North American Revolution when many royalists left the young United States and set up a colony in the Bermudas under the British government.

CHAPTER 2

Queen of the Caribbean

Highlights of Cuba

Discovered: By Christopher Columbus for Spain, October 28, 1492.

Population: 4,000,000.

Area: 44,164 square miles.

Language: Spanish.   *Capital:* Havana.

Government: Republic established in 1895.

Geographical Characteristics: Irregular mountain chains that cross the country in various directions form, between them, a number of fertile and healthful plateaus and valleys.

Climatic Conditions: Subtropical.

Principal Products: Sugar, tobacco, cigars, molasses, pineapples, bananas, cattle hides, rum, iron, and manganese.

O N October 28, 1492, just 16 days after Christopher Columbus had first sighted land of the New World at Watling Island in the Bahamas, his three ships dropped anchor in what is today the Bay of Nuevitas, Cuba. He described it as "the most beautiful land ever beheld by human eyes." The Queen of the Caribbean had been discovered. Columbus named it Juana.

The natives Columbus had taken aboard his flagship at Watling Island told him that this was the land of gold and riches he was seeking. Was it Cipango or Cathay, he wondered? Columbus would soon find out. He dressed in his most colorful and impressive costume and had himself rowed ashore. Instead of a delegation of stately mandarins to greet him, the few naked Indians, who had been watching, ran for the woods like frightened rabbits at his approach.

Not daunted by this lack of hospitality, Columbus kneeled on the shore, and took possession in the name of the King and Queen of Spain. Then he inspected the immediate wealth of the people of this new possession of the crown. He found that it consisted of a few miserable thatched huts, some crude household utensils, a fishing net, a fishing spear, and a small animal that looked like a cross between a dog and a large rat. Hardly the fabulous wealth of the Orient he had come such a long way to find.

Columbus gave orders for his ships to sail along the coast. A few days later he reached a large river and called it the Rio de Los Mares. He sailed up the river a way. The scenery enchanted him, the aroma of strange flowers pleased his nostrils, the seemingly endless variety of multicolored birds fascinated him. There was no denying that Juana was a lovely and beautiful land. But where were the silks and spices? Where was the gold and silver? Perhaps around the next bend?

The sailors of Columbus, however, fared rather well on that river journey. They saw the *hamacs*, or hammocks, in which the Indians slept. These swinging beds amused them, and they bought some, paying for them with colored beads. That was the beginning of the sailors' custom of sleeping in hammocks on shipboard, which persists to this day over the seven seas.

While Columbus was exploring the coast of Cuba, he heard of a city called Cubanacan. The name had a familiar sound to him. Surely it sounded like that of Kubla Khan, the fabulous potentate of Cathay. At last he was on the right track. At last he had reached the mainland of Asia. Immediately he sent an expedition to investigate.

For days he waited impatiently for his men to return. When they did, they reported that Cubanacan was a miserable

Indian village of some fifty huts. It stood on the site of present-day Santa Clara. The natives were kindly and hospitable. They invited the white men to stay and looked upon them as gods. They offered them what little food they had and taught their visitors how to puff on black rolls of leaves they lighted at one end and called tobacco. But they had neither silks nor spices, gold nor silver.

In vain, Columbus took samples of spices ashore. He showed them to the Indians in the hope that they would recognize them and lead him to where such spices grew. But the Indians did not understand him any more than he understood them. They brought him something that looked like cinnamon, but it was not cinnamon; something that looked like nutmeg, but it was not nutmeg.

On November 12, Columbus decided that the land of gold and spices must lie elsewhere. Cuba had been a great disappointment to him. Although Columbus returned to Cuba on his second voyage and sailed up and down its coast in his search for the golden cities of the East, he never did know that it was an island. That simple fact, which might have cleared up Columbus's mistaken belief that Cuba was the mainland of Asia, was not discovered until 1508 when Sebastián de Ocampo sailed completely around Cuba.

The writings of Christopher Columbus disclose that he found Cuba a land of almost unbelievable peace, serenity, and beauty, and that its people lived in an ideal state of contentment and harmony. They did not possess a high degree of culture, but they were industrious. They grew much the same kind of crops that rural Cuba does today: squash, beans, corn, yams, and last but not least, tobacco. These native Cubans were a mild people, possessing no weapons beyond spears for fishing and rough lances. In every way they were the exact opposite of the fierce Carib Indians who came on raiding expeditions from the South American mainland. These Caribs, or cannibals, were the Huns of the New World, roaming the peaceful Caribbean in their huge war canoes and unleashing their bloodthirsty cruelty on islands such as Cuba.

But Cuba was soon to know a scourge far worse than the Caribs. Columbus's stories of the fertile lands, good harbors, and deep rivers fell as seeds among those who came in his wake, and the fruit they bore was bitter with cruelty, oppression, and greed.

Columbus wrote the first chapter in the recorded history of Cuba. His son, Diego, who succeeded him as Admiral of the Indies, began the second, in 1511, when he appointed Captain Diego Velásquez as lieutenant governor of Cuba.

Captain Velásquez had been to Cuba with Columbus on the second voyage of that valiant navigator and had proved his worth as a fearless and competent leader of men. He had settled in Santo Domingo, Haiti, and made quite a sizable fortune. The doughty captain leaped at the opportunity to establish a Spanish colony in Cuba and decided to make the most of it. If there were gold and silver in Cuba, very well. If not, then Velásquez knew that the fertile soil of the island could be made to produce wealth. Hence, when his four ships sailed from Santo Domingo in November, 1511, they carried farming tools, seeds, cattle, horses, and building materials.

Unfortunately, the human cargo of 300 recruits for colonizing Cuba was not so innocent as the cargo in the holds. Among the adventurous noblemen were Pánfilo de Narváez, as cruel an oppressor of Indians as ever sailed out of Spain, and Hernando Cortez, who frankly proclaimed that he had come to the New World, not to work, but to gather gold. On the other hand, among the motley company, was Las Casas, a gentle priest, the friendly but futile protector of the Indians and outspoken historian of Spaniards in the New World.

Almost from the very day of landing on the northeast coast of Cuba, the Velásquez expedition ran into trouble. For reasons that puzzled the good captain, the Indians who had

been so friendly to Columbus and his crew were now antagonistic and defied the settlers. For the story of this useless
resistance on the part of the mild-mannered and peaceful
people it is necessary to go back a few years in the history of
the West Indies.

The lives of the Indians of Haiti, where Spain established
the colony of Santo Domingo, had been far from happy.
Almost from the first, they had been enslaved by the Spaniards
and forced to work at tasks strange and burdensome for them.
They were beaten and treated as animals in many instances.
Many fled in fear of their lives. Among those who escaped
from slavery in Haiti was an Indian chief by the name of
Hatuey. He made his way to Cuba, and there he became the
first advocate of New World rebellion against the conquistadors. In Cuba, Hatuey spread the story of Spanish cruelties
among the Indians of Haiti. He warned them that their turn
was next to feel the grinding heel of the conqueror.

Velásquez soon traced the cause of the Indian's hostility to
Hatuey. The Indian chief was captured and executed. A
number of his fellow rebels were seized, and then released with
a warning. In the light of his times, Diego Velásquez was
neither cruel nor vindictive. He wanted no trouble with the
Indians, for that would interfere with the work he had in
mind: the building of a settlement that would make Spain,
the colonists, and himself rich as Caesars.

Cuba prospered under Velásquez. By 1515, he had extended his colony from the first settlement at Baracoa to seven
Spanish-built towns, including Havana and Santiago. But a
great deal of the good he accomplished was undone by the
hotheaded and wild Pánfilo de Narváez who, under the pre-
text of bringing the benefits of civilization to the Indians,
carried on a ruthless campaign of extermination against the
helpless natives. Early he learned that the Indians stood in
great fear of the Spanish horses. One of his favorite tricks was
to tie a string of bells around the neck of a spirited steed and

gallop at full speed through an Indian village, frightening the natives half to death.

This sport of Narváez helped keep the Indians in submission. It also made an impression on the mind of young Hernando Cortez, who filed the knowledge of this native fear of the horse away for future reference. He used it to good advantage in his conquest of Mexico a few years later.

At this time Cortez was the private secretary to Governor Velásquez but his ideas and ambitions went beyond a secretary's job. When the nobles began to complain of the governor's refusal to institute a system of enforced Indian labor, Cortez became one of the leaders in a plot against his own employer. When Velásqeuz discovered this treachery, he decided to hang his disloyal secretary. Cortez not only talked his neck out of the hangman's noose but also argued himself into the job of mayor of Santiago de Cuba.

At this period of his life, as later, Hernando Cortez seems to have believed in having many irons in the fire. Besides being secretary to the governor, conspirator, and mayor of Santiago, he was a planter. It is in this latter role that Cortez is credited with bringing wheat to the New World.

Time and again, shipments of wheat seeds had been sent from Spain to Cuba, but when they arrived they were always found to be mildewed and useless. About 1517, so the story goes, a Negro slave on the Cortez plantation was emptying a bag of rice while Cortez was looking on. As the slave was about to throw the bag away, Cortez noticed three grains of wheat in the lining of the bag. They seemed firm and dry and sound. He had the seeds planted. One never sprouted, another went to stalk, but the third seed grew into a lusty and healthy plant that produced 180 perfect grains of wheat. These, in turn, were planted on the Cortez plantation. From the resulting crops came the seed grains that later sprouted on the mainland.

Governor Velásquez' foresight in fostering agriculture and

the breeding of cattle and horses in Cuba was soon to bear fruit of high value. Through this reserve of food supplies, Cuba was able to organize expeditions for new Spanish conquest. In 1517, Francisco de Córdoba sailed forth and returned with news of Yucatan, which juts like a thumb out into the Gulf of Mexico. In 1518, the crown granted Velásquez permission to carry on further explorations at his own expense. In the same year, Juan de Grijalva, a nephew of Velásquez, sailed along the Mexican coast and took possession of Yucatan in the name of Spain. When he returned to Santiago in Cuba, he told tales of golden wealth and temple cities in the new lands to the west and of two white men who were slaves of the Indians of Yucatan.

Velásquez immediately organized an expedition to explore and exploit this new territory, and incidentally to effect a rescue of the two white men. Hernando Cortez saw his opportunity and talked the governor into making him captain general of the expedition.

It took a lot of food to provision an expedition such as Cortez planned, but, as mentioned, under the wise guidance of Velásquez, Cuba was producing an abundance of food. Preparations were well under way by the middle of November in 1518. Then the governor began to have misgivings about Cortez. If he discovered the golden riches Grijalva had described in Yucatan, would Cortez return to Cuba? No! Better countermand the order and put a man more tractable in command.

The idea was a good one from Velásquez' point of view, but it came too late. Cortez got wind of it, and, on November 18, 1518, although preparations for the fleet were only about half completed, Cortez gave the order to sail to Havana. Velásquez heard the news, and ran shouting down to the waterfront, only to see the ships leave Santiago harbor. At the stern of the flagship stood Hernando Cortez, waving a mocking good-by. The governor's frantic demands for the ships to drop anchor were answered by a jeering laugh.

When Cortez sailed his fleet into Havana to complete preparations, the governor, Pedro de Barba, had received orders from Velásquez to arrest him. Cortez only laughed and forced de Barba to supply added provisions and the best horses in the town. He got what he wanted. And so it was that on February 10, 1519, Hernando Cortez, with eleven ships, 633 men, and sixteen horses, sailed out of Havana. How that expedition under the leadership of Cortez, a man who let nothing stand in his way, conquered Mexico, is another story and another chapter in New World history.

But Cortez' Mexican adventure had a sequel in Cuba. Velásquez, infuriated, prepared another expedition to sail after the impudent upstart who had been his secretary, to arrest him. To outfit that expedition, under the leadership of Pánfilo de Narváez, he all but impoverished the Cuba to which he had brought prosperity. The only result was that Cortez took Narváez prisoner in Mexico, talked Narváez' men into joining him, and sent Narváez back to Cuba, defeated and dejected. Some years later, Narváez lost his life as the leader of a luckless expedition to Florida.

Cuba had no treasures to compare with those of Mexico, it is true, but there was wealth in cattle raising and the few gold mines produced a small but steady stream of the precious metal. These mines were worked by slaves. At first Indian slaves had been sufficient, but by 1550, ill treatment and over-work had taken its toll until not one Indian was left. As early as 1521, Negro slaves were imported from Africa. Rebellions in the gold mines and the copper mines brought much bloodshed to Cuba. Then piracy lifted its head over the Cuban horizon. In 1537, a French raiding corsair sacked and burned Havana. Then, in 1538, Cuba took renewed hope when it was honored by having the famous Hernando de Soto appointed as its governor.

Hernando de Soto had gained fame and great wealth with Pizarro in Peru. But, like Cortez, his ambitions knew no bounds, nor his desire for greater riches. Never had Cuba seen a fleet such as that which brought de Soto and his company of nobles and grand ladies to the New World—a magnificent armada, a distinguished company.

The new governor also bore a commission as military governor of Florida, and it was for the conquest of Florida that Cuba was to serve as a base. With de Soto was his beautiful wife, Lady Isabella de Bobadilla, who subsequently won a name for herself in the history of Cuba.

While preparing for the grand expedition to Florida, de Soto built a fort to guard Havana against future pirate raids. When the fort was completed, not far from where La Fuerza stands today, Lady Isabella was put in command by de Soto who, at the same time, appointed her acting governor of Cuba during his absence. Thus the feminist movement got off to an early start in the New World.

On May 12, 1539, de Soto and his followers bade farewell to Cuba—many for the last time. Martial music filled the air as the impressive armada sailed out of Havana bound for Florida.

It was not long before bad news came back to Cuba from Florida. Reinforcements and more supplies were needed. As had happened before, in the case of Velásquez and his punitive expedition against Cortez, Cuba was drained of food and cattle and horses and men to satisfy the Spanish urge for conquest. Then the months passed. No news about de Soto came, either good or bad, until almost five years later, in October, 1544, and then from the Mexican capital. De Soto was dead, buried under the waters of the Mississippi River he had discovered. Dead, too, were most of his followers. De Soto's dream was over. Lady Isabella died of grief and Cuba buried another broken heart.

From the very beginning, Havana was one of the best and safest harbors in the New World; by the middle of the sixteenth century, it was the most important shipping center. Havana became a port of call for the plate fleets carrying their precious cargoes of gold and silver from Peru and Mexico to Spain. But the advantage also had its drawbacks.

Raiders and pirates flying the French, Dutch, and English flags cast envious glances on the rich and bustling seaport. In 1555, Havana was completely destroyed by the notorious Jacques de Sores. Then the dreaded Sir Francis Drake, who hated Spain with every drop of blood in his body, sailed the Spanish Main. He took the riches of the treasure ships, boldly sacked the strongest of the cities, including the fabulous treasure house at Panama. Havana waited apprehensively. When would Drake strike at the Queen of the Caribbean? Santo Domingo was razed by Drake in 1586. Surely, it would be Cuba's turn next.

Every able-bodied man in Havana left his usual occupation to help strengthen the defenses of the port. Volunteers came from every corner of the island. On May 29, six English ships were sighted offshore. Then came twenty-four more. Was Drake getting ready to strike? But day followed day, the thirty ships rode at anchor and nothing happened. The citizens of Havana could not believe their eyes. They did not know that the plague had broken out among Drake's fleet, and that his men were dying by the score. They did not know that Drake's ships rode so deep in the water because they were practically overflowing with golden treasure. But when Drake's fleet suddenly sailed away the Cubans did not care why. They gave prayers of thanks that they had been saved from a terrible fate.

Drake, however, did Cuba one good turn. His raids in the West Indies resulted in the building of better fortifications. The famous Spanish engineer, Bautista de Antonellie, was sent to Cuba to build two strong fortresses at Havana, Morro Castle and La Punta, one on each side of the harbor's entrance.

The seventeenth century was the heyday of the buccaneer. Outstanding among these Brethren of the Coast was the notorious pirate Morgan—later Sir Henry Morgan. He attacked Cuba in 1662 and was so enraged because the inhabitants fled to the hills without putting up a fight that he shouted contemptuously that he could have defended Havana against any force with one gun and a dog. Again after sacking the Spanish treasure house at Panama, Henry Morgan landed in Cuba to divide a million-dollar loot among his followers before returning to Jamaica to be arrested for piracy and taken to England for trial, only to be knighted by the king.

Another Englishman, Lord Albemarle, came to plague Cuba in 1762, when France and England were at war with Spain. On June 6, the first contingent of a fleet of almost 200 British warships and transports appeared off Havana under command of Admiral George Pocock. The English landed 14,000 soldiers under the leadership of Lord Albemarle. They faced less than 3,000 armed Cubans, all inexperienced fighters. Despite the overwhelming odds, the Cubans gave battle to the British, but the outcome was inevitable. On August 14, 1762, Havana capitulated to Lord Albemarle and the British occupied Cuba.

For almost a year, Cuba remained an English possession. In a way, it was a happy period for Cuba. Lord Albemarle opened the island to world trade. Under Spain, commerce with the colonies had been closed to other nations. Under the new regime, wealth poured into Cuba. At the end of the Seven Years' War between Spain and Britain, England gave Cuba back to Spain in exchange for Florida. A poor bargain that was for England. Not only did Cuba serve as a base for harassing the British during the North American Revolutionary War, which was only a few years off, but when she gave up Cuba, England lost the key to the Caribbean and the control of western world trade. What New World history would have been if John Bull had been a shrewder bargainer on that occasion, we shall never know. As it was, England did not keep Florida very long. In 1783 it returned Florida to Spain. In giving up Florida, the English suffered another attack of shortsightedness.

Even as early as the time of Lord Albemarle's conquest of Cuba the people of the island began to regard themselves as Cubans rather than Spaniards. Occasional revolts against the heavy taxes and oppressive policies of Spain flared up as early as 1717. It was then that yellow fever, soon to be known to Cubans as the Great Patriot, came to the rescue of the creoles. The Great Patriot, a deadly force of murderous mystery, fought silently but with deadly certainty on the side of the Cubans. During the English occupation, yellow fever killed more British soldiers than Cuban steel and lead. Oh, yes, the Great Patriot was a great friend of the Cubans, but a deadly enemy of all outsiders.

Yellow fever first came to Cuba from Central America about 1750. It killed the English. It killed the Spanish. But the native Cubans were relatively unscathed. The reason: Most native Cubans were immune. The majority of Cubans probably caught yellow fever in childhood. If they died, that was that. If they lived through it, they seldom caught the disease again.

During the Ten Years' War between the Cubans and Spaniards, which began in 1868, about 50,000 Cubans died as against over 200,000 Spaniards. Most of the Spaniards were killed by the Great Patriot. This Ten Years' War was the first concerted and sustained fight of Cuba for liberty. Its beginnings were small. On October 10, 1868, a group of 147 patriots met at the Yara plantation in the province of Oriente and solemnly declared the independence of Cuba from Spain.

From that memorable date followed ten terrible years of destruction, ravage, and guerrilla warfare during which nearly all the patriot leaders were slain. The United States was almost involved. But although the people of the United States sympathized with the Cubans, the government felt that the fight was no concern of the United States.

The one thing Cuba gained from this long, wholesale slaughter was training for the next and successful fight for freedom. This began with the Insurrection of 1895 and ended in victory and liberty in 1898. The end did not come until the United States became involved as a result of the tragic blowing up of the warship *Maine* in Havana harbor on February 15, 1898. In this incident, 252 American sailors were killed. The United States declared war on Spain on April 24, 1898. Spanish-American War veterans, who battled side by side with the Cubans in their desperate fight for freedom, know how valiantly the Cubans fought.

Peace was declared on July 16, 1898, and Cuba at last was free. In 1902, Estrada Palma took office as the first president of the new Republic of Cuba. The great patriots of Cuba, including Narciso López, José Martí, Bartolomé Maso, and Máximo Gómez, had not lived, fought, and died in vain.

The years that started a new life of freedom in Cuba also marked the death of the Great Patriot, yellow fever. That brings us to the dramatic story of Dr. Carlos Finlay and his mosquitoes, to Major Walter Reed and his conquest of yellow fever.

The War of Cuban Independence over, immigrants began flowing to Cuba, especially into Havana. General Leonard Wood of the United States Army was governor general pending the completion of details of the new Republic of Cuba. Under Wood's command was a large force of American soldiers.

The newcomers to Cuba, civilians and soldiers, were not immune to yellow fever. They caught the dreaded disease and died by the hundreds. It had always been believed that yellow fever was a filth disease, bred by dirt and caught by contact with fever victims through their presumably infected clothing and bedding. Cuba had no monopoly on this deadly disease. In the United States, Charleston, Mobile, New Orleans, and Galveston had become its victims. In the more than two hundred years since it first invaded the United States, it is estimated that yellow fever had claimed 100,000 victims in North America alone. Boston, New York, and Philadelphia suffered horrible yellow fever epidemics, during which hundreds of people dropped dead in the streets. Down in Panama, where French engineers had started to dig a canal across the Isthmus, men died of yellow fever and malaria almost as rapidly as they landed from France.

Up to the start of the twentieth century, science was helpless to do anything when yellow jack struck. Everything had been tried without success. In 1900, yellow fever ran wild in Havana. The highest authorities believed that a clean city was the best way to combat the scourge. To this end General Wood ordered Major William Gorgas to scrub Havana as bright as a new penny. Havana got such a cleaning as she had never experienced. General Wood and Major Gorgas sat back and waited for the result. It came in the form of the worst epidemic of yellow fever in 20 years.

On June 25, 1900, Major Walter Reed, of the United States Army Medical Corps, arrived in Havana with orders to fight the disease. His first act was to form a yellow fever commission composed of himself, Dr. James Carroll, Dr. Jesse Lazear, and a Cuban yellow fever specialist, Dr. Aristede Agramonte. These four set out to find the microbe or bacillus of yellow fever. After weeks of strenuous work studying the blood and bodies of the worst cases in the Yellow Fever Hospital at Quemados, the commission reported utter and complete failure. As Dr. Carroll put it, "How can you fight something you can't even see?"

But in Havana was another yellow fever specialist, Dr. Carlos Juan Finlay. He should have been given a place on the yellow fever commission. Dr. Carlos Finlay was born in Camaguey, Cuba, in 1833, the son of a Scottish father and a French Creole mother. He studied medicine in the United States, set up practice in Cuba and, in 1872, decided to devote his life to discovering the cause of yellow fever. Nine years later, in 1881, Dr. Finlay in an address before the Academy of Sciences in Havana announced his discovery that yellow fever was carried by the female of a certain mosquito, later named the stegomyia.

His audience listened attentively, but no one took Dr. Finlay seriously. He kept repeating his theory, often and loudly—so often and so loudly that he became the laughingstock of Havana. Oh, people laughed in a friendly way, just as they smilingly dubbed him the Theorizing Old Fool, a prophet without honor in his own country.

Dr. Carlos Finlay was no longer shouting his mosquito theory when the yellow fever commission conducted its first investigations almost twenty years later. He had become tired and embittered. Who could blame him? But Major Reed heard of Funny Old Finlay and his mosquitoes. Maybe there was something in the idea. Anyway, in July, 1900, Major Reed and his colleagues called on the venerable Cuban scientist "because there was nothing else they could think of doing."

When they left Dr. Finlay's house a few hours later, Dr. Lazear carried a jar containing some tiny black objects shaped like microscopic cigars. These were the eggs of the mosquitoes Dr. Finlay had insisted for so long were the carriers of yellow fever. The eggs were hatched in pure water into wiggling silver-winged mosquitoes. The yellow fever commission was ready to start a new attack on yellow jack.

To test the mosquito theory, it was necessary that the newly hatched insects be fed on the blood of yellow fever victims and then allowed to feed on healthy human beings. The theory was that, in this way, yellow fever is transferred from person to person. At that time, all attempts to produce yellow fever in animals had failed, although today certain types of monkeys have been found that can contract yellow fever. Reed wanted to turn man into a guinea pig. Was such a dangerous series of experiments justifiable? The members of the commission decided to experiment on themselves first. Near the end of August, 1900, Dr. Lazear applied to Dr. Carroll a mosquito that he had hatched in his own laboratory and that had made hearty meals on the blood of four yellow fever victims. Four days later, Carroll was ill with yellow jack. Fortunately, he recovered.

Dr. Lazear was not so lucky when he was bitten one day by a stray mosquito. He thought nothing of it, deciding that it probably was not the dangerous type of mosquito anyway, for out of about 400 different kinds of these insects, chances were that only one kind was the comrade in arms of the Great Patriot. Dr. Lazear was wrong. He had underestimated a serious enemy. A few days later he died, a victim of yellow fever.

Major Reed had unfortunately been called back to Washington during this period of early experimentation on human beings. When he returned to Cuba, he began the series of airtight experiments that have made history. Backed by the authority of General Wood and with the assistance of several American soldiers who offered to be bitten, Major Reed was at last able to prove to the world that yellow fever is carried in one way and one way only—by the stegomyia mosquito.

The next step was up to Major Gorgas and his sanitation division. The yellow fever mosquito is a very fastidious creature. The murderous female that carries yellow jack will lay its eggs only in fresh, still water. And what a breeding ground all Havana was, with its every house containing vases, water jars, cisterns, tin cans, soap dishes, little tin cups under table legs to keep off ants—all ideal breeding places for the stegomyia mosquito.

"Get rid of, or cover up every single water receptacle in Havana that might serve as a breeding place for these mosquitoes! Spray oil on stagnant pools and creeks and swamps," ordered General Wood.

Being a good soldier, Major Gorgas obeyed orders. This

time, when Wood and Gorgas sat back and waited for results, it was a different story. In 90 days there was not a single case of yellow fever in Havana. The breeding places of the stegomyia had been dried up or covered up, or films of oil on quiet waters had cut off the air supply the larvae needed.

The Great Patriot was dead. Dr. Carlos Finlay was vindicated after 20 years of abuse and ridicule. Cuba was free from Spain and free from yellow jack.

In the United States and other New World nations, yellow fever was swept out of existence by the same vigorous methods as those employed in Cuba. Down in Panama, after the French gave up the battle against yellow jack, Uncle Sam was able to build the canal because the conquest of yellow fever led to the conquest of disease in the Canal Zone. Thus, through the defeat in Cuba of the Great Patriot, better health conditions and new progress came to the Americas—Cuba's gift to the New World.

On May 20, 1902, the Lone Star Flag of Free Cuba was raised over Havana. It was the anniversary, to the very day— the three hundred ninety-sixth, to be exact—of the death of Christopher Columbus, who, on first beholding the green mountains of Cuba, said that: "It is the most beautiful land ever seen by human eyes!"

CHAPTER 3

Land of Golden Empires

Highlights of Mexico

Discovered: By Francisco Fernández de Córdoba for Spain in 1517.

Population: 19,154,000.

Area: 758,258 square miles.

Language: Spanish. *Capital:* Mexico City.

Government: Republic established October 10, 1824.

Geographical Characteristics: Two mountain chains traverse the country in a northwest-southeasterly direction, forming between them a number of valleys and plateaus of differing altitudes. The plateau valley of Mexico is the country's outstanding topographical feature.

Climatic Conditions: Owing to the varying altitudes as well as to the country's location in both the tropical and temperate zones, the climate is highly diversified. The mean temperature in the warm lowlands varies from 80 to 90°F., while the temperate plateau, at an average altitude of 6,000 feet, has a mean temperature ranging from 70 to 80°. The mean temperature of the cool regions, over 8,000 feet, is about 60°.

Principal Products: Oil, silver, lead, copper, henequen fiber, coffee, vegetables, gold, zinc, sugar, chicle, bananas, cotton, vanilla beans, hardwoods, nuts, rubber, and tobacco.

T HE story of conquest in Mexico begins long before the coming of the European conquistadors. In the ruins of ancient empires that ceased to exist many centuries ago, archaeologists today read a story of civilizations that rose and fell on the tides of time. The history of early Mexico thus put together shows a series of ruthless struggles for wealth and power with conqueror following conqueror in swift and spectacular succession.

The scene of this saga of conquest lies in the lofty and mountain-locked valley of Mexico. The valley itself is about 7,500 feet above sea level. Many of the towering peaks that look down upon it lift their snow-capped tops high among the clouds. It is a place of great natural beauty; the climate is healthful; the soil is rich and fertile. From time immemorial, the valley of Mexico must have been ideal for human existence.

More than one thousand years ago, this valley of Mexico was occupied by a people known as the Toltecs. They had a high degree of culture, mostly borrowed from the more ancient Mayas of Yucatan and Guatemala. These Toltecs practiced the cultural arts and human sacrifice with an equal and remarkable degree of proficiency. To rule the valley of Mexico they had conquered tribes known as the middle cultures. Then some ten centuries ago, into the valley came a people destined to conquer the Toltecs. These were the Chichimecs. A few hundred years later, they were in turn pushed from power by the Aztecs, a nomadic people from the north. Scientists believe these latter were members of the Shoshonean group of North American Indians. At any rate, their language was similar to the Shoshone tongue.

At first the Mexicans looked upon these wanderers from the north with contempt, Aztec barbarians who dressed in skins and hunted for their food with crude bows and arrows. To the cultured Mexicans, the manners of these Aztecs were as rough and crude as their weapons. They were decidedly undesirable immigrants.

For generations, the Aztecs wandered around Mexico in search of a place of permanent settlement. But all the good lands were occupied. Finally, they made their homes along the shore and in the reed-filled, shallow swamps at the western end of Lake Texcoco. This was about the year 1325.

Of the five lakes in the valley of Mexico, the central one, Lake Texcoco, became the main stage in the drama of the Aztecs and of Mexico. Upon its waters was enacted the dramatic sequence of one of the greatest human triumphs and one of the most heart-rending human tragedies of all time and of all people. The first act of this drama might very well be called: "The Struggle to Live."

We usually think of the Aztecs in a setting of golden splendor. But their beginnings were humble and full of haunting misery and soul-searing hunger. During their early days as homesteaders in the dismal swamps of Lake Texcoco, they had no land to cultivate, no decent shelter. For many decades the future rulers of Mexico lived half naked in hovels made of cane and reeds. Their only foods were fish and insects and a few plants that grew in the mud bottom of the lake.

Perhaps it was while hungrily eating some particularly tasty root plucked from the shallow lake bottom that an Aztec got the idea that started a unique type of agriculture. The root he ate was good. And why not? The mud in the bottom of the lake in which it grew was composed of the richest topsoil of the valley, washed down during centuries of rains. Under the waters of Lake Texcoco lay the richest farm lands in all the valley!

But what good are farm lands, however rich, beneath the waters of a lake 25 miles long and 20 miles wide, even if it is a shallow lake? Draining the lake was out of the question. What other alternative? Perhaps the lake bottom could be lifted to the surface. But how? No doubt the Aztecs sought long for the solution to that problem before the nameless inventor thought of the chinampa, or so-called floating market basket.

The chinampa was remarkably simple for an invention of such epoch-making importance. Huge baskets were woven from the reeds that grew in the swamps. Some of these baskets were from 200 to 300 feet long and from 50 to 100 feet wide. They were filled with rich soil dug up laboriously from the lake bottom. In these baskets, the Aztecs planted corn, beans, sweet potatoes, and other foods they had never before been able to grow. They even raised cotton and were able to make clothes for themselves. These great food-producing market baskets rested on the bottom of the lake and homes were built on them.

So successful were these chinampas that soon there were thousands of them. By the year 1370, the man-made garden patches had grown into a prosperous town. Through farming, the Aztecs acquired wealth and with it a small degree of power. The town slowly grew into a great city on the lake. This city was called Tenochtitlan. It stood on the exact site of present-day Mexico City.

As the Aztec tribe expanded and prospered, the earlier Mexicans in the valley went into decline. When their strength finally snapped under the strain of almost continuous internal strife, the Aztecs took control.

By this time, Mexico City was becoming a great and glittering metropolis. One of the first improvements undertaken by the rising city was in the matter of water supply. The brackish water of Lake Texcoco was unfit to drink, so the Aztecs secured rights to the waters of the famous spring of Chapultepec, a mountain close to the lake. A double water main of terra cotta carried the water from the spring to the city.

The city was built, not in one solid mass, but in a grouping of islands that grew out of the original chinampa idea. It was crisscrossed by broad avenues and wide canals, a Venice of the New World inhabited by nearly half a million souls. Broad causeways swept across the lake from the mainland to the island city and each of these was protected by drawbridges. There was a great city wall upon which were lighthouses to guide fishermen and traders who sailed the lake at night. There were splendid palaces, great market places, and nearly 60,000 homes. The focal point of this great city was a beautiful central plaza called the Tecpan. Here, behind lofty walls, were the principal temples, the palaces of the ruler, of priests and nobles. The Tecpan was dominated by the great temple pyramid or Teocalli (God House).

Following the lead of the Toltecs and Chichimecs, the Aztecs got their wealth from trading and taxes; the taxes they imposed chiefly in forms of tribute upon weaker tribes, from Sinaloa in the north to Chiapas in the south. This meant training a large, citizens' army, whose task it was to see to it that a constant stream of gold and goods and food was kept flowing into Mexico City.

As the culture adopted by the Aztecs may have been taken from the Mayas, a comparison has been made between the Mayas and the Aztecs in the New World and the Greeks and Romans in the Old, as regards character, achievements, and relations to each other. The Mayas, like the Greeks, were an artistic and intellectual people. They developed sculpture, painting, architecture, astronomy, and other arts and sciences to a high plane.

The Aztecs, on the other hand, were, like the Romans, brusque and warlike. They built their empire on the structures of earlier civilizations. Their improvements upon their acquired culture were mainly in the scope of military and commercial organization and efficiency of government.

To strengthen their position, the Aztecs entered into an offensive and defensive alliance with two neighbors, the powerful rulers of Texcoco and the weaker Tlacopans, whose city-states were near by on the shores of the lake. Although the original agreement provided for a division of the spoils of war, two parts each to the Aztecs and Texcoco and one part to Tlacopan, the Aztecs were soon in a commanding position and more or less took what they wanted. In time, they established full sway over their allies.

Conquest and commerce went hand in hand with the Aztecs' rise to power. War was their principal business and the by-product of this business was increased trading territory for the many caravans of Aztec merchants and traders. Slaves were another essential Aztec product of war. The dark and sinister gods of the Aztecs demanded frequent and abundant sacrifices of human lives. Much has been written about the cruelty of human sacrifice by the Aztecs. It is told that in one instance alone, 20,000 prisoners were horribly mutilated and then killed as an offering to the gods. From this it would appear that the Aztecs held life cheaply. But just the opposite was the case. The Aztecs considered human life the most precious of gifts and as such the only one worthy of offering as tribute to their gods.

Since wars were fought to obtain living offerings for the bloodstained altars of the Aztec temples, prisoners had to be taken alive. This developed a battle practice that was to act as a boomerang against the rulers of the valley of Mexico when they were confronted by the conquistadors. The Spaniards fought to win. To win, they believed in killing their enemies in battle. This system of warfare was strange and disconcerting to the Aztecs. They fought only to take prisoners.

The Aztecs had a calendar. It was arranged in a cycle of 52 years. At the end of this period, the people always expected the end of the world to come, as had been foretold by some prophecy. On the last day of each 52-year period, all fires throughout the land were extinguished. Shortly before midnight on this last day, a procession of priests marched from the temples in the city on the lake to the sacred hill outside Mexico City. They waited, watching the heavens. If certain stars appeared (as they always did) it was a sign that the gods were willing to let life go on for another 52 years. A new fire was kindled. Torches were lit from a great bonfire and runners sent to every part of the empire to light the fires of temples and hearths anew.

It was during the rule of Montezuma the Great, from about 1440 to 1469, that the Aztec nation became the dominant force in Mexico. His grandnephew, Montezuma II, took the throne in 1502. By then, the days of greatest Aztec glory had passed.

The city on the lake was still fabulously wealthy and all-powerful in Mexico, but there are indications that the golden empire of Montezuma would have collapsed of its own accord, even if a fair-skinned young man with a beard had not come along to change the course of New World history.

In the chapter on Cuba it was told how Hernando Cortez sailed out of Havana harbor in defiance of the orders of Governor Velásquez. That was in February, 1519. His little fleet of eleven ships, carrying 110 sailors, 553 soldiers, and sixteen horses, headed west across the Caribbean and into the Gulf of Mexico. But a storm scattered the ships and drove them south. The fleet finally united at Cozumel Island, off the coast of Yucatan.

From Cozumel, Cortez sent two small ships to the Yucatan mainland with a message to two Spaniards held captive by Mayan tribes. He also sent along some green glass beads so that they could buy their freedom. When no word was received from the captive Spaniards, the fleet got under way again. One of the vessels sprang a leak and the ships returned to Cozumel. After making repairs, and as they were about to sail again, a canoe put ashore. A lone man, naked and in Indian paint, ran up to Cortez and kneeled. He was Padre Gerónimo de Aguilar, one of the two captives Cortez had hoped to rescue. The story of Father Aguilar and his companions is told in the chapter on Yucatan. What is of vital importance here is that Aguilar joined Cortez and later proved of inestimable value as an interpreter. During his 8 years of Indian captivity, he had mastered the language of Yucatan.

From Cozumel, Cortez sailed northward to the mainland, where according to the stories of Córdoba and Grijalva, gold was to be found.

Despite his anxiety to find the fabulous Azetic Empire of Mexico, Cortez stopped on the way to explore the Tabasco River and to visit the great town reported to stand on its banks. This decision was unfortunate for the Indians of Tabasco. On March 25, 1519, Cortez fought the first battle in his conquest of Mexico against these Indians.

It was during this battle, where a few hundred Spaniards faced about 40,000 Indians, that the Spanish battle cry of "St. Jago and at them!" was first heard in Mexico. The foot soldiers were being worsted by the overwhelming hordes of Indian warriors when that cry rang out and Cortez and his small detachment of cavalry galloped into action. That was the end of the great battle of Tabasco and the first victory of Cortez in America.

The prancing, plunging, pounding horses terrified the Mayas, who had never seen horses before. Above and beyond that, the combination of these strange beasts and warriors in shiny armor struck fear into their hearts. The Indians were sure that horse and rider were one, a terrifying creature half man, half animal. Cortez had known all along that he was fighting against great odds. Only ten of his soldiers had guns. Thus it is easy to imagine what confidence it gave him when he saw his sixteen horsemen rout 40,000 armed warriors.

The Indian chiefs who came to make peace after the battle brought gifts of gold ornaments. Cortez asked them where the gold came from. "Mexico," they replied. That must have been sweet music to his ears. So far he had heard only rumors of gold and a place called Mexico. Here was proof that it existed.

It was at this time that Cortez received a gift far more precious than gold. Among the slaves presented to him by the defeated Indians as a peace offering, was a young, intelligent girl by the name of Malinche. She was an Aztec who had been sold into slavery by her mother, so that a half brother might gain her rightful inheritance. An Aztec merchant had bought Malinche and then sold her to a Tabasco chief. To posterity, this woman is known as Doña Marina.

It was not for her beauty or her intelligence that Cortez valued Marina. Her mother tongue was the Aztec language. During her residence in Tabasco she had learned how to speak

Mayan. Aguilar, the prisoner Cortez had rescued, spoke Mayan too. Thus Cortez suddenly had a way of communicating with the Aztecs. He spoke Spanish to Aguilar who translated it to Marina in Mayan who, in turn, translated it into the Aztec language. This ready means of making his wishes known to the people of Montezuma was to prove of great value to Cortez.

On Good Friday, April 21, 1519, Cortez landed where the city of Vera Cruz now stands. There the Spaniards built huts, mounted their guns, and made plans for the march on Mexico City. From this settlement Cortez sent word to Montezuma that he wished to see the emperor of the Aztecs.

In Mexico City, meanwhile, Montezuma was much disturbed by the news of the arrival of strangers on the coast of Mexico. The warrior part of the emperor told him that he should drive out the intruders, but the priest part of Montezuma warned him that this fair-skinned and bearded man might be the god Quetzalcoatl returning as he had promised according to ancient legend. Here was indeed a problem for the Aztec emperor. Indecision was the great weakness of Montezuma. It finally cost him his life and his empire.

While waiting at Vera Cruz for word from Montezuma, Cortez got ready for action. First he received the chiefs of the Totonacs, a nation that had recently been conquered by the Aztecs. They told Cortez that they hated Montezuma and his taxes and oppressions. It was pleasant for Cortez to hear that the Aztecs had such bitter enemies. The Totonac chiefs offered to join Cortez in his march against Mexico City. It was even more pleasing for Cortez to learn that he could count on allies among the enemies of Montezuma.

When the emperor sent word refusing Cortez permission to come to Mexico City, it had little effect on his plans. Cortez was never a man to take "no" for an answer. The large gifts of gold the emperor sent to soften the refusal only made Cortez the more anxious to set foot in the Golden City.

Nothing short of death could have stopped Cortez from marching on Mexico City. To prevent his own men from deserting him, he ordered all his ships but one burned. The troops were stunned when they learned that their leader had destroyed the ships and thereby cut off retreat. Cortez had many enemies in his expedition. They took this opportunity to fan the fires of revolt. They flickered faintly and died quickly.

On August 16, 1519, the march on Mexico City began. There were 400 foot soldiers, fifteen cavalry and seven artillery pieces, 1,300 Totonac warriors, and 1,000 Indian porters. As guides and hostages to guarantee the good faith of his Indian allies, Cortez took along forty chiefs.

Along the road to Mexico City lay the kingdom of the Tlascalans, perhaps the fiercest and most warlike of all the Indians of the country. Theirs was the only nation that had remained free of Aztec dominance. Cortez sent envoys ahead with requests for permission to pass through the country of these Tlascalans whose mountain stronghold was protected by a stone wall 9 feet high, 20 feet broad, and 6 miles long. The answer was: "No!"

Cortez and his army had to fight their way through every mile of that country. The small losses of the Spaniards were more than offset by the added strength Cortez obtained when the Tlascalans finally joined forces with him. Marching onward, they reached Cholula, the Sacred City of the Aztecs. There Cortez and his men narrowly escaped a deathtrap set by the allies of Montezuma. Fortunately, Marina discovered the plot in time, enabling the Spaniards to turn the tables. Thousands of Cholulans were trapped in the market place by the Spaniards and killed as a warning to others not to try similar tricks.

The march went on. Every day every man kept on the alert for another attack. Every night every man slept fully armed. Danger surrounded the Spaniards at every turn on the 200-mile march from the sea to the lake. On November 8, 1519,

almost three months after he had left Vera Cruz on the coast,
Cortez and his army crossed the magnificent causeway of
Iztapalapan, broad enough for ten horsemen to ride abreast.
The weather-beaten and bedraggled Spaniards lifted their
weary heads and beheld, with disbelieving eyes, the strange,
beautiful, and wonderful sights that met them on all sides. It
put new hope into their heavy hearts, new strength in their
weary muscles. As they marched over the causeway, they came
to a drawbridge. Later on—another drawbridge. Cortez made
no comment, but surely he must have realized that if those
bridges were drawn up, retreat from Mexico City would be
completely cut off. And he was entering a hostile city of almost
half a million souls. It took courage to march straight onward
without blinking an eye. No wonder men have called him
Stout Cortez.

As the Spaniards approached the city, Montezuma himself
came out to meet them. He was carried in a litter made of gold
and covered by a canopy ablaze with jewels. There was every
outward gesture of cordiality in that first meeting between
Cortez and Montezuma.

Thus, Cortez and his army made their triumphant entry
into the City on the lake. They marched to the great central
plaza. There, behind thick walls, stood the palace of Axayactl,
built by the father of Montezuma. This was put at the disposal
of the Spaniards and their allies.

The days that followed were as a dream for Cortez and his
men. Never had they expected to find such a city. The vast
market place was not overcrowded with 50,000 people buying
a greater variety of foods and flowers than could be had in the
finest market in Spain. The streets of the city were kept clean
by a street-cleaning force of a thousand slaves. With amazement, the Spaniards watched a strange game played with a
ball that bounced. This game, much like our basketball, was
played with a ball made of rubber, a substance they had never
seen. Policemen patroled the streets, avenues, and canals.

Richly dressed nobles were carried in golden litters. Wherever the Spaniards turned were signs of riches, more riches than any of them had even visualized in their wildest dreams.

But the wonders of Mexico City did not make Cortez forget that he and his handful of followers were alone in a strongly fortified city. Montezuma was friendly enough, but there were lesser chiefs who did not hide their hostility. Cortez knew that to capture the golden treasures of the Aztecs, he must make a bold and decisive move. His only course was to kidnap Montezuma and his family. This he did. They were taken to the palace occupied by the Spaniards. The people of Mexico City were stunned when they realized what had happened, but Montezuma told his subjects that he was a friend of Cortez and that he was visiting the white men of his own accord. The Aztecs knew that their ruler was a prisoner of the Spaniards, but there was nothing they could do. The word of Montezuma was law. The Spaniards were safe—for the time being.

As the months went by and Montezuma realized that his self-invited guests had no thought of going back whence they had come, he tried to buy them off. To do this, he imposed extra taxes calling for payment in gold and silver. To this he added his own vast hoardings of the precious metals. When the treasure was weighed and counted, it was found to be worth more than $6,300,000 in our money!

This wealth might have been enough for an ordinary man, but not for Cortez. He wanted more than just gold. Power! An empire! When he had conquered all Mexico, and only then, would his work be done.

By this time, Cortez had more or less forgotten Diego Velásquez, the governor of Cuba, against whose orders he had sailed to Mexico. But Velásquez had not forgotten. In April, 1520, an expedition from Cuba arrived in Mexico with orders to found Spanish settlements and to arrest Cortez. The commander was Pánfilo de Narváez. He had a fleet of sixteen ships and 1,200 men.

Feeling that a war of Spaniard against Spaniard would ruin his cause in Mexico, Cortez hurried to Cempoala where Narváez had pitched his tents. Captain Pedro de Alvarado was left in charge at Mexico City. Alvarado was a brave soldier, but impetuous and hotheaded. In addition, there was a deeply rooted vein of cruelty in his make-up. Cortez had had to discipline him on several occasions. Leaving Alvarado in command at the capital was one of the gravest mistakes Cortez ever made.

At Cempoala, Cortez had little difficulty with Narváez and his army. Cortez, with only a handful of men, made a surprise attack. He captured Narváez and his officers and talked and bought Narváez' men into believing that it would be more profitable for them if they left Narváez and joined Cortez. This they did with the result that Narváez and some of his officers were sent to Santa Cruz on the coast in chains. Cortez, with the newly acquired and much-needed additions to his army, felt sublimely happy. This bright frame of mind ended when news came of what Captain Alvarado had done when left on his own in Mexico City.

On an Aztec feast day, shortly after Cortez had left, a group of leading nobles had asked Alvarado for permission to perform a ceremony in the courtyard of the palace occupied by the Spaniards. Alvarado consented. When the warriors were going through some ceremonial dances, Alvarado ordered his men to attack them. It was merciless murder. Not a single one of 600 Aztecs escaped.

As a result of this massacre, the whole city was up in arms against the Spaniards. They were besieged in their palace stronghold. Only 140 Spaniards surrounded by tens of thousands of armed Aztecs. Hardly pleasant news for Cortez. A less stouthearted leader might well have thought it wiser to abandon them to their fate. Instead, Cortez gathered up his new forces and hurried back to the city on the lake.

By sheer daring, Cortez managed to lead his men across the

causeway into Mexico City and through the quickly opened gates of the palace where the Spaniards were cooped up. He took stock of the situation and conferred with Montezuma. The spirit of the emperor had been broken by grief for his own people and by the treachery of the Spaniards he had befriended. Montezuma maintained that there was nothing he could do. He feared that his people would no longer believe that he served their interests.

Through May and into June the siege lasted. The Spaniards were running low on food and ammunition. There were fierce fights almost daily. The Aztecs broke into the palace several times, but were beaten off. Cortez tried to break through the Aztecs' lines and escape from the city. But after fierce street fighting, he was driven back.

At last, when Cortez promised to leave Mexico City at once if the Aztec mobs would give him and his men safe passage, Montezuma consented to plead with his people once more. He spoke from a low tower on the palace wall. It was a broken and bowed figure of an emperor who made that last appeal for the safety of the invaders. But the people had had enough of Montezuma's friendship for the white men. His words were drowned out by shouts and insulting cries. Words were followed by a volley of stones and arrows. The nobles standing near Montezuma rushed forward with shields to protect him. They were too late. Montezuma fell. His body was pierced by two Aztec arrows. His head bled from the blow of a rock. This was in June, 1520.

When the people realized what they had done, they fled in every direction, fearing the destruction the gods might send down upon them for this terrible deed. After Montezuma's death, Cuauhtemuc became head of the Aztec army. Under his vigorous leadership, the Aztec pressure on the Spaniards became stronger. Realizing that he had to escape or perish, Cortez planned a final desperate effort to get out of the water-bound city. He constructed wooden forts on wheels, resembling primitive tanks. He had a portable bridge built to be laid across the breaks in the causeways, and he trained men in their use. With these means, the Spaniards tried to escape. The attempt failed.

On the night of June 30, while the Aztecs were arranging the funeral of Montezuma, Cortez decided to try to break away. Plans were made hurriedly but carefully. The Spanish would attempt to reach the mainland over the less heavily guarded Tlacopan causeway and then march in haste for the friendly walls of their allies, the Tlascalans.

When all preparations had been made, the Spaniards turned to the treasure. After the King of Spain's share and Cortez' own portion had been loaded on pack horses, there was still a huge pile of gold left on the floor. Seeing some of his men looking greedily at the yellow metal, Cortez told them to take what they wanted. As they fought over the gold to fill their pockets, he added: "But be careful not to overload yourselves. Remember, he travels fastest in the dark night who travels lightest."

At midnight, on June 30, 1520, the palace gates swung open and the Spaniards, hardly daring to breathe, stole out into the city. Across the deserted square they marched, and out onto the broad Tlacopan causeway. Soon they came to the first of three drawbridges. It was open. The portable bridge that Cortez had built was put across the gap.

Hardly was the bridge in place when a shrill cry split the silence of the night. An Aztec sentry had discovered them. As the Spaniards dashed across the makeshift bridge, the wails of the priests were heard, followed by the booming of the huge snakeskin drum on the top of the temple—a signal for the Aztecs to attack.

At first the Spaniards went forward in order. But as raging, yelling Aztecs leaped at them from all sides, they broke ranks. Order gave way to confusion. Soldiers slipped on the muddy banks and fell into the water to be drowned by the weight of their armor or the gold stuffed in their pockets. A man who fell only slightly wounded was immediately trampled to death by his fellows. Horse after horse fell, either with arrows buried in its body or with a leg broken in a fall. Banners, guns, gold, clothing, were thrown away by the Spaniards in their mad scramble to escape death, or, what was worse, capture and torture before being sacrificed to the Aztec gods.

Dawn came. The rising sun was greeted by shrill blood-curdling Aztec shouts of victory. But the Spaniards had gotten through, that is, about one-third of them. The rest were strewn along the causeway. It had been a horrible, terrible nightmare of a fight. After Cortez had sadly reviewed the shattered remains of his army, he sat down under a tree and buried his face in his hands. Tears streamed down his face. More than 700 Spaniards, over 3,000 Tlascalans, and half a hundred horses had been killed.

That night of June 30, 1520, has gone down in history as the Melancholy Night.

Despair was a short-lived emotion with Cortez. He had hardly recovered from the serious wounds he received in that terrible battle, before his head was awhirl with the new plans for the conquest of Mexico City and the realm of the Aztecs.

There were many things to be done. The support of Indian allies had to be assured. Indians had to be trained in European methods of fighting. Ships had to be built, for Cortez planned to attack from both land and water. Fresh soldiers and horses and supplies were recruited or forcibly taken from ships that put in at Vera Cruz on the coast. Ammunition had to be made. In this latter connection there is a story that illustrates how Cortez could inspire his men to risk their lives at his command. The Spaniards ran out of gunpowder. Cortez believed that he could make as much as he needed if he could only get sulphur. Now, among the mountains that stand guard around the valley of Mexico are several volcanoes. Where there are volcanoes, there is sulphur. Cortez needed sulphur. He got it.

One gallant Captain Montano and four brave men climbed

up the steep and lofty sides of Popocatepetl, the largest volcano. They peered over the edge into the huge, smoking pit
and watched with awe the flaming, fiery furnace about a
thousand feet below. Sulphur-laden steam rising from the
depths had formed sulphur deposits around the crater's edge.
To get the precious stuff, now more precious than Aztec gold,
Montano had himself lowered 400 feet into the crater with a
large basket. He made several trips before he had enough
sulphur for their needs.

The Aztecs, in the meantime, were not idle either. Cuitl-
huac, who succeeded Montezuma, after only 4 months on the
throne, died of smallpox. Cuauhtemoc, the young army leader,
took his place. This leader of the Aztecs had been an enemy
of the Spaniards from the start. He was ready to match Aztec
swords with Spanish steel.

It was almost a year after the Melancholy Night, namely
April 28, 1521, that Cortez' fleet of thirteen brigantines, built
under almost impossible conditions, was launched on the
waters of the lake. The general was ready to make his great
effort to capture Mexico City and defeat the Aztecs. For
several months, Cortez laid siege to Mexico City. Then at
dawn on August 13, 1521, the great attack by water and by
land began. All day long, the Spaniards and the Aztecs fought
desperately. There were victories on both sides. But as the sun
was setting, Emperor Cuauhtemoc was brought a captive to
Cortez. With the capture of their emperor, the fight went out of
his people. A daring wild dream had come true. Cortez had
completed his conquest of Mexico.

The glorious golden empire of the Aztecs became a Spanish
possession. Hernando Cortez, his greatest ambition fulfilled,
turned his eyes toward new horizons. He rebuilt Mexico City,
which had been reduced to ruin and rubble during and after
the long siege.

Immediately following the conquest of Mexico, the enemies
of Cortez tried to undermine his power. For a time, they

seemed successful but in October, 1522, word came from Spain that Cortez would serve as governor and captain general of New Spain. This was the name bestowed by the king on Mexico. Many other men would have rested on their laurels, but not Cortez. He sent expeditions into Central America; built a shipyard on the Pacific coast at Zacatula; and established the first trade route between Mexico and the Orient in 1527, when he sent three ships to the Moluccas under Alvaro de Saavedra.

Believing that a strait might exist between the Atlantic and Pacific Oceans, he sent one of his captains, Cristóbal de Olid, to investigate the coast of Central America.

In Honduras, Olid betrayed his trust and set up a colony of his own. Cortez, bent on punishing the traitor, fitted out an expedition and fought his way southward through the jungle wilderness to seize Olid. On the way, Cortez brutally killed Cuauhtemoc, the Aztec emperor, and two other Aztec princes he had brought along as hostages to ensure peace in Mexico City. On reaching Honduras, Cortez found that Olid had already been killed.

When Cortez returned to Mexico City in 1526, he found his enemies in control of the Government. Finally in 1528, Cortez returned to Spain where he was received with great honors, given a title, and granted much territory in New Spain. He returned to Mexico in 1530 and continued his exploratory expeditions, which included the discovery of southern California in 1533. Two years later, he established a colony called Puerto de la Paz in Lower California, but it was short-lived.

Meanwhile in Spain, the winds of royal favor swept in all directions and eventually they swept Cortez into oblivion. He left Mexico in 1540, discouraged and downhearted, and he died in Spain in 1547, as broken, as forgotten, and as poverty stricken as Columbus, two-score years before him.

Mexico, under the name of New Spain, was ruled from 1521 to 1821 successively by five governors, two royal commissions (*audiencias*), and sixty-two viceroys. The last of these, Juan O'Donoju, did not assume control. During the administration of the first viceroy, Don Antonio de Mendoza, who ruled from 1535 to 1550, discoveries were actively prosecuted in the north, the first money was coined in Mexico, the University of Mexico and several colleges were founded, and the first printing press in the New World was introduced. The School of Mines was founded by a later viceroy, the Marquis of Branciforte. The construction was begun in 1797, and the building was completed in 1813. Its total cost was about 2 million dollars.

The modern history of Mexico and the commencement of the almost continuous civil wars may be said to date from *el grito de Dolores* on the night of September 16, 1810, by the parish priest of Dolores, Don Miguel Hidalgo y Costilla. This patriot gathered about him many trusty followers under his banner to the cry of: "Long live religion! Long live our Most Holy Mother of Guadalupe! Long live America, and death to bad government." This cry is known as *el grito de Dolores*. Several efforts to cause a rebellion against the Spanish authorities had been made previous to this date, the first in 1798, but they were all suppressed. Don Hidalgo marshaled a considerable force and was victorious in several engagements, but he and his lieutenants—Allende, Aldama, and Jiménez—were captured and put to death in 1811. The bullets that ended their lives also ended the first stage of Mexico's war for independence.

José María Morelos y Pavón, the parish priest of Caracuaro, one of the greatest figures in Mexican history, then came to the front. Through his audacity, valor, and military sagacity, he led the cause of independence. After many notable engagements, in which he was almost always victorious, he captured Acapulco on April 12, 1813. In September, 1813, in the town of Chilpancingo, the first Mexican Congress was installed. Two months later it issued the declaration of independence and decreed the emancipation of the slaves. The first provisional constitution was adopted October 22, 1814. Morelos was eventually betrayed by a deserter named Carranco. He was taken to Mexico City, tried, and executed at San Cristóbal Ecatepec in December, 1815.

But the fires of independence continued to smolder in different parts of the republic. One of the patriots was Francisco Javier Mina, a Spanish officer. He disembarked at the port of Soto la Marina on April 15, 1817, with 500 men recruited in the United States, and marched rapidly into the interior, gaining many victories. His career ended when he was captured and killed in November, 1817. Many other patriot chiefs arose to lead the independent movement, but most of them met the fate of their predecessors. More successful was Guerrero, who, after many hazardous exploits and brilliant achievements, finally, in January, 1821, held a conference with Agustín de Iturbide, brigadier general in command of the royalist forces. The two leaders agreed to proclaim independence. The latter proclaimed what is known as the Plan of Iguala, on February 24, 1821. Next, Iturbide, assuming command of the forces, marched on Mexico City where the Viceroy Apodaca was deposed July 5, 1821. Spanish domination in Mexico, which had lasted three centuries, closed forever on September 27, 1821, when Iturbide made his triumphal entry into the capital.

The Mexican Congress elected Iturbide emperor in May, 1822. He was crowned and anointed with great pomp and ceremony in the great cathedral of the capital as Agustín I, Emperor of Mexico. His reign was short. General Santa Anna started a revolutionary movement in Vera Cruz, proclaimed a republic form of government, and compelled Iturbide to abdicate and leave the country. Iturbide made a return visit shortly after, only to be arrested, condemned to death, and executed. This was on July 19, 1824, just 5 days after he landed.

General Santa Anna dominated Mexican affairs for a good

many years. He is best remembered in the United States in connection with the battle of the Alamo in San Antonio. This episode was directly responsible for the independence of Texas. General Santa Anna played an erratic and rather tragic role in the fight for the liberty of his native land. He died in Mexico, old, lame, and blind, on June 20, 1876, and was buried without official honors. But his name, whether honored in Mexico or not, is part of Mexican history.

Now enter upon the Mexican scene two figures of tremendous contrast, Benito Juárez, who humbly began life in a squalid Indian hut, and Archduke Maximilian, a member of the rich and famous House of the Hapsburgers, brother of Francis Joseph, Emperor of Austria. The dramatic and tragic chapter of Mexican history in which these two men played leading roles began in 1858, when Juárez came into power. His administration was troubled by many political and economic crosscurrents. In 1861, France, Great Britain, and Spain occupied Vera Cruz because Juárez announced a 2-year suspension of the payment of foreign loans. England, Spain, and France had formed an alliance to make war on Mexico. However, England and Spain soon withdrew. France decided to carry on alone.

When large French forces were sent to Mexico by Napoleon III, Juárez declared war on France. On May 5, 1862, the French were defeated in battle. But their defeat was only temporary. In June, the following year, French troops entered Mexico City. On July 8, a monarchy was declared. In May, 1864, Archduke Maximilian landed at Vera Cruz to become Emperor of Mexico under the sponsorship of Napoleon III.

Meanwhile, French troops continued to pour into Mexico. In the summer of 1865, the French had driven Juárez north to the United States border. His forces were badly disorganized and his government without funds. Despite the fact that the crowns of Mexico sat on the heads of Maximilian and his Empress Carlota, Juárez never gave up his claim as the constitutional chief of the Mexican government. He surrounded himself with other Mexican patriots and worked constantly for the restoration of the republic.

The empire of Maximilian was having a hard time. The Mexicans did not endorse it. The United States opposed it. France saw how useless the whole project was. And Maximilian ran out of funds. All of this was good news to Juárez and his fellow patriots, but the best news they received during this trying period was word that the Civil War in the United States had ended and that Secretary of State Seward demanded that France withdraw her troops from Mexico. Seward abruptly said that the United States would go to war with France if the order was not obeyed. As France was not in a position to risk a war with the United States, the French troops went back to France.

This move was a blow to Emperor Maximilian. It put to an end the elaborate and gay balls and receptions given by the Empress Carlota. She returned to France to plead with Napoleon to stand by her emperor-husband. He refused to help the emperor. The unhappy empress was turned down everywhere she went. Eventually she lost her reason.

Back in Mexico, Maximilian faced a mountain of difficulties. In 1867 he was induced to lead an ill-fated army in a futile fight against Juárez to maintain his right to the empire. Deserted by his soldiers after a short time, Maximilian found himself besieged by the Mexicans. He was betrayed by one of his own trusted officers and captured. After a quick court-martial, Maximilian was executed on June 19, 1867. His last words are Mexican history: "May my blood be the last shed in sacrifice for this country; and if more is required, may it be for the good of the nation and never on account of treason."

And thus the scene between Juárez, the humble Indian, and Maximilian, the European prince, came to an end. Juárez once more became the head of a free Mexican republic, though not a peaceful one. A great deal of blood was shed before Mexico adjusted her domestic problems. But few countries have ever won lasting freedom any other way. Today, the United States of Mexico is one of the great republics of the New World, rich in heritage, in tradition, in natural resources, in history, and in heroes: Hidalgo, Morelos, Juárez, Diaz, Cardenas—her long line of patriots marches on.

If Hernando Cortez could return to the scene of his glory— Mexico City—today, he would undoubtedly be a little sad. For he would see descendants of the very people he thought he had conquered, ably guiding the affairs of a nation greater and richer than even his golden dreams of conquest could conjure up.

CHAPTER 4

Lands of the Spanish Main

Highlights of Central America

Population: 7,000,000.

Area: 225,000 square miles.

Language: Chiefly Spanish.

Countries: Guatemala, Salvador, Honduras, British Honduras, Nicaragua, Costa Rica, Panama.

Climatic Conditions: Ranging from tropical to subtropical, owing to variations in altitude.

Governments: Excepting British Honduras, which is a crown colony, the Central American countries are republics. They gained their independence from Spain in 1821.

THE chain of countries that form Central America is about a thousand miles long. It consists of seven links that vary in width from 40 to 600 miles. These links are: Guatemala, Salvador, Nicaragua, Honduras, Costa Rica, British Honduras, and Panama. At two points these connecting links of the two American continents trim down to comparatively thin strips of land between the two oceans. One of these points is the Isthmus of Panama in Panama. The other is the Isthmus of Tehuantepec in southern Mexico.

Between these two points lies the ancient and lost empire and bygone spheres of influence of the Mayas. Panama was beyond the frontier of Mayan influence, and its story is told in another chapter. But the chain of seven links will be kept intact by substituting Yucatan for Panama in this chapter. Although

64

Yucatan is part of the Republic of Mexico, it is closely knit to Honduras and Guatemala. This is because Yucatan's historical background is the key piece of the gigantic picture puzzle of Honduras and Guatemala in the lost culture of the early Mayas.

On the map of Central America there is no place called Maya-Land. And yet, only a few hundred years ago, a mighty people, creators of a splendid culture, spread their influence from Mexico City to Panama. These people were the Mayas. Their culture had its beginning in Guatemala and Honduras more than three thousand years ago. It made its last stand on the flat, arid plains of northern Yucatan with the coming of the Spaniards and the crumbling of the Maya Empire.

Where did these ancient empire builders develop? Myths have it that they came from the sea aboard large canoes. As their numbers increased, the ancients divided into tribes, each with laws and customs of its own. In time, they peopled the land from the Isthmus of Tehuantepec almost to the Isthmus of Panama.

The great family tree of the Mayas took root in the high mountain valleys of what today is Honduras and Guatemala. Established in a healthful climate on fertile land, with an abundance of water, the great Mayan cities of Tikal in northern Guatemala and Copan in western Honduras, flourished. In these large cities, built of stone, and in many smaller cities like them, lived a people who developed an elaborate system of hieroglyphic writing that enabled them to make a record of their history. They were accomplished astronomers and knew how to predict the seasons and compile an accurate calendar by observing the stars. They were splendid artists and craftsmen; skillful farmers and able merchants.

The resources of the country were abundant. It had fertile soil, and the greater portion of the people were engaged in agricultural pursuits. They traded for gold, silver, and other metals. Their architects, sculptors, and builders were equal in skill and taste and in mechanics to those of Babylon and Nineveh. The streets of their cities were paved. Water was brought in massive aqueducts from the mountain streams to the fountains in their communities. Their crops were cultivated by irrigation.

The greatest prosperity and highest achievements of the days when Maya-Land was in Guatemala and Honduras, dates back from 1,300 to 1,600 years. Then suddenly, for reasons unknown to us, the Mayas left their homes, their palaces, and their temples. They abandoned their trade routes. Their farms and gardens went back to the jungle. Maya-Land ceased to exist.

What happened? There is no answer. There must have been good reasons for a whole people to pack up and leave. Was it some sudden change in climate that made the land impossible to live in? Did a dreadful epidemic of malaria or yellow fever drive them out? It might have been earthquakes or volcanic outbursts. Or did the soil become exhausted after centuries of intensive farming? No one knows.

The abandoning of the ancient strongholds of the Mayas may have been sudden, but centuries passed before the people settled down to found another empire. The location of this new and mighty Maya-Land was Yucatan, the huge peninsula that divides the Gulf of Mexico from the Caribbean.

Yucatan is about 400 miles long and some 200 miles wide. It covers about the same area as the state of Minnesota. To the south, where it joins the mainland, Yucatan is rich in lakes and rivers. There the climate is even; the land rich. But northward on the peninsula, the country is very different. There the land is a flat table of limestone, with no rivers to create green meadows along their banks, although some bush does grow. There are but few lakes to ensure water supply in time of drought. For moisture, this region depends entirely upon rain. Strange features of this land without lakes and rivers are the deep, natural wells, or *cenotes*, in which the rainfall is stored far underground.

It was to this rather stern and forbidding country that many of the Mayas migrated from their ancestral homes in Guatemala and Honduras. They included two principal Mayan tribes—the Itzaes and the Xius. The former built the great city-state of Chichen Itza. The latter created the equally imposing metropolis of Uxmal. These city-states were about 100 miles apart and were ruled by priests and hereditary chiefs with despotic powers. As the city-states expanded, the rivalry between the Itzaes and the Xius grew. The result was that the two tribes were almost constantly at war. This situation became so serious during the last half of the twelfth century that it threatened to wreck the Maya civilization for a second time.

During this period of struggle and strife, one of the most remarkable figures in ancient American history entered upon the scene. His name was Quetzalcoatl. He was a member of the ancient Toltec nation that occupied Mexico to the north long before the Aztecs rose to power.

Quetzalcoatl is half history, half legend. According to history, he came to Maya-Land as a member of a Toltec war party. He was captured by the Mayas, but instead of serving as a slave, he became a man of great influence. In the course of the years, he rose in power and finally brought peace to Maya-Land by ending the disputes between Chichen Itza and Uxmal. He did this by establishing the neutral city-state of Mayapan, which virtually became the capital of Maya-Land.

So much for Quetzalcoatl as a man in human history. In legend, he is known to the Toltecs and the Aztecs as the Quetzal bird serpent, God of the Air. To the Mayas, he was known as Kukulcan, the Feathered Serpent and the God of the Air. Whether the god was a deified human being or the Toltec hero was the namesake of a god, remains a mystery. But man or god, Kukulcan, to call him by his Mayan name, played an important part in Mexican and Mayan history. In fact, he helped the Spanish conquistadors considerably. He was supposed to have been tall, fair-skinned, with golden hair and beard. Moreover, it was predicted that he or his children would return some day. Therefore, when the tall, bearded, and fair-skinned Spaniards arrived, they were taken to be the expected children of Kukulcan or Quetzalcoatl.

Kukulcan is supposed to have lived until close toward the end of the twelfth century. He is held responsible for the strong and steady Toltec influx from Mexico into Yucatan. The Toltecs were intelligent and quick to learn. They adopted all the best features of the Maya civilization and added a few touches of their own. Up to the time of the Toltec infiltration, the Mayas had not practiced human sacrifice to any great extent. After the coming of the Toltecs from Mexico, the offering of human beings to placate the gods began to play an increasingly important part in the religious life of the people.

Although, under Toltec influence, the culture and civilization of the Mayas reached great heights, the system of numbers and hieroglyphic writing was perfected, astronomical observatories built, a calendar more accurate than the one then in use in Europe was developed before the Mexicans arrived. There was intense interest in sports. A game very much like our basketball and played with a large rubber ball became popular. The soldiers wore armor of thickly quilted coats and helmets. Their wooden swords were edged with sharp obsidian, a hard, volcanic glass. The Mayas, too, used one of history's strangest hand grenades, a thin and fragile gourd filled with live hornets.

The city-states, such as Chichen Itza, Uxmal, and Mayapan, were built virtually alike. In the center stood the magnificent temple pyramids surrounded by the palaces of nobles and priests. On the edge, spread out the simpler homes of the common people.

For generations after the death of Kukulcan, life was rather peaceful in Maya-Land. There were wars, but they were mainly fought to obtain slaves for work or for sacrifices. As the years went on, a family by the name of Cocom rose to power in Mayapan. When Hunac Ceel of that clan became the ruler of the capital city, he made life so miserable and difficult for the other city-states that they rose in rebellion. Civil wars raged throughout the land. Finally, in 1441, the soldiers of Uxmal and Chichen Itza attacked Mayapan and destroyed it. That was the end of the league established by Kukulcan.

Individual governments broke down. Civil wars, droughts, and plagues took their toll. The Itzas abandoned their splendid city and founded Peten Itza far to the south. The Xius of Uxmal moved on to a place they named Mani, meaning the end. And that was indeed the beginning of the end of the glories that had been the Mayas.

The decay of the Maya Empire was well under way when Christopher Columbus unknowingly discovered the outpost islands of a New World in 1492. The Great Admiral did not reach the mainland until 10 years later. He first set foot on the continent of America in Honduras. A few days before he did that, opportunity for rich discovery knocked on the door of Columbus' cabin, but he did not hear the call. This is what happened:

On an August day in 1502, as his ship rode at anchor near the coast of Honduras, Columbus was surprised to see a huge canoe, manned by twenty-five Indian paddlers, coming toward him from what is today the Island of Pines, in the Bay Island group. The canoe itself was enough to draw exclamations of amazement from the gaping Spanish sailors. It was 8 feet across and almost as long as their own caravel. In the center of this craft was a rich canopy. Under it sat a dignified chief in fine dress, surrounded by members of his household.

Columbus was impressed. Because his mind was concerned solely with finding a water passage to the Orient, he asked the tall and stately Indian chief if he knew the way to Cathay or

Cipango. In reply, the Indian muttered something that sounded like "Mayam." That did not interest Columbus. His son, Fernando, however, examined the contents of the Indian canoe. To his amazement, he found that it contained cloth finely woven in many colors, feather capes, copper hatchets, copper bells, knives of flint, and corn bread. The owner of the canoe was a Mayan trader.

The only spark of enthusiasm Columbus showed was when he saw some trinkets made of gold. He asked where the gold came from. The chief told him that it came from a rich city far away to the north where there was much gold. But tales of rich cities far away had become tiresome fables to Columbus. He had been misled too often by Indians to take stock in this tale. Instead of sailing north as the Mayan trader suggested, Columbus headed his little fleet toward the east.

If Columbus had sailed north, he would undoubtedly have discovered Yucatan. Chances are that, from there, he would have gone on, as did Cortez later, to the wealth of Montezuma in Mexico City. As it was, his eastward course led Columbus into howling hurricanes, torrential rains, and roaring winds that all but crippled his poor fleet. That chance meeting could have prefaced a glorious new beginning or, at least, a spectacular ending for Columbus. Instead, the Admiral sailed toward more disappointments.

The next contact of Spaniards with the Mayas of Yucatan had far-reaching effects. In 1511, a Spanish ship bound from Panama to Haiti was wrecked on a reef near Jamaica. It was commanded by Diego de Nicuesa. Some twenty of the crew survived. They drifted for days in a tiny open boat which eventually was washed ashore on Yucatan. The exhausted Spaniards were captured by a Maya tribe and taken to a village where they were imprisoned in a large wooden cage. The Mayas fed the Spaniards well. As they fattened, their numbers steadily decreased. Then two of the prisoners, Gerónimo de Aguilar, a priest, and Gonzalo Guerrero, a soldier, realized that their luckless companions were being sacrificed to the bloodthirsty gods of the Mayas. With several others, they escaped from the prison by burrowing under the wall of their pen. All but Aguilar and Guerrero died in the jungle.

These two men would undoubtedly have met the same fate if they had not run into a friendly chief named Ahkin Cutz. He made the two Spaniards his slaves, but he treated them well. They soon found themselves favorites with the whole tribe. In time, Father Aguilar was made an honored member of the chief's household. Guerrero, as an extremely valuable warrior, was traded to a neighboring chief, Na Chan Caan of Chetemal.

Six years after these two Spaniards were shipwrecked and captured, in March, 1517, Francisco de Córdoba explored the coast along Yucatan in search of Indians to bring back to slavery in Cuba. He saw the tall pyramids of a Maya City and named it Great Cairo. After a skirmish with the Indians at Cape Catoche, Córdoba sailed westward and reached a large city. There the Indians, who appeared friendly enough, kept repeating the word: "Castilian! Castilian!" meaning Spaniard. On investigating, the Spaniards learned that two bearded white men, like themselves, were held captive by Indians in another part of the country.

Córdoba hoped to rescue his countrymen, who were none other than Father Aguilar and Guerrero, the soldier. The Indians, however, turned hostile and Córdoba was badly defeated in a battle at Champoton, in which fifty Spaniards were killed. It was not a very triumphant expedition that Córdoba took back to Cuba. But the news he brought of large cities with lofty pyramids and of having met Indians who spoke the word: "Castilian!" started the first gold rush to the American continent.

Juan de Grijalva, nephew of the governor of Cuba, was the next Spaniard to venture into Yucatan. He sailed in April,

1518. Among his captains were men who were to make their mark in the history of New World conquest: Francisco Montejo, Bernal Díaz, Pedro de Alvarado, and Alonso de Ávila. Grijalva reached the Island of Cozumel, off Yucatan, and then sailed on to Champoton where Córdoba had lost the first major battle of attempted Spanish conquest. He, too, saw great cities. He, too, heard of white men held captive. But what was more important, Grijalva got his hands on 20,000 pesos worth of gold. Eager to let his uncle, Governor Velásquez, know of his success, Grijalva sent the gold back to Cuba with Pedro de Alvarado.

When Velásquez saw actual gold he prepared an expedition to explore and exploit this new land of golden promise, and incidentally rescue the two white captives. Hernando Cortez was put in command.

The historic Cortez expedition sailed from Cuba in February, 1519. A few days later it put in at Cozumel Island. From some Indians, Cortez learned that the two whites were being held captive by Indians 2 days' journey in the interior on the mainland. He immediately sent a letter by messenger to the Spanish captives informing them that a ship would wait for them for 10 days on the coast. Cortez also sent along some green glass beads with which the Spaniards could buy their freedom.

Cortez waited for 10 days but when the rescue ship returned without news of the white prisoners, he set sail. Fortunately, as it proved, one of the vessels sprang a leak and the whole fleet returned to Cozumel. After repairs had been made, and as they were about to sail again, an old and bent man, his brown, half-naked body covered with paint, came ashore in a canoe. In halting Spanish, he explained that he was Father Gerónimo de Aguilar, one of the Spaniards for whom Cortez had sent ransom. When asked about his fellow captive, Father Aguilar told how he had tried to persuade Guerrero to come with him, but that the shipwrecked soldier, now an honored and powerful military leader among the Mayas, flatly refused to be rescued. Guerrero, it seems, had achieved far greater success as a slave of the Mayas than he ever would as a soldier of the Spanish king. He even told Aguilar to warn Cortez that he would be ready with his Indian army to defend Yucatan against Spanish invasion.

With Cortez was one Bernal Díaz, already a veteran Yucatan voyager. Díaz had sailed with Córdoba in 1517, and with Grijalva the following year. It was as a member of the Grijalva expedition that Bernal Díaz, believing that a colony was to be established in Yucatan, brought along some orange seeds. These he planted at Tabasco. When the seeds sprouted, the Maya priests saw that they were different from any plants they knew and carefully tended them. From these seeds came the first oranges in America.

Leaving Cozumel Island and Yucatan behind, Cortez sailed on to the town of Tabasco to fight his first battle against the Indians and to win his first victory in the conquest of Mexico. That was in the year 1519.

Mexico had fallen long before the forces of Spain began the conquest of Yucatan. In 1527, Francisco Montejo was given a royal grant to conquer and colonize the country. He founded the city of Salamanca that year and started on a grand tour of Yucatan, going from one Maya town to another, but never stopping long in any one place. It was an instructive and educational tour, but a costly one. When Montejo returned to Salamanca he had only seventy-two of his army of 382 soldiers left, fever and hostile Indians having done for the rest.

While exploring along the coast looking for a harbor, Montejo put in at Chetemal. There he captured an Indian who told him about a white man who commanded the Mayan army in that country. And so, Gonzalo Guerrero enters the picture again. Montejo sent a letter asking this "renegade" to surrender. Guerrero sent a polite but a firm "no thank you." From that time on, Guerrero became an active enemy of the

Spaniards. He taught his Indian warriors Spanish methods of warfare: how to dig trenches and pits and how to fight from ambush.

Not having achieved any notable success on his first tour of conquest, Montejo next decided to establish an inland base of operations. For this he selected the ruins in the abandoned city of Chichen Itza. He renamed this ancient Mayan metropolis Ciudad Real. But the hostility of both the country and the Indians were too much for Montejo. At first the Indians in the vicinity of Chichen Itza were not openly antagonistic, but they soon refused to work for the Spaniards or to bring them food. Then the more organized Indians, under the able leadership of Guerrero, attacked right and left. On one occasion, the Spaniards sent a desperate message to Guerrero asking him to give them food. His reply was that all the food the Spaniards would ever get from him or his adopted people would be at the points of Mayan spears or on the tips of Mayan arrows.

This second venture of Montejo's was also a failure. About to be attacked by a vast Indian army that would probably have wiped them out, the Spaniards managed to escape from Chichen Itza with their lives only through a clever trick. The Spaniards knew that the Mayas would not dare to attack while the church bell was ringing, as that indicated that the Spaniards were together in a body at prayers, So, on a dark night, Montejo attached the bell rope to the collar of his dog. Then he placed a bone just out of the dog's reach. As the hungry dog jumped for the bone, hour after hour, the dog tolled the bell, thus keeping the Indians from attacking.

Saved by a hungry dog, the starved army of Montejo escaped that night. The trick was discovered by the Indians shortly after dawn the next morning, but by then Montejo and his men were well on the way to the coast.

After losing Chichen Itza, Montejo returned to Cuba. By 1535, Spaniards controlled Mexico, Peru, Honduras, Panama,

Guatemala, and many other lands. But the white man had still no foothold in the Yucatan of the Mayas.

In 1540, as governor of Tabasco, Montejo sent his son, Francisco the Younger, to have another try at conquering Yucatan. As his father before him, the son met with stiff opposition from the Mayas. But, even as civil warfare had broken up the League of Mayapan many years before, so internal strife caused the final collapse of the Mayan nation.

Montejo the Younger selected the ancient city of Ti-Ho as his capital in 1540. One morning a sentry cried out that a mighty army of Indian warriors was almost at the gates. The Spaniards feverishly prepared for battle when, to their amazement, the Indians dropped their arms just outside the city in indication of friendship. The chief, Titul of the Xius clan, offered to join the Spaniards in war against his arch enemies, the powerful Cocoms. The bargain was made.

On January 11, 1541, Machi Cocom attacked the Spanish stronghold with 50,000 warriors. A fierce battle, which lasted all day, took a terrific toll of life on both sides. But, when it was over, the Spaniards were victorious. Organized resistance to the white invaders ended with this battle. On January 6, 1542, when he founded the city of Merida, young Montejo completed the conquest his father had begun in 1527.

It is true that 1542 marks the date of the conquest of Yucatan, but isolated Mayan tribes held out and continued to fight the Spaniards. As late as 1850 there was a Maya uprising against the Mexicans. A force of Indians, led by Felipe Pat and Cecilio Chi, swept successfully over the peninsula of Yucatan. They were almost at the gates of Merida and had victory within their grasp, when the rains came. Suddenly the Indians abandoned the fight and returned to their homes to tend their fields.

Today archaeologists are still working to fit together the huge jigsaw puzzle of Central America's great ancient civilization. At times they have received help from the most unexpected sources. A notable instance is that of the late Edward H. Thompson. While United States consul in Yucatan many years ago, Thompson became the owner of the Chichen Itza plantation on which is located the ruins of ancient Chichen Itza, including the timeworn temple pyramids, the broken avenues, the wrecked palaces, and other tumble-down ruins. One of the features of this ghost city was, and still is, the Sacred Well of Chichen Itza. Intrigued by stories of human beings having been thrown into this well alive as offerings to the Rain God, Don Eduardo, as the American consul was known, decided to find out if the stories were true. First he dredged the Sacred Well. Later he actually went to its bottom in a diving outfit.

Thompson performed these operations under terrific handicaps, but his labors were richly rewarded. From the bottom of the Sacred Well he brought up scores of jade ornaments, golden bells, and copper dolls and idols. Not only that, but he recovered a number of human skeletons. Some were the thick bones of full-grown men, but many of the gruesome relics were the skeletons of young girls who had been thrown into the well as brides of the Rain God.

On the other hand, descendants of the Mayas themselves have been instrumental in bringing to light, in the almost impenetrable jungle, remains of the past glories of their people. And strangely enough, it is the habit of gum chewing that is responsible. Chewing gum is made of a substance called chicle. For years, the natives of Guatemala, Honduras, and Yucatan have gone into the deep jungles to draw this chicle from trees. Time and again, they have called the attention of Mexican and North American scientists to ruins of the bygone past that have been swallowed by the green tidal wave of the jungle. The broken picture of the life history of the Mayas is one of the world's greatest mysteries. Some of the clues have been found and fitted together, others are still hidden in the jealous grip of the jungles of Yucatan and Central America. Some day the missing pieces will be found. When they are put together, they will unfold a picture of a mighty people who built a high culture before it vanished on the current of time.

Guatemala

Discovered: By Pedro de Alvarado for Spain in February, 1524.

Population: c. 2,000,000.

Area: 48,290 square miles.

Language: Spanish.   *Capital:* Guatemala City.

Government: Republic established in 1839.

Geographical Characteristics: Extremely healthful and fertile high plateaus formed by the chain of mountains that traverses the country and mountain spurs that extend in every direction.

Climatic Conditions: Along the narrow strips of the coast line, conditions are characteristically tropical. But in the interior, where plateau elevations range from 4,000 to 11,000 feet, the climate is pleasant and moderate.

Principal Products: Coffee, bananas, chicle, sugar, woods, rubber, cattle, hides, and skins.

The news of the invasion and the fall of Mexico in 1521 spread quickly through Central America. Traveling Indian merchants told tales of armored men and amazing animals and the awful power of their arms. Scarcely had Cortez subdued the Aztecs, when some of the southern nations sent ambassadors to Mexico to seek his favor. The great conquistador entrusted the work of their subjugation to Pedro de Alvarado.

This famous soldier was no ordinary adventurer, but a man of good family. He was born in Badajoz, Spain, in 1485. At the age of twenty-five, he went to Cuba with Governor Velásquez. Alvarado was famous for his athletic feats. To a frank and amiable disposition was united craft, courage, and cruelty.

Alvarado left Mexico on December 6, 1523, with 300 infantry, 120 cavalry, four cannon, several hundred Mexican warriors, and thousands of slaves to carry the baggage. The

Quiches, who were the most powerful nation in Guatemala, would make no terms with the Spaniards and met them in battle, with the usual result. The Indians were defeated.

With occasional battles with the natives, who retreated before him, Alvarado continued his march until he was brought to a halt by an army of 20,000 warriors. A desperate fight took place on the plains before the present city of Quezaltenango. The water of the river, it was said, was tinted for days with the blood of the dead and the wounded. After a brief rest, Alvarado marched upon the city of Utatlan. There the Spaniards received a submissive and hospitable welcome.

Suspecting that the invitation to occupy the city was a trap Alvarado tried the two kings of the Quiches by court-martial for treachery, and condemned them to the stake. The sentence was executed and the town was burned. This happened on Good Friday, 1524. From Utatlan, Alvarado marched to Guatemala, and was as well received, according to his own account, "as if I had come to my own father's house."

But in the meantime, the chiefs gathered a still larger army, and another battle occurred near Lake Amatitlan. The slaughter of the natives was terrific, but the Spaniards, with the advantage of firearms, suffered little. Thereafter, resistance was feeble and disorganized. On July 25, 1524, Alvarado formally proclaimed the sovereignty of the King of Spain over Guatemala. He selected the native town of Almolonga as the site of his capital, which he christened, with great ceremony: "The City of St. James, the Gentleman."

While several thousand Indians were employed in building the city, Alvarado returned to Mexico, and thence to Spain to give an account of his conquests. The king made him governor *adelantado* and captain general of Guatemala. The new governor strengthened himself at court by marrying Doña Beatrice de la Cueva, the daughter of an illustrious and influential family. He returned with her to Guatemala accompanied by a large number of colonists and adventurers.

The new colony grew rapidly in prosperity and population. But the restless Alvarado heard of Pizarro's conquest of the Incas. He built a ship and sailed down the west coast to Ecuador where he proceeded to reap a share of the harvest Pizarro claimed for his own. The latter resented the intrusion, and the two invaders narrowly avoided combat. Alvarado, fearing the result of his impudence, discreetly allowed himself to be bought off with a liberal bounty. He left the greater part of his followers with Pizarro and returned to Guatemala about a quarter of a million dollars richer.

Doughty Alvarado next appeared in Mexico, in 1541, just at the time when the Spanish colony there was aflame over the reports of richer countries to the northward. Chances are that he would have gone with the famous expedition that Coronado led in search of the fabulous Seven Cities of Cibola, but for an accident that cost him his life. Alvarado went with a Spanish battalion to the province of Jalisco to subdue an Indian rebellion. His horse fell and Alvarado was crushed under a mass of falling rocks that the animal dislodged in its struggle.

When the news of Alvarado's death reached his widow in Guatemala, she called all the alcaldes and *regidores* to the palace and proclaimed herself *gobernadora*. She appointed her brother, Don Francisco de la Cueva, lieutenant governor and commander of the troops.

The capital was situated on the slope of the stately twin volcanoes, Agua (water) and Fuego (fire). The citizens were in a state of great excitement over the audacity of Doña Beatrice in taking control of the government, when a howling storm broke loose. Two hours after dark, the earth was shaken by terrible convulsions, and an avalanche of water swept down the mountainside, carrying with it vast quantities of earth, rocks, and trees uprooted from the forest. The water was supposed to have come from the volcano Agua, hence its name. A deep ravine, which can be seen today, marks the path of the destructive flood. The city was buried beneath the deluge and the debris. The ambitious widow of the conquistador sought safety in the chapel adjoining the palace. Here, while clinging to the crucifix, she was crushed by the falling walls.

Following the disaster, the capital was removed a few miles eastward, where are now the picturesque ruins of Antigua Guatemala. That city flourished and became the most populous, the most beautiful, and the most influential north of the Isthmus, Mexico City alone excepted. There is no grander group of ruins on the Western Hemisphere, for the city's architecture was stately and massive. At the time of its destruction by an earthquake in 1773, Antigua Guatemala had a population of 80,000. Buildings with foundations as deep and walls as massive as those of the Capitol of Washington were crumbled into dust and the magnificent palace of the governor was shaken to fragments. On Sunday night, July 29, 1773, the disaster came without warning. In the twinkling of an eye, one of the proudest cities in the New World was forever humbled. The dead were never counted. The wounded died from lack of relief. The living escaped to the mountains and plains. The present capital, Guatemala la Nueva, was founded by the survivors, 30 miles away, on a picturesque plateau.

For three centuries, Spain governed Central America by the *Audiencia Real*. There were spasmodic attempts at resistance, and formal protests against her tyranny as early as 1811. It was not until 1821 that the representative of the king, Gabino Gainza, surrendered his authority. On September 15 of that year, independence was proclaimed and obtained without bloodshed. But peace was soon broken when Mexico tried to annex Central America to the ephemeral empire of Agustín de Iturbide.

Mexican troops, commanded by General Filísola, occupied the city of Guatemala on June 12, 1822. But Mexican domination, which never was accepted by the country, was of a short duration. The fall of Iturbide compelled General Filísola to return to Mexico with his army. Before his departure, however, he called a national assembly for the purpose of organizing the government of the country. That assembly met on June 24, 1823. Seven days later, it issued a decree which, to this day, is considered as the solemn and fundamental act of the emancipation of Central America. In November, the assembly established the Republic of Central America, under the form of a popular and representative government. It decreed also the abolition of slavery, equality before the law, division of powers, liberty of the press, and religious tolerance.

This form of government was not, unfortunately, maintained for long. Party jealousies brought civil wars. Revolutions rent the whole country. Despite the efforts of numerous patriots, including the illustrious General Morazán, the federation was dissolved in 1839. The five republics, one after another, began their autonomy under the respective names of Guatemala, Salvador, Honduras, Nicaragua, and Costa Rica. Since that time, they have continued to govern themselves as sovereign and independent states.

Salvador

Discovered: By Pedro de Alvarado for Spain in 1524.

Population: 1,635,000.

Area: 13,176, square miles.

Language: Spanish.   *Capital:* San Salvador.

Government: Republic established in 1832

Geographical Characteristics: Large fertile valleys rest between numerous spurs sent out by the two mountain ranges that run through the country.

Climatic Conditions: Range from tropical heat on the Pacific coast to mild temperatures on the interior uplands.

Principal Products: Coffee, sugar, indigo, tobacco, rubber, rice, gold, silver, balsam, henequen, and hides.

In the summer of 1524, after he had swept like a tornado through Guatemala, Pedro de Alvarado crossed La Paz River into Salvador. At first, the conquistador was hospitably received by the natives. But, overcome by terror at the cruelties inflicted on them, the Indians fled and spread an alarm which resulted in desperate resistance.

In a fierce battle at Acajutla, Alvarado received an arrow wound which rendered him lame for the remainder of his life. He took such ample revenge for that injury that of all the great multitude of his opponents on that day, not one was left alive. The struggle between the mailclad, well-armed Spanish veterans and the poorly equipped and half-naked native warriors could have but one result—victory for the invaders. But the victory was delayed by the bravery of the Indians. Not until 1525 was Cuscatlan, the capital, finally captured. Salvador then became part of the viceregal kingdom of Guatemala. For nearly three centuries it continued under Spanish rule. The natives wasted away and diminished in the cruel slavery imposed on them, as they tilled the soil under the fierce tropical sun, or toiled in the mines for the benefit of their taskmasters.

Even so, Salvador suffered less from Spanish rule than some of the other provinces of Guatemala, because it was farther removed from the central seat of authority. When the first mutterings of the coming storm of revolution were heard in 1811, Salvador was ready. It was not until 1821 that the successful termination of the struggle for liberty in Mexico inspired the southern colonies to shake off the Spanish yoke. This was accomplished without bloodshed, and in September of that year, the territory comprised in the kingdom of Guatemala was declared free and independent. In the following year, an attempt was made to annex the country to the Mexican Empire, under the rule of Iturbide. The Province of Salvador resisted, but finally had to submit to a Mexican force commanded by General Filísola, and was incorporated in the Mexican Empire.

The following year, however, witnessed the downfall of Iturbide. Salvador next joined the Central American Confederation, and became an independent republic in 1832 when it withdrew from the federation.

Honduras

Discovered: By Christopher Columbus for Spain in 1502.

Population: About 960,000.

Area: 46,250 square miles.

Language: Spanish.   *Capital:* Tegucigalpa.

Government: Republic established in 1838.

Geographical Characteristics: Low coastal plains extend inland from both shores, while the country gradually rises in the interior to several thousand feet.

Climatic Conditions: Same as that of Guatemala; hot jungle climate in the lowlands along the seashore; healthy mountain climate in higher altitudes.

Principal Products: World's largest crop of bananas; hides; indigo; rubber; ivory nuts; sisal hemp; and food products.

Honduras was discovered by Columbus during his fourth voyage. The locality first seen by him was the island of Guanaja, the most easterly of the group now called the Bay Islands, where he arrived on July 30, 1502. He reached the mainland on August 14 at a point which he named Punta de Caxinas, a cape stretching out into the sea and forming what was afterward known as the Bay of Trujillo.

Here the great explorer's foot first touched the mainland of the continent of America. Some 50 miles eastward, at the mouth of a river which he named Río de la Posesión (now known as Río Tinto) Columbus again landed and took formal possession of the country for Spain.

We next hear of Honduras when Gil González de Avila, while on a voyage from Santo Domingo to Nicaragua in 1524, reached the coast near the bay now called Puerto Cortez.

Having lost some of his horses there, he gave it the name of Puerto Caballos (Port of Horses), but he made no settlement.

While Honduras was placed on the map by Christopher Columbus in 1502, its real story does not begin until 22 years later, when Hernando Cortez placed one of his captains, Cristóbal de Olid, in charge of an expedition to sail southward along the coast of Central America. Olid was to discover, and claim, new lands for the glory of Spain and the profit of Cortez. But above all, he was to search for a strait that connected the Atlantic Ocean with the Pacific, discovered by Balboa in 1513. Backed by Cortez' money and Cortez' prestige, Olid sailed from Cuba with an army of 400 men. While in Cuba, Olid developed a close friendship with Governor Velásquez, who had never forgiven Cortez for cheating him out of his rightful share of the Aztec plunder. Inasmuch as conspiracy and double-dealing were among the principal by-products of the New World at that time, Velásquez did not find it difficult to convince Olid that it would be proper for him to feather his own nest and forget his obligations to Cortez. The ambitious Olid saw virtue in this proposal and adopted it. The result was that, when he reached Honduras, Olid established himself as a conqueror in his own right in a town he called Triumph of the Cross.

News of this change of policy on the part of Olid reached Cortez in Mexico City. To punish his faithless follower, Cortez organized an expedition under his own leadership. It was made up of hundreds of Spanish soldiers and thousands of Indian warriors. The 1,500-mile march from Mexico City to the coast of Honduras was made under the most trying circumstances. There were mountains to climb, rivers to cross, swamps to wade, jungle to penetrate, and Indians to fight.

Scores of men dropped dead by the wayside. Horses died or were maimed. All for the sake of revenge upon a man who had built a squalid town in a swamp! Then, when after many months, Cortez reached the town of Triumph of the Cross, he learned that his efforts had been in vain. Olid, the man he came to punish, was beyond punishment. He was dead. He had been killed even before Cortez left Mexico City.

The Spanish settlement established by Olid has passed out of existence, but Puerto Cortez, founded by Cortez in 1524, is still a thriving town. From Honduras, Cortez hurried back to Mexico to end rumors that he had died.

From this time on, for nearly three centuries, as a province of what was called the Kingdom of Guatemala, Honduras was under the rule of Spain. War, pestilence, and enforced labor in the mines and plantations swept away the enslaved Indian people, until at last there remained but a mere fragment of its once teeming population.

Futile and desultory attempts to overthrow Spanish rule were made by the colonials from time to time. In 1810, there were even echoes in Honduras of the cry of freedom made in Mexico by the patriot priest Hidalgo.

At long last, freedom came to Honduras when the Republic of Central America was organized. Eventually, this Union was dissolved. On October 26, 1838, Honduras became a free and independent state.

British Honduras

Population: 55,000.

Area: 8,500 square miles.

Language: English.   *Capital:* Belize.

Government: British crown colony.

Geographical Characteristics: From rather swampy coastal region, land rises quickly to hills and low mountains.

Climatic Conditions: Generally subtropical, except along coast.

Principal Products: Mahogany and other lumber, bananas, sugar, coconuts, and citrus fruits.

In the olden days, when buccaneers sailed the Spanish Main, British Honduras was known as Belize. It was the favorite meeting place of pirates. In time, Belize became a settlement of retired buccaneers. Spain owned the territory; in fact it was really part of Guatemala. However, most of the pirates who settled in Belize were Englishmen. They regarded their colony as an English possession—and so did England.

The British grip on Belize was strengthened after the seventeenth century when the forerunners of the lumbermen, called baymen, came to the colony. They were lured there by the magnificent forests of mahogany and logwood. There were many bitter battles between the baymen and the Spanish. Finally, by the treaty of Paris in 1783, the colony of Belize became English property. In 1871, British Honduras was raised to the status of a British crown colony. It is the only region on the Caribbean Sea's mainland that has remained in English hands.

Nicaragua

Population: 820,000.

Area: 44,275 square miles.

Language: Spanish.   *Capital:* Managua.

Government: Republic established 1839.

Geographical Characteristics: The outstanding feature is Lake Nicaragua in the southwestern section of the country. This lake is linked to the Atlantic Ocean by the San Juan River and separated from the Pacific by a narrow strip of land.

Climatic Conditions: Hot and humid near the coast, the climate becomes more temperate in the high mountain valleys.

Principal Products: Bananas, hardwoods, coffee, sugar, and tobacco.

Columbus discovered Nicaragua in 1502, but the most prominent figure in its history was Gil González de Avila, who found the country under the rule of a chief named

Nicarao. The latter's capital was situated on the shore of the great lake, then called Cocibolca, near the site of the present city of Rivas. The Spaniards named this lake, Nicaraoagua, or water of Nicarao. The name Nicaragua was thus created, and it has since been bestowed on the whole republic.

The history of the long Spanish rule in Nicaragua is more or less that of the other Central American republics. In 1821, Guatemala, of which Nicaragua was a province, seceded from Spain. This movement was followed by Nicaragua and the other provinces, and the Central American Confederation was formed. After a few years, Nicaragua withdrew from the Union and proclaimed itself a republic. When General Morazán, the great advocate of the federation, died in 1840, the cause of the Union was lost.

The question of building a canal to connect the Atlantic Ocean and the Pacific came to the fore almost the very day Balboa discovered the Great South Sea from a mountain peak in Darien. The route through Nicaragua, by way of the San Juan River and Lake Nicaragua, has always been among those which offered the strongest claims for consideration. Such a canal was advocated by Baron Alexander von Humboldt, who spent 10 years in exploration and scientific research in South and Central America. The realization of this idea came close to its fulfillment in 1901 when the United States approved a report favoring the Nicaragua route as against that of Panama. The following year, the decision was reversed. In 1916, a few years after the completion of the Panama Canal, the United States paid Nicaragua 3 million dollars for the right to build a waterway across Nicaragua. This treaty has since been reindorsed.

The story of Nicaragua is not complete without reference, brief as it must be, to William Walker, the famous filibusterer. The dramatic exploits of this Tennessee-born nineteenth-century buccaneer came near rewriting Central American history. All this happened nearly a hundred years ago. Time has painted Walker as a romantic hero, whereas he was really an arch destroyer of the rights of others. This is the story. In June, 1855, William Walker, with a band of three-score fighting men, landed in Nicaragua on the invitation of the local revolutionaries to help them rise against the party in power. With further reinforcements from the United States, Walker attacked the conservative stronghold at Granada and took it.

Patricio Rivas, leader of the Liberals, was made president by Walker who appointed himself commander in chief of the armies. At this time, Juan Rafael Mora was president of Costa Rica. Mora, who deservedly is Costa Rica's national hero, saw the security of all the Central American republics endangered. He resolved to rid Central America of Walker and took the field against him.

The resourceful and ruthless Walker defeated the Costa Ricans in a strenuous campaign, but soon found himself face to face with an alliance of all the Central American states. Then Cornelius Vanderbilt joined the opposition. Vanderbilt controlled the Accessory Transit Line that ran across Nicaragua and made high profits carrying men, mail, and merchandise bound for the California gold fields. Vanderbilt was neutral until Walker seized his steamers on the San Juan River. This was stepping on tender toes, and Vanderbilt then supported Costa Rica and its allies. Walker and his followers were finally beseiged in the city of Rivas on the Pacific coast. They were saved from surrender only in a nick-of-time rescue through the intervention of the United States Navy. A gunboat brought Walker and his North American cohorts to California. But Walker continued to plot new filibustering expeditions. In 1860, he went to the Bay Islands to prepare an attack on Trujillo, Honduras. His attempt failed. Walker was captured and executed by a firing squad.

Costa Rica

Population: 500,000.

Area: 23,000 square miles.

Language: Spanish: *Capital:* San José.

Government: Republic established in 1848.

Geographical Characteristics: Two chains of continental ranges run through the country creating a series of highlands ranging from 3,000 feet to mile-high elevations.

Climatic Conditions: Virtually the same as other Central American countries.

Principal Products: Bananas, coffee and other agricultural products, wood, rubber, gold, and silver.

Columbus discovered Costa Rica on September 18, 1502. He disembarked at Cariay Bay, now the city of Limón. At the time of the discovery, it is estimated that there were about 27,000 Indians in Costa Rica. They responded to the friendly overtures made by Columbus, but offered a determined resistance to the conquistadors who came in his wake. The result was that by 1611 the entire population, including the Spaniards and Spanish Indians, was not more than 15,000. This was due to endless warfare that took heavy toll of life on both sides.

One by one, the conquistadors came to Costa Rica. They came, they founded colonies, and one by one they left. As they left, their colonies died. The first really important center of Spanish population in Costa Rica, which has lasted to the present day, was the city of Cartago. It was established in 1564 by Vázquez de Coronado, who, probably more than any other, advanced the conquest of the region by peaceful means.

Costa Ricans, during the next 200 years, faced extreme hardship and danger with hostile Indians in the jungles and bloodthirsty pirates on the oceans. They were continually ravaged by the raids of the Mosquito Indians of Nicaragua and by English and Dutch pirates. Perhaps the greatest burden the courageous Costa Ricans of that era had to bear was the stagnating effect of the Spanish trading monopoly in the New World. Unable to obtain goods from the outside and consequently dependent upon what they could raise or import from Spain, the early pioneers were, for the most part, poverty stricken. By 1707, conditions were so bad that the governor at Cartago authorized the use of cocoa beans for money. The last Spanish ruler was Don Juan Manuel de Canas. In October, 1821, he joined the independent movement and became an officer of the newborn state.

Costa Rica took part in the events of 1821, when Guatemala proclaimed its independence from Spain. Costa Rica withdrew from the confederacy and began new life as the Republic of Costa Rica in 1848. The country has had the good fortune to live in peace, with no other disturbances than those produced by the filibustering expeditions of William Walker in Central America. At that period Costa Rica crowned herself with glory for her heroic and successful efforts to maintain the independence of her sister republics. Costa Rica's leader at that time was Don Juan Rafael Mora, one of the most conspicuous and meritorious figures in Central American history. All Central America owes him a great debt of gratitude.

CHAPTER 5

Island of Romantic History

Highlights of Dominican Republic

Discovered: By Christopher Columbus for Spain in 1492.

Population: 1,581,248.

Area: 19,325 square miles.

Language: Spanish.   *Capital:* Ciudad Trujillo.

Government: Republic established in 1844.

Geographical Characteristics: Four thickly wooded mountain ranges cross the country. The valleys between these ranges are fertile and highly productive. The Dominican Republic occupies approximately two-thirds of the island of Hispaniola.

Climatic Conditions: There is considerable difference in climate due to variations in altitude. The temperature is lessened by the cooling effect of the sea and prevailing east winds.

Principal Products: Sugar, tobacco, cocoa, coffee, corn, mahogany, and gold.

Highlights of the Republic of Haiti

Discovered: By Christopher Columbus for Spain in 1492.

Population: 3,000,000.

Area: 10,700 square miles.

Language: French.   *Capital:* Port-au-Prince.

Government: Republic established in 1804.

Geographical Characteristics: Located on the western end of Hispaniola, the Republic of Haiti is made up of a rugged mountain area that covers about 60 per cent of its territory. Valleys and mountain slopes and well-watered plains form fertile soil for agriculture.

Climatic Conditions: The climate is tropical but changes with altitude. Even noonday heat is usually lowered by breezes from the sea.

Principal Products: Sugar, bananas, coffee, cocoa, cotton, logwood, sisal.

ABOUT 50 miles southwest of Cuba lies a lovely tropical island, the second largest in the West Indies group. It was discovered by Admiral Columbus on the morning of December 6, 1492. Because its rugged beauty reminded Columbus of Spain, he called it Hispaniola (Little Spain).

Today this island is divided into two separate and independent states: the Republic of Haiti, comprising the western third, and the Dominican Republic, taking up the eastern two-thirds. Although the smaller in area, Haiti is the more populous. It has the unique distinction of being the only French-speaking republic in the New World and the first Negro republic in the whole world.

Columbus discovered Hispaniola on Saint Nicholas Day, 1492, and gave the saint's name to the spot where he landed, the tip of a peninsula that juts like a pointing finger toward Cuba across the waters of the Windward Channel. Today there is a city on the spot still called Saint Nicholas. Columbus did not stay long at Saint Nicholas, however. He sailed along the coast until he came to an inlet where he went ashore. He called the place Concepción, put up a cross, and took possession in the name of the King and Queen of Spain.

Columbus found the Indian inhabitants a mild, kindly, and peaceful race. They had an easy existence for they did not have to work very hard because their island paradise supplied their few needs with lavish generosity. One native town, to which Columbus sent a landing party, consisted of nearly 3,000 houses. It has been estimated that, at the time of discovery, there were about a million Indians on the island. The Indians were expert fishermen and they were very clever at constructing small boats out of hollowed-out trees, called *canoas*, from which came our word canoe.

These Indians, the Arawaks, called their home Haiti (mountainous land). The various names of this island are a bit confusing. Columbus' original name, Hispaniola, was soon changed to Santo Domingo, and as the entire island was known by that name for many years and as the two present-day republics have practically the same history until 1844, it will, for the sake of clarity, be referred to as Hispaniola here.

While sailing eastward along the coast in search of the promised lands of Cipango and Cathay, Columbus suffered the loss of his flagship, the *Santa Maria*. It was wrecked on Christmas Eve, 1492, on a reef near where Cap-Haitien is today. Fortunately, Columbus was able to save most of the supplies and the ship's rigging and get them ashore with the help of the friendly Indians. This mishap left Columbus with only one ship, the small *Niña*, for the *Pinta*, commanded by Martín Pinzón, had sailed off following a quarrel between Pinzón and Columbus.

The *Niña* was too small to carry its own and the *Santa Maria's* crew back to Spain. As some of the men would have to be left behind, Columbus built a small fort with the salvaged materials from the *Santa Maria*. He named this first Spanish settlement in the New World, La Navidad, because the shipwreck had occurred on Christmas Eve.

Columbus built the new colony with the greatest possible haste, for he was eager to return to Spain with the news of his discoveries. In less than ten days the work was done and on January 4, 1493, he set sail for home in the *Niña*, leaving thirty-eight colonists at Fort La Navidad. He warned them to keep on friendly terms with the Indians and to live inside the stockade. They did neither, with tragic results.

When Columbus returned on his second voyage in November, 1493, and anchored off La Navidad, he was offended because there were no signs of welcome from the little party of Spaniards he had left behind—not even a cannon shot. On going ashore, he quickly learned the reason. There was no one there to fire a cannon or raise a shout of welcome. All the Spaniards were dead, killed by Indians or dead from disease. The fort was a ruin of ashes. From an Indian chief, Columbus learned that the Spaniards had brought their fate upon themselves by the cruelties they had heaped upon the peaceful and friendly Indians, who finally rose in revolt.

Deeply worried over the loss of his first colony, Columbus sailed on to try again. A new colony was founded on the banks of a placid, silvery stream. It was called Isabella, in honor of the Queen of Spain and the Admiral's patroness. Here Columbus laid out streets and built a church. Isabella was to be a real colony, and in fact, it was the cornerstone of Spanish expansion in America.

Unfortunately, Isabella was established near low marshy ground and it proved unhealthful. During the first days of the colony, an epidemic of fevers took the lives of many of the colonists. This did not stop Columbus in his search for the lands of silks and spices, which he always thought were just below the horizon. He heard of a place in the interior of the islands called Cibao by the Indians and immediately jumped to the conclusion that it was the fabulous empire of Cipango. He sent a party to explore, but as on previous occasions, the similarity was only in the name, for all the Spaniards found was a poor Indian village.

Despite tormenting body fevers that brought death, and gold fevers that brought mainly disappointment, the little colony did not fare so badly. In 1495, a gold mine was discovered on the Jaina River in the interior. Bartholomew Columbus, brother of the Admiral, was sent inland to establish a fort and work the mine, which was named Buenaventura.

It was at this period that Columbus gave evidence of his shrewdness. Captain Ojeda, who had been sent to establish a fort at Cibao, reported an uprising among the Indians. At Isabella, some of the younger and more strong-willed colonists were getting out of hand. Columbus wisely let one problem solve the other by sending 400 of the Spanish troublemakers at Isabella inland to quell the rebellious Indians at Cibao. When Columbus sailed home for Spain for the second time on March 10, 1496, he left his brother Bartholomew in charge of the colony.

Back in Spain, as on his first return, Columbus received a magnificent reception from the court and the populace alike. As he intended to remain in Spain some time, he sent orders to Bartholomew to move the colony to a more healthful spot, which he had selected before sailing, on the southern shore of Santo Domingo. This Bartholomew did. Thus the third Spanish colony in America was built on the banks of the Ozama River, near its mouth. According to Columbus' wishes, it was called New Isabella, but the name was soon changed to Santo Domingo. On August 4, 1496, the first stone was laid in the building of the oldest city in the New World. Today this city is known as Trujillo, capital of the Dominican Republic. With the founding of this famous city, began a career of glory and discovery in the New World destined to make immortal the names of so many Spaniards during the great era of exploration and conquest.

The welcome given Columbus on his arrival at Santo Domingo on his return from Spain on August 30, 1498, was not altogether a pleasant one. During his absence, Francisco Roldán, one of the leading troublemakers, had led a revolt against the administration headed by Bartholomew Columbus. He had even gone so far as to sack the public storehouse to feed his followers. The cause of this revolt was that Roldán, and many of the other Spaniards, wanted Indians assigned to them to do all their work as slaves. Bartholomew had evidently not been quick enough and generous enough in sending the natives into backbreaking bondage to suit the arrogant and greedy adventurers.

For the sake of the colony's welfare, Columbus made peace with Roldán. To that end, he created a system of slavery whereby Indians were allotted to work for the Spaniards without any pay. This was the beginning of the cruel *repartimientos* system, for all practical purposes the death warrant of hundreds of thousands of hapless Indians. The painful crushing force of slavery, in a few years, wiped the entire native Indian population out of existence and caused the introduction of Negro slaves from Africa, not only in Santo Domingo, but throughout the entire New World.

Despite hardships and petty quarrels among the settlers, Santo Domingo prospered in a small way. The gold mine and small farms, all worked entirely by Indians, were showing a good profit to the Spaniards who lolled in hammocks under the shade of trees and gave orders. By 1499, Santo Domingo and the other towns of Isabella, Concepción, Puerto Plata, and Bonao were all in a fair way of prosperity. Then came the year 1500, and with it important events in the history of Santo Domingo.

The enemies of Columbus in Santo Domingo had not been satisfied with causing him trouble on the spot. Many of them had returned to Spain with all sorts of accusations against the Admiral. These tales bore fruit at court, and in April, 1500, Francisco de Bobadilla arrived in Santo Domingo with royal orders to take command. This Bobadilla did with a vengeance. Columbus and his brother were arrested and sent back to Spain in irons. Columbus was able to clear himself of the charges against him and he sailed for the New World again in 1502, on his fourth and last voyage.

But the Columbus who sailed this time was a man shorn of his powers. His place as governor of Hispaniola had been taken by Nicolás de Ovando. On top of that, Columbus had been forbidden to land at Santo Domingo because it was thought his return might start trouble. As he neared the island, however, one of his ships became unseaworthy. Columbus sent a message to Governor Ovando asking for permission to enter the harbor of Santo Domingo to make repairs or to buy another ship. Ovando refused to grant the permission. He would not even yield when Columbus, seeing a hurricane blowing up, asked for safe anchorage. The Admiral took his pathetic fleet to the shelter of a near-by cove after warning Governor Ovando against letting the treasure fleet of thirty ships sail out of the harbor until the weather cleared.

Ovando laughed at the warning. Joining him in the laughter were Bobadilla and Columbus' old enemy, Roldán, both of whom were making ready to sail back to Spain with the treasure fleet. They never reached Spain, nor did the treasure. The storm, a terrific hurricane, wrecked most of the ships as Columbus had predicted, and also laid waste the colony of Santo Domingo, which was rebuilt by Ovando.

Once more did Columbus set foot on Santo Domingo soil, in 1504, on his way home to Spain after he had spent many miserable months on the inhospitable coast of Jamaica. Governor Ovando greeted the Admiral with outward courtesy, but he set free a number of Columbus' shipwrecked crew whom Columbus had charged with mutiny. This affront cut so deeply into the great discoverer's pride that he sailed immediately for Spain, never to return to the New World again —alive. Some time after his tragic death in 1506, his body was brought to Hispaniola, this time with honors he did not receive in life. With great pomp and circumstance his remains were placed under the altar in the great cathedral at Santo Domingo City.

The year 1506 was an important one for Santo Domingo, for it was then that sugar growing was introduced by Governor Ovando to supplement the not too productive gold mines.

Within a few years, sugar making was the principal occupation of the colonists and their chief source of wealth. It has been said that some of the finest palaces in Spain were built on the profits of sugar from Hispaniola. There was, however, a specter that haunted and harrowed the Santo Domingo plantation owners. That was the dying out of Indian man power. Year by year, slavery took its terrible toll of human life. More than a million natives lived on the island when Columbus landed there in 1492. By 1507—only 15 short years later, only 60,000 were left. The reason for this tragic decrease in the Indian population was slavery. To begin with, the Indians were not constitutionally strong. Hard work to which they were unaccustomed and epidemics of diseases caught by them from their white masters, caused widespread deaths. Then the cruelties practiced by the Spaniards on the Indians made them so miserable that thousands found release through suicide.

Indians became slaves. As slaves they died and the Spaniards cursed them in death, for they had to have slaves. The thought of ever exerting themselves at manual labor was too much for this motley crew of adventurers who had come to the New World for wealth and glory, not for work. Even men who, back in Spain, had never had a donkey to ride, now demanded to be carried in litters on the shoulders of Indian slaves.

The Indian supply having dwindled to practically nothing, Governor Ovando set out to renew it by sending an expedition to the neighboring Bahamas to recruit slave labor. Of course the matter was not stated that bluntly to the intended Indian victims. Ovando sent supersalesmen on that voyage, and the rosy pictures they painted of Santo Domingo as a heaven on earth induced some 40,000 trusting Indians to go to Hispaniola, where they quickly were made to carry the soul-crushing chains of bondage. These Indians soon died also. But there were more where they had come from. For years, Indian slave labor was recruited from all over the Caribbean. One by one the islands were robbed of the free and happy people that had lived there before Columbus came. The flow of miserable humanity went through the Santo Domingo slavery mill and was ground into the earth from which it came. Then came the shocking announcement from Spain that all Indians were declared free by a royal commission.

The planters had to turn elsewhere for human beasts of burden. They turned to Africa. Negroes from Africa were brought to Santo Domingo as early as 1511, but this royal proclamation started Negro slavery on a large scale. It increased so rapidly that, in 1522, the Negroes were strong enough to stage an uprising on the plantation of the governor, at that time Diego Columbus, the son of the Admiral.

This first Negro revolt was easily quelled, but not so an Indian rebellion at about the same time. Some 600 Indians rose in arms under Chief Enrique. They took refuge in the mountains. There they held out until 1533, when the famous Father Las Casas induced Enrique to sign a peace treaty whereby the Indians were allowed to settle down in an independent community. They all soon died, however, and that was about the end of the natives of the island. Today on Hispaniola there is not a single pure-blooded Indian of the stock first found by Columbus.

Curiously enough, it is argued that Father Las Casas, the great humanitarian and friend and protector of the Indians, was indirectly responsible for the bringing of Negro slaves to the New World. Seeing the Indians he loved dying by the thousands, as a result of the grueling work they were forced to do, Las Casas suggested that perhaps the Spaniards could find slaves of a stronger and sturdier race, men better able to endure hardships and toil under the hot sun. The Spaniards did find them in Negro slaves imported from Africa.

With this new source of labor, Santo Domingo reached a high degree of prosperity. By 1540 there were nearly fifty sugar plantations on the island and the gold mines were producing steadily. Then came a decline and a series of events that both depopulated and impoverished the island. Misrule from Spain and heavy taxes caused constant quarrels. The assigning of privileges to a few favorites and the ban against open trade with other nations stifled commerce. The great treasure ships that had once stopped at Santo Domingo put in at Havana instead. The glowing accounts of golden wealth in Mexico and Peru caused treasure hunters in Santo Domingo to leave by the thousands for new and more promising fields.

Then, in 1586, Sir Francis Drake, who had been sent to the Caribbean by the Queen of England to wreak as much damage on the Spanish as he could, did his best to obey that order at Santo Domingo. The entire city was burned and looted, until the English, tired of destroying, took $30,000 ransom for what remained of the place and sailed on to burn and pillage other Spanish New World cities.

Toward the close of the sixteenth century, the seas of America, especially around the West Indies, became thick with roving freebooters and privateers of all nations: French, Dutch, Portugese, English—all preying on the Spanish ships and towns as legitimate victims. This danger to sailing served practically to cut off commerce between Santo Domingo and the mother country. If it had not been for illicit trade with the foreigners, the colony would undoubtedly have shriveled into decay. A lively contraband trade in hides, cattle, sugar, and tobacco sprang up and flourished until 1606, when Spain ordered every port on the island except Santo Domingo to be closed. This was done to enforce the Spanish trade monopoly in the New World. If this had been intended to bring business back to Spain, the plan went into a most unhappy reverse. The people in the closed ports went into the interior where they became indifferent farmers. The towns ran to ruin, emigration to other colonies increased, and what little wealth there was left served only to attract the marauding buccaneers.

That these sea robbers played an important part in the history of Santo Domingo, the Spaniards had themselves to thank. The island of Saint Christopher was the chief port of call of English and French privateers until it was attacked and destroyed by the Spanish in 1630. Looking for new places to roost, many of the sea rovers settled on Tortuga, a small island off the northwest coast of Santo Domingo. The people of the colony soon became used to the colorfully dressed buccaneers who came over to the mainland to hunt cattle for hides or for meat to be dried slowly over small fires. This dried meat was called boucan, and from this harmless food product the vicious buccaneers got their name.

In 1654, England declared war on Spain, and the following year a large English expedition was sent out to take Santo Domingo. However, the island was saved by what many considered a miracle. A large British fleet anchored at Santo Domingo in April, 1655, with 9,000 men under the command of General Venables, who decided to surprise the Spaniards with a night attack. The Spanish garrison was composed of poorly armed irregulars, but General Venables did not know that. The night was dark as jet. The British were just about to launch their attack when, close to the shore, they heard a loud clatter like that of a troop of horses. They immediately concluded that a large force of cavalry was coming to the rescue of the Spanish. Fearing immediate attack, the English fled in disorder. They might have stood their ground. There was no attack. There was no rescuing cavalry. The noise the British had taken for the clatter of horses' hoofs was produced by the island's huge land crabs. These enormous animals, which burrow in the sand, had become disturbed by the footsteps of the British soldiers. The crabs had come out of their holes in great numbers and the noise they made coming over the dry leaves sounded like the clatter of hoofbeats. In honor of this curious ally, the Spaniards of Santo Domingo instituted an annual Feast of the Crabs, in which a gold land crab was carried in the procession.

In the course of the years, many of the buccaneers who lived on the little island of Tortuga moved over to the greener pastures of Santo Domingo to raise cattle and foodstuff for the pirate captains. By 1672, there were about 2,000 of these newcomers, mostly French, on the island. They established plantations along the seaside and became quite respectable. In time, the entire western part of the island was occupied by them. They set up a government and even had a governor, D'Ogeron by name. Under his rule, the French colonists increased in numbers and prospered; soon they more or less controlled the trade and commerce of the island. Many honest and hard-working families came out from Anjou and Brittany.

However, these intruders, for so the Spaniards regarded them, had to fight for every gain and work in the fields with firearms at their side ever ready to meet Spanish raiders. Finally Governor D'Ogeron decided to put an end to the hostilities between the two nationalities by the straightforward means of conquering the Spanish. In 1669, an army of 500 Frenchmen attacked and captured the second largest Spanish city, Santiago. The French collected a large ransom for not burning it. The French were so encouraged by this victory that they spread out over the beautiful plain of Limonade, near Cap François. Following the lead of the Spanish, they imported large numbers of Negro slaves from Africa for their Santo Domingo plantations.

The wars of the great European nations invariably had a telling effect on Santo Domingo. France and Spain declared war in 1689, and a miniature war broke out between the Spanish and French on the island. The Spanish killed great numbers of their French neighbors and destroyed their plantations. But when the peace of Ryswick was signed in

1697, France got the western part of the island which today is known as Haiti.

The story of Hispaniola for the next century is one of startling contrasts. The French progressed and increased in numbers, but the Spanish settlements went to pieces. As a matter of fact, from the moment the French rights were officially recognized by the home government, the Spaniards began to lose interest in Santo Domingo.

Up to the time of the French Revolution, the wealth of the French colony steadily increased. Ever-growing numbers of slaves were imported to work the indigo, cocoa, coffee, sugar, and cotton plantations. Many of the planters returned to France to display their colonial wealth. In France was born the expression "rich as a creole." But despite this prosperity, there were constant disputes between the French and Spanish over boundaries and straying cattle.

Strangely enough, the Spanish, whose cruelties during the era of conquest and colonization have been so widely condemned, became comparatively kindly in their treatment of their Negro slaves on Santo Domingo. One explanation is that the Spanish population had so thinned out that the Spanish masters had only slaves to turn to for help when their plantations were attacked by French raiders.

The French of the island were notoriously harsh and cruel in their treatment of the Negro slaves. This was due partly to the infamous *Code Noir*, or Black Law, which gave masters power of life and death over Negroes. One curious thing about the *Code Noir* was that, harsh as it was, it did allow a slave to purchase his freedom, at a fixed price, which the master had to accept. Thus many slaves became freemen. Some of them acquired large plantations and grew rich. A great many blacks also escaped to the Spanish part of the island, where they became free Spanish subjects. At one time, out of a population of 125,000 Negroes on the island, 110,000 were freemen.

But being free had its limitations for the Negro freemen of Santo Domingo. Although not bound in personal service to any one master, they were still considered public property and were at the mercy of the whites at every turn. They were forced to serve 3 years in the army, during which time they were employed mostly to run down and punish their runaway black brothers, or maroons, as these escaped Negroes were called.

At all times these freemen were liable to be taken from their homes and families to build roads without pay. Because of these many cruelties, there was a Negro uprising in 1687, under a slave named Padrejan, who killed his Spanish master. He escaped and incited the French slaves against their owners. He was finally caught and executed.

This brings the story of Santo Domingo to its great and tragic chapter of carnage and bloodshed—to a chapter of such human upheaval as the New World had never seen; to the swiftly moving, dramatic, blood-and-thunder chapter known as the Revolt of the Negroes!

In the fateful year of 1789, there were on Hispaniola approximately 40,000 whites, 50,000 mulattoes, and 500,000 Negroes. To understand the great revolution that had its inception in that year, it must be remembered that there were three distinct stages which led the revolt to its dreadful climax: (1) The revolution of the whites against the governments; (2) the uprising of the mulattoes against the whites; and (3) the revolt of the Negro slaves.

Three times the cry of freedom was raised, each by a different race. But each and every cry was followed by frightful massacres, burnings of towns and plantations, and inhumanities beyond description.

At this time, the French governor in Santo Domingo had absolute authority in all matters. The colonists had no voice whatsoever in the managing of their own local affairs. Taxes were high. More often than not, the governor did not understand the problems of the plantation owners, or did not care. Thus the administration hindered rather than helped the planters. Therefore, when word of the outbreak of the French Revolution with the storming of the Bastille on July 14, 1789, reached the colony of Santo Domingo, the planters received the epoch-making news with hearty approval.

If Frenchmen at home could declare their freedom from tyranny, why not the colonists? Without waiting for word from Paris, the plantation owners elected representatives and formed a local legislature. La Comb, a mulatto, asked that his people be allowed representation. He was promptly hanged for his "impudence." The "rights of man," so far as Santo Domingo was concerned, did not apply to men of dark color. No sooner had the white planters formed their assembly than they fought among themselves. Some wanted complete freedom from France, and became *patriots*. Others argued that there could be freedom and still loyalty to the motherland. These latter were called *aristocrats*.

It was while this dispute was going on that news came of a mulatto uprising in the interior of the island led by a young, wealthy, and educated mulatto named James Oge. He had gathered 200 men and marched to demand the rights of his people from the assembly at the muzzles of guns and the points of swords. But he was defeated. Oge fled to the Spanish city of Santo Domingo on the other end of the island. The Spaniards returned him to the French on the promise that his life would be spared. The promise was not kept.

The mulatto revolt having been put down, the whites went back to fighting among themselves. The governor sent for troops from France to uphold his authority. When the troops arrived, they joined arms with the rebellious *patriots* instead.

Then, in 1791, came the decree from France that really set off the explosion. The colonial assembly for Santo Domingo was approved by the mother assembly in Paris, but with the provision that people of color born of free parents should be admitted to representation. While the mulattoes shouted with delight, the whites raged and plotted and armed for what was to come. But they were arming against ruthless fate. Few planters realized that, for them, their world was near its end.

While this was going on, no one gave much thought to the huge masses of Negro slaves who went about their work in the fields and at night gathered in the hills to the accompaniment of beating drums. Plantation owners asked their overseers what was going on. "Oh, just their silly voodoo ceremonies," was the answer. "Nothing to worry about."

On the plantation of Breda, owned by Count de Noe, was a Negro slave who worried quite a bit about those voodoo meetings of his people in the hills. He disapproved of voodoo. His name was Toussaint. Later he was to add L'Ouverture to that name and make it immortal by his fight for the freedom of his people. While Toussaint was a lad, the plantation overseer, Bayou Libertas, took a liking to him and made him his coachman. This gave Toussaint leisure to learn to read and write, an unusual accomplishment for a slave.

Toussaint may have gotten the idea for freedom for his people in Santo Domingo when he read, in Abbé Reynal's *History of Philosophy*, these stirring words: "The Negroes lack but a chief. Where is the great man? He will appear; we have no doubt of it. He will show himself; he will unfurl the sacred standard of liberty."

Toussaint L'Ouverture probably never thought of himself as that great man, but in his soul was born a determination. Once, when the impossibility of the blacks gaining freedom from the whites appeared too discouraging to his fellow slaves, Toussaint filled a glass jar almost to the brim with black kernels of corn. He spread a few white kernels on top. Then he said: "See how those few white kernels are on top so you are hardly aware of all the black ones underneath?" Then he shook the jar until the kernels were well mixed, and said:

"Now look. The many black ones have completely swallowed the few white kernels."

On August 14, 1791, the drums in the hills served as a signal to a surging mass of blacks who met and made their plans to rise in revolt. Toussaint did not attend, for he did not think the time was ripe. But under the leadership of three black slaves—François, Boukman, and Bissau, the revolution was born. Eight days later, they met at the Turpin plantation and marched on Cap François, murdering, burning, and devastating as they went. This first revolt ended in defeat, and there followed as punishment, and to teach the Negroes a lesson, a wholesale slaughter of blacks by French soldiers and civilians.

At the time of this march on Cap François, the mulattoes, always hating their blacker brothers more than the whites, asked for guns to fight the advancing army of Negro rebels. Not only did the whites refuse them, but put the blame for the crisis on the mulattoes and killed them by the hundreds.

Although he had been invited to join in the first open act of revolt, Toussaint refused. During the early days of the uprisings, he put himself at the head of the Breda plantation slaves and defended his master's property. Several times, at great risk to his life, he saved the cane fields from being burned. But when, later on, he decided that the time had come to translate his ideas and ideals of liberty to action, Toussaint did not hesitate. The wife of the overseer, Madame Libertas, was on the plantation at the time. Toussaint put her in a carriage and gave the driver orders to get her to the safety of the city under penalty of drastic punishment if he failed. Then Toussaint gathered together the slaves of Breda and marched to join the revolution.

Jean François and the other black leaders at first were suspicious of Toussaint L'Ouverture, both for his delay in joining the revolt and for his friendly attitude toward the whites. Instead of being given a command, he was put in charge of the wounded, probably because of his supposed knowledge of medicinal herbs. But his abilities were so outstanding that he was soon promoted to brigadier general in the army of the blacks. Jean François had assumed the grand titles of Admiral and Generalissimo, while Bissau, not to be outdone in titulary grandeur, became Viceroy of the Conquered Territories.

History was made at a fast pace in the next few years. The Negroes were defeated at their first big battle at Limbe. Then the mulattoes again offered to help the whites. When their offers were rejected this time, the mulattoes joined forces with the blacks. With their combined strength, they defeated the white forces on March 28, 1792, and drove them within Port-au-Prince. On that occasion, the Negroes were led by Chief Hyacinthe. After gaining their victory, he commanded his slave soldiers to lay down their arms and go back to the fields. This they did, much to the relief of the white population which had expected destruction and pillage.

Having aided them to gain a victory, the mulattoes then turned on their black brothers and slaughtered them in turn. Comparative peace followed and it might have lasted if war had not broken out between France and England in May, 1793. The English were about to attack the French in Santo Domingo. The French governor knew that the *patriot* planters would side with the British. In order to get quick reinforcements, the governor appealed to the Negro slaves, offering them freedom, arms, ammunition, and clothing if they would serve against the English. While the offer was officially rejected by Toussaint L'Ouverture and the other Negro leaders, a great many blacks accepted—but with a reservation. After getting French guns and ammunition, they deserted and ran back to the mountains. There, far back in the hills, a sort of mountain republic was formed.

On September 19, 1793, the English forces landed under Colonel Whitlock. Saint Nicholas fell first, and then other towns in rapid succession. The plan was for the Spanish and

English to divide the island between them. It was for services rendered in this campaign against the French that Toussaint L'Ouverture was honored by the Spanish and made a colonel. Finally Port-au-Prince fell to the English.

These defeats put the French General Levaux in a tight spot. He was besieged by the combined English and Spanish forces. As a last resort he sent an appeal to Toussaint L'Ouverture to come back to the French cause. The Negro thought the matter over, and after deciding that the cause of his people could be served better under the flag of a free republic such as France, rather than those of the English and Spanish kings, he accepted and fought bravely and loyally for the French. In 1795 came the Peace of Basle, which gave the Spanish part of Santo Domingo to the French. This gave the Negro commander more troops and he renewed his fight against the English invaders. It was at this time that he adopted the name Toussaint L'Ouverture, saying to his black soldiers that he was going to "open to them the doors of a better future." In 1797 he was made commander in chief of all the island's French troops. At last he was able to force the English to leave Santo Domingo, after a tragic venture that had cost the British crown 100 million dollars and more than 45,000 dead from wounds and disease.

Toussaint L'Ouverture was now in supreme command of all the island but a small part in which a Spanish garrison still remained although officially all of Santo Domingo was French according to the treaty of 1795. Toussaint proved himself as able in times of peace as in war. A remarkable reign of peace, short as it was, followed. His fellow blacks looked upon him as a god. When he ordered his soldiers to return to the cane fields, they obeyed without question. They were no longer slaves, but cultivators receiving a wage of one-third of the crops they produced. Complete protection was given to the white planters, and many of those who had fled during the days of revolt returned to their plantations.

Toussaint was firm and strict, but he was not cruel. Once he sent the Negro General Dessalines to punish a troublesome community. When he learned that Dessalines had committed wholesale murder, he became angry and said, "I told him to prune the tree, not to uproot it."

Various French commissioners who came to the island from France believed the Negro was becoming too powerful. One in particular, General Hedouville, suggested that Toussaint had done his work and that he would be wise to retire, go to France, and receive the honors and peace due him. The Frenchman pointed to a ship in the harbor that could be placed at his service. Toussaint knew that the Frenchman wanted only to get rid of him so that the blacks could be enslaved again. He pointed to a tiny shrub and replied, "When that shrub grows big enough to furnish the wood for a ship, then I will go!"

The year 1800 saw peace on Hispaniola, although a mulatto named Rigaud held out against Toussaint in a small southern province, and the Spanish, under General García, were still in Santo Domingo City. Toussaint demanded the surrender of the Spanish. At first García put up a show of fight, but on January 3, 1801, the gates of the city opened to the Negro general and his troops. Toussaint took possession, still nominally acting for the French Republic.

In July, 1801, Santo Domingo declared its independence, with Toussaint L'Ouverture as supreme commander for life. While the constitution was being printed, a French commissioner, Colonel Vincent, warned Toussaint that Napoleon Bonaparte would not like that document, as there were provisions that suggested a desire of the Negro leader to assume dictatorial powers separate from those of France. Toussaint decided to find out and sent Colonel Vincent back to France with a copy of Santo Domingo's constitution and a letter to Napoleon.

It has been said that Toussaint incurred the enmity of

Napoleon by addressing a letter to the future Emperor of the French as "from the First of the Blacks to the First of the Whites." Be that as it may, Napoleon had no liking for the Negro liberator. He was enraged when he heard that Toussaint had been made the chief executive for life. Napoleon had no idea of abolishing slavery. Toussaint L'Ouverture and what he stood for must be crushed once and for all, was the decision of Napoleon.

Napoleon's decision became action in a very short time. On January 28, 1802, a fleet of fifty-four French ships, carrying 25,000 seasoned troops, and commanded by General Le Clerc, brother-in-law of Napoleon and husband of the beautiful Pauline Bonaparte, appeared off the shores of Hispaniola. The land forces quickly took several cities. But when the fleet tried to land at Cap François, Le Clerc had to deal with a man who was to become almost as famous as Toussaint in Santo Domingo history, the Negro General Henri Christophe.

Christophe refused to let the French land, and when they did so anyway, the Negro set fire to the city, and as it was being reduced to ashes, he withdrew to the hills with his troops and 2,000 white inhabitants.

Hispaniola was again to be ravaged by the horrors of war. Toussaint, from his mountain stronghold, declared the island in a state of siege.

At first the tide went against the French army of Le Clerc. But by March, the general was so sure of success that he openly announced that it was the intention of Napoleon to return the Negro slaves to their former owners, and that slavery was to be reestablished.

When this news reached Toussaint, he seized the opportunity to gather a large army of blacks to him. He joined his forces with those of Henri Christophe and drove the French into Cap François. Victory was again within the reach of Toussaint when, probably in good faith and believing it was best for their people, Henri Christophe and other Negro generals went over to General Le Clerc. Thus deserted, Toussaint L'Ouverture was forced to come to terms with the French. On May 7, 1802, peace was signed. The Negroes were declared free and many other conditions favorable for the blacks were included in the agreement.

Satisfied that he had done his best for his people, Toussaint L'Ouverture retired to his plantation at Gonaïves. But he was not finished with Napoleon and his brother-in-law, Le Clerc. Early in the summer, Toussaint was tricked into visiting a French plantation to talk over some important matters with a French general. Instead, he was placed under arrest and under the cover of night carried aboard a waiting French frigate. His wife and family were seized at the plantation and also imprisoned on the French ship.

On the ship's arrival in France, Napoleon ordered the Negro's imprisonment in the distant and isolated dungeons of Fort de Joux in the mountains of the Swiss French border. He was separated from his wife and children, all his possessions were taken from him, and he was given only enough food to keep alive. Rumors had it that Toussaint had 8 million dollars in gold hidden among the hills of his native island. Daily he was questioned about a hidden treasure that he swore existed only in the minds of his persecutors. Time and again he wrote appeals to Napoleon, pleading that his only crime had been a love for his own people. Napoleon was deaf to these appeals. The cold and rigorous winter was a tremendous hardship for a man who had never known anything but the mild climate of Santo Domingo. Broken in body and spirit, he spent 8 horrible months in prison. On April 7, 1803, Toussaint L'Overture was found dead in his cell.

The news of their beloved leader's death again aroused the Negroes of Hispaniola to action. A sea of black humanity arose from the mountains, and the whole island was once more overwhelmed by war.

General Le Clerc died on Hispaniola of fever shortly after,

and General Rochambeau assumed command. The Negroes were making a valiant but rather unsuccessful fight. They missed the leadership of Toussaint, although Henri Christophe and General Dessalines were both able and courageous leaders. Then, in July, 1803, England declared war on Napoleon Bonaparte. English ships appeared off the island to threaten the French, who were forced to give up the fight. On November 30, the French sailed for home and another war.

On January 1, 1804, the Negroes declared themselves an independent republic. The native name Haiti was adopted and Jean Jacques Dessalines was made governor general for life. But Dessalines was not content with being governor. He declared himself emperor. His reign was one of almost constant turmoil, until on October 17, 1806, he was ambushed and killed by his own soldiers.

After Dessalines came a period of divided allegiance in the new republic. While a Negro named Pétion was elected president, Henri Christophe appointed himself King Henri I of Haiti, ruling the north and west. Christophe governed his kingdom with an iron hand but proved to be an administrator of exceptional ability. He established schools, built roads, and developed the nation's agriculture. He built the famous palace of Sans Souci for his residence and erected on the summit of a mountain a fantastic citadel overlooking the sea. Henri Christophe reigned until 1820, when his people turned against him. One day, in his magnificent palace at Sans Souci, when news reached him that his own personal guard had betrayed him, he committed suicide.

Pétion, meanwhile, had been elected president in January, 1807. His administration of the other end of the island was marked by many notable achievements, including the distribution of public lands to officers and soldiers of the fight for independence; the establishment of a college at Port-au-Prince; and aid to Simon Bolivar, the Great Liberator of South America, in the form of arms and ammunition.

After Pétion's death in 1818, Jean Pierre Boyer was elected president of Haiti, and governed for 25 years. When Henri Christophe committed suicide, Boyer assumed authority over the entire island. In 1821, there was an uprising by the inhabitants of the eastern part of the island against representatives of Spain. Boyer went to their aid with an army of 22,000 men. This eastern or Spanish part of the island continued in a state of more or less stagnation until the 1830's when a young patriot, Juan Pablo Duarte, organized a revolutionary movement. In 1840 the inhabitants declared themselves an independent state under the name of the Dominican Republic.

Of all the men of many nations whose names have written Hispaniola's history, the greatest is that of the Negro slave, Toussaint, who rose from coachman to commander in chief and achieved the freedom of his people. Today, in the capital of Haiti, there stands a statue to this beloved national hero. It does not show him in a warlike attitude astride a huge stallion, as he is often pictured. It reveals a black slave placing a wreath on the head of the man who fought and died to gain the freedom of an enslaved people.

CHAPTER 6

Stronghold of the Buccaneers

Highlights of Jamaica

Discovered: By Christopher Columbus for Spain in 1494.

Population: 1,122,000.

Area: 4,450 square miles.

Language: English.   *Capital:* Kingston.

Government: British crown colony.

Geographical Characteristics: This, the largest British island in the West Indies, is crossed by a mountain range that runs from east to west.

Climatic Conditions: Subtropical and pleasantly cool.

Principal Products: Sugar, cocoa, bananas, pimento, and coffee.

JAMAICA, the largest of the West Indian islands, is one of the few that retains its original Indian name. When Columbus landed on its shores in 1494, he called the place Santiago. But the native name, *Jaymaca*, which means the Island of Springs, was accepted by the Spaniards who found the island dotted with mineral springs.

At first, the Arawak Indians of Jamaica were hostile to Columbus and his men, but the Spaniards easily gained the friendship of the natives with presents of beads and other trinkets. After 3 days of exploring, the Admiral sailed on to Cuba, and the island of Jamaica received no further visits from Europeans until Columbus returned 9 years later, in 1503.

115

On his last voyage, after having explored the coast of Central America in search of a strait to the Orient, Columbus' ships ran into a heavy storm off the coast of Jamaica. There the Admiral took refuge in a harbor he had named Santa Gloria on his previous visit. It was Saint John's Eve, June 23, 1503, when the vessels, "full of holes as a honeycomb," were beached to keep them from sinking. Diego Mèndez and Bartolomé Fieschi, two courageous members of the party, offered to make the long and dangerous journey in a canoe across open seas, to get help from Governor Ovando at the colony of Santo Domingo on the island of Hispaniola.

When Governor Ovando received the news of the Admiral's plight, he was highly pleased. He hated Columbus, and the Jamaica disaster presented an ideal opportunity for Ovando to get rid of his enemy. He pleaded that he had no ships to send to the rescue, secretly hoping that the delay would eliminate Columbus from the picture.

Ovando's plan nearly worked. The months Columbus spent in Jamaica were a trial of horrible suffering and humiliation. The strong and healthy members of his crew deserted, leaving behind their ill and disabled companions. The food supply gave out. For a time the friendly Arawak Indians fed the white men. Toward the end of January, 1504, however, the natives showed signs of hostility. A few weeks later, they bluntly announced that they would bring no more food. Columbus knew that he and his ragged and emaciated crew were at the mercy of the Indians. In their weakened condition the Spaniards would be an easy prey if the natives should decide to attack. The situation was desperate. There remained but one solution. Columbus must somehow play upon the superstitions of the Indians to induce them to bring food.

One day Columbus recalled having seen in his nautical almanac that an eclipse of the moon was due about that time. Eagerly he brought out the book. Yes, he had been right. A lunar eclipse was due shortly after sunset on the evening of

February 29. But just what time? If the trick was to work, Columbus had to know the exact hour. His pen flew over pieces of paper, making calculations. Fortunately, the Admiral was an excellent mathematician and astronomer. When he had the answer, Columbus summoned his few loyal officers and told them of his bold plan to "steal the moon" from the Indians.

Word was sent to the Indians that if they did not bring food to the white men, Columbus would take their moon-god away from them by powerful magic, shortly after sunset on that very day. The chiefs met and sent word back to Columbus that they did not believe that white men had magic powerful enough to take away their moon-god. But despite their scoffing, the appointed hour saw the Indians crowded around the ships, muttering and in an angry mood. The chiefs pointed to the moon, which was shining with its usual brightness.

Again Columbus warned the Indians that unless they brought food, he would blot out the moon. When the threat produced no results, the Admiral, scanning the sky anxiously, announced he was about to perform his great magic. He told the natives to watch the moon, for within a few minutes he was going to blot it out of the sky forever. The Indians, growing slightly uncomfortable, fell silent, their eyes fixed on the silver disk. Columbus was silent, too, and so were his men. In their hearts, they were praying that the trick would work. Suppose the almanac was wrong? Suppose the calculations of Columbus were wrong?

As they watched, a frightened cry came from the throat of an Indian. He pointed to the moon. The edge of the moon had begun to darken. Little by little the shadow crept across the disk. A great clamor arose from the terrified Indians. The chiefs pleaded with Columbus to give them back their moon-god. Yes, they would bring food, much food. The white men could have anything they wanted if they would only return the moon to the sky. The Admiral agreed, breathing a sigh of relief. If the Indians had waited until the earth's shadow began creeping off the moon, the trick would have been spoiled.

In gratitude for returning the moon to them, the Indians kept the Spaniards supplied with food until June of that year, when two ships finally arrived from Santo Domingo and took Columbus and his crew to Haiti. After a short and unhappy stay on that island, Columbus sailed for Spain. But if the New World had been hostile to the Great Admiral, the Old World he sailed back to was even more so. His enemies in Spain had done a thorough job of blackening his name. When death overtook Columbus two years later, the ungrateful people held him without honor both in his own country and in the new lands he had discovered.

Spain allowed Jamaica to slumber another 5 years. Then Diego Columbus, a son of the Admiral, and governor of Santo Domingo, sent Juan Esquivel to take possession of the island for Spain, under whose rule it remained for a century and a half. In Jamaica, as in the other West Indian islands, the Spaniards treated the Indians as beasts of burden. Within a few decades, the friendly Arawaks, who in the time of Columbus had been populous as "ants on an anthill," were practically exterminated. With the disappearance of the Indians, the Spanish planters began importing African Negro slaves, supplied mostly by English and Dutch slave traders. When the Jamaicans saw the huge profits in slave trading, they decided to get their share by acting as a distribution point for the other Spanish colonies. In time, Jamaica became one of the busiest slave markets in the world.

The trade in Negro slaves is one of the most shameful chapters in the history of the New World. Natives were hunted in Africa like wild animals and then packed like sardines into the dirty and steaming holds of blackbirders. At the source, in Africa, villages were burned so that the natives could be captured when they tried to escape. Many died in warehouses in which they were kept awaiting ships to take them to America. On the voyage an average of seventeen out of every hundred died, and less than half of the Negroes lived long enough to enter actual slave labor in the colonies.

During the voyages to Jamaica and other colonies, the bewildered blacks were given just enough food and water to keep them alive. Thus the weak and the sickly were automatically eliminated, dying on the voyage. When, in later years, slavery was outlawed by several European nations, other hazards were added for the Negroes. Their presence on a ship was the only evidence on which a captain could be convicted of illegal slaving.

When captains of slave ships found themselves pursued by naval vessels they could not outrun, they promptly got rid of the evidence. The Negroes were brought on deck roped together and made fast to the anchor chain. When capture seemed inevitable, the anchor was thrown overboard and with it went the helpless Negroes. One by one they would be pulled over the side and plummeted to a horrible, gruesome watery grave. If a captain was caught with slaves on his ship, he was severely punished. But if he could send the Negroes to the bottom of the sea before his ship was overhauled and searched —he went free.

When a ship laden with human cargo arrived at Port Royal in Jamaica, the town bustled with activity. Merchants filled the slave market to inspect the shipment. The Negroes were pawed and thumped. Their leg and arm muscles were felt, and their teeth examined as if they were cattle. Then the bidding began. Children were sold away from their mothers. Bids were made on only one basis: how much and how many years of hard labor would be returned for an investment in human misery.

It has been estimated that during one period of 85 years, more than 600,000 Negro slaves were brought to Jamaica. During the hundred years of greatest activity in the slave trade, from 1680 to 1780, an annual average of 20,095 Negroes were imported into the West Indies, making a total of more than 2 million. Such distinguished seamen as Sir John Hawkins and Sir Francis Drake made large profits from the trade in slaves and considered it a highly respectable business. Although the slave trade was legally abolished by most countries in 1807, illegal slaving continued for many years, until public opinion of civilized society wrote finis to this traffic in human lives.

During the early period of the slave trade, England had no colonies in the West Indies, but she was casting envious eyes toward the Spanish settlements in the Caribbean. In 1596, Admiral Sir Anthony Shirley attacked and looted Jamaica, but was unable to take possession of the island. Various minor British raids on Jamaica took place during the following years. It was not until 1643, when Captain Jackson captured the capital, Santiago de Vega, that England seriously began considering taking the colony away from Spain. In 1655, Admirals Penn and Venables, with 6,000 men, took the island and proclaimed it a British colony. As a reward for their deed, Penn and Venables were recalled to England and thrown into prison. The colonists they had left in Jamaica were abandoned to starve and to suffer attacks from the maroons.

The word maroon is a corruption of the Indian word *cimarron*, meaning wild. It was applied to runaway slaves. When England took possession of the island, the slaves of Jamaica, having been told fanciful stories of the brutality of the English by their Spanish owners, took to the hills. There these maroons organized raiding bands, and for many years they terrorized the plantation owners.

Jamaica in time became the seat of British power in the Caribbean. It also became the headquarters of those picturesque rogues of the sea, the buccaneers, who raised havoc on the Caribbean during the seventeenth century.

The buccaneers were the direct result of Spain's policy of

prohibiting the ships of any other nation from trading with her American colonies. Other countries naturally resented this monopoly and commissioned privateers to break the Spanish blockades. Sir Walter Raleigh, Francis Drake, Frobisher, and Clifford are examples of such privateers. The letters of marque carried by these adventurers made it legal for them to attack and loot Spanish shipping and settlements wherever found. The French and Dutch were also active in this legalized piracy against Spain.

So successful were the privateers and so rich their rewards, that many adventurers entered into privateering as a sure way to get rich quickly. These outlaws, not having the protection of a king, were forced to hide out between raiding expeditions on isolated islands where they would be safe from capture. Cattle and hogs ran wild on many islands that had been abandoned by the Spaniards. These animals furnished a ready means of food for the pirates. From the few surviving Carib Indians on the islands, the freebooters learned how to prepare and smoke meat. This meat was called boucan, from which comes the English word buccaneer.

This smoked meat, or boucan, was prepared by cutting the beef into long strips. These strips were salted and wrapped around lengths of green wood. Placed between two forked sticks over a wood fire, the meat was turned as on a spit. Pieces of fat were thrown into the fire from time to time, giving off a thick pungent smoke that acted to preserve the meat. The finished product was rather tough, reddish in color, but it tasted fairly good and it could be kept for weeks, even in the hot climate of the islands.

At first only those who actually made boucan were called buccaneers, but the term gradually spread to include the whole class of outlaw sea raiders. By the time the various bands of marauders united into a sort of confederacy as the Brethren of the Coast, the word buccaneer was known and feared throughout the entire Caribbean.

The Brethren of the Coast was a unique form of society. There was no private property among them. In order to leave themselves absolutely free and unhampered, they took vows not to marry. As their life involved great risks of disabling injuries, a scale of compensations was in effect. For the loss of both eyes, 1,000 pieces of eight were awarded; for a right arm, 600 pieces of eight; a left arm, 500 pieces of eight, and the same for a right leg; a left leg, 400 pieces of eight; an eye or a finger, 100 pieces of eight. It is significant that the right, or sword arm, entitled the sufferer to 100 pieces of eight more than the loss of a left arm. A piece of eight was the approximate equivalent of a dollar in our money.

Although the manners and methods of the buccaneers were shocking, their dress made them picturesque figures. A coarse and often colorful shirt was worn outside short trousers. Shoes were of rawhide and were homemade. Their hats were Spanish sombreros with the brim cut off except in front, where it acted as an eyeshade. In rawhide belts the pirates carried knives and pistols and a powder horn. Their muskets were huge affairs, with broad butts and long barrels, and with the kick of a mule. Their weapons, which shot heavy bullets that ran only sixteen to the pound, became known as buccaneer muskets. For the most part, the Brethren of the Coast were heavily bearded. They had long hair and usually wore large rings in their ears.

It is true that the buccaneers did not have the official approval of any government, but France, England, and the Netherlands all silently condoned their activities. Any act that gave trouble to the King of Spain was welcomed. In polite society and official circles the buccaneers were spoken of as privateers. The Council of Jamaica, in 1666, even defended the sea bandits in an official decree, giving twelve reasons why their operations should be sanctioned. Among the reasons given were: the pirates stimulated trade on the island; they brought slaves to cultivate the plantations; their ships provided a navy in case of attack; and they served as spies to keep the British posted of the movements of the Spaniards.

Among the buccaneers whose exploits made them infamous are John Davis, who sacked Saint Augustine, Florida; Michel the Brusque, who was with the fiend L'Olonnais in the attack on Maracaibo; Edward Mansvelt of Curacao; and last but far from least, Henry Morgan.

The picture of Morgan with a red handkerchief knotted around his head, flourishing a cutlass and shouting fierce oaths as he leads his cutthroats in a boarding party, is a romantic one. He had a handsome face, a keen brain, a clever tongue, and the will to get what he wanted. If Henry Morgan had been almost anything but Morgan the Buccaneer, he would probably have been an admirable figure. As the fates decreed it, nothing can be said of Morgan to temper the verdict of time that he was a cruel and heartless villain. But whatever Henry Morgan was, however black his deeds, he is a vital part of the history of Jamaica.

Henry Morgan was born in Wales, in 1635, the son of a prosperous farmer. The early boyhood years on a farm evidently did not prove adventuresome enough for young Henry. At sixteen he ran away to the nearest seaport. He wanted to go to America. Having no money to pay his fare, he stowed away on a vessel bound for the West Indian island of Barbados. Hunger and thirst finally forced Morgan to make his presence known when the ship was only a few days out. The captain promptly put him to work and sold him into slavery when the ship reached Barbados.

It may have been the cruelties the boy suffered as a slave that determined his later life and conduct. Certain it was that he frequently felt the sting of the lash and the pangs of hunger. Whether he ran away from his owner or was freed after a time, is not known. But in 1658, when he was twenty-three years old, Henry Morgan was in Jamaica, a free man, but penniless. He was offered a place in a buccaneering expedition and he readily accepted. Being an apt pupil, Morgan learned the ways of the Brethren of the Coast in short time. He saved his share of the plunder, and a few years later he was able to purchase a ship of his own. From that point on, his rise in the ranks of the pirates was rapid.

Things had been slow with the buccaneers because England was at peace with other nations, but in 1665, war with the Netherlands broke out and pirate business picked up. Wars were always welcome to the Brethren of the Coast, for they lent some degree of legality to their plundering expeditions. In July of 1665, three ships laden with rich plunder from the sacking of the Spanish town of Granada in Nicaragua, sailed into Port Royal, Jamaica, under command of Captain Henry Morgan, Buccaneer.

Tales of the young newcomer's daring exploit reached the ears of Mansvelt, who, as the chief admiral of the Brethern of the Coast, had been licensed to conduct raids against the Dutch. Mansvelt summoned Morgan and offered him the place of vice-admiral in a large expedition he was fitting out. Morgan, well aware of his abilities as a leader of lawless cutthroats, accepted on the condition that he be given a half share in the venture. An agreement was signed and the fleet sailed in January, 1666. The main objective, an attack on the Dutch island of Curaçao, fell through. Morgan suggested a raid on the Spanish island of Santa Catalina. This island lies between Jamaica and Panama. The raid was a complete success. After it, Morgan parted from Mansvelt and returned to Jamaica. Here he won the favor of Governor Modyford, probably by sharing his ill-gotten gains with him.

When Mansvelt arrived at Jamaica a short time later, the governor was cool in his reception of the old pirate. He sang the praises of Morgan, for whom he predicted a brilliant future. Mansvelt went to the Island of Tortuga, another stronghold of the buccaneers. There he died mysteriously and suddenly. Mansvelt's death found Morgan ready to step into the shoes of his former chief. He proclaimed himself Admiral of the Brethren of the Coast. The buccaneers accepted him as their leader. Governor Modyford also acknowledged Morgan's claim. Soon the pirate chief talked the governor into giving him an official commission for a raiding expedition, which sailed from Port Royal early in 1668.

Morgan swept down on Puerto Principe where he launched the policy of destruction and terror that was to mark his trail through the colonies lying on the Caribbean. Back in Port Royal again, Henry Morgan told a fine and fanciful tale to justify his pillage of a Spanish colony when the commission he held clearly stated that it applied only to naval warfare. Governor Modyford probably did not believe Morgan's story of having defeated a large Spanish fleet that had been on its way to attack Jamaica, or that the raid on Puerto Principe had been made only with the purpose of preventing another attack against the English. The governor was principally interested in his share of the spoils. But it is said that he warned Morgan to be careful, and if he had to take towns as prizes to refer to them as "ships," because the King of England was strongly opposed to robbing ashore.

Emboldened by the success of his first major venture, Morgan next set his eyes toward the plum of the Spanish colonies, Panama City. His plan to attack the strongly fortified settlement of Porto Bello on the Isthmus took the breath out of his fellow buccaneers. They had always considered Panama as too well defended for their taste. But Henry Morgan had a way with him. As one of his men put it, he "was so able to communicate vigor with his very words."

One night in 1668, Morgan landed his pirates under the fort at Porto Bello and gave the order for attack. His cutthroat army climbed over the walls. The fortress was blown up, more for its terrifying effect on the inhabitants than for any tactical advantage.

Another fortress, Santa Gloria, offered resistance. The only way of getting over the walls was by using scaling ladders. But the Spaniards were waiting to shoot anyone who came near the walls. Morgan then took action typical of him. At the points of guns he forced Spanish nuns and monks to carry the scaling ladders and place them against the walls. The defenders hesitated to shoot, but finally decided that the sacrifice had to be made. Fire was opened on the innocent servants of the church. But the moment of hesitation was enough for Morgan and his band. Porto Bello fell into the hands of the buccaneers, paying the Brethren a handsome loot of 250,000 pieces of eight and some 300 slaves.

Probably Morgan's most spectacular exploit was his attack on Maracaibo, on the Venezuelan coast, in 1669. For this venture, Governor Modyford even let his partner have a newly arrived British man-of-war, the frigate *Oxford*. It was sent to Morgan's base of operations in the Isles des Vaches. Unfortunately, the frigate was blown to bits by an internal powder explosion one day while Morgan was entertaining his officers on board. Three hundred and fifty English sailors and many French prisoners were killed. By some trick of fate, Morgan and his officers, although rudely tossed into the water, were unharmed.

Toward the spring of 1669, Morgan, with eight ships, sailed for Maracaibo, which lay on the shores of a lake or lagoon on the western banks of the triangular Gulf of Maracaibo. The only entrance from the sea to this lake is by a narrow strait. This passage was protected by Spanish forts of the islands of Vigilias and Palomas. Morgan led his ships through the strait under cover of night, but the first light of dawn found them directly under the fortifications. The Spaniards opened cannon fire.

After a fierce battle that lasted all day, the Spanish guns suddenly ceased firing. Mystified, Morgan stole ashore. He was amazed to find that the fort was deserted. Morgan was puzzled, until he heard a hissing sound and saw a long fuse leading to the powder magazine. He stamped out the dangerous spark with his foot, returned to his ship, and gave orders for the fleet to proceed to the town of Maracaibo.

Maracaibo proved disappointing as to loot. While Morgan was taking what he could find, news reached him that three Spanish men-of-war under Admiral del Campo had arrived and were guarding the seaward exit from the lake. The Spanish admiral sent a note offering to let Morgan and his men go free if they would give up their loot and release the prisoners they had taken. Morgan put the proposition up to his men. They voted to fight.

Morgan knew that his small vessels would be no match for the Spanish men-of-war, so he resorted to strategy. He set his men to converting one of his ships into a fire ship. Fire ships were vessels set ablaze and allowed to drift down on enemy ships in the hope that they would set them afire.

The practice was to load the hull of a fire ship with sulphur. Heaps of gunpowder were placed at intervals in the hold and on deck and connected by fuses. The planks above the water line were loosened, so that they would come apart easily when the explosion went off, and scatter their flaming debris in all directions. The cannons were removed and in their place were substituted wooden dummies. Manikins of logs were dressed in typical buccaneer costumes and stood up along the bulwarks. In this particular instance, an extra fierce-looking scarecrow was placed on the deck to represent Morgan himself. Then came the final detail, twelve flesh-and-blood men to sail the ship and set off the explosion. There was no lack of volunteers for this suicide duty.

On April 30, Morgan's fleet, with the fire ship in the lead, sailed for the mouth of Lake Maracaibo. As dawn broke on May 1, the freebooters bore down on the Spaniards. The fire ship swept down upon the frigate *Magdalena*. Suddenly there was a terrific explosion. The fire ship went up in flames that soon spread to the *Magdalena*. A second Spanish ship was maneuvered into shallow water by its crew and scuttled; the third Spanish vessel was captured by the buccaneers.

Admiral del Campo escaped to the fort and manned the guns guarding the strait. Morgan's only road to the sea was still blocked. But Morgan knew more than one way to skin a cat. Boatloads of pirates were sent ashore to a point in the rear of the fort. All day long the boats plied between the shore and the ships, going full and coming back empty for more buccaneers, all in full view of the Spanish garrison. Admiral del Campo became alarmed. He saw signs of an attack from the rear and ordered his heavy cannons moved from the sea side to the land side of the fort. What he could not see was that the boats were not really returning from land empty, as appeared. The trick Morgan employed was a simple one. The pirates sat up in the boats going ashore and then lay down on the bottom, out of sight, returning. Actually not a single man was landed.

From his ship Morgan joyfully watched the Spaniards moving their cannons to the rear of the fort. Then, in the night, as a bright moon danced on the still waters, the buccaneers hoisted sail and proceeded through the strait, while del Campo looked on with sheepish resignation. Before he could get the guns back into place, Morgan and his ships were safely through the passage. When they were out of range, Morgan fired a salvo of seven cannon shots to taunt the disappointed Spaniards.

Back in Jamaica, Morgan went to Governor Modyford with his most ambitious plan, an expedition against Panama City itself. In this town on the Pacific side of the Isthmus he hoped to lay his hands on the treasure of gold and silver from Peru. The governor was a little afraid. It was said that news of Morgan and his raids had reached the ears of the king, who was none too pleased. But in June, 1670, an excuse came. Some Spanish warships, in reprisal for the attack on Maracaibo, raided along the coast of Jamaica, burning homes and taking prisoners. Governor Modyford summoned the council and Morgan was legally commissioned to sail against Panama.

Morgan's Panama expedition consisted of twenty-eight ships and 2,000 men, one of the biggest pirate fleets ever assembled. On December 6, 1670, the marauding squadron sailed from the base at Isles des Vaches. Early in January, 1671, Fort San Lorenzo, at the entrance of the Chagres River, was blown up. Thus the way was opened to Morgan across the Isthmus to Panama City.

As the buccaneers marched upon the city, the Spanish Governor Guzman sent a herd of 1,500 bulls against the enemy ahead of the Spanish army. His idea was that the beasts would trample the Englishmen. The reverse happened. When the invaders opened fire, the startled bulls turned around and completely disorganized the Spanish army, trampling many of the soldiers to death. Morgan marched victoriously into Panama City and viewed the many fine buildings with a glow of anticipation. But before the buccaneers could get down to the business of looting, the powder magazine was blown up on orders from the Spanish governor. The flames spread, completely destroying the city.

When Henry Morgan left Panama after a stay of 28 days, the loot and ransom amounted to 400,000 pieces of eight in gold, silver, and jewels, and close to half a million in various merchandise. On March 12, 1671, the buccaneers returned to Port Royal, and Morgan was received by the people of Jamaica as a conquering hero.

But trouble awaited Morgan in Jamaica. Peace had been declared between England and Spain even before he had set out for Panama, and the charge was made that both the buccaneer and Governor Modyford were aware of this, and therefore knew that the expedition was illegal.

When the news of the Panama raid reached the home country, Sir Thomas Lynch was sent out to replace Modyford as governor of Jamaica. On Lynch's arrival, in June, 1671,

Modyford was arrested and sent back to England. In January of the following year, Morgan was also arrested and shipped across the Atlantic to stand trial for piracy.

Very little is known of Morgan's forced visit to England, except that the charges against him were dismissed and that toward the end of 1673 the buccaneer was summoned to Whitehall by King Charles II. The pirate kneeled before his majesty, was touched on the shoulders by a jeweled sword, and was knighted Sir Henry Morgan. Not only was he knighted, but at the beginning of 1674, Morgan sailed for Port Royal as lieutenant governor of Jamaica. Governor Modyford, his companion in buccaneering, was also cleared and made chief justice of the island.

Henry Morgan had left Jamaica a buccaneer. He returned Sir Henry Morgan, and a most respectable and honored subject of the king, outwardly, anyway. Several times, during the years that followed, he served as governor of the island for brief periods. During those times, Morgan was the most severe persecuter of his former Brethren of the Coast. There is no doubt that he rid Jamaica of the buccaneers, who had by that time become out-and-out pirates, with not even a shred of legality attached to their lawless adventurings.

On one occasion, when a ship Morgan suspected of being a pirate vessel put in at Port Royal, Sir Henry invited the captain and his entire crew of seventeen to dine at the king's house. They accepted gratefully, and under the influence of good food and heady wine, told Morgan all about their past deeds and future plans. The governor entertained his guests well, gave them beds, and in the morning fed them an excellent breakfast and even supplied them with new linen. The pirates left feeling that their old friend Morgan, the Buccaneer, had not changed much after all. But the minute they stepped outside the bounds of the governor's mansion, the pirates were arrested. Before the sun set they were hanged, all seventeen of them.

For almost fifteen years Henry Morgan enjoyed his position as the first citizen of Jamaica. But although he professed to have reformed, he did not give up the riotous way of living he had adopted when he joined the Brethren of the Coast. Disease racked his body, and in 1688 he was forced to leave Port Royal for the drier climate in the interior of the island. There he died toward the end of August, one of the richest land and slave owners in Jamaica. When news of his death reached Port Royal, a salute of twenty-two guns was fired from the British warships in the harbor.

Less than four years after the death of Henry Morgan, on June 7, 1692, a terrific earthquake shook Port Royal. Buildings toppled and vanished with their occupants into yawning cracks in the earth. Soon a tidal wave swept over the ruins and wiped out the cemetery in which Sir Henry's bones had been interred. It was as complete a disaster as the world has ever known. Port Royal was rebuilt, but hurricanes in 1712, 1714, and 1722 descended upon it until, after the last one, the capital was moved from Port Royal to Kingston.

CHAPTER 7

Where East Meets West

Highlights of Panama

Discovered: By Alonso de Ojeda for Spain in 1499.

Population: 500,000.

Area: 29,100 square miles.

Language: Spanish.   *Capital:* Panama City.

Government: Republic established in 1903.

Geographical Characteristics: From flat, swampy coast lines, the country rises to a mountainous interior.

Climatic Conditions: Wholly tropical.

Principal Products: Bananas, cocoa, hardwoods, and some gold mining.

THE Republic of Panama was established in 1903. It is the youngest New World nation. Nevertheless, this narrow barrier between the Atlantic Ocean and the Pacific has the oldest settlements on the mainland of America and a history that is as ancient as it is dramatic and important.

The coast of Panama was visited by Alonso de Ojeda in 1499 and by Rodrigo Bastida in the following year. With Bastida on this early voyage was a young Spanish adventurer, Vasco Núñez de Balboa, who was to return a few years later to play one of the most important roles in the drama of New World discovery.

In 1502, Columbus sailed from Spain on his last voyage to "The Indies." His purpose is quaintly put by a contemporary historian as: "to seek the strait which, as he said, did divide the land from the other side."

The discovery of this strait had become an obsession with Columbus. He sailed the entire coast from Honduras to the Gulf of Darien, exploring every indentation of land. The Admiral's enthusiasm reached its highest pitch when the Indians told him of a "narrow place between two seas." Columbus naturally interpreted it as meaning a waterway. The Indians no doubt referred to the Isthmus of Panama, that narrow strip of land that connects North and South America.

Columbus reached the Isthmus of Panama in November, 1592. He landed in the Bay of Porto Bello and explored the Chagres River. Had he only known it, Columbus was as close to finding the way to "The Indies," and to learning the truth about his discoveries as he was ever destined to be. Only a narrow wall of land separated him from that truth.

The first serious attempts to colonize the Isthmus were made in 1509, when the territory was divided between two favorites of the Spanish court: Alonzo Ojeda and Diego de Nicuesa. Ojeda was the first to sail, from Santo Domingo, steering his course southward. As he was about to give up the voyage and return after a series of mishaps, Nicuesa came along and helped his rival to continue the expedition. Nicuesa then sailed on to his own province, while Ojeda landed at the entrance to the Gulf of Uraba and established the little settlement of San Sebastian. Food ran low after a few months. Ojeda, leaving most of the colonists behind, sailed for Santo Domingo to get supplies. He never returned, for his ship was wrecked. By the time he was rescued, the colony of San Sebastian had shriveled and died.

Nicuesa, in the meantime, had run into even worse luck than Ojeda. Through shipwreck and sickness and hostile Indians only seventy of the original band of 700 men were left to build a blockhouse at Nombre de Dios in Panama. Then,

134 · *Lands of New World Neighbors*

when the party began to recover from the many hardships and sufferings, Nicuesa had news of another Spanish settlement along the coast of the Isthmus and within the limits of the province over which he claimed jurisdiction. He decided to investigate. Toward the end of 1510, Nicuesa and his men sailed in two ships for the Gulf of Darien where the new colony had been established.

The story of this new settlement is one of the most romantic in the history of New World exploration. In 1510 an expedition was being prepared in Santo Domingo to go to the rescue of Ojeda, who was still thought to be with his colony in San Sebastian. In charge of the relief party was a lawyer, Martín Enciso, a strict and sober man who had no sympathy for the many penniless young adventurers who begged to be taken along on the expedition as a means of getting away from the island of Hispaniola and their debts.

In Santo Domingo, in those days, restless and owing everyone money, lived one Vasco Núñez de Balboa. He could not openly join an expedition because his debts bound him by law to remain in Santo Domingo until they were paid. Enciso would have nothing to do with Balboa, who had the reputation of being a troublemaker of the first water, but Balboa was determined to sail with Enciso, law or no law. Knowing that the ship would be closely watched for attempted stowaways, Balboa decided to adopt a disguise that neither the officers of the law nor the stern Enciso would be able to penetrate.

When the ship was well out to sea and Enciso was complimenting himself on having thwarted every attempt of the rascal Balboa to board, a barrel marked "Provisions for Voyage" suddenly came to life. Out of it sprang Balboa, a smiling greeting on his lips but one hand on his sword hilt. Enciso was furious. He threatened to throw Balboa overboard or maroon him on a desert island. The lawyer might have carried out his threats if he had not been persuaded that Balboa, having sailed the coast of Panama before, might prove of value. Grudgingly, Enciso allowed the adventurer to become one of the company.

It was not long before Balboa was the most popular man on board. Soon he was looked upon by many as the real leader. After they reached the spot where the survivors of Ojeda's colony were picked up, the expedition ran into trouble at every turn—storms at sea and hostile Indians on land. From then on Balboa did indeed become the leader. Without him, the expedition would have floundered into failure. It was under Balboa's guidance that a course was set for the western shores of the Gulf of Uraba where, as he had learned on his voyage 10 years before, the Indians did not use poisoned darts. This was in Diego de Nicuesa's territory.

Here the Spaniards decided to establish a colony. While the town of Darien was being built, the settlers grew tired of the domineering but incompetent Enciso. They voted to dispose of him. But the choice of a new leader caused some dissension. A few remained loyal to Enciso. Others argued that since they had settled in the province of Diego de Nicuesa, he should be asked to take charge. Still others wanted to place Balboa in command.

The final decision was that Balboa should be recognized as the leader until Nicuesa arrived. Meanwhile word reached Darien that Nicuesa had threatened to punish the uninvited settlers by taking from them the little gold they had found. Therefore, when he arrived, Nicuesa was not allowed to land. After some wrangling Nicuesa put out to sea for Santo Domingo and was never heard of again. This turn of events left Balboa in complete command at Darien.

As Enciso was causing trouble, Balboa had him imprisoned, later to set him free on condition that he return to Spain on the first ship. Enciso accepted the condition. He went to Spain where he started a bitter whispering campaign against Balboa, who meanwhile continued his explorations of the Isthmus. In company with Francisco Pizarro, one of Ojeda's officers who had been stranded at San Sebastian, Balboa led a party on a gold-hunting expedition into the interior.

When some gold was found in the territory of Comogre, ruled by a friendly Indian chief, the Spaniards began to quarrel over the division of the treasure. The Indians, setting little value on gold, were amazed at this Spanish hunger for the yellow metal. The chief's son told them that there was no need for them to fight over the little gold they had. He knew a land, he said, where there was more than enough gold for everyone. He then pointed toward the mountains and added that a great sea lay on the other side, and that to the south there was a land where gold was so plentiful that the inhabitants used it instead of pottery for their household utensils. This is the first definite mention of the existence of the Pacific Ocean and the first inkling of the Inca Empire in Peru. It is significant that, among those who heard the words of the young Indian, were Balboa and Pizarro, whose dramatic roles in history were cast that day.

When Balboa returned to Darien, he could not get the thought of the great sea across the mountains out of his mind. He had been in the bad graces of the king ever since Enciso had told his story to the court. Balboa knew the price of royal forgiveness; some great discovery, especially one with gold at the end of the trail. It was either that, or to return home to disgrace and poverty.

On September 1, 1513, Balboa with 190 of his sturdiest men and a large group of friendly Indians set out across the Isthmus. He had been warned that it would be a difficult journey, but it proved to be even worse than he had expected. Every mile of the way was a heartbreaking struggle. Hostile Indians waylaid them. Thick jungles and tropical fevers took their toll of men and morale. When they finally reached a high hill on September 25, only sixty-seven of Balboa's companions were able to follow him. Balboa climbed to the summit, while his men waited anxiously below. First they saw him stop

and stand erect. Then he fell to his knees in prayer. Balboa
had seen what the others could not see, the vast expanse of the
Pacific Ocean—revealed for the first time to the eyes of a
European. At that moment, immortality cloaked Vasco
Núñez de Balboa. Unfortunately, the most beautiful and stir-
ring tribute to that mountaintop scene in Darien, a sonnet by
Keats, mistakenly gives credit for the discovery of the Pacific
to Cortez.

Four days later, on September 29, Balboa reached the shores
of the Pacific. With the banner of Spain in one hand and his
sword in the other, he waded into the waters until they reached
up to his waist. Then, as his followers looked on in awed
silence, Balboa claimed for Castile and Aragon the whole
extent of the greatest ocean in the world. He named it the
Great South Sea.

In January, 1514, Balboa returned to Darien, highly
pleased with his discovery. Surely, he thought, the gift of an
entire new ocean would make the king forgive him his highhanded treatment of Enciso. And there was gold, too; promises
of golden riches to the south. There was not yet any actual
knowledge of the land of the Incas, but the Indians along the
Pacific had confirmed the story of a land where gold was more
common than the steel of the Spaniards.

Balboa sent the news of his discovery to Spain and waited
impatiently for his reward. But instead of titles and honors
there came Pedro Arias de Ávila, better known to history as
Pedrarias, with 2,000 colonists and a royal commission re-
placing Balboa as governor.

Pedrarias is infamous in history. He was over seventy years
old when he reached Darien in June, 1514. The best that has
been said of him is that he was so old that his days of evil-doing
could not last long. His contemporaries, as well as later
historians, agree that he was the most cruel, vicious, and
brutal governor Spain ever sent to the colonies.

Almost the first act of Pedrarias on arriving was to arrest

Balboa for his actions against Nicuesa and Enciso. When the popular young adventurer was acquitted of the charges, Pedrarias could hardly control his fury. If he could not get rid of Balboa in one way, there were others. To accomplish this, the governor gave Balboa permission to form an expedition to explore the shores of the Great South Sea. To do this Balboa needed ships. As there were none on the Pacific side and no means for building them there, Balboa built the ships on the Atlantic side. His idea was to take them apart afterward and have them carried in sections through the jungle and over the mountains and reassemble them on the Pacific shores.

The plan was carried out and piece by piece the ships were loaded on the backs of Indians and the long dreary trek across the Isthmus began. Some 500 men, mostly Indians, lost their lives to bring the first European boats to the new ocean. But Balboa was not destined to conquer by sail the ocean he had waded into with such high hopes. He was supervising the rebuilding of the ships near the present site of Panama City when a party of soldiers under Francisco Pizarro arrived from Darien. He had orders from Pedrarias to arrest Balboa on charges of treason against the crown. Balboa was taken to Darien for trial. This time the governor made sure that nothing would go wrong. A verdict of guilty was brought in almost immediately. In January, 1517, Balboa was beheaded.

About two years after Balboa's execution, the first important settlement was established on the Pacific coast. On August 15, 1519, Pedrarias founded a town which he called Panama, from an Indian word meaning abounding in fish. With settlements on both the Atlantic and Pacific shores, the Isthmus of Panama soon became a center of expeditions and exploration.

Even before the discovery of wealth in Peru, a great deal of gold went to Spain from Panama. As early as 1519 a road, roughly paved with cobblestones and boulders, was opened between Panama City on the Pacific side and Nombre de Dios on the Atlantic. This curving road was about 90 miles long and had stations at regular intervals along its route. After Pizarro's conquest of the Inca Empire, this jungle highway became famous as the Gold Road. Over its rutted course traveled mule caravans laden with gold and silver from the palaces and temples of the Incas in Peru and Ecuador and from the fabulous Potosi mines of Bolivia.

Nombre de Dios was a quiet and sleepy town for the greater part of the year. But once every 12 months, a messenger came from Panama with news that the plate fleet from Peru had arrived at the Pacific port. Then Nombre de Dios came to life. A boat was dispatched to the captains of the Spanish galleons that rode at anchor in the harbor of near-by Cartagena. The huge ships reached Nombre de Dios a few days later to load the treasures into their holds and take them home to Spain.

While the ships were in port, the hustle and bustle of Nombre de Dios resembled that of some great fair. There was singing, dancing, and carousing. Everybody had money. Fortunes changed hand at the turn of a card. Plans were made for expeditions and ventures into unexplored lands. Then, one day, the galleons, deep in the water with their precious cargoes of gold, silver, and jewels, sailed out of the harbor. Nombre de Dios returned to its sleep, to wait another year and another messenger with the news from Panama.

The picture of this once-a-year activity of Nombre de Dios was a familiar one by hearsay to Francis Drake long before he set eyes on Panama. This English adventurer and self-appointed enemy of Spain sailed across the Atlantic in 1572, and planned to add a little excitement of his own to the yearly doings of the town.

Drake had sworn undying enmity against Spain when on a previous voyage into New World waters with his uncle, John Hawkins. Their ships had been attacked off the coast of Mexico after the Spanish had promised them safety. Drake's revenge took the form of a one-man war against the King of Spain that lasted till his dying day. The bold Englishman made it his mission in life to divert all the Spanish treasure he could into the coffers of England. His many expeditions were nominally private enterprises, though sanctioned and, even on occasion, partly financed by Queen Elizabeth.

Francis Drake was already known and feared on the Spanish Main in 1572, when he put into action his bold plan to attack Nombre de Dios, the treasure house of the New World. It was early one summer morning, before dawn, when Drake's ships put into the harbor of the Spanish town on the Atlantic side of Panama. No life was stirring. Silently the Englishmen, mostly young Devon lads still in their teens, stole upon the sleeping town. They put the cannons in the fort out of action by spiking them.

The Englishmen had reached the town square before the alarm was sounded and the church bell began its frantic clanging. Spanish soldiers rushed out of their barracks. There was a lively exchange of musket shots during which Drake was wounded. Disregarding his wound, Drake led the attack against the Spaniards who gave ground. Without delay Drake and his men rushed to the king's treasure house, planning to take all the gold they could carry. But when Drake fell to the ground, faint through loss of blood from his wound, the loyal sailors left the gold and carried Drake back to the boats.

Nombre de Dios went back to sleep, but not a very sound sleep. While Drake and his Devon boys remained in the vicinity, every Spanish soldier in the city slept with one eye open and his sword and musket by his side.

The failure of his first major attack upon Panama only convinced Drake that an even bolder plan was necessary. For the rest of the year, he looted numerous Spanish ships while he made his plans for a raid on one of the great treasure caravans on the Gold Road between Panama and Nombre de Dios.

The Spanish mule trains traveled in the cool of the night, and late one evening in 1573, Drake and a handful of his men lay hidden among the bushes along the Gold Road ready to pounce upon a treasure caravan. They could hear the tinkling of the bells on the gold-laden mules as they came over the road from Panama. Strict instructions had been given by Drake that not a man was to stir until he gave the signal for attack. As they waited, a lone horseman came riding by from Nombre de Dios. One of the Englishmen, overenthusiastic, imprudently rose up from his hiding place. At the same moment, the rider whipped up his horse and was off at a gallop.

Drake waited anxiously, fearing that the Spaniard had become alarmed. But no. The sweet tinkling of the mule bells kept coming closer and closer. When the laden mules were directly in front of his hiding place, Drake gave the signal. The bushes came to life and the treasure train was quickly surrounded. Eagerly the Englishmen tore into the mule packs, only to find that there was no treasure.

One of the muleteers, trembling with fear, explained that the lone rider who had passed in the darkness had become suspicious when he thought he saw a man rising in the bushes. He had galloped ahead to raise the alarm. The mules carrying the treasure were sent back to Panama while only mules laden with a few supplies were sent ahead as a decoy.

Always patient when there was no other course, Drake awaited his time and chance. He knew that Peruvian treasure would be sent through to the Atlantic side sooner or later. Months later, his Indian spies told him that a treasure train had arrived in Nombre de Dios. That was what Drake had been waiting for. With only fifty men he descended on the town for the second time.

The Spaniards were taken completely by surprise, never dreaming that even the bold Drake would have the audacity to make another try for the treasure. Just how much of the treasure the Englishmen carried off is not definitely known, but accounts say that it amounted to 30 tons of silver and large quantities of gold and jewels. In any case, the loot was so great that some of it had to be buried, as it was too heavy to carry away. Much of this plunder was recovered by the Spaniards, who considered themselves lucky and hoped they would never see or hear of Francis Drake and his Devon lads again.

But Panama did hear from Drake again, in 1595, when he unsuccessfully attacked Porto Bello, which by that time had taken the place of Nombre de Dios as the Atlantic terminal for the treasure trains. It was Drake's last battle in his personal war against Spain. Fever seized him, and he died on board his ship. In a leaden coffin he was lowered to his last resting place under the waters of New Spain that he had so often terrorized.

The site that had been chosen for Panama City by Pedrarias back in the days of Balboa was far from an ideal one. The harbor was poor and the locale extremely unhealthful. Still the colony grew and prospered. The wealth of Peru had to come there for transshipment. Thousands of men worked gold mines that had been discovered in the province. Thirty brigantines and hundreds of men were kept busy working the rich pearl fisheries off the coast. All merchandise from Spain bound for the Pacific colonies had to pass through Panama. At its height, the colony was the most important one in the New World, having jurisdiction from Mexico to Peru. But gradually, as the other colonies gained in wealth and importance, Panama lost control and its influence; it shrank to more or less the present area of the Republic of Panama.

In 1575 there were 400 buildings and some 500 Spanish residents in Panama City. Epidemics and fires retarded its growth after the heyday, and the colony never completely recovered from the devastating fire of February 21, 1664. The seventeenth century also brought the buccaneers. The notorious Morgan was the scourge of Panama. The story of his raids in 1668 and 1671 is told in the chapter on Jamaica.

The destruction of Panama City by this extraordinary pirate was so thorough a job that instead of trying to rebuild it, a new city was built on another and safer site. The new city rose from a volcanic rock jutting a mile into the Bay of Panama from the foot of present-day Ancon Hill. It was planned to defy future Morgans and Drakes, with great walls 20 to 30 feet high, and in places as much as 60 feet thick, with moats, drawbridges, and the heaviest of fortifications. To build this new colony, Spain actually spent a mountain of money.

It is said that the King of Spain was standing in his palace looking out of a window one day. One of his courtiers asked him why he was peering so intently into the west. The king replied: "I'm looking for the walls and fortifications of Panama. For the vast sum of money they have cost me, certainly I should be able to see them from Spain."

Toward the end of the seventeenth century, the Isthmus was threatened by a different kind of invasion, a peaceful one by canny Scotchmen. William Paterson, the founder of the Bank of England, had learned from the pirate Lionel Wafer that a colony on the Isthmus would give him control of world trade. He probably also recalled the instructions of Queen Elizabeth to Raleigh, when he said: "By seizing the Isthmus of Panama you will wrest the keys of the world from Spain."

Paterson was a loyal Scotchman. He decided to give his countrymen the opportunity to profit by his scheme. He raised almost 5 million dollars and gathered 1,200 colonists in the highlands. They sailed for the New World in 1698 and landed at Darien. They planted their colony in New Caledonia Bay, which today is Puerto Escoces. They named the two towns they founded New Edinburgh and Saint Andrews. Hardly had the Scotch settlers landed when fever broke out, killing them by the hundreds. Their supplies ran out and starvation would have destroyed the entire colony if it had not been for the friendship of the San Blas Indians who came to their rescue. Early in 1699 the survivors sailed back home.

But far from being discouraged by their horrible experiences, these survivors recruited more of their countrymen and returned later the same year, 1,300 strong. The second try was a tragic repetition of the first. Before the end of the year, they were on their way home to Scotland again. In 1700, a third contingent of stubborn and hardy Scotchmen set out to control world trade by gaining a foothold in Panama. This third attempt might have resulted in a New Scotland on the shores of the Caribbean if the Spaniards, jealous of the control-of-trade idea, had not driven them out.

Panama Canal Zone

Population: 30,000.

Area: 554 square miles.

Language: English.

Government: Territorial possession of the United States.

Geographical Characteristics: The Panama Canal Zone is a narrow strip of land and lakes and rivers which combine to form the canal system.

Climatic Conditions: Tropical.

The idea of a canal across the Isthmus of Panama can rightly be said to have begun with the discovery of the Pacific Ocean. It is claimed by some authorities that Balboa considered the idea of a man-made canal across the narrow strip of land. Whether he did or not, one of his followers, Alvaro de Saavedra Ceron, did. In 1529 he proposed and drew plans for a canal to connect the Atlantic and Pacific Oceans, suggesting both Panama and Nicaragua as suitable routes. Six years later, in 1535, King Charles V of Spain ordered a survey to be made for a canal across the Isthmus. The survey was probably never made, for Pascual de Andagoya reported that it was an impossible project.

Until the actual completion of the Panama Canal, Nicaragua continued a strong rival for a waterway connection between the two oceans. Philip II of Spain had a survey made for a possible Nicaragua canal in 1556. When an unfavorable report was submitted, the king protected his pride by declaring that he did not want a canal anyway. He even forbade the discussion of such a project. Having disposed of the canal idea, the king went one better and ordered that not even new land routes should be opened up. These royal injunctions delayed any further serious considerations of a canal for almost three hundred years.

When the famous naturalist, Alexander von Humboldt, visited the Americas at the beginning of the nineteenth century, he traveled through Central America and brought the idea of a canal to life again by suggesting nine places suitable for the practical cutting of artificial waterways between the Atlantic and Pacific Oceans. Humboldt's views were so widely publicized that, in April, 1814, Spain passed a decree for the construction of an Isthmian canal. Various delays held up the project. Before any action could be taken, the Spanish colonies rose in revolt and declared their independence.

Panama gained her independence from Spain as a province of New Granada (now Colombia). With the passing of Spanish control in the Americas, the United States began to take serious interest in the possibilities of a canal. The first definite plan, however, was for a Nicaraguan canal. This was sponsored by a group of businessmen in 1825. After a year of futile effort to interest capital in the venture, the plan was abandoned.

Between 1824 and 1840 there were a number of investigations and proposals for canal projects, but nothing concrete resulted from any of them. The first actual survey of a route across the Isthmus of Panama was made by an English and a Swedish engineer in 1829, at the order of Simon Bolivar, the South American liberator. Although nothing came of it, the route surveyed by Bolivar later became the right of way of the Panama railroad, the first transcontinental railroad in the world.

The first contract for a railroad across the Isthmus was granted to a French Company in 1847, but as work was never started, the rights were obtained by a group of American businessmen, headed by William Henry Aspinwall, in December, 1848.

Before work started on the railroad, news of the great California gold strike at Sutter's mill broke upon the world. The mad rush of the forty-niners, who wanted to get from the Atlantic to the Pacific side of the continent in a hurry, sent a stream of humanity across the Isthmus of Panama. There was no railroad and no roads across the United States, and the overland journey in North America was long and difficult. Cape Horn saw many new faces during the years of the gold rush, but the voyage was far too slow, anywhere from a hundred days up. The narrow strip of land across the Isthmus of Panama offered the quickest route from east to west.

Enterprising steamship companies opened offices on the Atlantic and Pacific terminals of the Panama railroad. On arriving at the Isthmus, the gold seekers went by boat up the Chagres River to Cruces or Gorgona. From there a tiresome mule journey took them to the Pacific terminal. If the railroad had been in operation in those early days, it would have been a gold mine almost as rich as those of California. And yet, although it was not completed until January, 1855, the railroad is reported to have earned some 2 million dollars during the construction period as a result of the gold rush. The total cost of the road was 7 million dollars, or $140,000 a mile, for its 50 miles of rails. To that price must be added the cost in human lives, through the ravages of disease. There are various stories of how many workmen died, mostly exaggerated. It is true, however, that of 1,000 Chinese laborers imported in 1850, only about 200 were alive a few months later. When the road was finished, it was a complete financial success, returning enormous dividends for years. And no wonder. The first-class fare for the 50-mile run was $25. If a prospective passenger protested against the high rate and decided to walk, he gained nothing. The only passable route across the Isthmus was the railroad bed, and the company charged $25 for the right to walk.

With the completion of the transcontinental railroad across the United States, the Panama railroad suffered a severe setback. In 1887 it was bought by the French Company of Ferdinand de Lesseps for 25 million dollars as a part of the French canal project across Panama.

When Ferdinand de Lesseps tackled the job of building a sea-level waterway across the Isthmus, he was still basking in his triumph of constructing the Suez Canal. His prestige opened the pockets of his fellow Frenchmen in all walks of life to the tune of 60 million dollars. Work was begun in January, 1882, after a series of costly and ridiculous stunts on the part of de Lesseps to arouse interest in his venture.

On one occasion the ceremony of digging the first shovelful of dirt at the Pacific entrance to the canal turned into a farce when prolonged celebrations on board the official boat delayed the ceremony until the outgoing tide made it impossible to get within 2 miles of the digging site. A mock ceremony of digging in a sandbox aboard the boat was accompanied by many long and serious speeches. For months champagne flowed while not a spadeful of earth was dug.

The extravagance and waste of the French canal administration were mountainous. A mansion was built for the director-general at a cost of $150,000. Before it was ready to be occupied, the director's wife, daughter, and son died of fever. The official returned to France, where he died of a broken heart. A private railway car was constructed for $42,000; a bath-house cost $40,000; $2,700,000 was spent for personal servants of officials.

But the greatest waste was in human lives. Estimates of deaths from all causes, during the 8 years of the French effort, range from 16,000 to 22,000, the greater part from yellow fever and malaria. It is tragic to note that to protect the sick in hospitals from the annoyance of ants, bowls of water were placed under each foot of the beds. The French had no means of knowing it, of course, but in those very bowls of water bred the deadly stegomyia mosquito that carried yellow fever from infected patients and passed it on to others.

The French canal bubble burst in 1889, when there was no more money. What work had been done had been done well, especially in Culebra Cut, according to American engineers when they took over the job. One engineer said that if the Americans had had to tackle the job under the same conditions as the French, he doubted if they could have done better.

While the French canal effort was nearing its tragic end, a lively controversy was raging in the United States between the practicability of the Panama route for a canal as against Nicaragua. In June, 1890, under direction of a Maritime Canal Commission, work was begun on an American canal at Nicaragua. Operations were continued for three years, when the 6 million dollars of private capital was exhausted. The sponsors were then forced to give up, unable to interest either the government or new capital in the project.

The canal idea was allowed to slumber until 1902 when the United States, after receiving a favorable report on the Panama route for a canal, purchased the Isthmian railroad from the bankrupt French Canal Company for 40 million dollars. The next step, before operations could begin, was to buy a strip of land on each side of the proposed canal route from the Republic of Colombia.

Trouble with Colombia over the price of various concessions needed to begin the canal continued for more than a year, until the question was tabled by the adjournment of the Colombian Congress at the end of October, 1903, amid rumors of revolt in Panama, which, as has been explained earlier, was a province of the Republic of Colombia. The Isthmus naturally stood to lose the most if the treaty with the United States for construction of the Panama Canal fell through. In June, 1903, Panama threatened to break away from Colombia unless favorable action was taken on the canal proposition. On November 3, matters came to a head when Colombian troops were landed in Panama to suppress an impending revolt.

The Panama garrison was under the command of General Esteban Huertas. He was in sympathy with the Panamanians. Of three Colombia gunboats in the harbor, two immediately raised the new flag of Panama. The third halfheartedly shelled the city. From this resulted the only casualty of the revolution, the death of a Chinaman who was accidentally struck by the fragments of a shell in the streets of Panama.

On the afternoon of November 4, 1903, the declaration of Panama's independence from Colombia was announced in the Cathedral Plaza of Panama City. The new republic was recognized by the United States 2 days later, on November 6. On February 13, 1904, the constitution of the republic of Panama was signed and Dr. Manuel Amador was elected the first president.

When the United States began work on the Panama Canal, it had a tremendous advantage over the French. Methods for controlling malaria were known, and the dreaded yellow fever had been conquered in Cuba a few years before. It was really man's victory over yellow fever that made the building of the Panama Canal possible. The story of this great victory is told in the chapter on Cuba.

Disease and death were the first problems faced by the United States in accepting the challenge of the canal. The very first commission that journeyed to Panama for preliminary investigations in April, 1904, was accompanied by Colonel William Gorgas, who as chief sanitation officer of Cuba had rid Havana of the last trace of yellow fever.

Sanitation and mosquito control became the battle cry of the canalers. By the end of 1906, Panama, once the pest spot of the Americas, was as healthful as any place in the tropics. Modern houses were built, raised off the ground and screened.

Sewers and waterworks were constructed. Yellow fever was banished and malaria restricted until its ravages were negligible. If it had not been for the thorough cleanup job performed by Gorgas, the big ditch could never have been dug.

The railroad was brought up to date. Instead of going blindly into the work of digging, or as many United States newspapers demanded, "let the dirt fly," the work on actual canal construction was carefully planned.

At first, the work of construction was put in the hands of civilian engineers. After a few years, this system was found unsatisfactory. There were constant disagreements as to policy. When an engineer grew tired of his job, he simply resigned. Finally President Theodore Roosevelt announced that he was tired of delays and replacements. He turned the job over to the United States Army.

"I'll put men in charge who will stay until I'm tired of them," announced the President. On February 26, 1907, Lieutenant Colonel George Goethals, United States Engineering Corps, was appointed chief engineer of the Panama Canal. From that time on the dirt really did fly.

When Goethals assumed his duties on April 1, 1907, one of his first acts was to let the canal force know who was the boss. But despite his iron rule, he was popular with the men in the vast army of workers. They knew that so long as they did their jobs, they would get a fair deal. Favoritism was abolished and the petty tyranny of foremen and minor officials was done away with.

One of the famous institutions of this era of the canal work was the informal court held by Colonel Goethals every Sunday morning. At this court, any employee could present his grievances. Goethals was the judge and jury. Once, when a man had heard the colonel's decision on his case, he protested that he would appeal. "Appeal? To whom?" boomed Goethals. The man looked sheepishly at the boss for a moment and then, laughing, went back to his work.

The physical work of canal construction is too vast a subject to be covered here. Probably the best-known phase of the canal is the famous Culebra Cut (now Gaillard Cut) and its terrible slides, which in a few moments completely undid the labor of months or years.

When the French came up against the great Cucaracha slide in 1887, they simply shrugged their shoulders and gave up work on that part of the canal. The United States engineers refused to be licked. They waged a constant battle against overwhelming odds, and won. Before work was finished there were twenty-two major slides, involving 25 million cubic yards of earth.

When the United States engineers took over they were able to take advantage of some of the French work, principally in the Culebra Cut. But the machinery that had been abandoned was for the greater part either ruined or outmoded.

At the height of canal construction 100 steam shovels, doing the work of 10,000 men, were in operation. More than 100 locomotives were in constant use. Single dynamite blasts sometimes used 40,000 pounds of explosive; more than a million blasting cartridges were employed to set off charges in a single year.

The Panama Canal was completed on October 10, 1913, when President Woodrow Wilson pressed a button in the White House in Washington, D. C., blowing up a dike that let the waters come pouring in. Then came a period of testing and trial operations. On August 15, 1914, the canal was opened to commercial traffic.

The canal is in reality not a canal for its whole length. A ship enters the Atlantic side and continues at sea level for a little less than 7 miles to the Gatun Locks, where it is lifted up three steps to Gatun Lake. Although the vessel is towed by electric locomotives through the locks, it continues under its own power for some 20 miles across Gatun Lake to Gamboa, and through the stupendous Culebra Cut for 7 miles to the

Pedro Miguel Locks and dam, where a drop of 30 feet brings the ship to Miraflores Lake. A mile across, this lake leads to the Miraflora Locks, where two drops bring the vessel back to sea level, and into a 7-mile channel to Balboa, with the Pacific Ocean ahead.

The entire length of the canal is 34 miles. Contrary to popular belief, it does not run from east to west, but almost due south from the Atlantic entrance at Limon Bay to the Pacific exit at the Bay of Panama. At one place in Panama, as a matter of fact, the Pacific Ocean is east of the Atlantic.

The canal has a minimum width of 300 feet and a maximum of 1,000 feet. Its depth varies from 41 feet to 80 feet in Gatun Lake. The locks are 1,000 feet long and 110 feet wide, and about forty-eight ships a day can be accommodated. Gatun Lake, which has been called one of the greatest works of man, is artificial. It was made by damming the waters of the Chagres River. It is 165 square miles in area, contains 183 billion cubic feet of water, and furnishes water power for a great part of the canal's operation. The total canal cost was $366,650,000.

If Balboa were to come back to visit Panama today, he would no doubt gaze at the gigantic canal with unbelieving eyes. But if he were to visit the San Blas Indians living on the tiny islands along the northern coast and high among the forbidding mountains, he would see practically no change in their way of life, except that many of them would be wearing bowler hats sold by enterprising American merchants.

The San Blas Indians, living for the most part in their almost inaccessible mountain stronghold, have adopted practically none of the ways of the white man. They are still racially pure, and live under the rule of a cacique, or chief, as they did in the days of Columbus. These Indians are perhaps best known from reports that there are white Indians among them. This mistaken notion of white Indians is due to exaggerated cases of hereditary albinism.

Although the San Blas Indians are friendly today, and the

men are frequently seen in the streets of Colon where they come to sell coconuts, hides, tropical fruits, and a little gold, they resent intrusion within their own domain. It is said that white men who penetrate into San Blas territory for trade or curiosity, are treated courteously, but firmly told to leave at night. The Indians are expert canoemen, and around the waters of Panama it is a common sight to see a San Blas Indian skillfully sailing his canoe through seas that even large boats have difficulty in battling.

Puerto Rico

Discovered: By Columbus for Spain in 1493.

Population: 1,800,000.

Area: 3,435 square miles.

Language: English.   *Capital:* San Juan.

Government: Territorial possession of the United States.

Geographical Characteristics: The island is broken up by fairly low mountain ranges that run northeast to southwest.

Climatic Conditions: Generally temperate.

Principal Products: Sugar, coffee, fruits, and tobacco products.

To the northeast of Panama, on the fringe of the Caribbean, lies a curve of islands, forming a sort of bulwark against the Atlantic Ocean. The northernmost of these is Puerto Rico, one of the most important island possessions of the United States.

Puerto Rico was discovered by Columbus on November 17, 1493, but it was given its name (Rich Harbor) in 1508, by Juan Ponce de León, who in the following year founded the city of San Juan de Puerto Rico. It was from this port that Ponce de León set out on his famous and romantic quest for the Fountain of Youth and discovered Florida. Puerto Rico remained under Spanish domination until December 10, 1898, when it was ceded to the United States by treaty.

Virgin Islands

Population: 22,000.

Area: 133 square miles.

Language: English.   *Capital:* Saint Thomas.

Government: Territory of the United States.

Geographical Characteristics: Typical mountainous Caribbean islands
of volcanic origin.

Climatic Conditions: Tropical tempered by cooling winds.

Principal Products: Sugar, bananas, and other fruits.

Fifty miles east of Puerto Rico lie the Virgin Islands. They
were named after the Virgins of Saint Ursula by Columbus
who sighted the islands on his second voyage in 1493. In the
days of the buccaneers the names of many of these islands were
changed to suit the taste of the Brethren of the Coast: Rum
Island, Dead Man's Chest, Salt Water Money, Rock Island,
and Beef Island were some of the names bestowed by the buccaneers. Saint Thomas of the Virgin group became a Danish
crown colony in 1666, as did Saint Croix and Saint John later.
In 1917 these three main islands and fifty smaller ones were
sold by Denmark to the United States for 25 million dollars.

Leeward Islands

Population: 89,300.

Area: 410 square miles.

Government: British colony.

Next in the curve are the Leeward Islands, the most north-
erly group of the Lesser Antilles. This group, known as the
British Leewards, is of volcanic origin. It is composed of a
great many islands, the largest of which are: Aguilla, Antigua,
Barbuda, Dominica, Nevis, Montserrat, Redonda, Saint Kitts,
Sombrero, British Virgins, with the seat of government at

Saint John, Antigua. The Island of Nevis is important to the history of the United States as the birthplace, in 1757, of the famous American statesman, Alexander Hamilton.

Windward Islands

Population: 165,000.

Area: 515 square miles.

Government: British colony.

Curving southward and into the easternmost extremity of northern South America are the Windward Islands. They are called that because they are exposed to the northeast trade winds. The British possessions in this group are Grenada, Saint Lucia, Saint Vincent, and a number of smaller islands known as the Grenadines. Saint Lucia was once so infested with poisonous snakes as to be almost uninhabitable.

Then someone remembered that the mongoose, a small Asiatic mammal, is a deadly enemy of even the most poisonous Indian snake. The tiny snake slayers were transported from India to Saint Lucia and not even Saint Patrick did a better job of chasing the snakes out of Ireland than the mongoose did in destroying the serpents of Saint Lucia.

French West Indies

Population: Guadeloupe and Martinique combined, 500,000.

Area: Guadeloupe and Martinique combined, 1,073 square miles.

Language: French.   *Capital:* Guadeloupe—Basse-Terre.
Martinique—Fort-de-France.

Government: French colonies.

Geographical Characteristics: Typical mountainous Caribbean islands of volcanic origin.

Climatic Conditions: Tropical with frequent hurricanes.

Principal Products: Sugar, tobacco, and bananas.

When Columbus in 1493 discovered the Islands that today compose the French West Indies, he landed on Guadeloupe, where members of the crew to their amazement found iron cooking pots and part of a European vessel. One might wonder what happened to the crew of this nameless ship. If it had not been wrecked, if members of the crew had lived, some now nameless sailors and not Columbus would have the honor of discovering the New World.

Guadeloupe, and its companion, Martinique, were settled by the French in 1635. Martinique, the birthplace of Empress Josephine, the first wife of Napoleon Bonaparte, was the scene in 1902 of one of the greatest natural disasters in recorded history.

Forty years ago on the Caribbean coast of Martinique, there was a thriving city of 30,000 souls. Its name was Saint Pierre and it stood on a crescent-shaped stretch of land about half a mile long and a quarter of a mile wide. On one side rolled the blue-green billows of the Caribbean Sea. On the other, green hills rose swiftly into mountains. About 4 miles back from Saint Pierre and reaching almost a mile into the sky, stood Mont Pelée, a towering but harmless volcano. So the people thought. For generations, Mont Pelée was a playground for the people of Saint Pierre. From its slope they could see the city down below with its narrow, winding streets, lined with houses that had walls as yellow as butter, and roofs as red as the hibiscus, and through it all were scattered stately palms, ancient tamarinds, and gay flowers, all drenched in sunlight, all wrapped in contentment and peace.

Then, suddenly, toward the end of April, 1902, the picture changed. Mont Pelée, which only twice in the course of a century had lifted its volcanic voice, began a deep-throated growl, like a beast awakened from sleep. Day after day, the grumblings and growlings of the volcano grew angrier and more threatening. Great clouds of ashes released from the crater drifted over the city and fell like a gray and dismal rain.

Time and again, the earth trembled. Houses rocked. Windows were broken, and pictures fell from the walls. One would think that the people of Saint Pierre would have tried to escape to other parts of the island. Some did leave, but most of them felt more secure in their homes than anywhere else.

Early in May, the downpour of ashes grew thicker. The rumble of wagon wheels and the clop-clop of donkey's hoofs were no longer heard in the streets, for the cobblestone pavements were covered with a thick blanket of ashes as white and as fine as flour. The wind swept ashes from roofs and awnings and blew them into houses. Gone was the gay and colorful life of the city. The only sounds were the whispered prayers of the people and the increasing roar of the volcano. And yet, the people of Saint Pierre clung to their homes as havens of safety. Then, on Monday, May 5, the volcano served a last but forceful warning. At noon, a flood of boiling mud was flung out of the crater and hurtled down the mountainside along the course of the White River.

Now, at long last, some of the people were awake to the danger. All day, on May 7, and throughout the night, there was a steady stream of people fleeing north or south along the coast, climbing into the hills or boarding ships. The next morning, May 8, the town clock of Saint Pierre was 10 minutes slow. Its hands were at 7:52—when the drums of volcanic doom began their roll. The clock never struck eight, for in Saint Pierre time ceased to exist at 7:52 A.M. At that hour, out of the depths of Mont Pelée, came swift and certain death to the 30,000 souls in the City of Doom. Nothing was saved. Only one was spared. The fiery breath of the volcano put a blight on everything it touched. In less than a minute after the eruption, Saint Pierre was a citadel of the dead. Its houses crumbled. Its blue waters were black with boiling mud. Its slopes were treeless and bare. A city, once pulsing with life, was blanketed with ashes with nothing to indicate that anything in that spot ever lived. Only one man, a prisoner in the city jail, lived to tell the story. Today Saint Pierre is still a ghost town, sleeping under a blanket of lava and ashes.

Throughout New World history there are chapters where volcanoes have taken terrific toll of life and property. But even as volcanoes take toll, they also give bountiful gifts. Most of the islands in the Caribbean and the Pacific have been pushed above the sea by volcanic pressure and the soil of many New World lands owes its fertility to volcanic ash.

Barbados

Population: 190,000.

Area: 166 square miles.

Language: English.   *Capital:* Bridgetown.

Government: British crown colony.

Geographical Characteristics: Mainly coral reefs, sandy clays, and brown sandstone.

Climatic Conditions: Tropical tempered by cooling winds.

Principal Products: Sugar and cotton.

In the Atlantic proper, east of the Windward Islands, and the most easterly of the West Indies, lies the British island of Barbados. The island was discovered by Portuguese navigators but claimed for England by Captain Cataline in 1605. It was first settled by the English in 1626 when forty colonists and a few Negroes founded Jamestown. During the days of the buccaneers Barbados was a favorite pirate port of call. But the visits were for the purpose of friendly and profitable trade, and not for plunder.

CHAPTER 8

Land of the Conquistadors

Highlights of Colombia

Discovered: By Alonso de Ojeda for Spain in 1499.

Population: 8,368,540.

Area: 476,916 square miles.

Language: Spanish. *Capital:* Bogotá.

Government: Republic established December 17, 1819.

Geographical Characteristics: The country, which has coast lines on both the Caribbean and the Pacific, is crossed by three chains of mountains. Its predominating feature is the Magdalena River, which is navigable for over 900 miles.

Climatic Conditions: From tropical along the coast lines to delightfully temperate in the high plateaus.

Principal Products: Bananas, coffee, petroleum, tobacco, tagua (ivory nuts), Panama hats, emeralds, gold, rubber, platinum, cattle, and hides.

ALTHOUGH Colombia is the only country that bears a name honoring that of the discoverer of the New World, Columbus never set foot on the soil that comprises the present-day Republic of Colombia. Indeed its coast had been explored several times before 1502 when the Admiral sighted its shores on his fourth voyage. It was after Columbus' discovery of Cape Gracias a Dios, on September 14, 1502, that he sailed along the Colombian coast for a con-desirable distance, but without landing.

Three years before, in 1499, two Spaniards visited Colombia, although neither of them founded any settlements. Early in that year, Alonso Ojeda discovered the easternmost part of the country, La Goajira. In the fall of the same year, Rodrigo Bastida discovered the mouth of the Magdalena River, where he barely missed being shipwrecked.

In 1509, Ojeda returned with a royal grant of lands lying east of the Darien River. He called it the Province of Uraba. He established himself on the coast and attempted the conquest of the country. Ojeda spent most of his time fighting the Indians. He did manage to subdue the coast tribes to some extent, but all attempts to conquer the Chibcha Kingdom, situated on the high Andean plateau, proved futile. Colonization, however, had begun. In 1525, the important port of Santa Marta was founded by Bastida.

Despite the early start of colonization, Colombia was neglected by Spain for a long time. Although it later proved to be one of the greatest treasure houses of the New World, the fabulous golden empires of the Aztecs and the Incas overshadowed Colombia for a good many years.

The history of Colombia really begins in 1536, with the appearance of Gonzalo Jiménez de Quesada, a staid young lawyer, who was to write one of the most thrilling and extraordinary chapters in the dramatic story of New World conquest.

In that year, Don Pedro Fernández de Lugo arrived in Santa Marta as governor with a force of 1,500 men, among them his son, Alonso, and as chief justice, the young lawyer, Gonzalo Quesada. Troubles soon beset the colony in the form of disease and starvation. De Lugo sent his son to explore the Indian country in the hope of securing food, or gold with which supplies could be purchased in Santo Domingo. Young de Lugo, however, betrayed both his father and the colony by sailing back to Spain with some $200,000 in treasure he had seized from the Taironas Indians.

By the spring of 1536, the situation in the colony at Santa

Marta was desperate. Unless the unexplored country behind the mountains and up the great Magdalena River could be made to produce either gold or food, the settlement was doomed. Governor de Lugo was too old to head an expedition himself, and among his officers there was not one he deemed capable of handling such a difficult assignment. More than courage was needed for the task of persuading a force of already discouraged and undernourished men to fight their way into an unknown and dangerous country.

The old governor finally decided that a smooth tongue would be of more use in bringing such an expedition to a happy conclusion than a sharp sword. Hence, he drafted the mild-mannered young lawyer, Quesada, for the job of saving the colony and conquering the Indians.

On April 6, 1536, Gonzalo Quesada, promoted to the rank of general, set out at the head of an expedition consisting of 600 foot soldiers and seventy-five mounted men. The official objective was to explore and discover the sources of the Rio Grande de la Magdalena. Quesada was thirty-seven years old, and he was in supreme command, Governor de Lugo having granted him "all the power I have and hold from his Majesty."

While Quesada marched overland with part of his expedition, the rest, some 200 men aboard seven ships, sailed up the Magdalena River. The two forces had arranged to meet at the town of Tamalameque, about a hundred miles up the river. But only two of the ships, under the command of Captain Chamorro, managed to reach this point. The others were disabled.

At this meeting place, Quesada had to use his smooth tongue to prevent his weary and disheartened army from deserting in a mass and returning to the coast. The result justified the governor's trust in Quesada. Where the shouted threats of a hard-boiled campaigner would only have brought the mutiny to a head, the lawyer's persuasive words filled even the weakest and most timid with new life and courage. The members of the expedition marched on, hacking their way, yard by yard, through what is even today some of the most impassable country in South America.

Slowly they advanced along the banks of the Magdalena River, battling hostile nature at every turn. The men had to fight their way through swamps and jungles. Unbearable heat, torrential rains, and sickening dampness took their toll. Fighting the tortures of insects and the ravages of fever, men dropped in their tracks. Sick men, struggling to keep to their feet, fell easy prey to jaguars of the jungle and crocodiles of the river. Continuous rain ruined their gunpowder and rusted their swords. And then, too, hostile nature had her ally in warlike Indians, whose poisoned arrows fell upon the Spaniards in showers of death.

The horrible variety of trials catalogued by Don Juan de Castellanos, a contemporary historian, gives a vivid picture of this historic march. He tells how Quesada and his soldiers were reduced to eating the leather of their shields and the sheaths of their swords boiled in water.

After many months of almost intolerable suffering, with no signs of gold or of country that held any promise of rich rewards, an advance party returned to Quesada with strange news. They had found bricks of salt in an abandoned hut, together with some clothing that had been made by people who could hardly be savages. Although a poor substitute for gold, this find gave them new hope. Captain San Martín, one of Quesada's most trusted officers, was sent ahead to investigate.

In a few weeks, he came back with more good news. He had found more of the salt, this time wrapped in finely woven reed blankets. Pressing on, he had seen in the distance, stretches of cultivated land and the roofs of large towns. Sickness, exhausttion, and despair were forgotten. Every man, from Quesada down, remembered the enormous riches of Mexico and Peru, and the general, although ill, ordered the advance.

Fortunately, the glowing description of a rich land given by

Captain San Martín proved to be true. Within a short time, the army found itself in a land that was as a paradise compared with the inferno they had emerged from. Not only was there an abundance of food, but as they climbed higher and higher on the plateau, the climate became invigorating and pleasant. But of the 800 men who had started, only 166 were left to enjoy that bracing air of the highlands. The horses had done better, however, for of the seventy-five that had pranced out of Santa Marta, sixty were still alive.

The reason for the high percentage of survival among the horses was that General Quesada, realizing that the success of an invasion of a great Indian nation might very well depend upon the four-footed animals, took every precaution to safeguard them. To protect them from poisoned Indian arrows, each horse was covered with a special blanket with a 3-inch thickness of cotton padding, making it virtually arrowproof. Even at times of greatest hunger, Quesada would not permit the slaughter of a single horse for meat. On one occasion, a soldier, half-mad with hunger, killed a sick horse for food. As an example to his men, Quesada had the man executed on the spot.

As Quesada advanced ahead of his small and ragged army, he saw vast plains covered with thickly populated towns. Some of the Indians came to greet the stangers. They were friendly, and brought presents. The effect produced on them by the horses was even more than the general could have hoped for, but in one way, it was almost too good. Seeing the mounted cavalrymen looking like half men, half beasts, the Indians, here as in Mexico, believed them to be supernatural monsters, and were sure that they were cannibals. To appease them, one Indian chief sent the Spaniards a present of a man, a woman, and a deer to be fed to the horses. The Spanish soldiers naturally ate the deer with relish, but Quesada wisely returned the man and the woman unharmed. A little later, some of the soldiers helped the Indians put out a fire in one of the towns.

The result of these two incidents was that the Indians, called the Chibchas, began to trust the invaders of their land, although they held them in awe. They regarded them as some sort of strange gods.

One day Quesada learned about the great chief of the Chibchas, Bacata (Bogotá), and that this chief was determined to defend his country. The first sign of hostility came when Chief Bacata sent out 500 warriors, carrying the mummies of chiefs who had distinguished themselves in battle, to attack the Spaniards in the rear. Quesada was prepared and easily repulsed the Indian attack.

Bacata, although taking care not to show himself, sent his warriors to attack again and again, but without success. Finally, about a year after he had left Santa Marta, Quesada led his men into the fortified town of Chia. There he had his first view of the real culture and wealth of the Chibcha empire. The walls of the houses were covered with gold plates that glittered in the sunlight. The minor chiefs of Chia proved friendly, and Quesada ordered his army to rest during Holy Week (April, 1537).

The Chibcha Indians of Colombia had developed a remarkable type of culture. Their civilization, however, was not so advanced as either that of the Incas of Peru or the Mayas and Aztecs of Mexico. Their buildings were of wood instead of being constructed with massive stones. Also, these dwellings were rather simple compared with the magnificent palaces and impressive temples of Peru and Mexico.

The Chibchas, however, did have a well-organized society, with social institutions and a store of ancient traditions and legends. Much to the disappointment of the Spaniards, their greatest treasure was not gold, but salt. As it turned out, however, the salt of the Chibchas was more than worth its weight in gold. Salt was almost unknown among neighboring tribes, whose land were rich in gold and emeralds. As the Chibchas had an inexhaustible source of salt in their mines they could buy whatever goods they wished at more or less their own price. Although the expedition to conquer the Chibchas did not become as well known as the more sensational conquests by Pizarro and Cortez, the fact is that the soldier conquerors of Colombia found more gold and jewels over a period of years than either Pizarro or Cortez in Peru and Mexico.

Perhaps the most interesting thing about the Chibchas is their connection with that snare and delusion of the Spaniards, El Dorado, the Gilded Man. While there is no authentic record of a Spaniard ever having actually witnessed the ceremony, it is believed that the very Chief Bacata, who opposed the advance of Quesada and the Spaniards, was transformed into a man of gold during certain tribal rites.

This fantastic ceremony of the Chibchas is said to have taken place on the shores of Lake Guatavita. Early in the morning, the high chief, or Bacata, was stripped of his royal robes and his body was covered from head to foot with an oily substance, and then completely sprinkled with gold dust, until he looked for all the world like a statue carved from solid gold. Bacata was then carried in a litter to the edge of the lake where a raft awaited him. This raft was poled by young nobles to the middle of the lake, where, at noon, the Bacata washed off the gold dust while the nobles threw great quantities of gold and emeralds into the lake.

There is every reason to believe that this ceremony actually did take place among the Chibchas. Some think that it was the origin of the Spanish belief in a promised land of El Dorado, which continued to lure adventurers to their death for many, many years after the Chibchas had been completely conquered. It is claimed that some gold and emeralds were recovered from the bottom of Lake Guatavita. There are still men who believe that those who succeed in dredging that lake will find on its bottom one of the greatest treasures ever discovered by man.

General Quesada, having rested in Chia during Holy Week

of 1537, decided to seek this El Dorado in the royal treasure house of Chief Bacata. He ordered his army to attack the capital. To his surprise, they met with no resistance; but to their disappointment, when they entered the city, there was no sign either of the fabulous chief or of his great treasure. Although at this time Quesada learned about the rich emerald mines at Somondoco and sent an expedition to investigate, it was a good many years before the Spaniards were able to operate the mines to any profit.

Disappointed in not getting his hands on the wealth of Bacata, Quesada decided to attack the near-by stronghold of Tunja, where the second greatest and wealthiest chief of the Chibchas was reported to live. The Spaniards set out with a will for what proved to be Gonzalo Quesada's greatest adventure, and perhaps the most spectacular two-man drama of all New World history.

On August 20, 1537, the Spaniards first caught sight of the Chibcha city of Tunja, and it was a cheering sight, for in the distance they saw a town even more impressive than the city of Bacata. At Tunja, there was a large palace covered with golden plates that glittered in the afternoon sun. As the Spaniards approached, Indians came with presents from the chief, who also sent a message explaining that he was ill. He asked the Spaniards to delay their entry into Tunja until the following day. Quesada suspected some trick, and decided to enter without delay. Seeing the way to the palace lined with thousands of hostile Indians, he held a conference with his officers. While some advised an attack in full force, Queseda decided that the best strategy was for only a few of them to go ahead. His theory was that while the Indians would attack a large force, the sight of a few Spaniards boldly marching into the stronghold would both puzzle and confuse them. Taking but ten horsemen and Captain Olalla with him, Quesada rode calmly and unfalteringly through the surging mass of muttering Chibchas, straight for the gold-covered palace.

When they came to the king's palace, a heavy gate barred their way. With his sword, Quesada cut the cords that held the barricade fast. He instructed his soldiers to wait outside and went into the palace with only Captain Olalla at his side. The threat of sudden death surrounded them. A wrong move would have brought thousands of armed warriors rushing at them. But the very audacity of Quesada's plan dumbfounded the Indians. Slowly, expecting a rain of spears and arrows at any moment, the two Spaniards walked toward the throne where sat the Chief of Tunja, eyeing them suspiciously, not knowing what to make of these strangers who came two against thousands.

When they were within speaking distance, Quesada calmly asked the Chibcha chief to acknowledge and recognize the authority of the King of Spain. The chief was friendly enough, but replied that he knew nothing about any king across the sea. He invited the white men to retire for the night to a house that would be prepared for them, and declared that he and his nobles would be glad to discuss the matter in the morning. Again the Indian chief insisted that he was not feeling well.

At that moment, something, perhaps a gesture or look on the part of the chief, made Quesada suspicious. The invitation to remain overnight might well hide a trap. Quesada's instinct told him that the time had come for a bold stroke, and he took a page out of the book of Cortez and Pizarro. Whispering quick instructions to Captain Olalla, Quesada drew his sword. He rushed at the Chibcha chief and grabbed him by the scruff of the neck. Olalla was at his side. There was a surging movement through the sea of Indians, but the natives were afraid —afraid of what these amazing men would do to their chief. They waited to see what would happen—waited for the king to speak. And when the Chief of Tunja did speak, it was with the sharp edge of Quesada's sword close to his bare throat. He spoke only a few words, but their effect was a great relief to the Spaniards. The Chief of Tunja told his people that he surrendered the city to the white men and that his subjects should go to their homes in peace.

And so it was that Gonzalo Quesada, almost singlehanded, surrounded by 10,000 of the enemy, conquered the stronghold of Tunja. News of his bold victory spread like wildfire throughout the empire. From that moment on, the Spaniards met with little resistance. But, as in the case of the capital of Bacata, the Chief of Tunja managed to smuggle out the greater part of the royal treasure. As it was, however, when the wealth of Tunja was piled in the square, it was so high that the horsemen on one side could not see those on the other.

General Quesada and his army followed up their victory in Tunja by attacking one Chibcha stronghold after another. Few of them offered much resistance. Finally, the great chief Bacata was killed by a Spanish musket ball as he was trying to escape from a besieged town. With Bacata dead, discord broke out among the Chibchas. The royal successor, Sagipa, made an alliance with Quesada for a joint attack upon the neighboring Panches. Rich presents of gold and emeralds persuaded Quesada to help the Chibchas, and with 12,000 Indian warriors and a handful of Spaniards, he marched against the Panches and easily defeated them.

Quesada again tried to find the hiding place of the fabulous royal treasure of the slain Bacata. Sagipa, although friendly to the white men, guarded the secret. In the end he suffered tortures and death at the hands of the Spaniards without revealing the location of the treasure. To this day, it has not been found.

The Chibchas conquered, General Quesada looked around for a likely place to found a colony. After surveying the land, he chose a location where the soil was fertile, water abundant and pure, and building materials available. There he set about erecting a church and twelve huts, one for each of the Apostles. The settlement was formally occupied on August 6, 1538, and proclaimed the domain of the King of Spain. The town was named Santa Fe. The colony, because it reminded Quesada of Granada in Spain, he called New Granada (Colombia). A few years later, the name of the town was changed to Santa Fe de Bogota, in honor of the Chibcha Chief Bacata. In time this was shortened to Bogota.

The almost singlehanded conquest of the Chibchas by Quesada is perhaps an extreme example of the tremendous odds faced by the conquistadores. These men have been accused of many faults and sins, but no one could ever charge them with lack of courage or will. Many of their deeds may appear cruel and brutal today, but it must be remembered that such conduct is an indictment of the age rather than the men. History must be judged according to the standards of the age in which it was made. And according to the standards of the age of conquest in the New World, Cortez, Pizarro, de Soto, Balboa, Quesada, and many others were great men. In the light of any standards, they were outstanding leaders, fearless fighters, and explorers extraordinary.

Quesada had fulfilled his mission of conquering the Chibchas and saving the colony of Santa Marta from extinction through starvation and poverty, and in May, 1539, returned to Spain. As the years passed, the mountain-hidden city of Bogota prospered. But even the towering Andes could not hide the colony from the eagle eyes and grasping hands of Spanish taxgatherers. Soon tobacco and salt became government monopolies; the exportation of agricultural products was discouraged; gold, silver, platinum, and emeralds were closely watched and heavily taxed. Despite these restrictions, Bogota, at an early date, became one of the main centers of Spanish American culture. The country was rich; the climate was healthful; and its mountain-locked location protected the city from the costly and destructive ravages of pirates.

One of the drawbacks, however, was the difficulty of communication with the outside world. The only avenue of transport between Bogota and the coast was the treacherous and turbulent Magdalena River. For many centuries, it remained the only means of carrying passengers and cargo between the coastal ports and the inland capital. Thus, the inaccessibility of Bogota had both its advantages and disadvantages.

For a while the colony was governed by *audiencias* sent out from Spain, but this system proved cumbersome. It was replaced by presidents appointed by the king. The first of these presidents, Venero de Leiva (1564–1574), distinguished himself for his kind treatment of the Indians and his just government of the colony of New Granada. During his rule, known as the Golden Age of the colony, schools for Indians were established, roads and bridges were built, and operation of the Muzo emerald deposits begun.

In later life, Gonzalo Quesada returned to New Granada from Spain. Although he was over seventy years old, he led a futile 3-year expedition in search of the Man of Gold. It was an expedition as magnificent in size as it was pathetic in its failure. Over 300 soldiers, some 1,500 Indian and Negro slaves, over 1,000 horses, 600 cows, 800 pigs, and large supplies of other foods made up the expedition. When, after having reached the Orinoco River, Quesada returned to Bogota empty-handed, his party had been reduced to fewer than a hundred soldiers, a mere handful of Indians, and eighteen horses. In 1579, past eighty, Gonzalo Quesada, the conqueror of Colombia, died—poor, bitter, and forgotten.

As its inland mountain capital progressed and prospered, so did Colombia's coastal ports of Santa Marta and Cartagena. But they also suffered setbacks which Bogota was spared. In 1586, Sir Francis Drake, the English terror of the Spanish colonies, sailed into Cartagena harbor with nineteen ships, looted the city, and extracted a ransom of 200,000 golden ducats. Ten years later, he destroyed Santa Marta, but let Cartagena escape with a threat of future vengeance. Then came the age of the dreaded buccaneers. Cartagena and Santa Marta both received painful visits from the fierce and brutal

Henry Morgan. In 1679, Cartagena was sacked by the notorious French pirate, Jean Baptiste Desjeans, who took 10 million pesos and stripped the port of its defensive armament of eighty cannons.

It was as a result of these raids that the strong and magnificent fortifications of Cartagena were built. These defenses consisted of a wall 40 feet high and more than 50 feet thick, surmounted by heavy cannons, extensive underground fortresses, and elaborate harbor protective measures. The cost to the crown of Spain was some 70 million dollars, and the fortifications took almost a hundred years to build. But what is most important is the vital part they were to play in the later history of Colombia.

In 1739, the year war broke out between England and Spain, the system of presidents in the colony of New Granada gave way to a viceroyalty. In the following year, Cartagena was attacked by a strong British fleet under the command of Admiral Vernon, but the stout defenses of the city withstood the furious storm of English attack. Admiral Vernon sailed away, only to return again in 1741, with fifty-one warships, 135 transports, and 28,000 men. The full force of more than 2,000 cannons bombarded Cartagena, which beyond its solid, gun-studded fortifications was defended by fewer than 3,000 soldiers and only seven ships. On March 13, Admiral Vernon again had to give up, having lost some 18,000 men, mostly from disease. It is interesting to note that taking part in this siege was one Captain Lawrence Washington, a half brother of George Washington.

The social conditions that prefaced the fight for freedom in Colombia were similar to those in the other Spanish American colonies. In 1780, during the rule of Viceroy Florenz, a large debt had been accumulated by the colony. Even more harsh and ruthless taxes were imposed on the people of New Granada, already burdened to the breaking point. Instructions for additional taxes were published on October 12, 1780, and led to the first outbreaks among the people. In Mogotes, 400 men gathered to protest against the abuses of guards and tax collectors, but the most famous of the early uprisings took place in Socorro on March 16, 1781.

A notice of the new taxes had been posted in the town on market day. In protest, a group of people, led by a drummer, marched on the mayor's house. While the spokesman announced that the people refused to pay the tax, a woman, Manuela Beltrain, tore down the official decree and smashed the board on which it had been posted. Her action was a signal to the crowd, which set up a cry of, "Death to the Regent!" Although the Mayor, finding himself helpless, agreed to suspend the tax, it was too late. The spirit of revolt had been aroused. On April 16, some 6,000 citizens met in Socorro to decide on a plan of action. Juan Francisco de Berbeo was chosen leader of the revolutionary movement. An open revolt was avoided when the Spaniards agreed to abolish the most objectionable taxes, but it was a temporary triumph for the revolution. The conditions were eventually disapproved by Viceroy Florenz at Cartagena, and 500 troops were sent forth to suppress the opposition.

A few years after these early uprisings, in 1783, a cultural movement was inaugurated in Colombia that was to play an important part in the stirring events of the next few decades. This was the unique Botanical Expedition of José Celestino Mutis. It began as a project to study native plants. Soon, however, Mutis, a scientist of great ability, enlarged his plans to include the establishment of a complete center of scientific learning in Bogota. New trends of thought were started. They led to an intellectual stimulus that spread throughout the country. Under the influence and instruction of Mutis, men were being trained for important roles in the coming outbreak against oppression. One of the most important and brilliant of these men was Antonio Nariño. He was the first Colombian to speak for the independence and freedom of the people.

In August, 1794, he printed and distributed parts of the declaration of the French Revolutionary Assembly dealing with the rights of man. He was arrested and sent to an African prison camp. He escaped. In the years that followed, he spent half his time in royalist jails and the other half fighting for liberty.

In 1808, Napoleon deposed the Spanish King Ferdinand VII. The effect of this on Spain's American colonies through the efforts of Simon Bolivar to set the New World free, are given in detail in the chapter dealing with Venezuela. But one of the percussion caps that led to the explosive outbursts of revolution was a bloodless uprising in Quito (Ecuador) on August 10, 1809. It helped stir up the people of Colombia. The people of Quito invited other patriots to follow their lead. A convention was held in Bogota in September of that year. Two months later, Torres wrote his famous declaration addressed to the government, which ended with the prophetic words . . . "heaven grant that other ideas less liberal may not produce the fatal results of an eternal separation!"

Then, on July 20, 1810, the storm of the revolution broke in Bogota, as the result of a trivial incident.

Llorente, a Spanish merchant, insulted a group of creoles who had come to borrow some articles to be used in welcoming a royal commissioner. The term creole, by the way, was used to distinguish American-born men and women of pure European stock as against European-born Spaniards. The Spanish policy was to ignore and oppress the native-born creoles. Francisco Morales and his son, Antonio, took offense and attacked the merchant. That was all that was needed to fan a long-smoldering fire into flame. Mobs gathered in the streets and the prison guards were disarmed. The royalist commander of the militia, Juan Sámano, asked the viceroy for permission to use his troops in an attack on the people, but the viceroy, to his credit, refused to take such drastic action. Instead, some of the soldiers joined the patriots.

All night long, the people met in open assembly, and by dawn of July 21, a supreme popular council, or junta, of the people of New Granada had been organized. The movement spread to the provinces, and on December 22, 1810, a united congress met in Bogotá and elected Manuel Bernardo de Álvarez as first president.

This revolt was not against the authority of the King of Spain, but a fight for recognition as a full province of the Spanish crown. The first city to declare absolute independence from the rule of Spain was Cartagena, with an uprising on November 11, 1811. Instruments of torture that had been used in the Inquisition were publicly burned in the plaza and a Declaration of Independence was signed. Other provinces followed suit, Santa Marta alone remaining a royalist stronghold. Santa Marta was not taken by the revolutionists until January, 1813.

Toward the end of 1812, at a most critical time in Colombia's desperate bid for liberty, Simon Bolivar appeared on the scene. The part played by Bolivar and his brave associates, Páez, Santander, and Sucre is outlined in the chapter on Venezuela. But it is important to remember that Colombia gave refuge to and supported Bolivar at a most vital period in his fight for New World liberty. If it had not been for the help and encouragement Simon Bolivar received from the people of Colombia, his magnificent dream of liberation for five South American countries might never have been realized.

Colombia's Declaration of Independence was signed in Bogotá on July 16, 1813, and the free government almost immediately sent its armies to drive out the Spanish forces from every part of the country. All went well until July, 1815, when news came that General Pablo Morillo, with a large fleet and 15,000 royalist troops, had landed at Santa Marta and was planning to attack and occupy Cartagena, which immediately began preparations for a siege.

The heroic resistance of Cartagena has gone down in history

as a tribute to the courage and loyalty of its people. Although there was discord among the commanders, no thought of surrender entered the heads of the populace. The royalist blockade by land and sea prevented the Cartagenans from getting food, and hunger soon became acute in the city. A heavy bombardment began in October, to which were added the horrors of pestilence. The besieged inhabitants were reduced to eating dogs, cats, leather, and rodents. Soldiers dropped dead of starvation at their posts. For 4½ months the terrible siege continued, until one night most of the survivors escaped from the city in small boats under cover of a storm. Thus, on December 4, 1815, death and starvation gave General Morillo the city of Cartagena—but a city as empty and hollow as his victory. The revolution in Colombia was all but over for the time being, with only isolated guerilla resistance to the royalist forces in some of the more remote provinces.

Bogota was soon occupied by Morillo and his army, and the colony of New Granada once more became a viceroyalty by decree from Madrid. Then followed a reign of terror in Bogotá. Patriots were arrested by the dozens every day. When the jails were no longer large enough to hold the prisoners, a college and a convent were converted into jails for the rebels. Private property was confiscated. General Villavicencio, a former royal commissioner, was executed by being shot in the back. Then began a series of brutal executions which included among its victims Camilo Torres, the spokesman of the people, and the patriot scientist, Caldas, who pleaded in vain for a little time, not just that he might live longer, but in order to complete his scientific work.

On November 16, 1816, General Morillo left Bogotá to take the field against Simon Bolivar in Venezuela. He turned the command of the capital over to General Juan Sámano, a heartless executioner and tyrant. Although the outlook for the revolution appeared pretty hopeless, the torch of liberty was being kept ablaze on the llanos, or plains, of the Casanare province. This vast territory of huge cattle ranges, where rough and ready "cowboys" held sway, the royalists had been unable to subdue because they did not have enough cavalary to make a thorough campaign.

At this stage of Colombia's fight for independence, one of the greatest and bravest patriots of the revolution appears on the scene, a woman, Policarpa Salavarrieta. She is better known in history as La Pola. She gave her life for her country's freedom, and today her name is honored as one of Colombia's most revered patriots. She is, indeed, the Joan of Arc of Colombia. La Pola came to Bogotá in 1813, at the age of eighteen. She saw the birth of a new country, and pledged her allegiance to a free and independent Colombia. When the royalists recaptured the capital, she was employed as a seamstress by the wealthy and noble ladies of the city, many of them royalists by birth and sympathy.

La Pola's occupation gave her an excellent opportunity of learning the plans of the royalists. She took every advantage of her position, passing whatever information she secured along to the revolutionists who then were making their last stand in the Casanare province. By the time General Morillo left Bogotá and General Sámano took command, La Pola was the center of revolutionary espionage. She not only passed along news of the enemy's movements, but found ways to send much-needed supplies through the royalist lines to the desperate forces of the revolution. Chief among La Pola's fellow conspirators was her fiancé, Alejo Sabarain.

General Sámano and other Spanish officers, alarmed by the information leaking through to the enemy, became suspicious of the young and pretty seamstress. They had her watched, but the secret police were unable to find any conclusive evidence against her. Then, in the latter part of 1817, La Pola realized that she was under constant watch, and securing important information for the cause, she helped her fiancé and other fellow conspirators to escape from Bogotá to

Casanare. It was a great blow to the revolution when Sabarain and his friends were captured on the road by royalist troops. Even worse, papers involving La Pola in a plot against Spain were found on the prisoners. Sámano, without delay, arrested La Pola and she was condemned to death before a firing squad. On November 14, 1817, La Pola, her fiancé, and five other condemned revolutionists, were led to the execution wall in the Plaza Mayor in Bogotá. As an added disgrace, Sámano had ordered all rebels to be shot in the back. La Pola refused to be thus humiliated and defiantly faced her executioners. When a Spanish soldier offered her a glass of wine, she calmly refused it, saying that she would not accept even that "from the hands of a Spanish tyrant." Then, as the soldiers raised their rifles and waited for the command to fire, La Pola, loudly and bravely spoke her last immortal words to the people of Colombia. This is what she shouted to the crowds that stood back of Spanish soldiers with bayonets on their rifles:

"Indolent people! How different would your fate be if you would realize the value of liberty! Look at me; although a woman and young, I have enough courage to suffer death, and a thousand deaths more; and do not forget this example!"

Hardly had she finished when the drums of death drowned out her words. She smiled as the volley of shots rang out. And so died La Pola. But her stirring words lived, and so did the fight for liberty. The spirit of independence was on the march again. Two years later, on August 7, 1819, as Simon Bolivar watched from his black charger and shouted orders, the army of the revolution fought and won the famous Battle of Boyaca, completely routing the royalists and regaining the independence of Colombia. On December 17 in that year, the free and independent Republic of Colombia was established, with Bolivar as its president.

CHAPTER 9

Cradle of New World Freedom

Highlights of Venezuela

Discovered: By Christopher Columbus for Spain in 1498.

Population: 3,491,159.

Area: 352,170 square miles.

Language: Spanish.   *Capital:* Caracas.

Government: Republic established July 5, 1811.

Geographical Characteristics: Range from a mountainous area in the northwest to densely forested area in the southeast. Between are the broad, grassy plains of the Orinoco Valley, well watered by the Orinoco River and its tributaries.

Climatic Conditions: Tropical and subtropical.

Principal Products: Petroleum, fruits and vegetables, coffee, cocoa, cattle and hides, meat, tonka beans, lumber, pearls, and gold.

O N July 31, 1498, six battered vessels under command of Admiral Columbus, approached the coast of South America. Neither the Admiral nor his crew was very cheerful. It was hot. Everyone was discouraged. This third voyage had not proved so fruitful as Columbus had hoped it would be. Then a sailor cried out from aloft, "Land! Land to port!"

The cry was as welcome as the sight that greeted the men who rushed to the rail: an island with three prominent peaks. When one of the sailors recalled that it was Trinity Sunday, Columbus named the island Trinidad. Surely, they all thought, this must be one of the Spice Islands. They sailed on. During one night, they heard a great roaring of water, like the sound of thundering breakers. Standing on deck throughout the dark night, Columbus saw the sea rolling past his ships from west to east like a mighty current. He ordered a sailor to lower a bucket into the sea, and he found that the water was fresh. Although he did not know it, Columbus had discovered the mouth of the Orinoco River.

Nor did Columbus know that he was on the threshold of a great and unknown continent. He still thought that he was in Asiatic waters. Instead, he was at what today is Puerto Colón, Venezuela. Sailing westward along the coast, Columbus reached another island where the Indians willingly traded large quantities of excellent pearls for worthless beads. The Admiral named the island Margarita (pearl), and with a lighter heart sailed back to his colony at Santo Domingo.

That part of the New World did not see Columbus again. But in the next year, a former companion of the Admiral, Alonso Ojeda, led an expedition along the northern coast of Venezuela as far as the Goajira peninsula. The main accomplishment of the Ojeda expedition seems to have been one of bequeathing names, for Ojeda sailed into Lake Coquivacoa (Maracaibo), and there the Spaniards were amazed to see Indian villages built on piles above the swampy shores. It reminded them of Venice, so they called the country Venezuela (Little Venice).

Although Venezuela was discovered early, colonization was slow at first. In 1520, Gonzalo de Ocampo founded New Toledo on the present site of Cumaná, but hostile Indians made short shrift of the colony. Two years later, Ocampo returned, and reestablished Cumaná. It became the first permanent settlement on the South American continent. In 1527, Coro was founded farther west along the coast. In its early days, colonization in Venezuela was conducted by the Welsers, a house of German bankers. The King of Spain gave them a charter in payment for money that he had borrowed from the Germans.

The Welsers developed the natural resources of the new land and did much valuable exploring, but their cruel and brutal treatment of the natives so horrified the Spaniards that their contract for exploiting Venezuela was revoked in 1556. Colonization again proceeded slowly under Spanish patronage.

One year after the Welsers took over, an adventurer, Ambrosio de Alfínger, sailed from Coro to Lake Coquivacoa with 150 soldiers to found a settlement. He met with opposition from an Indian chief Mara. When the chief was killed in a battle, the soldiers shouted *"Mara cayo!"* (Mara has fallen). From that day on, it is said, that lake has been known as Maracaibo. Alfínger's settlement was not so permanent as the name he gave to the lake, for it was soon destroyed by the Indians to avenge the death of their chief.

Coro was the first capital of Venezuela, but in 1577 the seat of government was moved to Caracas, a town that had been founded high up in the coastal range of the Andes just 10 years before. The new capital had two great advantages: the climate was cool and healthful and the city was safe from any pirates who might come raiding Venezuela way.

By this time, the search for El Dorado, the fabulous Gilded Man, was well under way in the New World. Rumor had it that the Golden City of the Gilded Man was located far up the Orinoco River at a place called Maroa. The city did not exist, any more than El Dorado did, but many an adventurer lost his fortune or life, or both, in quest of this fabled land of the Gilded Man and easy riches. Among these was Sir Walter Raleigh, famous figure in the days of Queen Elizabeth.

In 1595, the gallant Sir Walter was a prisoner in the Tower of London, having incurred the displeasure of Queen Elizabeth. He secured his release on the promise to head an expedition to the Orinoco and bring back the wealth of El Dorado.

Needless to say, Raleigh did not find El Dorado. But the Queen forgave him anyway.

Almost a quarter of a century later, Raleigh was again a prisoner in the Tower of London, this time on orders of King James, who had succeeded Queen Elizabeth. The plan that had worked once, worked again. Raleigh promised James to outfit and head another expedition to the Orinoco, and this time he would bring back the gold of El Dorado without fail. King James said that he had best do so, because if he failed, he would have Raleigh beheaded.

When the Raleigh expedition reached Trinidad, off the coast of Venezuela, Sir Walter was too ill to head a party in search of a rich mine that his chief officer, Captain Keymis, claimed to have located some years before, along the banks of the Orinoco. In his stead he sent Keymis, and his young son Walter, with orders to avoid any Spanish colonies along the river. One of the conditions on which King James had let Raleigh sail, was that he promised, under penalty of death, not to set foot on Spanish-claimed territory. That was a difficult feat in those days, when Spain claimed about everything in the New World.

Raleigh had been tricked and betrayed before he even left England. The Spanish ambassador to England had seen Raleigh's secret maps. The king himself showed them to him. A Spanish colony quite high up along the Orinoco had been deliberately moved down the river so as to be right in the path of Raleigh's party. On New Year's Day, 1618, the English force was ambushed by the Spaniards. Young Walter Raleigh was killed, and Keymis gave up his search for the gold mine. When the captain returned with this sad news, Sir Walter accused him of treachery. Keymis killed himself. Raleigh returned to England and the Tower of London where he eventually was beheaded.

During the years following the era of conquest, Venezuela settled down to the routine life of a Spanish colony. For about two and a half centuries dozens of Spanish governors came and went. Some were good. Some were bad. All did their best to take for Spain as much as possible in return for as little as possible. In 1731, Venezuela ceased being a part of the Viceroyalty of Peru, and became a captaincy general in its own name.

The Spanish colonial policy during the eighteenth century was one that begged for trouble. It is true that Spain had her hands full of European problems, and the neglect of her colonies can perhaps be charged to that. But to neglect were added high taxes and highhanded policies. The colonists had no voice in the government. Education was discouraged. Commerce was regulated in favor of Spanish merchants. In fact, a private enterprise, the Guipuzcoana Company, had a monopoly on both exports and imports. To this company, under royal charter, the Venezuelans had to sell their coffee, cocoa, sugar, indigo, hides, and minerals at low prices. On the other hand, they had to purchase everything they needed at high prices.

In 1778, as a result of protests against the hardships imposed by the Guipuzcoana Company, the monopoly was abolished. But this relief, important as it was, did not cause general jubilation. Thoughts of freedom and liberty were in the air. They were born of the successful fight of the North American colonies for freedom from England and the epoch-marking French Revolution. By the end of the eighteenth century, Venezuela was a powder keg waiting for a spark to touch it off.

During these years of readjustment in France and the United States to new ways of life, a boy was born to one of the oldest and wealthiest families in Caracas, on July 24, 1783. He was christened Simón José Antonio de la Santíssima Trinidad Bolívar y Palacio, but the world came to know him as Simon Bolivar, or more simply as the Liberator.

Bolivar's father died when the boy was only three years old.

It fell to his young and beautiful mother to raise her headstrong and independent young son. He was what today would be called a problem child. It is told that Simon's mother once sought the advice of the kindly Judge Sanz of Caracas about her difficult offspring. The judge, who knew young Bolivar (then not more than six or seven), said that the youngster was a *polvorin*, horn of gunpowder. On hearing this judgment, little Bolivar shouted: "Then be careful not to come near me. I might explode!"

When he was nine years old, Bolivar's mother died. There were relatives enough to look after him but Simon was pretty well able to look after himself. As the youth grew older, a tutor was engaged for him, one Símon Rodríguez, who played an important part in shaping the ideas and ideals of the future liberator of Venezuela and other countries.

Rodríguez was a dreamer and a visionary, with revolutionary ideas and revolutionary friends. As master and pupil walked through the woods of the vast Bolivar hacienda at San Mateo, the boy heard about Aristotle and the glories of ancient Greece; about freedom and liberty, the French Revolution and the rights of man. He learned with avid interest about George Washington, the father of the United States, and Napoleon Bonaparte, First Consul, the symbol of a strong, independent France. Both were his ideals. But young Simon Bolivar also learned many other things: to ride the fieriest horses, to lasso the fiercest bulls, and to fight with pistols, sword, and lance. Then Rodríguez the tutor became involved in a serious revolutionary plot and fled from Venezuela just a few steps ahead of a firing squad.

Some time later, the Bolivar family decided that Simon needed a bit of polish, and he was sent to Spain to stay with an uncle. He sailed from La Guaira during a time of pitiful and futile revolutionary attempts, all of them ending in failure and horrible bloodshed. That was in 1799. On the way to Spain, the sixteen-year-old Simon Bolivar stopped in Mexico and Cuba, where he heard and absorbed ideas of freedom and independence similar to those he had heard Rodríguez express.

Bolivar soon forgot about those ideas amid the gaiety and luxury of court life in Madrid. By 1802 he was married and back in Venezuela. Then, in 1803, eight months after their marriage, his lovely bride died. Bolivar, brokenhearted, returned to Spain. For several years, his life was a series of adventures and escapades that made fashionable Europe sit up and take notice of the rich and handsome young man from Venezuela —for Simon Bolivar was a striking person. He was rather short of stature, about 5 feet 6 inches tall, but the strenuous life of his native plains had given him a figure that was more than once compared to that of a Greek god; and then there were his eyes, deep-set, dark, and brilliant. In those flashing eyes, even as a youth, there was a hint of the great internal fires that someday would break into roaring flames.

At last, in 1805, Simon Bolivar tired of his life of gaiety, and just about that time he met his exiled tutor, Rodríguez, the firebrand revolutionary. At this particular period, Bolivar's faith in revolutions was somewhat shaken. In December of the previous year, he had seen one of his heroes, one of his personifications of the ideal of freedom, Napoleon Bonaparte, crowned Emperor and Dictator of France. To Bolivar this was a crime against dearly won liberty that could not be condoned.

Almost ill through his disillusionment, Bolivar sought advice from Rodríguez, who was an advocate of long walks to clear the brain. He proposed a walking tour through Italy and Bolivar accepted the idea with pleasure. He was not a very cheerful companion, however. As they walked the roads to Rome, Bolivar maintained a morose silence most of the way. They reached Rome in August, 1805. One day they climbed to the top of Monte Sacro, the great hill that stands close to Rome. At first Bolivar stood silent as the older man spoke of the glories that had been Rome, of Caesar and his ambitions, and of the rise and fall of the Roman Empire. While he was speaking, young Simon interrupted him, and put into a few fiery and trembling words all the thoughts that had crowded his mind during their walking tour.

"Rodríguez!" he said, "I swear that I'll free America from the Spaniards and not leave one of the oppressors there!"

Simon Bolivar then and there dedicated his life to humanity. He was twenty-two years old. His life of leisure ended that August day on the hill above Rome. About a year later, in September, 1806, he sailed for Venezuela by way of North America. He visited New York, Washington, Boston, Philadelphia, and other cities in the United States to study a working democracy at firsthand. In December, he stepped ashore on his native soil, and heard the name of Francisco Miranda, and learned that the idea of liberating Venezuela was not his alone.

Francisco Miranda was also a pioneer in the quest for freedom in the Americas. Born in Venezuela, he had left his native land long before Bolivar was born, with memories of his father being persecuted by the Spanish authorities. Perhaps it was this early memory of oppression that led Miranda to serve in the North American Revolution under Rochambeau. At any rate, the idea of freeing his native land from the yoke of Spanish domination became firmly rooted in his mind. His idea extended far beyond Venezuela, grew into an almost fantastic vision of a vast Indian empire, from Mexico to Cape Horn, to be ruled under a grand hereditary Inca, and to be patterned after the empire of the Incas of ancient Peru.

After the North American Revolution, Miranda fruitlessly tried to win support for his idea in Europe. Discouraged, he returned to the country he had helped gain freedom. In New York he found a group of merchants ready to give an ear to his scheme. Miranda talked eloquently from the very depths of his soul. The merchants listened and dreamed of the profits they would reap if they could smash the Spanish colonial monopoly. They agreed to finance an expedition, and, early in 1806, Miranda sailed with three ships and 200 American adventurers, most of whom hardly knew where they were going or why.

Arriving off the Venezuelan coast in March, two of his ships were seized, but Miranda managed to escape to Trinidad in the third. There he raised a small army to restore his depleted American force and sailed once more for the Venezuelan mainland where he attacked and took Coro. It was a bright beginning for his noble adventure, but it soon began to dim. To his utter amazement, Miranda found that the people of Venezuela were not so enthusiastic about gaining their liberty as he was in fighting to give it to them. Success depended on his countrymen rallying to his brave cries for freedom. All he heard was an empty echo—and the victorious shouts of the Spanish army that completely broke up and routed his small and halfhearted mercenary group. Bitter, discouraged, and with a price on his head, Francisco Miranda turned his back on a dream and sailed for England. Venezuela was not yet ready for freedom. The gunpowder was there, but it was not for Miranda to set the spark.

Simon Bolivar took up life again in Caracas in the winter of the year of Miranda's failure. He studied the situation and realized the wisdom of keeping his revolutionary ideas to himself. He became an officer in the militia, rising to the rank of colonel by 1810. But never for a moment did he lose sight of his purpose. Freedom for Venezuela! Gradually Bolivar gathered around him a group of men who felt as he did and dreamed of freedom. They met at night in the various patios of Caracas, and under the stars talked of the future and discussed ways and means of translating their dream of liberty into living reality.

Then, in 1808, Napoleon Bonaparte unwittingly set off the spark that was to explode the powder keg, not alone in Venezuela, but in all South America. The spark blazed quickly and furiously through a fuse that ran all the way from Paris to Venezuela by way of Madrid.

Napoleon had gone a long way since Bolivar had seen him crowned Emperor of France in Paris in 1805. All Europe had become Napoleon's chessboard and many kings his pawns. One of the kings who was checkmated was Ferdinand VII of Spain. He had to renounce the Spanish throne in favor of Napoleon's brother, Joseph Bonaparte. When this humiliating news reached Venezuela and the other colonies, indignation rose high. French deputies who came to proclaim French domination over Venezuela had to flee for their lives. The spark, at long last, had reached the powder keg. The first explosion roared in 1810 when the city council of Caracas voted the captain general, who had pledged loyalty to the Emperor Napoleon, out of office and set up a junta, or popular council. The council, however, solemnly declared its allegiance to the deposed Ferdinand VII. This was a long way from the realization of Bolivar's dream of independence for Venezuela. But it was a start, and following the lead of Caracas, similar juntas, or councils, were soon formed in Bogota, Buenos Aires, and Santiago de Chile.

In July, 1810, Simon Bolivar went to London to win the approval and support of England for the provisional government that had been set up in Venezuela and to prevail upon Francisco Miranda to return to Caracas. England did not give Bolivar the support he wanted, but Miranda agreed to go back to Venezuela. It was on July 5, 1811, that the congress at Caracas took the final step in renouncing Spain by declaring the complete and absolute independence of Venezuela. In December, the first constitution was adopted and General Miranda, at sixty, became the leader of the free country. Thus Venezuela was the first colony of Spain to revolt and declare her independence through an elected congress.

Although it was Bolivar who had persuaded Miranda to come back to Venezuela and head the government, conflict between the two began quite early. At first, perhaps, it was just a matter of old age against youth. On one occasion, Bolivar was showing off his horsemanship, and when General Miranda gave a command, Bolivar ignored it. This breach of discipline enraged Miranda, who told the executive committee that Bolivar was not temperamentally fit to lead troops. The trouble was smoothed over, however, by Bolivar's uncle, who took him along in his command to lay siege to royalist troops at Valencia, which surrendered on August 13, 1811. Bolivar was complimented for his part in the siege by General Miranda himself, who admitted he was mistaken about the military ability of the young colonel. As a token of his sincerity, Miranda sent Bolivar to the capital with the royalist prisoners to announce the news of victory to a jubilant Caracas.

At this time Miranda wanted to press his advantage and drive all the Spaniards out of Venezuela. But the congress decided otherwise. It summoned the general back to Caracas. On the other hand, the royalists took advantage of the letup on the part of the rebellious patriots and sent an expedition into the field under Domingo Monteverde, who quickly took the town of Carora. He was marching on Barquisimeto, pillaging and killing as he went, when disaster struck the young republic from another and more terrible source.

The news of Monteverde's successful raids had barely reached Caracas, when at 4 P.M. on Holy Thursday, March 26, 1812, a rumbling sound filled the air. Bolivar was at prayers in the Chapel San Jacinto with some friends. The ground began to tremble. At first they thought Monteverde's artillery was bombarding the city. Then the walls of the church started to shake and tremble, and they realized that this was an attack against which they were helpless—an earthquake.

As screams filled the air and buildings toppled to the ground, Bolivar and his friends ran into the street. Tearing off his coat, and working in his shirt sleeves, choking with dust, Bolivar led the work of pulling tortured victims from under the debris. He lifted stones that would have defied any three ordinary men. When one of the victims cried out that it was vengeance from heaven for the revolt against Spain, Bolivar drowned him out with this defiant shout: "Even if Nature must oppose us, we will battle with her too, and compel her to obey!"

Ten thousand people in Caracas alone died in that earthquake. Many other republican cities and towns were destroyed. Strangely enough, cities that were royalist strongholds were spared. Then came the aftermath of the earthquake—Monteverde! He was advancing victoriously and relentlessly through Venezuela, a tidal wave of vengeance dyed red with blood. The young republic that had started out so bravely only a year before was sinking to its knees. Miranda, although given dictatorial powers and placed in full command of the army, was discouraged. His self-confidence was gone. The desertion of so many of his soldiers to the royalist cause after the earthquake had lessened his faith in the sincerity of the Venezuelans. In that frame of mind, he marched against Monteverde and his Spanish army. On July 25, General Miranda surrendered to Monteverde at La Victoria. The first Venezuelan republic was dead after a year of life. Bolivar joined with the other patriots in turning against Miranda. In their eyes, the general had betrayed the republic to the royalists. When it was discovered that he planned to escape to England from La Guaira aboard a waiting British vessel, whatever leniency remained toward him disappeared.

On the night of July 30, 1812, Simon Bolivar and a self-appointed committee met in the house of Governor Las Casas at La Guaira. While Miranda was asleep in an adjoining room, they held an informal trial. In the morning they arrested Miranda on a charge of treason, and he was turned over to the Spaniards. Glad enough to make an example of a rebel leader, they sent Francisco Miranda to the dreaded

Spanish prison of La Carraca. There he died, 4 years later, chained to a wall like a beast.

As for Bolivar, he escaped from La Guaira, in disguise, and made his way through the Spanish lines to Caracas, where rich and influential friends prevailed upon Monteverde to give the young man a passport to the Island of Curaçao, off the Venezuelan coast. That was probably the most serious mistake Monteverde ever made. From the Spanish viewpoint it would have been better if he had sent young Bolivar to La Carraca too. Instead, Monteverde let the Firebrand of Venezuela slip through his hands, and when Bolivar sailed on August 27, 1812, he was more determined than ever to rid his homeland of Spanish rule. Only one thought burned in his mind, day and night, and that thought was liberty for his country.

From Curaçao, Bolivar looked toward the South American mainland. He must find a starting point for his second onslaught against Spain. After long study, he decided that there was only one such point, the port of Cartagena in New Granada (Colombia), the colony adjoining Venezuela. Cartagena was one of the few cities still held by the patriots who had risen against Spain in Colombia. Before the year was out, Bolivar presented himself to the government at Cartagena. He was given a commission and command of the near-by village of Barranca. It was there Simon Bolivar composed his famous Cartagena Manifesto, which, when it was issued on December 15, 1812, had a tremendous effect on the people of New Granada. It began, as one historian put it, "a flow of eloquence which was to continue for eighteen years."

In this manifesto, Bolivar put into words for the first time his idea of the Colombian Republic, combining the colonies of Venezuela and New Granada. He stressed the common interests of the colonies, and pointed out that so long as there was Spanish domination in one, the other could not be free.

Bolivar quickly backed up his words with action and

victories, and in a short time had freed the entire province of Cartagena of Spaniards. Then, from his headquarters in Ocana, he gathered his little army of 200 men and told them of his plan to march east to take Caracas. Early in February, 1813, he began the first of the many great marches that made the name of Simon Bolivar immortal in military annals as well as in human history.

The way to Caracas lay nearly 500 miles to the east, across almost impassable mountains, through jungles inhabited by hostile Indians; a vast desolate wilderness where neither food, nor shelter, nor arms could be obtained. The hardships and sufferings of that heroic march would have proved too much for human endurance if the men had not been continually fired by the courage and driving force of Bolivar.

It is small wonder, after what he had seen his army go through, that Bolivar was in a grim mood when he reached Trujillo, Venezuela, in June, and heard that the Spanish commander had issued orders to his troops that no quarter be given and no mercy shown to the rebels. It is understandable why Bolivar, after pacing the floor of his room throughout the night of June 14, issued on the following morning his defiant reply to the Spanish, his proclamation of "War to the Death!"

"Venezuelans!" Bolivar proclaimed. "Every Spaniard who does not actively conspire against tyranny in favor of the cause of justice, shall be considered an enemy, punished as a traitor to the patria and in consequence immediately put to death!"

Simon Bolivar's march on Caracas continued, a triumphant progress of victories as the royalists retreated before him. At last, Monteverde, cooped up in the capital, was forced to flee. The city was surrendered at La Victoria. Bolivar had taken a tremendous gamble, but he had won. The whole western part of Venezuela had been reconquered. To the greatness of Bolivar, let it be said that his terms to the Spaniards were most generous and in complete negation of his harsh decree of "War to the Death!" The Liberator never did a deliberately cruel deed in his life.

Bolivar entered Caracas on August 6, 1813, to the wild acclaim of an adoring populace. On October 14, he was named captain general of the armies and given the title Liberator of Venezuela. This title he treasured above all other honors that were later heaped upon him. He shared the honor by forming the famous Order of Liberators among his brave and loyal officers.

The republic made ambitious plans while Bolivar drove out isolated Spanish forces. And then, when the outlook for peace and liberty was better than it had ever been, the rumbling of another earthquake were heard in Caracas—of a human earthquake this time—in the form of José Tomás Boves, a ruthless Spanish pirate smuggler from the great plains of Venezuela.

Boves had gathered together, under his renegade standard, an army, or rather a huge murdering band, of 7,000 lawless raiders. They roamed the plains like a dreadful plague under the appropriate name of the Infernal Legion. They ravaged the important city of Calabozo. Encouraged by the success of Boves, royalist Spaniards rose in arms. Venezuela was again in the throes of a horrible civil war.

Although the patriots fought bravely under Bolivar, they suffered defeat after defeat, until on July 6, 1814, Bolivar led 10,000 of his people out of Caracas to escape the terrors and tortures of Boves and his merciless army. For 20 endless days and 20 grueling nights, the Liberator led his flock of 10,000 men, women, and children over the mountains, urging them on at every step. Many fell by the wayside; only a small fraction of those who had started reached refuge at Barcelona. When Bolivar saw that the cause had once more been lost, he secured ships for his little group of refugees and sent them to the safety of the West Indies.

Meanwhile, in Europe, the star of Napoleon had ended its

meteoric dash. As a result of the Congress of Vienna (1814–1815), Napoleon was overthrown. Ferdinand VII again sat on the throne of Spain. He was determined to regain his American colonies. No expense was to be spared to this end. A fleet of seventy-six ships and 15,000 men under General Pablo Morillo was dispatched to "pacify" the liberty-minded colonials. Given a 60-day schedule of conquest, Morillo was instructed first to subdue New Granada (Colombia) and Venezuela. Next he was to put down rebellions along the coast south to Buenos Aires, and to follow that up with the quelling of the Mexican spirit of revolt.

When the news reached Bogota early in 1815, Bolivar was sent to prepare the defense of Cartagena, which was then under the command of General Castillo. But the old general had a grudge of long standing against the Liberator and refused to turn his command over to Bolivar no matter what the consequences. The Liberator promptly laid siege to Cartagena but the walls of Cartagena, 40 feet high and 50 feet wide, built in the seventeenth century as a protection against pirates and other freebooters, proved impregnable. On May 10, Bolivar, once more thwarted by his own people, resigned his command and sailed for Jamaica on a British ship. General Morillo landed his 15,000 Spanish troops on Venezuelan soil and promptly took about 5,000 soldiers to Colombia where he starved Cartagena into submission and took possession of Bogota. Many of the patriots escaped to Hispaniola. Once more there was no independent government left in northern South America. The only resistance was the guerrilla warfare of a roving and unknown advocate of freedom, José Antonio Páez, a rough and uneducated cattle rancher who sent his loyal llaneros (cowboys) to harass the Spaniards at every turn, thus keeping alive the cause of liberty until the Liberator himself was again ready to take a hand.

Bolivar spent several months in Jamaica, made plans, outlined his scheme for a Pan-American Union of independent

American nations, and published his famous Jamaica letter. In December, 1815, Cartagena, desperate and in death agonies, sent for Bolivar to come back and take command. He agreed, but on the way to Cartagena, he learned that the city had fallen, and that the refugees were on their way to Hispaniola. Bolivar immediately ordered his ship turned about, and headed for the Haitian port of Aux Cayes. At Haiti, the president of the Negro republic, Alexandre Pétion, offered Bolivar arms and ammunition. With this help the fight for independence was reborn.

On March 31, 1816, Bolivar left Haiti with seven ships and 250 men. He also had ammunition for 4,000 more troops. Landing on the Island of Margarita, Bolivar, for the third time, declared the independence of Venezuela and set up a government. Then he embarked for the mainland to put his declaration into effect. The patriot army succeeded in winning some victories over the Spanish forces, but were finally defeated at Ocumare.

While Bolivar was away fighting, two of his officers began plotting against him. When the Liberator returned he was horrified to hear shouts of, "Down with Bolivar!" This treachery was too much for him. He washed his hands of the whole affair and sailed back to Haiti.

Two months later, the plotters changed their minds and pleaded with Bolivar to return. The Liberator, putting the cause of freedom above petty personal bickerings, raised another expedition in Haiti and landed in Venezuela on December 31, 1816.

When a desperate dash to capture Caracas with 700 men failed, Bolivar decided to change his tactics, and to attack from the rear by gaining control of Angostura (Ciudad Bolívar) and the Orinoco. After that he would operate from the great plains, where his troops could move quickly and where there was an abundance of beef cattle. As this plan formulated in his mind, it grew until it no longer stopped at the freedom of Venezuela and New Granada, but laid open the way for a march over the Andes to free Quito (Ecuador) and Peru.

The army that marched on Angostura was a strange one. It consisted of some 2,000 men, poorly armed, mostly untrained, and hardly a match for a fraction of their number in trained troops. Still, this motley force gave battle against the royalists on the banks of the Orinoco. There were 500 rusty muskets for 2,000 soldiers. The rest were armed with bamboo lances and bows and arrows, against a unified and fully armed force of 1,600 Spanish veterans. And yet, Angostura fell to the republicans in the spring of 1817. This meant that Bolivar was in command of navigation of the Orinoco and held the key to the back doors to all of northern South America—to Venezuela, to Colombia, to Ecuador, and to Peru.

At this stage of the story José Antonio Páez played an important part. Páez was a master of guerrilla tactics whose untrained but efficient cowboy soldiers had opposed Boves in 1813 and had made life difficult for the Spaniards ever since. Bolivar, at Angostura, needed this Lone Wolf of the Llanos. He sent word to Páez at San Fernando de Apure that he was marching to join him. On January 31, 1818, these two men, as opposite as men can be, met for the first time on the banks of the Apure River. Bolivar, thirty-five, an aristocrat to his finger tips, and a scholar; Páez, twenty-seven, rough, illiterate, and uncouth. But there was a common meeting ground, for both men had undying courage and belief in an ideal, although Páez was at times a bit vague in his interpretation of liberty.

As Bolivar made a profound impression on Páez when they first met, so did Páez on the Liberator. As the two generals were riding along the river, Bolivar asked how the two armies could cross to the other side without boats. "That's easy," said Páez, calling a halt and pointing to three Spanish gunboats that were lying at anchor in the middle of the river. "We'll use those gunboats."

Bolivar could think of no way to capture the strongly armed boats. But Páez quickly showed the way when he commanded fifty of his horsemen to follow him into the river. As Bolivar looked on open-eyed, a detachment of horsemen captured the gunboats.

From about the time of the meeting with Páez, Bolivar saw his dream slowly but surely come true. He sent General Santander to New Granada (Colombia) to spread rumors that the Spanish were being defeated and that the republican army was sweeping everything before it. The object of this bit of strategy was to prepare the ground for his march into that country. Bolivar trusted that his optimistic picture, although at the time composed mostly of hopes, would induce Granadan fighters to join his army.

Bolivar chose the rainy season for his march on the Spaniards in New Granada. He knew that no one would expect a military expedition to be undertaken at that time of the year. On May 26, 1819, he set out at the head of an army of 1,300 foot soldiers and 800 mounted men. Day after day the men waded waist-deep in swamps, and constructed crude rafts to carry them across flooded lagoons.

As the republican army advanced, the Spaniards bowed before it, hardly putting up a fight. The decisive battle of Boyaca was fought and Bogota saw the entry of Bolivar and his ragged, dirty, but victorious troops on August 10. One of Bolivar's first acts was to seize 600,000 piasters from the treasury of the Spanish viceroy and give the money to his soldiers.

On June 24, 1821, came the great Venezuelan victory of Carabobo, where Bolivar had won another battle in 1814. The plan of battle was drawn up by the Liberator, but it was executed by Páez. Out of 6,000 Spanish troops, fewer than 400 escaped to Puerto Cabello. In recognition of his victory,

Bolivar designated the Lone Wolf of the Llanos as the commander in chief of all the armies.

When the congress of Colombia met in special session at Rosario de Cucuta, it was to acclaim Bolivar and to declare the date of the victory of Carabobo a national holiday. Colombia and almost all Venezuela was at last free from Spanish oppression.

Bolivar's next move was toward Ecuador, where one of his brilliant young commanders, General Antonio José de Sucre, had already won the battle of Pichincha and entered Quito. On July 31, 1822, the liberation of Ecuador was announced by the popular assembly, and union with Colombia effected.

A few days before the declaration of Ecuador's independence, the famous meeting between Simon Bolivar, Liberator of the North, and José de San Martín, Liberator of the South, took place in Guayaquil. San Martín had come up from Argentina with his Gauchos and freed Chile and part of Peru.

San Martín's plans for liberating South America were different from Bolivar's. If the two men had stubbornly stuck, each to his way, there might have been a clash and perhaps an explosion that would have undone the good accomplished by both through years of fighting and bloodshed. It was to avoid such a tragedy that San Martín came to Guayaquil to meet Bolivar. For two days, July 26 and 27, 1821, the two great men talked behind locked doors. Little is known about what they said, but the outcome was that San Martín stepped out of the way to let Bolivar carry out his project of liberation in Peru and Bolivia. Even if San Martín had not already proved himself a great man, he did so by that decision. He abandoned his ambitious and cherished plan at the height of his career. He did it because he believed it was the best thing for the people of South America. After this meeting, General Sucre defeated the Spanish General Cauterac, and Bolivar was made Dictator of Peru. He hated that title but accepted it in the hope that his prestige would have the effect of ending the internal problems of Peru.

For a while Bolivar rested, but Peru again became the scene of Spanish activity. The Battle of Ayacucho was fought on December 9, 1824, when Sucre, with 6,000 men, opposed Viceroy Laserna's 10,000 Spanish troops. Bolivar had instructed Sucre that he wanted a full and complete victory. Sucre obeyed orders, and although wounded, defeated the enemy. He then pursued them, giving no quarter. By evening the Spanish army had been destroyed. The victory raised Bolivar almost to the height of a god. Of all the gifts and honors offered him, Bolivar accepted only one, a gift of several million pesos; this money he distributed among his soldiers. When Upper Peru established itself as an independent free state, it asked for the right to call itself Bolivia, after the Liberator. Bolivar gave his consent on the condition that the new capital be named Sucre.

The last Spanish flag on the South American continent came down with the surrender of the Spanish at Callao, Peru, on January 25, 1826. From that day on, Spanish domination became only a memory. Bolivar was spoken of as the George Washington of his country. And in that very year he received, from Marquis Lafayette, a miniature of George Washington, sent to him by request of the Washington family. From that day to his death, Bolivar always wore this miniature on a chain around his neck. It was his most treasured possession.

For the next few years, Bolivar traveled through the countries he had liberated, supervising reconstruction and making plans for the liberation of the West Indian Islands of Cuba and Puerto Rico. Although he was the head of Venezuela, Colombia, Peru, Ecuador, and Bolivia, his only title was that of Liberator.

It was not long, however, before Bolivar's dream was to be rudely shattered. Venezuela fell prey to internal dissension, forcing Bolivar to proclaim a state of siege from Bogota.

Again he took to the field, this time not to drive out the Spaniards but to disperse conspirators and malcontents who were trying to destroy the republic by their bickering and jealousies. His former friend and ally, Páez, turned against him, demanding the separation of New Granada (Colombia) and Venezuela. Bolivar told Páez that he had already put that matter before the congress, and Páez, ashamed of his conduct, offered himself to be court-martialed. Bolivar, generous as always, publicly thanked Páez for his past services and implored him to continue to serve his country as he had in the past.

The sad realization had come to Simon Bolivar that freedom from Spain and oppression did not necessarily mean peace for the Americas. One after another, civil wars broke out. They extended from Mexico to Cape Horn. It sickened Bolivar to see his people fighting among themselves, and on January 15, 1830, he issued an appeal imploring South Americans to respect and treasure their dearly bought freedom. The reply was a barrage of accusations heaping the blame for their troubles on the head of the man who had given all his life and his entire fortune to set them free. There were plots against his life and conspiracies to undo all he had accomplished.

Matters finally came to a head and on September 22, 1830, Bolivar was once more called to the supreme command of the army. But he was ill, worn and exhausted in body and soul. An injury caused by a fall made him an invalid, and he was carried to Santa Marta, Colombia, where it was believed the waters would do him some good. When he arrived there on December 1, he could not walk. Only a few loyal friends were with him. For 2 weeks he suffered, not only from physical pain, but from a broken heart. Death came on December 17, 1830. On that day the great Liberator was himself set free.

Bolivar was almost alone, and unhonored when he died. But 12 years later, in 1842, a large fleet of warships filled the harbor of Santa Marta. The colors of all the countries he had liberated were flying side by side with those of England, France, and Holland, all draped from their staffs at half-mast. It was a momentous day, for Simon Bolivar was at last going home—home to his last and permanent resting place in his beloved Caracas in Venezuela.

Trinidad

Discovered: By Christopher Columbus for Spain in 1498.

Population: 500,000 including the Island of Tobago.

Area: 1,976 square miles including the Island of Tobago.

Language: English.   *Capital:* Port-of-Spain.

Government: British crown colony.

Geographical Characteristics: Typical mountainous Caribbean islands of volcanic origin.

Climatic Conditions: Tropical tempered by cooling winds.

Principal Products: Asphalt, fruits, and oil.

The most striking feature of Trinidad is the huge pitch lake of La Brea. It is the largest of all the asphalt lakes in the world. It bubbles and boils over an area of more than a hundred acres. Its asphalt is exported in large quantities and used for road making.

Trinidad was discovered by Christopher Columbus on July 31, 1498. It was the first sight of land on his third voyage to the Indies. Originally claimed for Spain, the islands were used as footballs in overseas international politics for many years. The inhabitants of Tobago Island have seen the Spanish, Portuguese, French, and Dutch flags flutter over their heads in bewildering procession.

Among those who visited Trinidad was Sir Walter Raleigh. He attacked the Spanish colony there in 1595, when he headed an expedition to the Orinoco River in Venezuela. Raleigh's object was to find the golden riches of the fabled Gilded Man. Failing in this, Raleigh attacked and destroyed the city of

San José de Oruna on Trinidad. The island was ceded to England in 1802 by Spain. Tobago has been a British possession since 1814.

Dutch West Indies

Discovered: By Alonso de Ojeda for Spain in 1499.

Population: 91,000 (combined population of six major islands).

Area: 403 square miles (combined area of six major islands).

Language: Dutch.   *Capital:* Curaçao.

Government: Dutch colony.

Geographical Characteristics: Level terrain of islands, broken up by infrequent and low hills.

Climatic Conditions: Tropical.

Principal Products: Orange liqueurs.

One of the first visitors to the Dutch West Indies was Amerigo Vespucci, who at that time had no idea that a whole New World would be named after him. Although discovered by Ojeda, the famous Spanish navigator, in 1499, Curaçao was not settled by the Spanish until 1527. Some seven years later, the Spanish were ousted by the Dutch. The Hollanders held sway until 1807, when the British took control. In 1815, the islands were restored to the Netherland government.

During the days of Dutch control, Curaçao was the headquarters of the powerful Dutch West India Company. This company also owned and operated a thriving colony in North America, the principal town of which was called New Amsterdam. Today it is New York. About three hundred years ago, Indians were giving the Dutchmen in New York quite a lot of trouble. To put the red men in their place, the Dutch sent troops from Curaçao to New York. That was in 1643 when Peter Stuyvesant was governor of the Dutch West Indies. Later Peter Stuyvesant went to New York where he remained in charge until he surrendered New Amsterdam to the English.

CHAPTER 10

Land of Vast Horizons

Highlights of Brazil

Discovered: By Pedro Álvarez Cabral for Portugal in 1500.

Population: 44,002,095.

Area: 3,285,319 square miles.

Language: Portuguese.   *Capital:* Rio de Janeiro.

Government: Republic established in 1889.

Main Geographical Features: Brazil roughly falls into three general geographical areas—the lowland, tropical Amazon Basin, comprising the major portion of north and northwestern Brazil; the higher northeastern states, parts of which consist of scrubland and desert; and the central and southern coastal upland.

Climatic Conditions: From tropical temperatures in the Amazon Basin to the warm and dry northeastern section and to the cooler climate of the southern and coastal regions.

Principal Products: Cocoa, fruits, tobacco, coffee, rubber, cotton, yerba maté, hides and skins, carnauba wax, oil seeds and nuts, meats.

B RAZIL is unique among the nations of the New World. In area, it is larger than any republic in the Western Hemisphere, including the United States. It covers more than 3,285,000 square miles. This is nearly half of the total area of South America. Brazil's capital, Rio de Janeiro, was for many years the seat of government of a great European power, Portugal. Also, within the memory of people still living, Brazil was an independent empire in its own right. Lastly, whereas Spanish is the national language of all the other Southern American republics, Portuguese is the national language of Brazil.

But to start at the beginning: Columbus returned to Spain in 1493 with the amazing news of his discoveries. At that time, Spain believed with Columbus that he had discovered a westward route to the fabulously rich Spice Islands of the Orient. Naturally Spain claimed these lands to the west across the Atlantic. At the same time, Portugal was extending her exploration southward along the coast of Africa. Both Portugal and Spain were in a globe-girdling race to reach and claim the Spice Islands of the Indies.

In an attempt to keep all this new territory for herself, Spain prevailed upon Pope Alexander VI to establish a boundary line which would keep Portugal out of the western seas. The result was that the Pope issued a papal bull establishing a north and south Line of Demarcation 100 leagues west of the Azores. All lands and oceans discovered west of the Line of Demarcation were to be the property of Spain. Those east of the line would belong to Portugal.

When news of this reached King John II of Portugal, he protested that it was unfair to Portugal. So, in 1494, under the Treaty of Tordesillas, the Line of Demarcation was moved to 370 leagues west of the Cape Verde Islands. On the map, this famous line would run from the tip of Greenland down through the Atlantic, enter the South American continent near the mouth of the Amazon, and continue down toward Antarctica.

Although this casual dividing up of the whole world by two nations seems fantastic today, it was a masterly stroke on the part of the Pope. With a line drawn on the map, he averted jealousies that might have made the arena of New World exploration one of bloody conflict between Spain and Portugal. It is also to the credit of the two nations that they respected the provisions of the treaty. Whenever differences regarding the Line of Demarcation arose, a peaceable adjustment was made.

As a result of this allotting of separate spheres of influence between the two countries, Portugal had to seek a way to the Spice Islands by sailing east around Africa. It was while on this route, in 1500, that Cabral was blown off his course and accidentally discovered Brazil. The year before, the coast had been sighted by Vicente Pinzón, a former companion of Columbus, but as he made no attempts at exploration, he is not credited with its discovery. Pinzón, however, did make an important and interesting find. Several miles out in the ocean, he noticed that instead of being salt, the water was fresh enough to drink. Curious, Pinzón sailed westward and came to the mouth of the Amazon River. He was the first European to tell of this mighty waterway that discharges such a great volume of water through its many mouths that the ocean is fresh for some 50 miles out to sea.

Confining their explorations to an eastwardly direction, Portuguese explorers bent their efforts to find a way to the Spice Islands around the southern tip of Africa. Success came to Vasco da Gama who rounded the Cape of Good Hope and sailed on to India, returning to Lisbon in July, 1499, with his ships laden with the riches of the East. This triumph put the discoveries of Columbus in the shade for the moment.

King Manuel of Portugal lost no time in following up the da Gama discoveries. Early in 1500 he sent Pedro Cabral with a fleet of thirteen ships to establish Portuguese settlements in the East and to monopolize the trade of the Spice Islands. Following Vasco da Gama's advice to keep well off the west African coast, Cabral's ships sailed far off their course and on April 22, 1500, a strange new land was sighted. This region later became known as Brazil, after a native dyewood similar to the brazilwood of the Orient.

Cabral sailed south along the coast and on May 1 anchored

his ships in a harbor he named Port Seguro. Going ashore, he took possession in the name of Portugal. Cabral's instructions, however, were to bring back spices and silk from India, so sending one ship back to Lisbon with the news of his discovery, the Portuguese navigator continued on his voyage to the Orient by way of Africa. A year later, he returned to Portugal, his ships filled with spices and other treasures of the East.

The news of Cabral's accidental discovery came as a pleasant and unexpected surprise to the Portuguese. They had more or less resigned themselves to the belief that all the lands in the new "Indies" were to the west of the Line of Demarcation, and therefore the property of Spain. But Brazil was obviously to the east of the line and Portugal was quick to take advantage of this. The king made immediate plans for an expedition, which required the services of a navigator and pilot who had sailed the western seas. Amerigo Vespucci had just returned from a voyage with Ojeda to the northern coast of South America under the sponsorship of Spain. When King Manuel of Portugal invited him to go as chief pilot on the expedition, Vespucci accepted. In May, 1501, with Vespucci as chief pilot, an expedition of three caravels set out from Portugal to explore the as-yet-unnamed Brazil.

The little that is known about this voyage comes from two letters written by Vespucci, one to Lorenzo de Medici and another to a former schoolmate. Unimportant in themselves, these letters, through a curious set of circumstances, led to the adoption of the name America for the continents of the Western Hemisphere. Considering how important the name of Amerigo Vespucci is to us, it is amazing how little is generally known either of the man or his travels or, for that matter, just how and why America is called America.

Amerigo Vespucci was born in Florence, Italy, on March 9, 1451. His father was a well-to-do notary. He was educated by his uncle, a Dominican monk, who instilled in him an interest in the sciences. At an early age young Vespucci became so absorbed in the study of geography and the theory of navigation that he acquired great skill in practical astronomy. He also became expert in the calculation of latitude and longitude as practiced in that day. His education finished, he found employment with the wealthy Florentine commercial house of Medici. Sometime before 1492, he was sent to Spain as a confidential agent of the Medici.

Even as a businessman, Vespucci spent his leisure time studying geography, collecting maps, charts, and globes, and perfecting himself in the art of map making. There is no doubt that he followed the doings of his fellow countryman, Christopher Columbus, closely. By 1493, Amerigo had formed a connection with the Seville commercial house of Juanoto Berardi, who was a friend of Columbus. It is believed he met the Admiral on the latter's return to Spain after his first voyage across the Atlantic. It is equally possible that during the following years, he heard much about the discoveries in the New World. If one is to believe the stories told about Vespucci and his travels, it seems that by 1497 he was no longer satisfied to hear about the adventures of the daring navigators of new oceans but embarked on an expedition of his own in May of that year. Accounts of this voyage are vague. Some doubt that it ever took place. But, according to Vespucci, the expedition reached the waters of the Gulf of Mexico, sighted Florida, and returned to Spain in October, 1498. The following year, Vespucci sailed with Alonso Ojeda on a voyage of exploration along the coast of Venezuela and into Lake Maracaibo. It was on returning from this voyage that Vespucci was called to the service of Portugal and sailed for Brazil.

On this, Amerigo Vespucci's third voyage, the coast of Brazil was sighted on August 16, 1501. Sailing slowly down the coast, a good harbor was reached on November 1 and named Bahia de Todos Santos. Two months later, the party put in at another fine harbor. Because it was discovered on January 1,

1502, and thought to be the mouth of a river, it was named Rio de Janeiro, the River of January. Actually, the River of January turned out to be a bay. From this point, the expedition sailed south as far as the island of South Georgia, off the coast of Argentina.

Another voyage to the Brazilian coast with Vespucci as pilot followed in 1503. The purpose was to find a water passage to the Spice Islands. At about the latitude of the present-day S˜o Paulo the ships ran into heavy storms. They were forced to return to Portugal without having accomplished their purpose.

In his letter to Lorenzo de Medici, written from Lisbon in 1503, Vespucci describes the nature of Brazil and gives a long account of the natives and the climate. So strange are the wonders he has seen that the letter writer uses the Latin phrase *Mundus Novus* (New World). This is generally accepted as the first hint or suggestion that the newly discovered lands to the west across the Atlantic might actually be a new world. It must be remembered that Columbus, to his dying day, believed he had reached the Spice Islands and Asia. It is unlikely that Vespucci actually suspected the truth, but by using the expression New World he planted the idea that a great new continent lay between Europe and the Orient.

Vespucci's second letter, written in 1504 to his old schoolmate, Soderini, is even more explicit on this point. Both of these letters were translated into French and Latin. They circulated all over Europe and were widely read among the learned men of the day.

It so happened that a young French scholar by the name of Ringmann Philesius edited one of Vespucci's *Mundus Novus* letters. In 1507, Ringmann became associated with Martin Waldseemüller, a professor of geography at Saint Dié College in Lorraine, in the preparation of a new and complete geography that would include all the latest geographical discoveries.

There was not much trouble with the three old divisions, Europe, Asia, and Africa. But the two young men wanted their map to be up to date, so they added a fourth part to their map, based on Vespucci's letters. This fourth part was more or less the coast line of present-day Brazil. They called it America, or the land of Amerigo. This was no intended slight to Columbus. As has already been explained, Columbus made no claims at all of ever having discovered a new continent.

The *Cosmographie Introductio* of Ringmann and Waldseemüller was published in April, 1507. It was the first time the name America appeared on any map, and then it applied only to the section of the New World that is today Brazil, the land that had been so enthusiastically described by Amerigo Vespucci.

When, in 1520, Ferdinand Magellan sailed through the strait that now bears his name and proved that the Orient lay thousands of miles to the west of the land discovered by Columbus and across an entirely new ocean, geographers were faced with the problem of naming a new continent. America was already there on the Waldseemüller map, so map makers took the easiest way and spread the name over two entire continents. In one map of this date the letters AME are printed on the North American continent and the letters RICA across South America.

Many accusations have been made against Amerigo Vespucci, including one that he made false claims in an effort to establish discoveries prior to those of Columbus. The evidence against this is that they were friends and that there was a most cordial meeting between the two men shortly before the death of the Admiral. The record of the latter years of Vespucci's life indicates that he was a man of both distinction and talent. In 1508, he was appointed to the high position of chief pilot of Spain, with the responsibility of examining all pilots and checking and revising maps and charts brought back by navigators and explorers. This post he held until his death in 1512, when unknowingly, he bequeathed his name, Amerigo, to a New World.

Despite Amerigo Vespucci's glowing accounts of Brazil, Portugal was not deeply interested in it. Brazilwood and parrots had no appeal to a nation that was growing rich with Spice Islands' trade and profits from newly acquired mines in Africa. For 30 years the Portuguese did nothing to establish colonies in Brazil. It was known that private adventurers, mostly French, came to Brazil and sailed off with cargoes of brazilwood, but nothing was done to stop them. Then came rumors of silver discovered to the south, in La Plata, by Spain. At the very mention of this precious metal, Portugal took notice. Brazil became important overnight. The king realized, at last, that if he wanted to retain hold on the country he would have to establish colonies.

Martin de Sousa was sent with an expedition to look for silver and to found colonies. Sousa waged a successful war against French corsairs and destroyed French establishments near Pernambuco. In 1532, he founded São Vincente, the first permanent colony in Brazil. But Sousa did not find silver, so when the colonists asked for help from the mother country to fight off foreign invaders, Portugal took no action. However, the problem was met by dividing Brazil into estates, or captaincies. These were granted to private individuals of wealth who were willing to finance their own settlements even to the point of hiring soldiers to protect them.

The captaincy system failed because there was no coordination or unity. Finally, in response to a desperate plea from the colonists that the whole enterprise would be snatched away by foreigners unless prompt aid was sent, Portugal appointed a governor general. In 1549, Thome de Sousa took office as the first appointee. He arrived in Brazil in March and founded São Salvador (Bahia), which remained the capital of the colony for many years.

Although the country prospered in a small way, the French were not driven out of Brazil until 1567, by Governor Mem de Sa, who also founded Rio de Janeiro.

The year 1580 was a turning point in Brazilian colonial history, for in that year Dom Enrique of Portugal died and Philip II of Spain assumed the throne of both countries, thus becoming the ruler of Brazil as well as the rest of South America. Up to this time, Brazilians had been careful lest they settle too far west, on the western or Spanish side of the Line of Demarcation established by the Tordesillas Treaty which was still in effect. But as a colony of Spain, this invisible boundary line was wiped out and a westward move began. These gains were zealously held on to when Portugal regained her independence in 1640. They are largely responsible for the vast extent of Brazil's territory today.

A spirit of national unity and pride took root at an early date in Brazil. The threat of a common enemy acted as a magnet to draw people together. For almost a century, from 1520 to 1615, Brazilians had fought the constant threat of French invaders in quest of dyewood.

Hardly had the French been driven out when the Dutch West Indian Company cast greedy eyes on Brazil, followed by an attempt at conquest. Dutch forces attacked and captured Bahia in 1624 and little by little gained control of the greater part of settled Brazil. An appeal was made to Spain, still holding on to the throne of Portugal, but the stepmother across the Atlantic was too occupied with European wars to pay attention.

Left to their own resources, the Brazilians sharpened their swords and wits and declared war on the Dutch. It was a proud day when, in 1654, the last of the Dutch forces were driven out. The Brazilians had proved their worth and gained a great victory without help from Spain, or Portugal, which was by then ruled by its own sovereign.

The expulsion of the Dutch marked an important date in the history of Brazil. From that date on, the colonists felt themselves equal to the Portuguese in Europe. Brazil was an element to be reckoned with, and the colony played an ever-increasing role in Portuguese politics and policies.

In 1640, when King John IV regained the throne for Portugal, the first viceroy was sent out to Brazil, although the colony was not declared a viceroyalty until a century later.

Portugal was now beginning to take more interest in the colony. Little by little, Brazil began to pay dividends. The people were industrious and the soil was good. Some gold was discovered in the south as early as 1694, with the promise of more to come. Then came the rich gold strike in Minas Geraes.

Although the El Dorado of Brazil had been long in the finding, it proved to be a bonanza that made the waiting well worth while. News of the strike set in motion a gold rush similar to the later ones to California in the United States and to the Klondike in the Yukon. In 1719, more gold was found in Matto Grosso. Six years later, there was another gold strike in Goyaz. Then, in 1729, to top this outcropping of fabulous wealth, enormously rich diamond fields were discovered in a part of Minas Geraes that had been abandoned by gold prospectors.

When not enough Indians could be found to work the mines and diamond fields, large numbers of African slaves were imported. Bahia, although it remained the official capital, lost most of its population and trade to Rio de Janeiro, the natural port for Minas Geraes. But the news of this new-found wealth spread beyond Brazil and Portugal, with the result that it drew pirates and raiders as honey draws flies. Time and again, Rio de Janeiro had to pay a king's ransom to escape destruction at the hands of the roving Brethren of the Sea.

From all over the colony, people headed for Minas Geraes. As a result of this gold rush, the state of Minas Geraes has to this day the largest population of any state in Brazil.

In return for the wealth Brazil was pouring into the coffers of Portugal, the colony demanded the right to play an important role in the affairs of the mother country. A case in point is the Treaty of Madrid between Spain and Portugal which, to a great extent, was drawn up by Alexander de Gusmão, a native of Santos, Brazil. In 1763, Brazil was formally elevated to the honored status of a viceroyalty, with its capital at Rio de Janeiro.

But an event more exciting than the discovery of gold and diamonds awaited Brazil. Portugal was invaded by the armies of Napoleon in 1807. On November 29 in that year, the French forces were marching on Lisbon. King John VI, who had no idea of surrendering to Emperor Napoleon, sailed from the mouth of the Tagus River that very day, with thirty-six ships carrying the royal family and several thousand nobles and courtiers. Their destination was Rio de Janeiro. For the first time in history, a colony was about to become the seat of government of the mother country.

Rio de Janiero and all Brazil were both flattered and honored to become the seat of the empire. King John and his followers were received with wild acclaim. All believed that it was the dawn of a new and better day for the colony. At first it seemed that they were right. The king abolished restrictions on foreign commerce. This began a brisk and profitable trade in coffee, sugar, hides, and tobacco.

But, all too soon, it became apparent that kings and courts are expensive luxuries. The cost of administration was heavy. Positions had to be found for the thousands of hangers-on who had trailed along in the royal wake. In addition to these burdens, the queen launched a long and expensive war against Uruguay and Argentina. But these drawbacks were in a small degree compensated for in 1815 when the Congress of Vienna raised Brazil to the status of a kingdom.

Lisbon, by this time rid of the French occupation, resented this turn of affairs. With the land in America a kingdom and the king in Rio de Janeiro, Portugal was practically reduced to the level of a colony of Brazil. The parliament in Lisbon demanded that King John return the seat of government to Lisbon. The king had become fond of Brazil and expressed a desire to remain in the colony. However, his loyalty to Portugal forced him to deny his own preference. On April 26, 1821, he sailed for Lisbon, leaving behind him as regent, his son and heir apparent to the throne of Portugal, Dom Pedro.

Dom Pedro was an intelligent but willful young man of twenty-four when he assumed the role of regent in 1821. He was never very popular, but as the head of the government he was respected. When Portugal enacted various laws and measures to reduce Brazil again to the level of a subservient colony, the people looked to Dom Pedro to take their side. This he did but in a halfhearted way. When Lisbon demanded that Dom Pedro return to Portugal late in the year 1821, he hesitated. It was a crucial moment in the history of Brazil. So long as Dom Pedro, heir apparent to the throne of Portugal, remained, certain prestige and rights could not be denied by the mother country.

When, on January 9, 1822, Dom Pedro was finally forced to face the situation, he declared that he would remain in Brazil for the good and happiness of the colony. His decision, greeted with joyous acclaim, was no doubt to a great extent influenced by the Patriarch of Brazilian Independence, José Bonifacio de Andrada e Silva, who was chosen head of a new ministry. This move was in open defiance of Portugal, and the Brazilian drive for independence had won its first bloodless battle.

When Portugal sent orders that the ministers who had defied her authority be arrested and tried as rebels, Brazil was ready to fight. Dom Pedro was at Ypiranga, near São Paulo, at the time. When he read the dispatch that his ministers had agreed to defy Lisbon, Dom Pedro is reported to have thrown his hat into the air and shouted: "Independence or death!" This was on September 7, 1822.

After this evidence of his love for Brazil, Dom Pedro's popularity reached new heights. He was elected constitutional emperor of an independent Brazil. At first, Portugal refused to recognize the new empire. But with the fact accomplished, there was nothing much she could do. On March 10, 1826, King John IV, the father of Dom Pedro, died in Portugal. The crown was offered to Dom Pedro of Brazil. He accepted it and then immediately abdicated in favor of his daughter, Maria de Gloria.

Although Dom Pedro accepted the throne of Portugal only to bestow it upon his daughter, the act stirred up a hornets' nest in Brazil. Suspicions that a son of the royal line would favor Portugal gained ground. The emperor lost nearly all his popularity.

At this time, Brazil was engaged in a war with Uruguay. In 1828, with the help of Argentina, the Brazilians were driven out of that country. On August 27, the Republic of Uruguay was born at a peace conference in Rio de Janeiro.

The loss of Uruguay tended to make Dom Pedro even less popular. Unfortunately, he resented criticism, and continually dismissed his ministers. Finally, on April 7, 1831, a deadlock came when Dom Pedro refused to appoint a cabinet acceptable to the people. Instead he abdicated in favor of his five-year-old son, also named Dom Pedro. As shouts of "Viva Dom Pedro II!" rang out in the streets of Rio de Janeiro, Dom Pedro I was aboard a British warship in the harbor, waiting to return to Portugal. There he died 4 years later.

As the young emperor, Dom Pedro II, was only five years old, a regency was established to rule until he should be of age at eighteen. But internal strife broke out almost immediately and continued year after year, threatening to disrupt the country completely. The need for the authority of a strong government became a matter of life or death by 1839, when the boy emperor was only fourteen years old.

A proposal was made in congress that Dom Pedro II be declared to have reached his majority immediately. It was argued that the boy had been carefully educated and that his judgment was mature for his age. The proposal was defeated, but as matters went from bad to worse, it became obvious that a leader, even a boy leader, was needed to save Brazil from anarchy. On July 23, 1840, Dom Pedro was declared to be of age, and thus assumed his duties as constitutional emperor. A year later, on July 18, 1841, Dom Pedro II was crowned Emperor of Brazil in magnificent ceremonies in the Cathedral of Rio de Janeiro.

The boy emperor began his reign. A cabinet of liberal and popular ministers was appointed. All political prisoners were freed. As the boy grew to manhood he gave more and more of his time and efforts to the welfare of his people. Gradually, internal unity was established after 20 years of bitter civil war. From an absolute monarchy, Brazil became a liberal and constitutional government with an elected parliament.

True, there were troubles both internal and external during the long rule of Dom Pedro II, but a steady advance was made along every line of activity under the kindly guidance of an emperor who was simple in his ways; a philosopher and student. Perhaps his greatest act, and the one that did most to cause his downfall, was the complete abolition of slavery on May 13, 1888.

The freeing of the slaves had come to a head gradually over a period of years. For obvious reasons, it was bitterly opposed by the rich landowning class. The younger element in the army also turned against their aging emperor, who knew and felt that he was outliving his time. If it had not been for the love of the people of Brazil for their gentle ruler, there can be no doubt that the revolution would have come long before it did. On November 15, 1889, the Republic of Brazil came into being. It was a bloodless revolution, with the only casualty one man slightly wounded in the leg.

Two days later, on November 17, Dom Pedro and his family left Rio de Janeiro and boarded a ship waiting in the harbor. It was all done on the friendliest basis, but the old emperor was sick at heart. He loved his country and his people and he did not quite understand what had happened. Two years later, on December 5, 1891, Dom Pedro II died an exile in Paris.

Among the heroes of Brazil who stand high-lighted against

the days of the empire is José Bonifacio, one of Brazil's great national heroes. He was born at Santos, Brazil, June 13, 1763. At the age of twenty he attended the famous University of Coimbra in Portugal, graduating 6 years later. He became one of the leading scientists of the day. Learned societies in London, Paris, and Berlin invited him to membership and from his pen poured forth numerous reports on a great variety of subjects.

Bonifacio returned to Brazil in 1819 to devote himself to scientific research, but he soon found himself drawn into and playing the leading part in the momentous political events that occurred in the following few years. As already mentioned, when King John VI returned to Lisbon in 1821, Portugal tried to reduce Brazil to its former colonial status. This met with intense opposition and Dom Pedro was proclaimed Emperor of Brazil. Dom Pedro named Bonifacio Minister of Interior and of Foreign Affairs. He held this post for 18 months.

With his two brothers, Bonifacio founded a newspaper in which he vigorously attacked the succeeding cabinet's policy of excessive leniency toward the Portuguese. In consequence, not long afterward, the three of them were arrested and exiled to Europe. He was permitted to return to Brazil in 1828 and 3 years later when Dom Pedro I abdicated, he named Bonifacio tutor of young Dom Pedro II. The venerable Patriarch of Independence held the post only 3 years. His enemies succeeded in having him imprisoned on the island of Paqueta, in the harbor of Rio de Janeiro. There he died on April 6, 1831.

No story of Brazil would be complete without an account of Francisco Orellana's amazing journey down the Amazon River from near its source high in the Andes along its entire length to where it empties into the Atlantic at Para, Brazil.

Orellana was a Spanish adventurer and companion in arms of Francisco Pizarro, the conqueror of Peru. In 1540 he was captain general of Guayaquil, Ecuador, when Francisco Pizarro's younger brother, Gonzalo Pizarro, came to Quito as governor. Gonzalo had heard of a fabulous Land of Cinnamon in the unknown territory east of the Andes. This was also believed to be the home of the Gilded Man who bathed himself in liquid gold. Orellana and Pizarro joined forces. Toward the end of February, 1541, a large and well-equipped expedition crossed the Andes and invaded the Amazon Basin under Pizarro's leadership.

Gonzalo Pizarro had done himself well. Under his command were 220 Spaniards, 4,000 Indians, and 1,000 mastiffs to hunt jaguars and hostile natives. He also had 2,000 hogs for food and a large quantity of munitions and supplies. Orellana was second in command, and the spiritual welfare of the party was in the hands of a priest, Father Carvajal. The account by Father Carvajal of what happened during this expedition is a unique chapter in the story of exploration and conquest in the New World.

For almost a year the expedition struggled through the jungles, fighting disease, wild beasts, fever, and starvation. There was no sign of the Land of Cinnamon or of the Gilded Man. By December, 1541, a sad and sorry remnant of the original party was encamped on the banks of a small river, discouraged and desperately in need of food. Orellana had supervised the building of a large boat. He offered to take some men and go downstream in search of food. Gonzalo Pizarro agreed on the condition that Orellana would return within 12 days whether he discovered food or not. Toward the end of the month, Orellana, with some fifty Spaniards and a number of Indians, headed down the river in the boat and several canoes. Among those who went was Father Carvajal.

Gonzalo Pizarro waited for twice 12 days without any sign of Orellana's return. Finally, he decided that his friend and second in command had deliberately deserted. There was nothing for Pizarro to do but to make his way back to Quito. This he did with great difficulty. In Peru he accused Orellana of treason. This story has gone down in history as the "Treason of the One-Eyed Man," for Francisco had lost one of his eyes in the service of the conqueror of Peru.

What really happened is told by Father Carvajal. As the party under Orellana sailed down the river, the current grew swifter and swifter. At last it became obvious to the Spaniards that it was impossible for them even to attempt going back. The current was too swift for a journey up the river. The jungle was too thick to permit a return overland. There was only one course: to continue downstream until they reached the sea.

After some weeks, the Spaniards came to a broad river, but friendly Indians warned them of the many dangers ahead. They talked fearfully about a clan of fierce woman warriors, or Amazons, who would be sure to kill them all. Orellana and his comrades laughed at this story. They continued their journey down the great river, which grew wider day by day. Almost every day they had running fights with hostile Indians. Food was scarce and every morsel was gotten at the risk of a volley of poisoned arrows. The fantastic story of the women warriors was repeated at the few villages where the natives proved friendly.

Late in June, 1542, the predictions of the natives came true, according to Father Carvajal's story. As the Spaniards were passing an Indian village, they were attacked by bands of Indians led by women warriors armed with bows and arrows and blowguns. These women were tall and broad-shouldered and with long hair hanging down their backs. Father Carvajal wrote that they fought with more savagery than the men. The Spaniards managed to escape only after many casualties. Father Carvajal, himself, lost an eye in this encounter.

That Orellana actually met a tribe of Amazons or women warriors is highly doubtful. What is more likely is that some women fought with the men, which is not at all unusual. Also, it is believed that the Indians who attacked at this point were the Tapuyas, whose habit it was to wear their hair long in the fashion of women. But, whatever the truth, the fact remains that from that encounter the greatest river of South America got its name, the Amazon.

After the fight with the so-called Amazons, Orellana and his men almost despaired of ever seeing civilization again. But, by the end of August, they reached the mouth of the river. They sailed into the Atlantic and up the coast of South America to a Spanish settlement on an island off the coast of Venezuela.

Orellana's journey down the entire length of the Amazon was one of the great feats of New World exploration, but it attracted little attention. For many years, the mighty river was more or less ignored. What really called the attention of the world to the vast Amazon jungles was the boom in rubber some three hundred years later.

The Indians who lived along the Amazon in northern Brazil were familiar with the properties of rubber long before the coming of Europeans to the New World. They knew how to extract the milk from the trees and how to smoke-cure the rubber so that it could be manufactured into various simple articles. One of the popular sports among the Amazon Indians was a game played with a rubber ball.

The white man, for some strange reason, took a long time to appreciate the useful qualities of rubber. It was not until 1743 that a young French scientist, Charles de Condamine, called the attention of Europe to this amazing and useful product of nature. He had been sent to South America by the French Academy of Sciences to measure an arc of the meridian at the equator. Having accomplished this highly technical task, he set out for home via the Amazon. Along the river he picked up several rubber articles of Indian manufacture, and even experimented with rubber as a waterproofing. So pleased and enthusiastic was he that he wrote several papers on the subject of Brazil rubber.

As a result of Condamine's publications, a small rubber trade was established along the Amazon. But there was one great drawback. Rubber was found to be an excellent waterproofing material, but even with the best smoke-cure it became brittle in cold weather and sticky in the summer. When this was discovered, the enthusiasm for rubber lagged. The Amazon jungle would probably have gone back to its peaceful life after a mild boom if it had not been for Charles Goodyear, a Yankee with an inventive mind and endless patience.

In 1839, after many years of experimenting, Goodyear discovered the secret of vulcanization by mixing sulphur with the crude Brazil rubber and then applying just the right degree of heat. This process ended the ruinous effects of heat and cold on rubber. By 1840, rubber was booming again—and so was the Amazon. At that time it was practically the only source of supply for the crude product.

With rubber bringing a high price, Brazil guarded her monopoly carefully, making it unlawful to export either young trees or even the seeds of rubber trees. Several unsuccessful attempts were made to smuggle seeds out. The few that did reach Europe, mostly England, failed to grow. Britain's object in trying to get seeds was to raise shoots that could be sent to India, Ceylon, and the British East Indies for transplanting. The climate of those parts of the British Empire is much the same as that of Brazil. Great success had been met with the transplanting of quinine from the South American jungle to the East Indies. Similar success might be had with rubber if seeds could only be smuggled out of Brazil. Many adventurers tried this, but none succeeded.

A rare opportunity, however, came to a young Englishman, Henry Wickham, who was located on the Upper Amazon, near the Rio Negro in 1876. A British steamer, the *Amazonas*, had sailed from England to Manaos, a city 1,000 miles up the river, with a cargo to trade for crude rubber. The goods were put ashore in the charge of two rascally rubber traders. They made off with the wares and left the ship's captain, Thomas Murray, with an empty ship and no way of returning to England with a cargo of rubber to pay for the journey.

That was the opportunity Wickham had been waiting for. He made a deal with Captain Murray and soon had the vessel loaded with 70,000 seeds of the rubber tree. When the ship was boarded by Brazilian inspectors, the wily Wickham not only persuaded them not to inspect the illegal cargo, but convinced them that he was carrying orchids and other rare tropical plants as a present for the Queen of England. Impressed, these officials did all they could to speed the *Amazonas* on its way.

The seeds reached England in good condition and were planted at the London Botanical Gardens at Kew, where 2,500 sprouted and produced healthy plants. These were distributed among the British Empire's possessions in the East. The original plants grew and multiplied. Thus the rubber plantations in the British and Dutch East Indies today sprang from the seeds smuggled out of Brazil by Henry Wickham.

The Amazon was still to see its greatest rubber boom, however. It roared from 1903 to 1910 when the mass production of automobile tires skyrocketed the price of rubber. From an original low of 5 cents a pound, crude Brazil rubber jumped to $3.07 a pound. In 1825, less than 30 tons of rubber had been exported from the Amazon. In 1903, more than 30,000 tons were sold at prices that made everyone who touched rubber rich. Para, at the mouth of the Amazon, became a thriving metropolis overnight. The jungle town of Manaos mushroomed into a magnificent city with a $5,000,000 opera house.

Far in the interior of the jungle, where nothing more elaborate in the way of a dwelling than a palm-thatched hut had ever been seen before, magnificent marble and tile mansions were built. Caviar and champagne were the regular diet of illiterate rubber traders. Grand pianos were carted on the backs of Indians for scores of miles over jungle trails, never to be played. Then the Brazilian rubber bubble burst. The rubber plantations of the East Indies had matured and began to supply first-grade Brazil rubber in any quantity and at a mere fraction of the price for which it could be produced along the Amazon.

Today, profiting by the mistakes of earlier years, Brazil is bringing the rubber industry back to its vast Amazon territory. It is estimated that there are still 300 million untapped rubber trees in Brazil. The plantation system of the East Indies is also being introduced.

What future wealth lies hidden in the steaming jungles of the Amazon and Mato Grosso, no one knows, for the immense region has hardly been explored. The possibilities are vast, but the problems to be solved and the obstacles to be overcome are many and difficult.

The country that first bore the name America on any map is eloquently and adequately described in one phrase by Rudyard Kipling, who wrote: "The United States of Brazil is a world in itself."

British, French, and Dutch Guiana

Discovered: By Christopher Columbus for Spain in 1498.

Population: British, 340,000; Dutch, 175,000; French, 35,000. *Total:* 550,000.

Area: (In square miles) British, 90,000; Dutch, 58,000; French, 35,000. *Total:* 183,000.

Language: Chiefly Spanish and Portuguese, together with languages of respective governments.

Governments: British, Dutch, and French colonial governments respectively.

Geographical Characteristics: Cut by many rivers, the Guiana country rises from low coastal regions to lofty mountains by way of a series of steadily rising hills and plateaus.

Climatic Conditions: Tropical but tempered by cooling winds.

Principal Products: Sugar, aluminum ore, rice, rum, diamonds, timber, copra, coffee, gold, and cocoa.

North of the Amazon and south of the Orinoco River lies Guiana. This region is divided between Venezuela, England, Holland, France, and Brazil. Columbus reached the Orinoco Delta and the Guiana coast in the summer of 1498. This was on his third voyage. When Columbus reached the shores of this land, he called it the Continent of Eden. The reason for this was that, instead of finding a burning hot tropical country so close to the equator, Guiana was a place with pleasant, cooling breezes. This was in sharp contrast to the furnacelike heat he and his men had endured in the doldrums on their journey across the Atlantic.

Columbus could not understand how such a pleasant climate could exist so close to the equator. He concluded that it must be due to the shape of the earth. Instead of being round, like a ball, the earth might be pear-shaped, Columbus concluded. He pictured the earth as being shaped like a plump kind of pear that was nearly spherical in its lower part, but with a short stubby apex in the equatorial region somewhere beyond the Guiana country.

Now we know that the earth is neither shaped like a ball, nor like a pear, but rather like a grapefruit. Columbus did not know that. He actually believed that he had sailed uphill from the furnacelike heat in the doldrums behind him to the balmy climate along the green shores of Guiana. As for the Orinoco River, Columbus speculated on the possibility that it might actually flow from the Garden of Eden.

The subsequent story of the Guianas is rather unexciting. During the days when Spanish, Portuguese, English, Dutch, and French adventurers went in quest of El Dorado, the Gilded Man, Guiana was widely explored and thoroughly exploited.

In contrast to the continent of Eden visualized by Columbus is the French prison at Cayenne. This penal colony, where French criminals are kept in harsh exile, virtually for life, was established in 1852, Nearly all the members of the white colony at Cayenne are either convicts or descendants of convicts. This is due to a peculiar arrangement whereby convicts, after serving their terms in the prison, are doomed to remain in exile for many years in the penal colony. The basic idea of this system was to colonize French Guiana. It has not been very successful.

CHAPTER 11

Liberators of the South

Highlights of Argentina

Discovered: By Juan Díaz de Solís for Spain in 1516.

Population: 12,400,000.

Area: 1,080,000 square miles.

Language: Spanish. *Capital:* Buenos Aires.

Government: Republic established in 1816.

Geographical Characteristics: Reaching westward from the eastern boundary of Argentina, stretch grass-covered plains or pampas toward the Andes. These mountains run north and south in two almost parallel ranges. Towering among these is Aconcagua, an extinct volcano. It reaches a height of 22,834 feet and is the loftiest peak in South America.

Climatic Conditions: From tropical temperatures in the northern interior, the climate ranges from temperate on the pampas to cool in southern Argentina.

Principal Products: Meats and dairy products, livestock, cereals, flour, linseed, cotton, and wool.

JUAN DÍAZ DE SOLÍS, chief pilot of Castille and veteran navigator in the uncharted waters of the West Indies, sailed out of the harbor of San Lúcar, Spain, in 1515, to find a southwest passage to the Orient. Two years earlier, Balboa had discovered the Pacific Ocean after crossing the Isthmus of Panama. But some 40 miles of swamps and jungles, mountains and forests, separated the two oceans. Hence, the discovery of the Pacific was of no value to Spain until some way was found for ships to reach it. De Solís thought he might find a waterway around or through the New World by sailing south along the coast of America. The course he steered after leaving Spain took him to the coast of Brazil. There he turned southward, looking hopefully into every bay and inlet on the chance it might be the waterway to the Orient. In 1516, de Solís sailed into what he thought surely must be the strait connecting the two oceans. Then he tasted the water. It was sweet water. Instead of finding a strait, he had reached the mouth of a great river.

Disappointed, but mindful of his duties to the king, de Solís took possession of all the adjacent lands in the name of Spain and named the body of water Mar Dulce (Sweet Sea). Then, with eight of his men, he landed on an island. There he was attacked by a band of Charruan Indians and killed. The rest of the Spaniards, seeing their leader fall dead, hoisted anchor and set sail as fast as they could.

In time, the lands Juan de Solís claimed for Spain on the shores of the Sweet Sea at the cost of his life, became one of Spain's largest and most troublesome colonies. The territory today takes in the republics of Argentina, Paraguay, and Uruguay. The body of water de Solís called Mar Dulce is today known as La Plata River, on which lie the great modern cities of Buenos Aires and Montevideo.

Ferdinand Magellan was the next caller in this part of the world. He, too, was looking for the strait to the Indies. He, too, explored La Plata River. This was in January, 1520. Magellan did not tarry long in the Sweet Water region. He was convinced that the waterway to the Pacific lay farther to the south. He was right. Ten months later, on October 21, 1520, Magellan sighted the narrow water passage at the extreme southern tip of Argentina that today bears his name, the Strait of Magellan.

Magellan's history-making discovery should have stimulated Spain's interest in the Argentine, but that was not the case.

Six years went by before another Spanish expedition touched Argentine soil and then it was under the leadership of Sebastian Cabot, son of John Cabot, who discovered North America in 1497. Sebastian Cabot had not only sailed twice with his father across the North Atlantic, but was known as a first-class navigator and astronomer in his own right. He was given the post of chief pilot of Spain and went out to learn a little more about the Strait of Magellan and to determine if the lands above the strait were on the Spanish or Portuguese side of the Line of Demarcation, mentioned in the chapter on Brazil. However, instead of following his instructions, Sebastian Cabot, fascinated by the Mar Dulce, sailed inland along the coast of Argentina and up the Paraná River. He founded Fort Espíritu Santo and proceeded up to the river's junction with the Paraguay River.

On this journey, Cabot and his men noticed the Indians wore silver ornaments. When questioned by the Spaniards, the natives told them that there were rich silver mines up the river. Therefore, Cabot called this waterway the Rio de la Plata (Silver River). The silver deposits the Indians referred to were in all probability the rich silver mines of the Incas in Upper Peru (Bolivia). There is no doubt that Sebastian Cabot's reception in Spain would have been different had he reached Peru and tapped the fabulous wealth of the Incas. But that, as will be told in another chapter, was left for Francisco Pizarro. Instead, Cabot retraced his steps and returned to Spain with glowing reports of riches and a few handfuls of silver trinkets to substantiate his claims.

Spain's first expedition for the purpose of colonizing La Plata was headed by Pedro de Mendoza, a Basque nobleman. He sailed his ships up the Silver River to Riachuelo in February, 1536. There he founded the city of Buenos Aires. The story is told that the first man ashore was Sancho del Campo. After taking several deep breaths, del Campo shouted, "Buenos aires!" (good air), and thus the city got its name. Less colorful historians say that the city was named in honor of La Virgen del Buen Aires, patroness of Mediterranean sailors.

Mendoza landed 2,500 men and 72 horses, and set about establishing a colony. From the very beginning, troubles beset the settlement. There was neither gold nor silver. Indians attacked almost daily. The horses, on the other hand, grew fat on the good green grass of the pampas. Many animals were stolen by the Indians. Others strayed from their masters and ran free on the vast plains of Argentina. Thus began the great herds of wild horses in the Argentine.

Although the Indians along the east coast of South America were not so civilized nor so organized as those of the west coast, they made up for those shortcomings in ferocity. The natives of Argentina were particularly fierce and warlike and they delayed Spanish colonization for many generations. It is also interesting to note that the descendants of these Indians, who were at first terror-struck by the white men's horses, became in time the world's finest horsemen.

As the colony at Buenos Aires suffered from disease and hunger and death, Mendoza desperately sent expeditions in search of gold and silver. One of these, led by Juan de Ayolas and Martínez de Irala, went up the Paraná and Paraguay Rivers and out of sight and existence, so far as Mendoza was concerned. When Mendoza heard no news from them by April, 1537, he sailed for Spain, ill and discouraged. He left instructions that Ayolas was to act as lieutenant governor until his return. But Pedro de Mendoza never returned to La Plata. He died on June 23 and was buried at sea.

The main events of Argentine history now shift to the Paraná River and Paraguay. Ayolas, leaving Irala behind, continued up the Paraná River into Upper Peru. There he obtained large quantities of gold and silver, but on his return journey with the treasure, Indians attacked and killed the whole party. Irala, in the meantime, had established a town on the Paraná River, near its junction with the Paraguay. This town he called

Asunción. For many years it was the center of the colony. News of the demise at sea of Mendoza and of Ayolas' death in the upriver jungles, reached Irala at virtually the same time. Being a decisive and quick-thinking leader, he assumed command on July 31, 1539, and the development of Asunción became his pride and purpose.

The development of a colony was far from easy, for disease, hunger, and Indians took a steady toll. In 1541, Irala decided to bring the colonists at Buenos Aires to Asunción. He did a thorough job, moving not only the people, but the church, all the houses, and the Spanish ship that served as a fortress. By the middle of 1541, the only living things in Buenos Aires were scores of abandoned horses. Thus, under the rule of Irala, Asunción became the only Spanish settlement in the Argentine.

In 1541 appeared a man who played a brief, dramatic, and tragic role in the history of La Plata. That man was Alvar Núñez Cabeza de Vaca, one of the most interesting and unusual figures in Spanish American conquest. He was given the post of governor of the province to succeed Mendoza. This was resented by Irala's friends who naturally expected Irala to get the post. It was this same de Vaca who, beginning in 1528, wandered through the southwestern part of the United States for more than six years, as described in a later chapter. It can truly be said that de Vaca was unique among the conquistadors. He firmly believed in treating the Indians kindly. He had an almost exaggerated sense of justice in his latter years and this, together with lofty, at times almost fantastic ideals, was to be his downfall as governor of the Spanish colony of La Plata. Cabeza de Vaca's principal fault, surrounded by sterling virtues, was that he lacked the ability to get along with the type of Spaniards who inhabited the New World in those days.

When Cabeza de Vaca arrived at the island of Santa Catalina, off the coast of Brazil, in May, 1541, he was told that Martínez de Irala had forced most of the inhabitants of Buenos

Aires to move to Asunción against their will. As governor of the
colony, de Vaca had to go to Asunción, a journey of many
months by boat, first to Buenos Aires, and then up the Paraná
River. His travels across the continent of North America had
taught de Vaca that the shortest and quickest route between
two points is a straight line. So he decided to go to Asunción
overland. When he was told that this route lay across impenetrable jungle wilderness, swamps, and mountains, de
Vaca only smiled and reminded his listeners of his North
American cross-country trek.

True to his promise, de Vaca did what everyone told him
could not be done. On May 11, 1542, after an amazing journey
of 120 days through a dense wilderness populated by hostile
Indians, he arrived in Asunción. There he assumed the
governorship, reprimanded Irala for his highhanded behavior
in uprooting Buenos Aires, and then made him his lieutenant.

Next on the program was to clean up Asunción according
to de Vaca's ideas and ideals. Indian slaves were freed; taxes
were reduced; dozens of Irala's highhanded companions were
thrown into jail. Having arranged things to his own satisfaction,
at the expense of creating powerful enemies, de Vaca set out to
open up an overland route to Peru. As an administrator, de
Vaca showed poor judgment, but as an explorer, he revealed
rare gifts. He ascended almost the whole length of the Paraguay River and was nearly within reach of the riches of Peru.
There he was forced to return because of the difficult country
and the hostility of the Indians, who neither understood his
overtures of friendship nor his promises that the Spaniards
would do them no harm.

On returning to Asunción, de Vaca found that his enemies
had undone all his reforms. Indians were again slaves, taxes
had climbed, and riots had disrupted the peace and prosperity
of the colony. On Saint Mark's Day, April 25, 1544, Governor
de Vaca was arrested and thrown into prison by the Irala
faction. In short and swift order, Irala was elected lieutenant

governor. For 10 months, de Vaca languished in the vermin-infested jail of Asunción, fed and kept alive by an Indian woman. In March, 1545, he was sent back to Spain to stand trial. In Spain, as elsewhere in those days, the wheels of justice often revolved rather slowly, so that it was not until many years later that de Vaca was found innocent. But by that time, he had been stripped of all honors and his fortune was gone. As so many other conquistadors, he died in oblivion.

Martínez de Irala has often been criticized for his part in the conspiracy against de Vaca, and quite justly at that. On the other hand, Irala's rule as governor, which was confirmed in 1552, brought progress and prosperity to the colony. Also, Irala was the first governor in whose election the colonists themselves took part, true proof of the early birth of the democratic spirit in La Plata colony.

Several unsuccessful attempts had been made to recolonize Buenos Aires, both under de Vaca and Irala. The great metropolis of the future got its second start in 1580. Juan de Garay, who might be called the real father of Buenos Aires, reached the long-abandoned settlement on June 11, 1580. He succeeded where others had failed. First of all he decided to subdue the warlike Querendi Indians. That done, he divided the surrounding country into great ranchos, and allotted Indians to work for the Spaniards. Under this system, great cattle ranches came into being and soon Argentina began to ship meats, hides, and other cattle products to Spain. This was the actual founding of Argentina's vast cattle industry of today.

When de Garay was stabbed to death by an Indian one night while he slept, the command of Buenos Aires fell to Hernandarias Saavedra. Under the governorship of Saavedra, the colony progressed rapidly. He was an able and wise administrator to whom even the Indians turned for protection and help.

Up to this point, there had been little interference in the affairs of La Plata colony from Spain. Perhaps the reason was that La Plata contained silver in its name only. But Spain soon began to realize that the complete conquest of the colony was even more important than if it had been rich in minerals. The reason was that Spain saw the need of a strong and loyal buffer state in Argentina against the growing Portuguese colony in Brazil. There were almost endless boundary disputes between the Argentines and Brazilians. They kept the two colonies in an almost constant turmoil for some two hundred years. One of the storm centers was the Banda Oriental (East Side). The everlasting boundary bickerings finally led to the liberation of that province as the Republic of Uruguay. Spain and Portugal let Uruguay have its freedom rather than see it belong to one or the other.

The conquest of La Plata and its type of government differed from those of Spain's other American colonies. First, there was no organized and highly cultured Indian civilization in the Argentine, such as that of the Incas or Aztecs, to conquer. Then, as there was no mineral wealth, but only the produce of the soil and the labor of the settlers, there was more true colonization in the La Plata region than elsewhere in South America.

In 1617, the King of Spain divided La Plata into two districts: La Guayra, comprising present-day Paraguay, with Asunción as the capital; and Buenos Aires, or Rio de la Plata, including more or less what we today know as Argentina and Uruguay.

By the beginning of the seventeenth century, Spain's rule was firmly rooted in Buenos Aires and Asunción, with many prosperous settlements in the interior. The future of Argentina and its neighboring countries was to a great extent determined by the geography of the land, especially the plains of Argentina —the vast treeless pampas, where grass often grows to the height of a man. This pampas extends nearly 500 miles in width. That cattle raising and agriculture were to be the occupations of the settlers in this great plain which did not need even to be cleared of forests, was a foregone conclusion.

It was the pampas that gave birth to the famous and picturesque Gauchos, or cowboys. The Gauchos are more or less the same today as they were in the colonial days, a hardy stock of mixed Spanish and Indian blood. They still live on horseback, fight, eat, work, and even play in the saddle. Impatient of temperament, tough in body, and absolutely fearless, the Gauchos were an independent lot, caring little for the rules and regulations sent across the Atlantic from Spain. Their extraordinary horsemanship—equaled only by the cowboys of the western plains of the United States—became a powerful and telling military factor when the struggle for Argentinean freedom began. The Gauchos were born cavalrymen.

Like the other Spanish American colonies, the Argentinos in time became restless under the rule of Spain. Trade was restricted and taxes were heavy. Worst of all was the bitter hatred between the creoles, native-born Americans of Spanish parents, and the Spaniards. The creoles had no voice whatever in the government or management of the colony's affairs. Only Spanish-born aristocrats could rule and administer. Another injustice against which the colonists rebelled was that the Argentines were made dependent on the distant viceroyalty of Peru. This, among other things, meant that all European merchandise destined for La Plata was shipped from Spain to Panama, then to Peru and, lastly, overland to Buenos Aires. The prime result was that the goods were sold in the Argentine at six to eight times their original cost. Thus, restrictive trade regulations, high prices, high taxes, and no voice whatever in the conduct of the affairs of the colony tended to create a strong demand for freedom.

Another contributing factor to the early spirit of democracy in Argentina was that the wealth of the land lay in the tilling of the soil and the tending of cattle and not in idly sitting back and raking in wealth from mines and plantations worked by Indian slave labor. This common interest made for an equality unknown in the other colonies. The great division between the very rich and the very poor did not exist in the Argentine. Also, the fusion of a hardy type of Spaniard with the high-spirited Indians produced a definite type of independent and liberty-loving Argentino. A man who spent his life riding over the wild, open pampas, the master of his horse and his destiny, could hardly be expected to submit quietly to the petty authority of Spanish officials.

It was the English, however, who gave impetus to the revolutionary movement in La Plata. In 1806, England and France were at war. To punish the Spanish colonial government for sending aid to her enemy, England decided to seize Buenos Aires. On June 24, news reached the city that a British force, under General Beresford, had landed on the coast. Viceroy Sobremonte heard the news while attending a theater performance. Instead of giving thought to the defense of the city, he lost his head and fled with his possessions. The result of this was that on June 27, 1806, General Beresford, with 1,560 troops, took possession of Buenos Aires, a city of 55,000.

The colony was offered freedom from Spain and the status of a British crown colony with liberal guarantees of free administration of justice, rights of private property protected, and freedom of trade. But the people of Buenos Aires, already dissatisfied with Spanish domination, had a different idea of freedom from the mere shifting from one dominating power to another. The colony's army, commanded by General Santiago de Liniers, and reinforced by a band of cowboys led by Juan Martín de Pueyrredón, retook the city on August 12, driving the British back to their ships.

The aftermath of this first English invasion was to strengthen the forces of democracy in Argentina. When, on August 14, General Liniers, in recognition of his services, was elected to be the governor's lieutenant, Viceroy Sobremonte refused to recognize the choice. Sobremonte's authority was not challenged openly, but the populace, nevertheless, looked upon Liniers as their true leader. A citizen militia was formed, serving as a training school for the patriot army to come.

On February 3, 1807, the English returned and captured Montevideo, the capital of La Plata's province of Banda Oriental (Uruguay). Viceroy Sobremonte was in charge of the fort at the time. He surrendered. When news of this reached Buenos Aires, Sobremonte was deposed, and his authority no longer recognized.

But Buenos Aires, and not Montevideo, was the real goal of the British. On June 28, a large English army marched on the city. While General Liniers fought to delay the invaders, Mayor Alzaga hurriedly fortified the city and organized a defense force composed of men and women, boys and girls. On July 5, when the British under General Whitelocke attacked Buenos Aires, the city was ready. As the British troops marched down the narrow streets toward the main plaza, women and girls and boys hurled down bricks and firebrands from the housetops. At the same time, Linier's "minutemen" kept up a steady fire from behind walls and doorways. The combined attack of regulars and irregulars was too much for the English. General Whitelocke gave up. He evacuated the city and also surrendered the fortress of Montevideo.

This defeat of the English made the colonists thoroughly aware of their own power. When news reached Buenos Aires that the French, under Napoleon, had removed the king from the throne of Spain, the Argentinos compelled Cisneros, the new viceroy, to call a popular assembly to decide on the colony's future course of action. On May 22, 1810, an assembly attended by 450 citizens convened in Buenos Aires. On May 25, the most famous date in Argentine history, the resignation of Viceroy Cisneros was accepted and the government was taken over by a junta, or popular council, selected by the people.

The people of Buenos Aires immediately voted to give the other provinces of the colony the benefits of their freedom. Patriot armies were sent into Upper Peru, Paraguay, and to Montevideo to spread the gospel of the bloodless revolution of May 25, using force if necessary to convince their fellow colonists for their own good.

Paraguay had been asked to send deputies to the Buenos Aires junta on July 24. When the offer was rejected, an army under General Belgrano marched against Asunción. The Buenos Aires force was defeated, but patriot prisoners captured by the army of Paraguay talked so eloquently of the advantages of the revolution, that on June 11, 1811, an assembly was called in Asunción. It followed the advice of the great Paraguayan patriot, Dr. José Francia, and declared the establishment of the independent Republic of Paraguay.

Uruguay, on the other hand, had been a little ahead of Buenos Aires. Because of the constant fight between Spain and Portugal over Brazilian boundaries, it had in fact, if not in name, been separated from the viceroyalty of La Plata for some years. In Uruguay, the patriot movement, under the leadership of José Artigas, had been advocating freedom from Spain since the close of 1808. The successful revolution in Buenos Aires injected new life into their fight for freedom. On May 18, 1811, the forces of Uruguay, led by Artigas, and with the help of an army from Buenos Aires, defeated the royalist forces at the famous battle of Las Piedras, forcing the siege of Montevideo. On October 20, the Spanish general surrendered the fortress of Montevideo, and Uruguay had won her first and most important battle in the fight for liberty.

The declaration of independence and the formulation of a plan of self-government, however, was only half the battle in the fight for liberty in Uruguay. The next step was to make Spain accept defeat and the loss of the colony. The patriots soon realized that the only way to accomplish that objective was to drive the Spanish forces out of the country; although with reinforcements always available to the royalists from Spanish garrisons in Chile and Peru, that was almost impossible. More than once during the years that followed the declaration of independence, it seemed as if the fight for liberty would be lost.

On March 9, 1812, a critical time in Argentina's struggle for freedom, a ship from London, the *George Canning*, arrived in Buenos Aires. On board was an obscure passenger, Lieutenant Colonel José de San Martín. He was thirty-four years old, returning to his native land after an absence in Europe of many years, during which he had served in the Spanish army.

Not only was Colonel San Martín well trained in the arts of war, tactics, and military discipline, but in his heart he carried a long-cherished plan for the liberation of his native land. While in London, he had joined the English branch of a secret society that had been formed by the patriots in Buenos Aires, the Lautoro Lodge. The primary objective of this organization was to fight for the independence of South America. The society's constitution contained the now-famous provision "to recognize no government in South America unless it has been elected by the free and spontaneous will of the people." To this creed, San Martín subscribed with all his heart and soul, and it has been said of this great Argentine liberator, that he was not a man, but a mission.

Although San Martín's name was hardly known in Buenos Aires, within 8 days of his arrival in the city San Martín accepted a commission of lieutenant colonel in the patriot army. His first task was to organize a cavalry squadron. He also established a military academy for the training of Argentine youths. San Martín's first regiment was formed of men picked by himself. As he told his friend, Carlos María de Alvear, "we shall have only lions in this outfit." This regiment became the famous Argentine Mounted Grenadiers. During the fight for Argentine independence, the Grenadiers was a training school that gave the Army of the United Provinces nineteen generals and 2,000 officers, and fought freedom's battle from San Lorenzo, near Buenos Aires, to Pichincha, in Ecuador.

On January 31, 1813, a general constituent assembly met in Buenos Aires and decreed absolute freedom from the sovereignty of the King of Spain. The royal colony became the free and self-governing United Provinces of La Plata. The Republic of Argentina was born.

At this stage of the revolution, the Spanish armies were making a strong fight to regain the colony. In Upper Peru, the royalist forces were gaining the upper hand. On the coast, the Spanish fleet was bombarding Buenos Aires and terrorizing the towns along the Uruguay River. At a council of war, San Martín urged that the patriot forces be concentrated in an attack against the royalist stronghold of Montevideo, which had been reoccupied by the enemy. It was with the aim of ridding Buenos Aires of this immediate threat, that San Martín fought the battle of San Lorenzo on February 3, 1813.

A young cavalry captain named Escalada had learned that the Spaniards planned to attack and loot the monastery of San Carlos at San Lorenzo, about 17 miles up the Paraná River. This news he brought to San Martín in time to allow him to evacuate the monks from the monastery and install his Grenadiers in their place. It was shortly after dawn when the royalists' commander led his soldiers up the high bluffs leading to the monastery. From the bell tower, San Martín watched them, a smile on his face, as he thought of what a surprise the Spaniards would get when, instead of helpless monks, they found a determined and well-armed force of patriot soldiers.

When the Spaniards were quite close, San Martín gave the signal to attack. Leading his little army, he galloped out of the monastery, taking the royalists by complete surprise. In the heat of the battle, San Martín's horse was shot from under him, but his life was saved by Sergeant Juan Cabral, who, by his act of heroism, assured the liberty of half of South America. The royalists were completely routed.

The battle of San Lorenzo was not much more than a skirmish. It had no great military importance, but it served three purposes: (1) it stimulated the cause of independence; (2) it reestablished the flow of trade between Buenos Aires and Paraguay by freeing the settlements along the Paraguay and Uruguay Rivers from Spanish attacks; and (3) the greatest result of all, there emerged from it a great general to take command of the fight for freedom—José de San Martín.

In the meantime, things were not going so well with General Belgrano and his campaign in Upper Peru. After winning the battle of Salta in February, 1813, there followed a series of defeats. Vilcapangio, called the bloodiest battle of the entire Argentine war, was lost on October 1. Retreating, Belgrano again clashed with the royalist General Pezuela at Ayohuma, on November 26, where the patriots suffered another serious defeat.

After Ayohuma, General Belgrano was relieved of his command, and San Martín took his place. San Martín found the remnants of Belgrano's army at Cochabamba under the command of Juan de Arenales, who was somehow keeping the spirit of fight alive among his soldiers despite lack of money, officers, and equipment. San Martín and Arenales became friends immediately, and the two men set to work reorganizing the troops. One of the difficulties was in securing new recruits for an army that had twice been badly defeated. San Martín overcame the obstacles by parading his well-trained and impressive Mounted Grenadiers before the populace, after which the young men of the countryside rushed to take up arms in the fight against Spain.

While reviewing the situation in Cochabamba, San Martín realized that if the fight for South American independence was to be won completely and for all time, the Spanish stronghold of Peru had to be wiped out. He knew that the poor patriot army of Upper Peru could not accomplish that victory alone; the Argentinos must have allies. Then it was that the great plan to liberate not only Argentina, but Chile and Peru, formed in his mind. But San Martín also knew that while he took time to prepare his plan, the upper frontier section could not be left undefended. Fortunately, there was a ready-made army, irregular but tough, that could be trusted to hold back the royalists—the Gaucho, or cowboy, army of Martín Güemes, in whose leather-tough hands San Martín placed the safekeeping of the new republic while he retired to work out his great idea.

San Martín's plan, in its simplest form, was to assemble a strong army in the Cuyo district, on the Chilean frontier, where the Andes Mountains drop eastward to the Argentina pampas; then he would march across the Andes into Spanish-held Chile and defeat the royalists there. That done, the third and final step was to join his Argentine patriot army with an army of free Chileans and to attack and drive out the Spanish army of occupation in Peru. In that way, and only in that way, San Martín believed the permanent independence of Argentina and of the rest of South America could be assured.

San Martín did not dare breathe even a word of his plan in Buenos Aires, as he feared it would be laughed at as well as opposed by the leaders of the republic. He needed time and secrecy to put the plan into effect. To achieve that end, San Martín pleaded an "infected lung," and resigned from active army duty to become governor of the Cuyo district, a district that was to be the heart of his daring campaign to destroy Spanish domination in Argentina, Chile, and Peru.

In 1814, San Martín arrived in Mendoza, in Cuyo, and immediately began to gather around him the nucleus of his glorious Deathless Army of the Andes. His Mounted Grenadiers were a start. Shortly after, a band of Chilean patriot soldiers, fleeing from Spanish armies in Chile, straggled into Cuyo and offered their services to San Martín. He welcomed them with open arms. Their leader, Bernardo O'Higgins, almost at once became San Martín's right hand man, with the rank of general.

Bernardo O'Higgins, now known in history as the Liberator of Chile, was the distinguished son of a distinguished father, Ambrose O'Higgins, who had come to Buenos Aires as an Irish immigrant. As a trader, the elder O'Higgins had worked his way across the Andes to Chile. There his rise to fame and fortune was rapid. His keen business instinct secured him army contracts that led to Spanish army commissions. Distinguished service in the Spanish army led to the rank of captain general, and eventually won for this great man of humble beginnings the exalted rank of Viceroy of Peru.

With General Bernardo O'Higgins, the son of the first O'Higgins, in command of Chilean refugees that continued to drift across the Andes into Argentina, San Martín went ahead with his plans. By 1816, the government in Buenos Aires was forced to recognize the assembled troops at Cuyo as the Army of the Andes, with San Martín as commander in chief.

The story behind San Martín's Army of the Andes is one of romance, hardships, loyalty, and determination. Help came from the most unexpected sources. One day Luis Beltran, a mendicant friar and a native of Cuyo who had served as an artilleryman in the Chilean army, sought out San Martín and offered his services. When he was asked what he could do, Beltran reeled off a long list of qualifications: blacksmith, cobbler, mathematician, draftsman, architect, chemist, and physician. In a sack slung over his back Padre Beltran carried his own handmade tools. San Martín took the friar at his own estimate, and set him to work establishing an arsenal, from which was soon flowing a steady stream of cannon, shot, and shells.

When money was needed, the people of Cuyo made voluntary contributions, and the ladies, headed by San Martín's wife, gave their jewels. Thousands of uniforms were made by the women without pay. When preparations were near completion, opposition from Buenos Aires threatened to wreck the whole project. However, the citizens of Cuyo overrode the government and unanimously elected San Martín governor, with full powers to go ahead with his project of liberation. This, San Martín set out to do.

The way to Chile led through two passes over the towering Andes: Uspallata and Los Patos, each over 12,000 feet. There were no maps, but San Martín had to get there. How? The Spaniards in Chile would certainly wipe out any small mapping expedition into their territory. But San Martín found a way. On July 9, 1816, an Argentine Congress at Tucumán confirmed the Declaration of Independence and had it published. Remote as that event may seem from a map of the Andes passes, it served San Martín as a tailor-made opportunity.

Alvarez Condarco, the chief engineer of San Martín's staff, was sent under a flag of truce to deliver a copy of this Declaration of Independence to the governor general of Chile. San Martín instructed Condarco to go by way of Los Patos, and to return by the Uspallata Pass. The plan worked. Condarco narrowly missed being taken prisoner in Santiago de Chile, but he returned to San Martín with rough but invaluable maps of the two mountain passes.

The great march across the Andes began early in January, 1817. The Army of the Andes consisted of about 5,000 men and 9,000 mules to carry ammunition and supplies. The forces were divided. Some went by Los Patos and others by Uspallata, but with strict instructions from San Martín to meet at an appointed place on the other side, in Chilean territory, between February 6 and 8.

Owing to San Martín's long and careful preparations and his military genius, the army crossed the Andes without any great difficulty. Many military authorities have considered it a greater military feat than the more famous crossings of the Alps by Hannibal and Napoleon.

Soon after crossing the snow-clad mountains, as scheduled, the Army of the Andes met the Spanish army and defeated it in the battle of Chacabuco. Forty-eight hours later, San Martín and O'Higgins entered Santiago de Chile at the head of their respective troops. They were wildly acclaimed by the people. At an emergency meeting of the assembly, General O'Higgins was elected governor.

The battle of Chacabuco, although it marked the beginning of the end for Spain in South America, was far from completing the ideas of O'Higgins and San Martín. There were still royalist forces in Chile, both in the north and the south. San Martín marched south first, where the patriots were defeated by the Spaniards at Cancha Rayada, on March 15, 1818. This defeat, after little more than a year of freedom, struck fear into the heart of Chile, but a fear that lasted only 2 weeks. On April 5, 1818, San Martín and O'Higgins gave battle to the Spaniards on the plains of Maipo, where the royalist forces were beaten and the spirit of Spanish resistance in Chile crushed.

Chile had been liberated, and the first and second steps in San Martín's plan had been accomplished. The third, the driving of Spanish troops and influence out of Peru, was considered by many to be impossible, but not by San Martín and O'Higgins. They set about to organize a Chilean army to be joined with that of Argentina for the supreme effort of ridding the entire continent of Spanish occupation and oppression.

This final part of the plan was strongly opposed by the Buenos Aires government, which considered the independence of Argentina an accomplished fact. But San Martín was convinced that, so long as Spanish rule continued in Peru, it would be a constant threat to South American freedom. He resolutely went on with his plan, As a thousand miles of impassable desert lay between the patriot army in Chile and the royalist stronghold in Peru, the only way of getting the troops into Peru was by water. That meant a fleet, and the patriots had no ships. Still, somehow, a fleet of sorts was gotten together in the harbor of Valparaíso. It was ready to sail on August 20, 1820, and consisted of two decrepit East Indiamen, a British corvette, a number of brigs, sixteen transports. Last, but not least, there were three Spanish warships whose crews had joined the patriots. In command was the famous English Admiral Cochrane, a stout sea dog often deemed second only to the great Nelson as a naval genius.

It was while inspecting the three Spanish warships that General O'Higgins remarked: "It was three ships that gave the Western World to Spain. Please God, these three will take it away from her!" And they did; not the ships, but the fighting spirit and the idealism of the men who sailed in them, inspired by the courage and undaunted faith of their leaders.

Before San Martín took command of the expedition to free Peru, he had been faced with a great decision. The Buenos Aires government sent instructions absolutely forbidding him to go ahead with his planned attack on Peru. San Martín hesitated, but he did not hesitate long. Although he loved his native Argentina, he loved liberty more. He resigned his commission as brigadier general in the army of Argentina, and it was as a general in the patriot army of Chile that he saw his plan of liberation to its conclusion.

The defeat of the Spanish in Peru was less difficult than San Martín had anticipated. Two victories by the armies, at Pasco and Nazca, spread the spirit of the revolution throughout the ancient realm of the Incas. Resistance melted before the patriot advance; hundreds of royalists pledged their allegiance to the cause of independence. On July 8, 1821, San Martín entered Lima, but as a liberator, not as a conqueror. On July 21, the independence of Peru was declared.

Where San Martín might have gone from there, no one can say. A year later, on July 26 and 27, 1822, the famous interview between San Martín and Simon Bolivar took place at Guayaquil, Ecuador. What is known of what happened at that meeting is told in the chapter on Venezuela. After their interview, San Martín virtually disappeared from the scene. He selflessly renounced any plans or ambitions of his own in order to leave Simon Bolivar free to carry out the final phases of the liberation of Peru. The final bitter blow came when San Martín, exiled from his native Argentina, sailed for Europe. There he died poor and forgotten in Boulogne, France, on August 17, 1850, at the age of seventy-two. Like Simon Bolivar, who died forgotten and unhonored, San Martín had to wait for the hands of time to place him in his true size of greatness. Today the memory of San Martín and his deeds lives as the personification of liberty and independence in the lands he aided in their quest for freedom.

South Georgia and Falkland Islands

Population: 4,000.

Area: 6,600 square miles.

Government: British colony.

Off the southeastern coast of Argentina at the entrance to the Strait of Magellan, lie a group of islands that history seems to have almost completely passed by: the Falkland Islands and South Georgia.

The Falklands have the distinction of having gone by many names. They were discovered by Davis, an explorer for Queen Elizabeth, in 1592, when he was almost wrecked attempting a passage through the Strait of Magellan. In 1594, the famous sea rover, Captain Hawkins, visited the Falklands and gave them the name of the Maiden Islands, to honor the English queen. Four years later, they were renamed the Sebald Islands by a Dutch navigator. On some Dutch maps, they still bear that name. Next, almost a hundred years later, they were given their present name, Falkland, by Captain Strong.

In 1764, the French established a settlement in the Falklands as headquarters in the whale-fishing industry. Some years later, the islands were seized by Spain, and compensation was paid to France for relinquishing her claim. The Spaniards founded the port of Soledad. The English resumed their interest in this group of rocky islands in 1766, and established a colony at Port Egmont, but were soon driven out by a punitive expedition from Buenos Aires. This act almost caused a war between England and Spain, but the matter was settled peaceably, and Port Egmont was returned to England. Although the British abandoned the islands in 1774, they reestablished their claim in 1833, and today the Falklands are a British crown colony, with a governor who is often called the King of Penguins, from the great number of these strange birds that inhabit the islands.

The climate of the Falklands and South Georgia is bleak and cold, with an almost steady wind blowing at gale proportions. No trees will grow; the skies are overcast and a heavy mist overhangs the islands for more than two-thirds of the year.

Considering these climatic and geographic conditions, it is remarkable that a small but happy and prosperous colony makes these islands its home, raising sheep and digging fuel out of the peat soil to keep the damp chill out of their bones. Although the whale industry is no longer what it was, these islands still export large quantities of whale oil and bone.

Perhaps the most important and exciting historical event in the life of these islands took place during the first World War, when a British fleet gave battle to and defeated a German fleet off the Falklands.

Highlights of Paraguay

Discovered: By Alejo Garcia, a Portuguese, who died on the Paraguay River in 1524. Explored by Sebastian Cabot in 1526 for Spain.

Population: 902,000.

Area: 61,647 square miles (excluding some 120,000 square miles of disputed Gran Chaco territory).

Language: Spanish.   *Capital:* Asunción.

Government: Republic established in 1811.

Geographical Characteristics: Paraguay has no ocean outlet whatever. It is divided by the Paraguay River. The country is mainly made up of great flat plains with several mountain chains and numerous rivers.

Climatic Conditions: Tropical in the upper third section which lies within the tropics. In the remaining area, the climate is temperate.

Principal Products: Beef products, hides, cotton, tannin, lace, oranges, tobacco, yerba maté, quebracho wood, and vegetable oils.

The first European in Paraguay was Alejo Garcia, a Portuguese explorer. In 1524, he set out from Santa Catharina on the coast of Brazil, traversed what is now Paraguayan territory, and finally reached Charcas in Upper Peru. On his return trip, he was killed by natives while making explorations along the Paraguay River. Garcia was followed by Sebastian Cabot. Some years later, Cabot was followed by an expedition under the leadership of Juan de Ayolas. He, like Garcia, met a tragic death at the hands of natives of Paraguay. For fuller data see the chapter dealing with Argentina.

The Jesuits began the work of establishing their famous missions in Paraguay in 1608. These grew to the proportions of a state separate from that of the Spanish. The missions were largely composed of groups of Guarani Indians who worked for the benefit of the Jesuits, under strict social discipline, and who, in return, received a religious education. The prosperity of the Jesuit missions caused a feeling of intense jealousy among the colonists in Paraguay. This was largely because Jesuit commerce was exempt from the heavy crown taxes that burdened all other colonists.

The discontent increased in time to such a point that, in 1721, armed rebellion broke out and continued at intervals for a period of 20 years. The original aim of the colonists had been the expulsion of the Jesuits, but the movement soon changed into a revolution against the Spanish authorities by virtue of the fact that they supported the Jesuits. Thus, this war was one of the first insurrections against the Spanish yoke in the New World. In the end the commoners were subdued, but the feeling of discontent persisted. Finally, in 1769, in order to preserve peace in his dominions, the King of Spain was obliged to order the expulsion of the Jesuits from Paraguay.

Much has been said about the influence of the Jesuits in Paraguay, but it was exercised largely over the Guarani in the missions. These Indians disappeared completely after the expulsion of the Jesuits. At the same time, the Jesuit missions were located far from the centers of population, and were spread not only over Paraguayan territory, but were found in lands which today belong to Argentina, Brazil, and Uruguay.

Paraguay originally included not only the present territory, but also large areas of land drained by La Plata River, together with an extensive region in the north which is now a part of Brazil. During the same colonial period, by various royal decrees, the province suffered important territorial reductions. By the time independence was gained, Paraguay was considerably smaller than the original province.

In 1810 the revolutionary movement inaugurated in Buenos Aires had liberated the provinces of the viceroyalty of La Plata River, among which Paraguay was included. The plan was to unite these provinces into a federation. The Paraguayans, with a sectional feeling of long standing, refused to take part unless certain guarantees were made eliminating taxes on commerce passing through various provinces on its way to the sea. At this sign of insubordination, the Buenos Aires government fitted out an expedition under the command of General Belgrano and sent it to Paraguay. The expedition met defeat in the battles of Paraguarí and Tacuary. Not many months later, on May, 14, 1811, the old Spanish regime at Asunción was overthrown and the independent life of the country began.

Prominent among those who will live forever in Paraguay's history are Dr. José Francia, a dictator with the habits of a hermit; Carlos Lopez, who brought progress and prosperity to Paraguay; and his son, Francisco Lopez, whose dreadful war against Brazil, Argentina, and Uruguay earned him the title "The Cruel."

In half a decade of ceaseless warfare under Francisco Lopez, nearly all the man power of the nation was exhausted. When the war ended, about 500,000 men or nearly half the country's population, had been killed. Those who lived to shiver at the memory of this dreadful war were mostly women, children, or old men.

Highlights of Uruguay

Discovered: By Juan de Solís for Spain in 1516.

Population: 2,040,300.

Area: 72,153 square miles.

Language: Spanish.   *Capital:* Montevideo.

Government: Republic established in 1828.

Geographical Characteristics: From a low, swampy or sandy coastal region, the country rises to high, grassy plains cut by chains of rocky hills called *cuchillas*.

Climatic Conditions: Generally subtropical.

Principal Products: Largely cattle and sheep; canned, dried, or frozen meat products; with such minerals as silver, copper, and lead.

Toward the end of 1515, when Spaniards first reached Uruguay, the natives were divided into two powerful tribes or nations—the Charruas and the Yaros. It was to a band of the former that the great navigator Solís fell a victim.

The Charruas belonged to the great family of the Guaranies. They were fierce and quarrelsome. In April, 1526, Sebastian Cabot reached the Rio de La Plata. He sent an expedition under his lieutenant, Juan Alvarez Ramón, to explore the country along the Uruguay, but the band was attacked by the Charruas, and its leader killed, with many of his followers.

Cabot directed the erection of the first fort constructed in the Banda Oriental of Uruguay. It was situated on the river San Salvador as a protection against the attacks of the natives, and was held until 1580, when it was abandoned by its garrison.

Captain Juan Romero was sent from Asunción in 1550 to make the first settlement within the present limits of Uruguay. He established himself on the San Juan River and called the settlement San Juan Bautista. Two years later, the place was abandoned by the colonists, who had become disheartened and unable to resist the continued attacks of the Indians. A settlement was begun in 1574 at the place where Cabot had established his fort, on the San Salvador. This, too, was abandoned by the settlers, who returned to Paraguay, worn out by the unrelenting warfare waged upon them by the natives.

Meanwhile, the Spanish conquerors had established themselves firmly in Paraguay and were pushing their settlements into Argentina. Repeatedly they tried to gain a solid foothold in Uruguay, whose rich pastures attracted the raisers of cattle. The opposition of the natives was, however, so fierce and so successful that little or no progress toward occupation was made for a long time. In 1603, a veteran Spanish force under Saavedra was routed in a pitched battle by the Charruas. In 1624, the first of the centers of population that now exist was founded. This settlement was made on the Rio Negro, by a monk named Bernardo de Guzmán. It was called Santo Domingo de Soriano. Later the Portuguese established the colony of Sacramento (Colonia) on the Rio de la Plata, almost opposite Buenos Aires. A lively trade sprang up between the two cities. In January, 1726, Montevideo was founded by a settlement of six families from Buenos Aires, who were joined during the same year by twelve more from the Canaries.

Soon after the dawn of the nineteenth century, the British made a determined effort to capture Buenos Aires and Montevideo. The first attack failed. A second attack was made on Montevideo on February 2, 1807. After a vigorous assault, by land and by sea, the city was taken by the English. Soon after this, the combined English forces on the river, under command of General Whitelocke, made an attack on Buenos Aires, but were disastrously defeated. Withdrawing from Montevideo, the English abandoned the Rio de la Plata.

Having successfully defended their soil from invasion, the people of Uruguay had learned their own strength and were prepared to take their government from the Spanish. The revolutionary party in Uruguay gained new strength in 1810 under the leadership of José Artigas. He organized a movement for liberation of the Banda Oriental. In April, 1811, he invaded that region with an armed force which many of the inhabitants joined. On April 26, Artigas routed a Spanish force of 600 men in San José. A month later, he gained a great victory over the Spanish army at Las Piedras. After varying fortunes and a succession of victories and defeats, the Uruguayans succeeded in expelling the Spaniards from their country, and a confederation of the provinces of Uruguay was formed under Artigas, who was titled the Protector.

When, in 1822, Brazil became independent of Portugal and the Brazilian empire was proclaimed by Dom Pedro I, Uruguay was formed into the Cisplatine province of Brazil. Artigas continued the struggle for freedom until, overcome by the superior force of his adversaries, he was forced to escape to Paraguay, where he remained until his death in 1850. The liberator of Uruguay and fervent patriot never returned to his native country. Uruguay continued to serve as the rope in the tug of war between Argentina and Brazil until 1828, when those two countries settled their boundary disputes and agreed that Uruguay should become an independent republic.

CHAPTER 12

Waters of Storm and Stress

Highlights of Chile

Discovered: By Ferdinand Magellan in 1520 and claimed for Spain by Diego de Almagro in 1535.

Population: 4,553,237.

Area: 286,322 square miles.

Language: Spanish.   *Capital:* Santiago.

Government: Republic established in 1818.

Main Geographical Features: Chile's outstanding features are its mountain ranges, the Cordillera de la Costa range and the Andes. In between lies Central Valley, the great agricultural section of the country. Chile has a 2,653-mile coast line, greater than the distance from Montauk Point on Long Island to the Golden Gate at San Francisco.

Climatic Conditions: Differences in latitude cause pronounced climatic variations. Going from west to east, one can pass from the temperate zone of the coast to the cold peaks of the Andes in the same latitude. Dry and hot in the north, temperate in the central region, and cold and tempestuous in the south.

Principal Products: Wool, frozen meats, copper, iron ore, nitrates, barley, wines, fruits, iodine, wheat, borax, beans, and silver.

W HEN in the days of Pizarro the Spanish conquerors of Peru tried to extend their conquest south into Chile, they met not only with forbidding obstacles of nature, but encountered stubborn resistance from the Indians. These tribes, although not civilized and organized as were the Incas, had been able to hold back invading armies of the great Inca of Peru in the days before the Spaniards came to the New World.

How Francisco Pizarro and Diego de Almagro quarreled over the ancient Inca capital of Cuzco, and how, to get Almagro out of the way, Pizarro sent him with an expedition to explore and conquer Chile, is told in the chapter dealing with Peru. Almagro, at the time he set out to explore Chile, was over seventy years old, but he had the heart of a lion, and the thought of golden Chilean riches, even greater than those of Peru, acted as a powerful magnet.

In 1535, Diego de Almagro started out with 500 Spanish soldiers and 15,000 Indians to claim for Spain the lands and treasures of the unknown country to the south, which then bore the name of New Toledo.

His route lay from Cuzco, over the Andes, and then, by way of Lake Titicaca, over the old Inca road. It was winter, and the expedition was totally unprepared for the bitter cold of the snow-covered mountains, whose narrow passes, swept by icy winds, proved to be deathtraps. When their food gave out, the barren country offered the Spaniards nothing. Many of Almagro's men lost toes and fingers through frostbite; others were blinded by the glaring snow. When the struggling, exhausted army reached the great deserts (now the famous nitrate districts) there was not even wood for fires, for neither trees nor shrub can survive in these barren wastes.

After suffering untold hardships in crossing this hostile territory, the survivors reached more hospitable country, the green and fertile Copiapó Valley. But still there was no gold, so Almagro, sending food back to those who had been left helpless and dying in the mountains, pressed on, reaching at last the central plains of Chile, not far from the River Maule. There, at the old outpost of the Inca Empire, the Spaniards met the fierce and warlike Araucanian Indians, whose attacks made the hardships of the snow-clad mountains and barren deserts seem almost mild in comparison.

After months of miserable existence, Almagro finally admitted himself beaten. With the pitiful remains of his army, he marched wearily back to Cuzco and more troubles with the Pizarros. In money, the expedition had cost 500,000 pesos; in life, 156 Spaniards, 10,000 Indians, and forty horses. Troubles in Peru kept the Spaniards too busy to bother with Chile, and anyway, the failure of Almagro to find gold caused Pizarro and his cohorts to lose interest in the country. Early in 1540, however, Pedro de Valdivia, a distinguished soldier, and one of Pizarro's most trusted captains, decided to try his luck in the south. In regard for his good services the Conqueror of Peru graciously made Valdivia lieutenant governor of Chile, with rights to explore and conquer—at his own expense.

Profiting by the mistakes of Almagro, Captain Valdivia marched his 200 soldiers across the desert region with all possible speed, and then took a course southward, nearer the coast, to avoid the high mountain country. Even then it proved a long and hard journey. It was not until the end of the year 1540 that Valdivia ordered his men, reduced to 150, to make camp on the banks of the Mapocho River at a spot where it flowed past a hill. There he immediately made plans for the building of a city. On February 12, 1541, the first Spanish settlement in Chile was finished, a few wooden houses with thatched roofs and a fort. It was called Santiago. The hill, now a park in the capital of Chile, was known to the Araucanian Indians as Huelen, or Misfortune Hill; but Valdivia did not know that.

Despite obstacles of one sort and another, principally Indian attacks, Valdivia and his settlers at Santiago stayed on, spending what time there was to spare from fighting the natives in looking for gold in the surrounding country. One day while Valdivia was away with most of the soldiers, a force of 6,000 Araucanians swept down on Santiago, forcing the inhabitants to take refuge inside the tiny fort. There are two stories as to how Santiago was saved. One is that a young and beautiful woman, Doña Inez Suárez, rallied the few soldiers in the fort around her, and at the head of a small detachment of cavalry routed the Indians. Another version of the salvation of Santiago is that Pedro de Valdivia himself returned in the nick of time and broke the Indians up with a cavalry charge.

Whichever story is the true one, the little colony was seriously weakened by the attack. Valdivia saw that he would either have to get reinforcements and supplies from Peru or abandon his efforts. The latter was not to his liking, for Valdivia was a determined man. On the other hand, he was also proud and hated to ask for help. He decided to send a messenger to Lima with the news that a rich gold mine had been found near Santiago. The trick worked, as Valdivia hoped it would, and in double-quick time colonists and supplies flowed into Santiago. Although some gold had been found by Valdivia, certainly no rich gold mine had been discovered. But once the newcomers arrived, it was a long and arduous journey back to Peru, so they stayed and helped rebuild Santiago.

Pedro de Valdivia proved himself to be as able a colonizer and administrator as he was a fighter. During the years that followed, he founded many other settlements, including Concepción and Valdivia City; he built a number of strong forts and tried to subdue the Indians. In this latter effort he met his death in 1553. The Araucanian Indians, flushed with their victory, once more threatened to wipe out the Spaniards. They would probably have succeeded if it had not been for the courage and ability of Valdivia's lieutenant, Francisco Villagra. When a new governor of Chile arrived, he found the war with the Araucanians still being fought. This governor, García de Mendoza, son of the Viceroy of Peru, managed to subdue the Indians for a while, but when he left after a brief term of office, there were new uprisings all over the colony.

It was due to the hostility and ferocity of the Araucanian

Indians that little progress of a permanent nature was made by the Spaniards in Chile for many generations. Although these Indians had achieved no civilization such as their neighbors to the north, the Incas, they proved a greater obstacle to the Spanish invasion. The Incas, having been for so long under the complete and absolute dominance of their kings, gave slight trouble to the Spanish conquistadors, who simply took over the reins. In the Araucanians, however, the Spaniards found themselves up against Indians whose intelligence and courage had, for generations, enabled them to maintain their independence in face of the powerful Inca Empire.

The Araucanians had a form of military organization among the various tribes. Each member tribe had its own chief, but in times of stress, they united under the leadership of an elected war chief, called the *toqui*.

Indian opposition to the Spanish in Chile lasted until 1640 when Governor Baydes negotiated a treaty with the Araucanians at Quillin, whereby the Bío-Bío River was established as a boundary line between the Spaniards and the Indians. But even then, to enforce the treaty, the Spanish had to build a long line of forts and maintain a permanent army along the boundary. Long after the Spanish conquest was an established fact in Chile, the Araucanians continued fighting until, in 1766, they won the right to have a representative minister at Santiago.

But to go back to the early days of the colony, Santiago and the other Chilean settlements grew and prospered in spite of trials and tribulations ranging from Indians to earthquakes. The worst of the latter occurred in 1575. It wrecked many of the cities and was followed by great tidal waves that swept 3 miles inland, leaving nothing living in its wake.

Chile had hardly forgotten its great earthquakes when a tornado appeared off the coast—a human tornado; Sir Francis Drake, the archenemy of Castile and self-appointed despoiler and plunderer of New Spain. Stories of his raids on the north coast of South America, through the West Indies, and even on Panama, the treasure house of New Spain, were told wherever Spaniards gathered.

After his famous raid on the treasure house of Nombre de Dios in 1572, Francis Drake and his friend, John Oxenham, explored some of the country of Panama. One day, upon reaching a hill, Drake climbed a tree to gain a wider range of vision. From its topmost branches, he saw the great South Sea. He was the first Englishman to view the broad expanse of the Pacific Ocean. He was awestruck by the sight. His heart beating faster and the blood throbbing in his veins, he said a silent prayer, beseeching the Almighty to give him "life and leave to sail once in an English ship upon that sea."

Six years later, in September, 1578, Francis Drake's prayer was answered. He sailed through the Strait of Magellan to the Pacific in his famous ship, the *Golden Hind*. But the western ocean was so raging and turbulent, that his crew changed its name from the Pacific to the Furious Ocean. The weather improved after a few weeks, however, and the *Golden Hind* steered her course northwest along the coast toward Peru and Spanish gold. Drake made frequent landings and one of his shore parties picked up an Indian who told about the Chilean port of Valparaíso. The Englishman at once decided to pay it a visit.

At noon on December 5, 1578, Drake's *Golden Hind* sailed boldly into Valparaíso. The captain of a Spanish ship, not dreaming that this new arrival could be anything but a countryman, hailed Drake and welcomed him to the harbor. When his ship was boarded by an armed party from the *Golden Hind*, and the Spanish captain heard them speak English, he was more dumbfounded than frightened, for he would sooner have expected to find men from the moon in the Pacific than Englishmen, and especially that one English-man, Francis Drake. Fortunately for the town, a Spanish sailor managed to swim ashore and warn the inhabitants, who fled in terror at the very mention of the name Drake. The result was that when Drake landed, he found his first loot in Chile exceedingly slim.

Leaving Valparaíso 2 days later, Drake steered his *Golden Hind* along the Chilean coast. At Arica, the port of the rich Potosí silver mines, he found a llama caravan loaded with silver bars and looted it. The lure of gold drew Drake steadily north, toward Callao, the port of Lima, capital of Peru and the shipping port for all the treasures of the conquered Inca Empire.

Drake's raid on Callao harbor was a bold and daring one, but it was motivated by a force even stronger than an itching for gold. The Englishman had been told that one of his old friends, John Oxenham, who had been with him that day when he had first sighted the Pacific from a tree in Panama, was a prisoner of the Spanish Inquisition in Lima, and Drake was determined to rescue him. Daring as he was, Drake knew that his forces were not numerous enough to attack the Spanish stronghold of Lima, but he planned to seize the treasure ships in Callao and hold them as ransom for the release of Oxenham. With this plan in mind and trusting his luck to the winds, he sailed on to Callao, where the winds failed him, as will be seen.

It was in the dead of the moonless and cloudy night of February 15, 1579, that the *Golden Hind* glided silently as a ghost ship in among the Spanish vessels anchored in the crowded harbor of Callao. At about the same time, an empty treasure ship from Panama arrived. The two entered the harbor side by side. An officer of the Spanish ship, anxious to learn who the other ship was, had himself rowed to the side of the *Golden Hind*. As he climbed aboard the ship and made his way across the deck in the dark, the Spaniard bumped into a cannon. No Spanish ships in Pacific waters carried weapons of that kind. This visitor in the night could be one thing only—a pirate. He jumped back into his rowboat, headed for safety, and shouted the alarming news at the top of his lungs.

Drake acted quickly. He made the rounds of the Spanish ships, cutting their cables, trusting the wind to carry them out of the harbor where he could seize them and use them to ransom his friend John Oxenham. He was not able to go ashore, but from captives he learned that there was little gold in the port, as a large galleon, the *Lady of the Conception*, nicknamed the *Spitfire*, had sailed for Panama some time before with a large cargo of Inca gold and silver. That was bad luck enough, but to add to Drake's fury, the wind died down. The Spanish ships he had cut loose in the hope of capturing them outside, remained becalmed in the harbor instead.

News of Drake's raid reached Lima early the following morning. The excited and bewildered viceroy, seeing his province threatened by a foreign nation for the first time, gave orders for the *Golden Hind* and its commander to be taken immediately, so that proper and drastic punishment might end the unexpected threat once and forever.

The *Golden Hind* was not so easily taken. When a stiff wind sprang up, Drake outdistanced his pursuers without difficulty. His plot to secure the release of Oxenham, however, had failed. To take the sting out of his disappointment, Drake decided to overtake and loot the richly laden *Spitfire*. The galleon had a 14-day start on the *Golden Hind*, but that obstacle only acted as a spur to Drake and his eager crew. Ordering every inch of canvas spread to push his ship along at top speed, Drake offered the prize of a golden chain to the man who first sighted the quarry.

On March 1, young John Drake, nephew and page of Francis Drake, shouted from the crow's nest of the *Golden Hind* that he had sighted a sail and claimed the reward.

The ship proved to be the *Spitfire*, lumbering along, low in the water with treasure. Drake realized that if he came up on the galleon too suddenly, she might become suspicious and dump her precious cargo. For that reason he checked his own speed by throwing water-filled casks overboard to be trailed behind on long ropes and act as drags. This braking device worked, and when night fell, Drake cut the casks adrift. The *Golden Hind* shot forward like an arrow, readily overtaking the enemy. For 3 days, the two ships sailed together, and when they parted company, Drake's vessel was heavy with gold and silver and jewels, while the *Spitfire* tossed and pitched as the empty hulk she was.

Although the rest of this famous voyage of the *Golden Hind* has really no place in this chapter, it is interesting enough to warrant a hasty survey. With the treasure of the *Spitfire* in the hold of his ship, Drake sailed north, raiding Spanish ships off Nicaragua and plundering the Port of Guatulco, Mexico. Next, the *Golden Hind* coasted northward along California and the coast of Canada, until ice floes made farther progress dangerous. Francis Drake had hoped to find a water passage to take him east around the northern tip of the continent as the Strait of Magellan had taken him west around the southern tip. But, luckily for him, he had to give up the search. Had he continued into the Arctic seas, in his flimsy craft, chances are that the story and the life of Drake would have ended in the cold polar waters.

The ship had all the treasures it could carry and the men wanted to return home to spend their booty. Many of them argued that the simplest way would be to sail south and make their way back through the Strait of Magellan. But Drake was taking no chances on running into a Spanish fleet expecting him to do just that. His decision was a bold one, as usual. Drake headed across the Pacific, direct for the Moluccas, in the East Indies. After a long and arduous voyage, the *Golden Hind* at last sailed into Plymouth, the richest treasure ship ever to reach England. His reputation was made, for Drake was the second man and the first Englishman to circumnavigate the globe. For this brilliant deed he was knighted Sir Francis Drake by Queen Elizabeth.

The loss inflicted by Drake's raid on the west coast of New Spain was slight compared with the havoc and confusion he caused among the colonies in Panama, Peru, and Chile. Troops were rushed to fortify weak ports, the treasure ships changed their routes, and many cursed the name of Magellan for ever having discovered the strait that now menaced their security. Along the Chilean coast, trade was paralyzed for a long time. Small vessels were afraid to venture to sea, and serious food shortages arose in many cities.

What the Spaniards feared most, other adventurers who would follow in the wake of the *Golden Hind*, came to pass altogether too soon. In 1586, Thomas Cavendish sailed through the Strait of Magellan. After raiding towns along the coast, he headed west and home, the third man to sail around the world. Richard Hawkins, in 1594, had the bad luck to run into a Spanish fleet; he was captured and sent to Spain and prison.

This victory over Hawkins gave heart to the Spaniards, but only for a brief spell. In 1600, the notorious Dutch pirate, Van Noort, looted and burned Valparaíso. It was Van Noort who introduced the good colonists of Chile to the many cruelties of the true pirate, including the buccaneers' ceremonial of making their victims walk the plank. This Dutchman was bad enough in himself, but what was worse, the word of his rich hauls spread and brought on a veritable deluge of pirates of all nations.

The haunt of the pirates of the west coast was the island of Juan Fernández, now a possession of Chile. On this Pacific island, they met to divide their loot and to provision with water and meat. The meat was provided by the herds of wild goats that inhabited the island. Early in the eighteenth century, the notorious pirate, Dampier, put in with several ships at Juan Fernández, where a member of the crew of one of the pirate vessels had a quarrel with his captain. As punishment, he was marooned on the island. He remained there alone for 4 years, until he was rescued in 1709 by Captain Woodes Rogers of the English privateer *Duke*. Curiously enough, Dampier was Rogers' pilot at the time. The name of this marooned sailor was Alexander Selkirk. It is believed that it was his experience that gave Daniel Defoe the inspiration for his immortal novel, *Robinson Crusoe*. The Chilean-owned island of Juan Fernández is perhaps better known today as Robinson Crusoe Island.

As was pointed out earlier in this chapter, the Peace of Quillin was signed between the Araucanians and the Spanish in Chile in 1640. At that time, the Indians agreed to help the Spaniards in fighting the buccaneers and pirates that were making life short and uncertain along the coast. This peace with the Indians was broken many times in the years that followed, but gradually the fights between the Spaniards and the Indians became less frequent and less intense. By 1766, when the Indians were allowed representation in the government, Chile was an established, prosperous, and thriving dependency of the viceroyalty of Peru. In 1788, Ambrose O'Higgins was appointed governor of Chile, an event that is significant both as an interpretation of the history of his time and as a preamble of history to come.

Ambrose, or Ambrosio O'Higgins, the father of Bernardo O'Higgins, the Liberator of Chile, was born in Ireland in 1720 and came to Buenos Aires, Argentina, in 1758. As a trader he made his way across the Andes to Chile. There, because of his engineering training, he was awarded some army contracts. After this came a commission in the army, followed by distinguished service, which was recognized by his appointment as governor of the colony.

The important factor in this appointment is that it shows how widespread liberal ideas were in Chile at an early date. If there had not been a tendency toward democracy throughout the colony, it would have been impossible for an Irish immigrant to rise from a humble trader to attain the highest office in Chile. Ambrose O'Higgins harbored no thoughts of independence, but he was liberal in his views and his uppermost thought was the good of his adopted country. During his rule many notable improvements were completed in Chile, including new roads and bridges, the rebuilding of forts, and peace with the Araucanian Indians, whose fight for independence persisted until it finally mingled with that of the Chileans themselves a few years later. At the age of seventy-six, Ambrose O'Higgins was appointed to the most exalted post in New Spain, the viceroyalty of Peru, which office he held until his death in 1801.

The background to the struggle for independence in Chile —injustices, trade restrictions, abuses on the part of Spain— is practically identical with that of the other Spanish American colonies already discussed and does not need repeating here.

Chile's fight for freedom centers around Bernardo O'Higgins, who was born in Chillán on August 20, 1778. He was sent to school in England where young O'Higgins met Miranda, the famous Venezuelan patriot and forerunner of Simon Bolivar. As a pupil of Miranda, O'Higgins absorbed his first ideas of liberty. On English soil was born his determination to dedicate his life to liberate his people. On the death of his famous father, O'Higgins returned to his native land and took up the cause of independence in earnest.

The movement for freedom in Chile had been gaining momentum and swelling like a balloon, needing only a pinprick to burst. The collapse occurred when news reached Santiago that Buenos Aires had deposed its royal governor and declared its independence on May 25, 1810. The governor of Chile at the time, General Carrasco, was willing to work with the junta, or popular assembly of Buenos Aires, and to extend the movement into Chile, but he was duty bound to

read, at an open assembly, a request from the exiled Ferdinand VII that Chile swear loyalty to Emperor Napoleon, who
had driven him from his throne.

The people of Santiago defiantly refused to recognize the
authority of Napoleon. On September 18, 1810, the royal
governor was ousted and a popular provisional government
set up, with the liberal Conde de la Conquista, who had been
governor of Chile in 1772, as its head. Although this government defied the Viceroy of Peru, it nominally claimed loyalty
to the throneless Ferdinand of Spain.

Conquista died a few months later, and was succeeded by
Dr. Juan Martínez, who called elections for a popular congress of Chile, to be held in 1811. This election was the signal
for open strife among a number of opposing factions. When the
first congress assembled in Santiago in July, 1811, Bernardo
O'Higgins was the deputy from Chillán. He soon became the
leader of a strong party that opposed the central Chile group
of Santiago, headed by José Miguel Carrera.

Internal quarrels occupied the legislators of independence
until December, when three Carrera brothers with the army
to back them up, assumed control of the government.
José Miguel Carrera dismissed the congress, exiled Dr.
Martínez to Mendoza, and placed himself as chief of government and president of a new junta. The cities of Valdivia and
Concepción set up rival popular councils. Bitter enmity and
heated accusations disrupted the entire movement for the
time being, and was no doubt watched with grim satisfaction
from the palace of the Viceroy of Peru in Lima.

Spain had no intention of losing Chile as a colony so easily,
and while the patriots were fighting among themselves, a
strong army was sent down from Peru to quell the rebellion.
But Spain had not counted on the underlying unity of the
bickering patriots. They forgot their disputes in order to face
the common foe in battle at Yerbas Buenas, about 15 miles
from Talca. With O'Higgins commanding the patriot force

in the field, the royalist army of General Pareja was defeated. Independence in Chile had won its first battle.

While José Carrera was away from Santiago with the army, the popular assembly took away his powers and voted complete control to General O'Higgins. But Carrera did not give up. The two factions continued their fight for control of the young government of free Chile. Then, in 1814, the arrival of another royalist army from Peru brought the two rivals together again. On October 1, 1814, the patriot army under O'Higgins met the Spanish forces of the king at Rancagua, where the cause of Chilean independence suffered a terrible defeat. So complete was the victory of the Spanish army that the patriots, expecting no mercy, fled over the Andes to Mendoza, where the Argentine General José San Martín was organizing his Army of the Andes. How O'Higgins and San Martín joined forces there is told in the chapter on Argentina.

The actual declaration of Chilean independence was not proclaimed until February 12, 1818, the first anniversary of the battle of Chacabuco, where the famous Army of the Andes, under San Martín and O'Higgins, defeated the royalists. Two months later, on April 5, the liberation of Chile was assured by the glorious victory of Maipo. General O'Higgins was wounded early in the battle, but despite his wounds, he displayed such courage and heroism in leading his men to victory as to make him forever the greatest national hero of Chile.

When the constitution of free Chile was adopted in October, 1819, Bernardo O'Higgins was elected governor with supreme authority. Then came the final campaign to drive the royalists out of their Peruvian stronghold. In this, the final victory of independence, San Martín and O'Higgins shared the honors with the admiral of the brave little Chilean navy, Lord Cochrane, whose daring and naval genius played an important part in the liberation of half of South America.

Diego de Almagro was the first European to explore Chile when he marched south from Peru in 1535, but the famous Portuguese navigator, Ferdinand Magellan, landed in Chile 15 years before, after his epic discovery of the westward passage from the Atlantic to the Pacific through the strait that today bears his name. With four ships, Magellan entered the strait from Atlantic waters in 1520 and began exploring the many channels, always working westward, hoping against hope that he would find an outlet to the Pacific.

During the lonely nights, Magellan saw a great number of fires burning across the land to the south of the strait. He named it Tierra del Fuego (Land of Fires). The reason for these fires was that some of the Indians of the section, although they had fires, did not know how to make fire anew, therefore never dared let their precious flames go out. On November 28, 1520, Magellan, after 5 weeks of battling headwinds and current, cleared Cape Deseado, and entered upon the Pacific.

In the years immediately following Magellan's voyages, there were many attempts to sail west through the newly discovered passage. In 1526 the Loaysa expedition with Captain del Cano, who had been with Magellan, as pilot, made the passage. In 1540, Alonso de Camargo, who made the voyage with the object of opening up a sea route to the coasts of Chile and Peru, was the first to reach Peru by way of the Strait of Magellan. Then, for almost forty years, the strait was empty of ships and sails until Francis Drake sailed through it on the wings of a wind that was an ill one for the Spaniards of the west coast.

The first effort to establish a colony in the Strait of Magellan was made by Spain in 1584 when Pedro Sarmiento founded the town of King Philip. The colony was a dismal failure and lasted only a few years. For many generations it was believed that colonization was impossible in the rigorous climate of the strait, but today, only a few miles north of Port Famine, stands the prosperous city of Punta Arenas, in justification of

Pedro Sarmiento's belief that a colony could live and prosper there.

During the century following its discovery, the Strait of Magellan became an increasingly important communicating link between the two great oceans. As a waterway, it became the almost exclusive route of ships owned by the rich, powerful, and dictatorial Dutch East India Company. Since only members of the company could sail through the strait, or, for that matter, around the tip of Africa, independent merchants and mariners found themselves facing a closed door so far as trade with the Spice Islands of the east were concerned. Among those who objected to this situation was Jacques Le Maire, a merchant of the city of Hoorn in Holland. Sharing this resentment was William Schouten, a veteran navigator who had sailed three times to the Indies. Both believed that as there was a way to sail to the Spice Islands around the bottom of Africa, so there must be a way to sail around the bottom of South America.

With the help of money raised by the people of Hoorn, Le Maire and Schouten outfitted an expedition. In the summer of 1615, the Dutch Captain sailed from Holland. On January 29, 1616, Captain Schouten sailed around the tip of South America and called the southermost wave-swept, wind-blown rocky point, Cape Horn, in honor of his native city.

This discovery was not so easily accomplished as this reads. When he reached the region of the Horn, Schouten and his men had to fight biting cold, razor-sharp winds, icy rain, and hail. As a matter of fact, in January, 1616, Captain Schouten was about to give up in despair. In his log, he wrote that his ship met "mighty waves that came rolling along before the wind." It was unlike anything he had ever experienced before. The howling wind all but tore his ship apart; the driving sleet cut into the faces of the sailors like thousands of knives; the seas were like mountains. But through it all, stout old

Schouten held his course until, at last, the furies of Cape Horn were behind him and he was safe on smooth Pacific waters.

The history of Cape Horn and those who have rounded it since that day of discovery would fill volumes, most of them telling the same tale of shipwreck and disaster, of hardship and suffering. Cape Horn can be gentle, but its peaceful moods are rare. More often, Cape Horn is in a stormy temper, demanding offerings of drowned sailors, wrecked ships, shredded canvas, and jettisoned cargoes.

At an early date after its discovery, Cape Horn became the gateway for exploration, conquest, and sea trade into the Pacific. The California gold rush of 1849 gave the fast Yankee clippers their most severe tests, and rounding the Horn they proved their worth to all the world.

Although Cape Horn is 1,300 miles farther south than Cape of Good Hope at the tip of Africa, it was a timesaver for ships bound for the Orient. Countless Yankee captains took the greater risks of sailing around old "Cape Stiff." In this battle between men and nature, the Cape won out time and again. In 1909, a vessel bound for a Chilean port from Argentina by way of Cape Horn was forced to turn east and go by way of Cape of Good Hope, taking 207 days instead of the 2 weeks' journey around Cape Horn.

In the roster of those who have given battle to old "Cape Stiff" are some of the greatest names in the annals of the sea: Anson, Cook, Gray, Dana, Melville.

There is no exaggerating the importance of Cape Horn to the United States before roads and railways opened up the west. It was the one connecting link between the two extremes of the young, growing, expanding nation. Cape Horn was the focal point of coast-to-coast trade and commerce until the Panama Canal was opened in 1914. Then old "Cape Stiff" retired, but even today, it stands ready to challenge any sailor venturesome enough to want a real battle with the elements. Her weapons are many and cruel: cold, salt, stinging seas;

bleak, roaring, howling, westerly winds; hail and sleet and snow that keep decks a sheet of ice; gloomy black clouds that rest on the tops of the spewing waves; huge and treacherous icebergs rising to heights of 1,500 feet—all standard features of the Cape. Yes, truly Cape Horn and the Strait of Magellan deserve their titles of Seas of Storm and Stress.

CHAPTER 13

The Realm of the Inca

Highlights of Peru

Discovered: By Pascual de Andagoya in 1522. Conquest for Spain by Francisco Pizarro begun in 1532.

Population: 6,762,881.

Area: 482,258 square miles.

Language: Spanish.   *Capital:* Lima.

Government: Seceded from Spain in July, 1821. Republic established in 1824.

Geographical Characteristics: Peru's main geographical feature is a high plateau traversed by three chains of the Andes Mountains which attain heights of more than 22,000 feet. The narrow strip of coastal land is mostly desert but the valleys between the mountains and the high plateau are very fertile.

Climatic Conditions: From the coast, where it rains but once in a lifetime, the climate changes with altitude.

Principal Products: Mineral ores and concentrates, petroleum and derivatives, llama and vicuña wool, sugar, gold, silver, copper, and cotton.

STRADDLING the boundary line between Bolivia and Peru, at a height of 12,000 feet among the towering, snow-capped peaks of the Andes, lies one of the world's loftiest lakes, the famous Lake Titicaca. It is the legendary birthplace of the Children of the Sun, the rulers of the ancient Inca people.

According to timeless Inca legends, it was on the sacred Island of Titicaca in this lake that Manco Capac and Mama Ocllo, his wife, were spoken to by their father, the Sun God, and told to go out into the land and instruct the savage tribes in religion and the arts. The Sun God gave Manco Capac a magic golden wedge and told him that the wedge would leave his hand and sink into the ground when they reached the site where they were to build a city.

According to tradition, the two Children of the Sun traveled northwest from the western shore of the lake until they reached a place where the wedge flew out of Manco's hand and sank deep into the earth. Manco Capac and his wife settled there and began instructing the savages in the various arts and in the worship of the Sun. Soon a great city rose. It was called Cuzco and here Manco Capac founded the mighty Empire of the Sun.

Tradition places this coming of the first Inca and the founding of the city of Cuzco at about the year one thousand. But the studies of archaeologists reveal that three distinct civilizations flourished in Peru hundreds of years before that time: the Chimu of the coastal plains, the Tiahuanacans of the highlands, and the Chancas of the northern forests. What happened to these earlier cultures we do not know, but on their ruins the Incas built their remarkable empire.

There has been much speculation as to what sort of people the early Tiahuanacans were. They lived in the highlands around Lake Titicaca and built massive stone buildings and temples. They have been called the Big Stone people because of the large boulders they used in their buildings. But their period is one of darkness that, so far, has not been touched by the searching beam of history.

The story of Peru, as we know it, begins over nine hundred years ago with the half-legendary, half-historical Manco Capac who became the Sapa or Chief Inca, of the Quechua tribe in Cuzco. Originally, the word Inca was the title of the king, or ruler. But, through popular usage, it came to be used both for the people and for the territory they occupied. The first Inca made his family supreme in the vicinity of Cuzco. He was followed by a long line of rulers, each of whom extended the boundaries of the Inca Empire. At the death of the Inca Huayna Capac, around the year 1528, the vast realm spread itself almost 2,300 miles from Colombia south to the River Maule in Chile. It was larger than the Roman Empire before Caesar.

The supreme and absolute ruler over this huge domain of nearly 400,000 square miles, with a population of around 15 million people, was the Sapa, or Chief Inca. The form of government was a pure despotism. The Inca was head of the priesthood, the maker and interpreter of laws, and commander of the army. As the direct descendant of the Sun, he owned everything and everyone. He was God.

The Inca Empire was rich in gold, but gold was not used as money. The metal was held precious because its yellow brilliance was associated with the Sun and because it was soft and could readily be worked into images and objects for both religious and practical uses. The accumulation of gold throughout the 400 years of Inca rule in the form of plates, idols, ornaments, and utensils of all sorts, was enormous beyond belief. All this golden treasure, as everything else, belonged to the Inca.

The genius of the Incas was for conquest and political organization rather than skill in the arts and crafts, although they did achieve an amazingly high degree of culture. The lands of the realm were divided into three parts. One part was set aside for the Inca, another for the support of priests and temples, and the third for the people. All lands were worked by the people in common. Those of the Sun were tended first; next those of the old and sick, of widows, orphans, and soldiers away from home, then the common peoples' own land; and, lastly, the lands of the Inca.

There was no money in Inca Land, and taxes were paid for in work or produce. Surplus foods were stored by the Inca in royal warehouses and distributed free to the needy in time of famine. Wool and cotton were given to the women as they were needed for making clothing for their families. There was no such thing as personal property to be handed down from parents to their children, except in the case of the Inca, of course.

As a result of this socialistic setup with no money, little trade, and almost nothing that could be called fixed property, there were few criminals in ancient Peru and not much need for laws. Those laws that did exist were harsh. Theft, murder, blasphemy against the Sun, and tampering with the irrigation system or burning a bridge were punishable by immediate death. The entire town of a lawbreaker was also punished, which acted as a great curb on crime. A high degree of peace was maintained throughout the land by the drastic method of completely destroying any rebellious city or province and exterminating its people.

The acquisition of new peoples and lands was a business-like procedure. In the conquest of a new province, the idols were taken as hostages to Cuzco. The chiefs were also brought to the Inca capital and there entertained while they were instructed in the Inca way of life and religion. When it was thought that these alien chiefs had been converted to the new way and order, they returned to their peoples where they ruled and behaved as they had been taught during their training course at Cuzco. No doubt the Inca's standing army of some 200,000 armed warriors helped in persuading conquered chiefs to subscribe to the laws of the Inca. In other cases, entire conquered peoples were moved into lands already under the Inca sway, while loyal Inca subjects were moved into the newly acquired territory.

Work was a virtue in the Inca Empire. Waste and idleness were crimes. There were government departments for the conservation of wild life, and for the preservation of the forests. Children were selected for careers at an early age. Marriage was compulsory. There was no unemployment. All in all, it was an ideal state of existence, except for one thing: The machinelike regimentation stifled all initiative and freedom of action among the millions of subjects of the Inca despot—a flaw in the system that was to prove its downfall.

The Incas fell short of the Mayas and Aztecs of Mexico in the higher intellectual culture. They had no written method of communication and only a crude knowledge of astronomy. On the other hand, they surpassed their northern neighbors in agriculture, the textile arts, and the construction of public works such as roads, canals, and aqueducts.

They were, for instance, master builders in stone, as remains of buildings still standing in Peru today testify. Their temples and palaces were constructed of stone blocks, some of huge size, weighing up to 20 and 30 tons apiece. How these enormous stones were transported dozens of miles and lifted to great heights to their places on top of buildings is a mystery as great as that of how the pyramids of Egypt were built. One suggestion is that an inclined plane was built at the side of the building and the massive blocks of stone were moved up inch by inch by means of levers. These great blocks of stone were perfectly fitted together without the use of mortar and clay. There are walls standing today in which not even a thin penknife blade can be forced between the stones.

The Inca civilization probably reached its highest level in agriculture. Their method of growing crops was scientific farming in every sense of the word. Among the chief crops were corn, yams, bananas, peanuts, tobacco, beans, and various native fruits. All these were grown under the greatest difficulties.

Nature offered little land for the Incas to cultivate. One part of the country is a roller coaster of rugged mountains, while the entire coastal region is mainly a vast desert where rain falls barely once in a lifetime. But the Incas overcame these handicaps in a way and on a scale that is truly remarkable. In the highlands, they lined the mountains with stone terraces and soil was laboriously carried up from the valleys. Thus, rich farms were literally built on the steep mountainsides.

The elaborate and gigantic irrigation system by which the Incas transformed their coastal deserts into fertile fields and growing gardens remains even today as a monument to their extraordinary engineering genius. Water from mountain streams and lakes was diverted into canals and carried for great distances to the coast. There the life-giving liquid was diverted into a complex network of irrigation canals. To store water during the highland's rainy season against the eternal coastal draught, huge reservoirs were built. In the valley of Nepena one reservoir was ¾ mile long and 1½ miles wide, with a massive stone dam 80 feet thick. One aqueduct alone is said to have had a capacity of 60 million cubic feet of water a day!

Farms, thus artificially created, were carefully tended and the soil enriched by adding small fish or guano, the bird fertilizer imported from the small islands off the coast of Peru. The ground was broken by a pointed stick drawn through the earth, the nearest thing to a plow found by the Spaniards in America. Men pulled the plow but women followed in the furrow, and broke up the bigger clods.

It was in large-scale public works such as this, and in road building, that the Incas outshone all other native American peoples. The Great Inca Road—a 2,300-mile highway from Quito down to Chile—ranks with the Great Wall of China as an engineering feat. Much of it was cut through solid rock. Deep ravines were crossed by swinging bridges. Some of these bridges were 400 feet long. A large part of this highway was 15 feet wide and paved with stones. Across the deserts where the shifting sands would bury any road, tall stakes were put up to guide travelers.

Over this magnificent road passed a steady and diverse stream of Inca traffic. Chiefs were carried in sedan chairs by servants. Every 10 miles there were tambos, or resthouses, with occasional more elaborate royal inns to serve the Inca when he made his frequent tours of the kingdom. Storehouses, well filled with food to supply armies on the march, lined the highway. At 5-mile intervals, runners were stationed as a part of the efficient express service of the Inca. Relays of these runners could cover the 1,000 miles from Cuzco to Quito in less than 8 days, and there is a record of the time having been cut down to 5 days in an emergency. By this means fresh fish, game, and fruits were rushed to the Inca's royal table from all parts of the empire.

Coordinating with this messenger service was a system of beacon fires for use when urgent news had to be sent from some remote point in the empire to the Inca. Using smoke by day and flame by night, this telegraph system could flash the news of an uprising a thousand miles away to Cuzco in a matter of hours.

It is strange that with a road like this, the Incas never hit upon the idea of the wheel as an easy means of transportation and hauling heavy loads over long distances. This failure to invent the wheel was a lack the Incas shared in common with all the other Indians in the Americas. Master potters as they were, they did not even use the wheel in their pottery making.

But the Incas did have the distinction of being the only people of the New World who domesticated a beast of burden, the llama, a small member of the camel family. This animal was used to transport cargoes over long distances. It also explains why the armies of the Inca were so powerful. With these llamas to carry supplies, the conquering troops were able to extend the empire in all directions. A llama could carry a 100-pound load from 10 to 12 miles a day, thus releasing man power for other work.

Two other animals, both of the camel family, played an

important part in the daily life of ancient Peru. These were the vicuña and the alpaca. They roamed wild in large numbers in mountain pastures belonging to the Inca. Every 4 years, great herds of them were driven into enclosures and sheared for their soft and valuable wool. Some were then killed and the skins and flesh divided among the people. The rest were set free until the next roundup.

Because they had the fine wool of the vicuña and alpaca the Incas developed their textile art to a high degree, some examples of which in weaving, color, and design have no rival even today. The spinning of thread from the wool of these animals was a very important part in the life of the women. Wherever they went, they always carried workbaskets, spinning fine threads as they walked or gossiped.

Although the Incas did not have any written form of communication or recording, they did have an unusual system of keeping accounts by means of a series of knotted cords, called quipus. A quipu consisted of a main cord to which were attached several hanging cords of different colors. Knots tied in these hanging cords at different levels, according to a sort of decimal system, served admirably for keeping the simple accounts needed for the Incas. Some of these quipus, however, were extremely complex, and specially trained Quipacamayas, or Keepers of the Knots, were needed to interpret them.

The Incas became expert metalworkers. They knew how to cast from molds and beat plates and cups from single sheets. They discovered the art of soldering and of plating or gilding a base metal with one more precious. The Inca craftsmen worked equally well in gold, silver, copper, or lead. They also had found that bronze, a combination of copper and tin, made a substance much harder and more serviceable than copper alone. Thus they used bronze in place of iron or steel.

Peruvian silver was mined in pits, while most of the gold was taken out of streams. In the dry season, the Incas built dams across rivers and creeks. These dams caught the gold-laden gravel when rains made the waterways run high. The gold was taken out the following dry season when the waters ran low again. Needless to say, both these precious metals were found in great quantities, but, as the mining of gold and silver was quite laborious, the people employed at this occupation were required to work only a few months a year.

Such was the vast and rich empire inherited by Huayna Capac—the last of the great Incas. He had added considerably to the realm himself, until it was so large that he could not keep in as close contact with his people as had been the custom of his ancestors. There was some unrest in the more remote regions. Some students believe that the Inca Empire had already passed its greatest glory by the time the conquistadors appeared on the horizon. In 1524, Huayna Capac, feeling that his end was near, summoned to his bedside his two favorite sons, Huascar and Atahualpa. Huayna loved both his sons, and wanted to make them both Incas. This he did by giving Huascar, his legitimate heir, the greater part of the empire, while he directed that his favorite, Atahualpa, should rule the northern kingdom of Quito. Having made this decision, Huayna Capac died. It is said that some 4,000 faithful women, pages, and servants, voluntarily gave up life and were buried with him.

Hardly had the period of mourning for the deceased Inca come to an end before civil wars broke out, Atahualpa sent 30,000 warriors against Huascar, who was defeated and taken prisoner by Atahualpa, who then assumed the royal title of Sapa Inca and settled down to rest on his hard-earned laurels. He was not to enjoy his glory for long.

As early as 1530, two strange bearded men with light skins are said to have come to the court of Atahualpa. They said they were Spanish sailors and told the Inca strange stories about a great king across a great sea. As they talked, Atahualpa probably remembered an ancient Inca legend that told how a stranger, fair of skin and beard, would one day come and destroy the people of the Incas. What happened to these two Spaniards, no one knows. Then, 2 years later, in 1532, news was brought to the Inca that a small army of these strangers was advancing from the coast toward his encampment outside Caxamarca. Atahualpa waited, half-curious, half-afraid, not being able to make up his mind what action to take. While he waited, this strange little band made its way across the mountains, led by Francisco Pizarro.

Francisco Pizarro was fifty years old when his great moment came. He was uneducated, of poor birth, and had been a swineherd in his youth. He came to Panama in 1510 and served in the Spanish army. His courage and ability as a soldier gained him the rank of captain.

On the momentous day of September 29, 1513, Pizarro was one of the small band of men who, with Balboa, were the first white men to sight the gleaming expanse of the Pacific Ocean. What probably interested Captain Pizarro more than the vast stretch of blue ocean was the hint of an Indian chief that there were lands of much gold to the south.

In 1522, Pascual de Andagoya arrived in Panama with news that he had reached a region to the south called Biru (Peru). He also brought definite information that a great rich Empire of the Incas existed. Andagoya discovered Peru, but with the news of his discovery, he passes out of the Peruvian picture and yields first place to Francisco Pizarro, who decided that the time had come for him to get his hands on some of the New World's riches. But expeditions cost money— and Pizarro was not rich. Therefore he took into partnership an old friend, Diego de Almagro, a few years his senior and a veteran New World campaigner, and Father Hernando de Luque, who besides having great influence in Spain and Panama, was the agent of the millionaire-banker, Gaspar de Espinosa. The three signed a compact, or rather Father

Luque did, for neither Pizarro nor Almagro could write. They only marked their crosses at the bottom of the famous contract that was the first step in the downfall of the Inca Empire and the beginning of the Spanish conquest of Peru.

In November, 1524, Pizarro sailed southward for Peru. He was followed a short time later by Almagro. This first attempt was a dismal failure. Both men returned the following year after months of suffering which had taken them only as far as the San Juan River, just north of Buenaventura, Colombia. But a small quantity of gold had been obtained.

Their second expedition, which set out in November, 1526, was a bit more pretentious. It consisted of two ships carrying 160 men and besides the two leaders, Pizarro and Almagro, one Bartolomé Estrada, who went along as pilot and navigator. At the San Juan River, the expedition split up. Pizarro went ashore to see what he could find in the soggy jungles of Colombia. Almagro took one ship back to Panama for fresh supplies and recruits. Estrada sailed southward in the other vessel to explore the coast line.

One day, off the Peruvian port of Tumbes, Pilot Estrada sighted a strange sort of sailing raft bearing Indians who wore ornaments of gold and garments of finely woven cloth. This craft, made of a peculiarly buoyant wood, interested the pilot, as did the Indian passengers, who were the first people of the Inca encountered by the expedition. After Estrada had satisfied his curiosity, taken some gold ornaments, and captured some of the Indians for the purpose of training them as interpreters, he turned his ship about and sailed northward to rejoin Pizarro.

One can readily imagine with what joy the tales of the pilot were received by Pizarro, who had met with nothing more encouraging than Indian arrows, insects, hunger, and disease-ridden swamps. The Inca Empire that had a few years before been only a rumor, was now a reality beyond question. The moment Almagro arrived from Panama, the Spaniards headed southward. But adverse winds made progress impossible, and they were forced to make a halt at the Island of Gallo.

At this time, Pizarro's followers, ill and hungry and having seen little of the promised gold, threatened to go back to Panama. Instead of shouting at them or pleading with them, Pizarro took out his sword, drew a line in the earth, and said: "Friends and comrades. On that side of this line lies Peru and riches. On this side of the line lies Panama and poverty. Choose each man for himself. For my part, I go south!"

With those words, Pizarro crossed the line in the direction of Peru. Thirteen men followed his lead and this small but determined band made its way on a raft to the Island of Gorgona. There they remained, suffering all kinds of hardships until a small vessel from Panama reached them many months later.

Again they sailed southward, toward Tumbes, where an Inca official invited the Spaniards ashore. Pizarro did not go ashore himself, but sent two of his men. They came back open-eyed with stories of a large city, gold-plated temples, forts, and armed soldiers. Pizarro was at last satisfied that he had struck gold. After a little more exploring, he returned to Panama, taking with him, from Tumbes, an Indian named Felipillo. This native was later to become Pizarro's chief interpreter and one of the greatest scoundrels in the wrecking of the Empire of the Incas.

When Pizarro returned to Panama from Tumbes, he found strong opposition to his idea of going to Peru again with a larger expedition. The Spanish governor was openly hostile and it became necessary for Pizarro to go to Spain to get the direct approval of the king for his proposed conquest of the Inca Empire. On July 26, 1529, after many trials and tribulations, including being thrown into jail for old debts, Pizarro at last received the royal commission for the conquest of Peru. Some time, in addition to a great deal of difficulty, was involved in getting an expedition together. Not until early in

1530 did Pizarro sail from Spain. At Panama, there were more delays. The actual start for Peru did not get under way until January, 1531.

When the expedition at last sailed south from Panama City, there were plenty of Pizarros in it. Besides Francisco, there were his three brothers, Hernando, Juan, and Gonzalo Pizarro, as well as a half brother and a cousin. The party consisted of 200 men and a few horses. Among the priests who sailed, Father Vincent Valverde was to play a prominent role in the drama about to be enacted in the realm of the Inca. Almagro, as on previous occasions, remained behind to gather together additional men and supplies.

Time could not have seemed very golden to Pizarro. At any rate, more than a year and a half passed before the Peruvian conquest actually began. After various adventures along the coast of Peru, Pizarro learned that Atahualpa, the Inca, was encamped at Caxamarca, fairly near the coast. Pizarro knew that in war, as in chess, the way to win is to corner the king, and he promptly set out for the royal encampment with his band of 190 stalwart Spaniards. That was on September 24, 1532.

Among Pizarro's captains was Hernando de Soto, who later was to discover the Mississippi River. This gallant explorer was sent ahead of Pizarro's main party. He returned with the first eyewitness account of the might and splendor of the Incas. He also brought word that Atahualpa had just defeated his brother in war and that the Inca Empire was in a state of unrest. That was indeed good news for Pizarro, who ordered his little army to march forward.

When the Spaniards reached Caxamarca on November 15, 1532, the city was deserted. But on a hillside beyond, Atahualpa and an army of 40,000 soldiers were encamped. On the following day, Saturday, November 16, the Inca, at Pizarro's insistent invitation, came to Caxamarca, borne on a golden litter and accompanied by several thousand soldiers. In accordance with orders from Pizarro, the Spaniards were hidden in the houses around the city square. With muskets primed and their swords drawn, they watched their leader, waiting for the signal to attack.

The only Spaniard who went out to greet the Inca was Father Valverde. Through an interpreter he told Atahualpa that he must, on the spot, become a Christian and accept the authority of the Spanish King. When the Inca laughed scornfully and knocked a Bible from the priest's hand, Pizarro gave the signal to strike. With their battle cry of "Santiago, and at them!" the handful of Spanish cavalry and foot soldiers rushed out of the houses and fell upon the surprised Inca forces. In the battle that followed, Atahualpa played his last role as Inca in the drama of the New World. When it was over, some 2,000 of the Indians had been killed and Atahualpa was Pizarro's prisoner.

To all intents and purposes, Peru was conquered by the Spanish on that day. The Incas, untrained in initiative, were lost. For so many generations had the people of Peru blindly obeyed orders that they were no better than puppets without their leader, and from that day on, Francisco Pizarro and his followers pulled the strings.

Three days after his capture, Atahualpa astounded Pizarro and his companions by offering to ransom himself by filling a room 22 feet long and 17 feet wide with gold as high as he could reach, in addition to filling two smaller rooms twice over with silver. Hardly believing their eyes or ears, the Spaniards nevertheless drew up a contract that was approved by the Inca on the spot. Then began such a series of gold shipments as Midas may have dreamed of. From all over Inca-land came an almost continuous stream of llamas and men weighted down with gold in every shape and form to be poured into the famous ransom room. It was not until May 3, almost six months later, that Pizarro was satisfied that the Inca had lived up to his promise and announced the royal ransom paid in full. Still

Atahualpa was not released, although he had paid many millions of dollars worth of gold and silver for his freedom.

Pizarro's partner, Almagro, had by this time come from Panama with much-needed supplies, additional horses, and more men who were thirsting for gold. On the Inca side, Huascar, the rightful heir to the Inca throne, had been mysteriously murdered in Antamarca, where he had been held a prisoner by his brother Atahualpa. Perhaps it was the death of Huascar that gave some of the Spanish captains the idea that if they did away with Atahualpa, there would be no Inca chief to lead the Indians in a revolt. Who first had the idea is not known, but the interpreter Felipillo helped matters along to their tragic climax. He spread rumors that Atahualpa, whom he hated, was secretly plotting to lead his people against the conquerors. The result was that Atahualpa, after a mock trial, was executed on August 29, 1533. It was later proven by De Soto that Felipillo's charges were false, but it was too late. Atahualpa had been killed. This last detail in the conquest of Peru completed, the Spaniards began squabbling among themselves.

Almagro had never trusted his partner Pizarro any too much, and now he suspected that Francisco was planning to take both gold and glory for himself and his brothers, half brother, and cousin. So when Hernando Pizarro went to Spain with the king's royal fifth of the Inca's ransom, Almagro quietly sent an agent of his own. The outcome was that when Hernando returned to Peru with royal titles and honors for Francisco Pizarro, including a marquisate and vast grants of land in New Castile, Almagro also received for his services rights to explore and conquer an almost equally vast territory to the south. This territory was called New Toledo, while the lands granted to Pizarro were called New Castile. The vagueness of the dividing line between these two territories soon led to open warfare between Pizarro and Almagro.

The focal point of the dispute was the Incas' capital city of

Cuzco, which, as early as 1533, had been looted by the Spaniards. Was it in New Castile and the property of Pizarro? Or was it in New Toledo and the property of Almagro? In 1535, a stalemate peace was made and Almagro set out on an ill-fated expedition to explore New Toledo from Peru far into Chile.

In the meantime, Pizarro had decided Cuzco was not the ideal capital for the Spanish, as it was too far from the coast. After some debate, a large level plain on a river in the Rimac Valley was selected as the city site by Pizarro. It was convenient to the parts of the Inca Empire the Spaniards most wanted to be in contact with and was only a few miles from the excellent harbor of Callao. On January 6, 1535, the City of the Kings was founded, better known as Lima, a Spanish corruption of the Inca word *Rimac*.

The expedition of Almagro to his southern domain resulted only in death, suffering, disappointment, and disillusion. Neither gold nor silver was found to pay for the hardships of crossing the snow-clad Andes inadequately clothed, of marching wearily across unknown country among hostile Indians. Some members of the expedition got as far south as present-day Santiago, Chile. Almagro set out in July, 1535. He returned to Cuzco in April, 1537, where more troubles awaited him at the hands of the Pizarros. Almagro's first thought was to secure his rights and fortune for his young son, Diego, known to history as Almagro the Lad. At his side, and loyal to Almagro, were the stout companions of his southern misadventure who called themselves the Men of Chile.

By this time, a half brother of the murdered Atahualpa, Manco by name, had been raised to the Inca throne by Pizarro, who intended using him as a puppet to subdue the Inca nation. This Manco proved to be less docile than Pizarro had expected. Over a period of years, he caused the Spaniards no end of trouble, besieging Cuzco, leading his Indian army in repeated attacks against the white men, waylaying Spanish traffic on the Inca Road, and generally harassing the invaders. But the people of Peru were too cowed and broken in spirit to rally in sufficient numbers around a ruler, who, at his best, was not a great leader. Years later, Inca Manco was murdered while playing games with a group of Spanish renegades.

Open warfare again broke out between Almagro and the Pizarros over the title to Cuzco, in which the brothers Hernando and Gonzalo Pizarro played important parts. Friends of Almagro advised him to kill the brothers when he had the chance, saying that "the only good Pizarro, was a dead Pizarro." But Almagro still remembered the days in Panama when he and Pizarro signed their first partnership and he hopefully waited for the good old days of friendship to return.

On April 8, 1538, the combined forces of Hernando and Gonzalo attacked an inferior army organized by Almagro, who was so ill at the time that he had to watch the battle from a sickbed. The Almagrites were defeated and Almagro was thrown in prison, where, a short time later, on July 8, he was put to death by the Pizarros.

Before the death and defeat of the elder Almagro, Francisco Pizarro had taken Almagro the Lad with him to Lima on the promise of treating him as a son. Events show that Pizarro had no idea of sharing either companionship or wealth with the son of his old partner.

Francisco Pizarro, wealthy beyond any of his dreams, enjoying the honored title of marquis, was growing old in the City of Kings he had founded. He was aware that he had many enemies, but he had never been a man to have fears, and he went about openly and defied those he knew would gladly kill him, if they dared.

Perhaps Pizzaro would not have been so confident had he known what was going on in the house of Almagro the Lad. This young man, although only nineteen years of age, was the leader of a group of weather-beaten and campaign-hardened veterans of his father's Chilean expedition. Story has it that they were so poor that they possessed but one cloak among them and had to take turns wearing it. For that reason, the populace of Lima saw but one of the Men of Chile abroad at a time.

Poor as they were, these deadly enemies of Pizarro must somehow have begged, borrowed, or stolen twenty more cloaks on June 26, 1541. On that day, as the Marquis Pizarro was eating his Sunday dinner, Juan Herrada and twenty Men of Chile broke into the palace with drawn swords and the cry, "Death to the Tyrant!" on their lips. In the terrific fight that followed, Francisco Pizarro was stabbed to death. Almagro was avenged. The man who, almost singlehanded, had conquered Peru, was at last conquered by a blade of steel.

Pizarro's death brought the days of Inca conquest to a close. They were followed by 300 years of rule under the harsh and rigid Spanish colonial system, with Peru serving as the seat of a vast viceroyalty extending from Panama to Chile. There was great prosperity for Spain, but little for the people of Peru. They were forbidden to trade with foreign countries or even other Spanish colonies. High taxes and oppressive measures were heaped one on the other. The cry for freedom raised its voice, and was encouraged by the success of the North American and French revolutions.

While the revolutionary movement spread rapidly through South America, Peru's participation was delayed because large forces of Spanish troops were permanently stationed at Lima, and thus Peru was among the last colonies to secure its freedom.

Despite this obstacle, futile but valiant attempts at freedom were led by such patriots as Gabriel de Aguilar, Hipólito Unánue, Antonio de Zela, and Mateo Pumacahua. However, it was not until 1820 that the famous general patriot, José de San Martín, after his victories against the Spanish in Argentina and Chile, began his fight to liberate the people of Peru. On July 21, 1821, San Martín and his army entered Lima and on July 28 raised the Peruvian flag and proclaimed the independence of Peru.

But even that did not win liberty for Peru. The country had a large population of royalist die-hards who kept the fires of conflict burning. Not until several years later, on December 9, 1824, did the combined Colombian and Peruvian forces of Simon Bolivar, under the command of General Antonio José de Sucre, defeat the royalists at the battle of Ayacucho, making possible the birth of the new republic of Peru. But, for all practical purposes, freedom from Spain in Peru began on that day in July, 1821, when the Peruvian national flag, for the first time, flew proudly over the roofs of the ancient City of the Kings.

CHAPTER 14

Land on the Roof of America

Highlights of Bolivia

Discovered: By Diego de Almagro for Spain in 1535.

Population: 2,911,283.

Area: 419,470 square miles.

Language: Spanish.   *Capital:* La Paz.

Government: Independence proclaimed on July 16, 1809. Republic established in 1825.

Main Geographical Features: From the loftiest and largest plateau in the Western Hemisphere, truly the roof of America, Bolivia slopes eastward and northward into the jungles and plains of the Amazon Basin and the rivers of La Plata system.

Climatic Conditions: Ranging from tropical heat to Arctic cold.

Principal Products: Coca leaves, quinine bark, rubber, hides, nuts, tin, lead, silver, and other minerals.

BOLIVIA at the time of the Spanish conquest was a part of Collasuyo, the southernmost province of the vast Inca Empire. But long before the first Inca was born, there flourished along the shores of Bolivia's lofty Lake Titicaca a rich and powerful civilization. This period is often referred to as the era of the Big Stone people. Little is known of this race except their ability as builders. Evidences of their skill are huge timeworn statues and the ruins of great stone temples and market places, marking the site of the long-forgotten city of Tiahuanaco.

With the rise of the Incas, the history of Bolivia, as of Peru, begins. The mountain-locked Lake Titicaca is the legendary home of the Quechuas, and birthplace of the mighty Inca dynasty. Along its shores, the Incas built their magnificent palaces and temples. In the mountains of Bolivia, the artisans of ancient Peru dug copper for their tools and mined the gold and silver to decorate their temples and palaces.

The story of the rise of the Inca Empire, and its conquest by a handful of Spaniards under Francisco Pizarro in 1532, is told in the previous chapter. As for the early colonial history of Bolivia, it is virtually identical with that of Peru, except that silver took the place of gold as an incentive for Spanish conquest and oppression of the Indians.

The first Spanish settlement in the country was Paria, near the present Oruro. It was founded by Diego de Almagro in 1535, when he passed through Bolivia on his disastrous march to Chile. Once the Spaniards gained a foothold in Bolivia and the Indians were subdued, life settled down to a cruel and grinding routine of transferring the mineral wealth of the mountains to the coffers of the King of Spain. With the discovery in 1545 of Potosí, one of the richest silver mines the world has ever known, Bolivia quickly overshadowed even golden Peru as Spain's chief source of wealth.

An Indian legend tells that in 1462, 70 years before the coming of Pizarro, the Inca Huayna Capac was returning from his silver mine at Porco. He rested at a tambo or royal inn, on the great Inca road near the foot of Potosí Hill. The innkeeper told the emperor that the hill was rich with a shiny metal "white as moonlight on the waters of Lake Titicaca."

Huayna Capac went to investigate. As he neared the hill, a strange loud voice called his name from the sky. The Inca gave answer that he had heard, and the voice from the sky spoke again, saying: "Huayna Capac, go back! The treasures of this hill are not for the people of the Inca! They must be left untouched for other men!"

Whereupon the Inca, true to the superstitions of his race, turned his back on a 5-billion-dollar mountain of silver. No Indian dared dig into the sacred hill. That is said to be the reason why its riches were unknown to the Spaniards until they had been in the land for many years.

One starlit night in 1545, an Indian, Gualca by name, was tending a herd of llamas on the hillside. It was cold, and with his dog by his side, the Indian was huddled close by a campfire. A rustling noise in the grass, perhaps a small animal, aroused the dog, who was soon pawing at and uprooting a bush. Gualca, the Indian, watched the animal, glad of something to occupy his mind. Then, by the light of the campfire, he saw something gleam among the roots of the bush—something gleaming that was "white as moonlight on the waters of Lake Titicaca." Gualca knew at once that he had discovered silver. He ran to the village and showed the silver-dusted roots to Don Juan de Villaroel. The very next day, Indians were set to work digging silver out of Potosí Hill.

The gold of Peru was becoming exhausted at that time, and the news of a silver strike in Bolivia spread like wildfire. By the end of the year, 170 Spaniards and 3,000 Indians were living at the bottom of Potosí Hill and working the silver deposits. The town of Potosí was founded by Diego Centeno. It still stands today, one of the highest settlements in the world, 14,350 feet above sea level.

When the first stream of silver from Potosí began to flow into the treasury of Spain, a current of humanity started in the opposite direction. For more than a hundred years, the silver mines of Bolivia made it the richest and most precious of Spain's colonies. During that century, Potosí was the most populous city in the Western Hemisphere. It is estimated that, at the peak of the boom, anywhere from a quarter to half a million Spaniards and Indians lived in Potosí.

As for the amount of wealth that was taken out of the silver mountain, it is impossible to make an accurate estimate.

During the first century after the flood of silver began to flow, the fifth share of the Spanish crown amounted to 3,240,000,000 piastres. The total estimated silver yield for that period is put at 6,000 cubic yards of bar silver which, if made into a column a yard square, would rise more than 3 miles high. At one period, this fabulous silver mountain of Bolivia supplied the metal for more than half the entire world's silver coinage.

Life in Potosí was the pattern of all boom towns of the great gold and silver rushes. The cost of living reached unbelievable heights. Plain flour was more precious than pure silver dust. The Spanish hidalgos wore costly embroidered tunics under armor encrusted with diamonds, emeralds, and rubies. The fashion in women's shoes was to trim them with pearls and precious stones. So keen was the rivalry among the grand ladies of Potosí to outdo each other that, in many cases, a single slipper alone represented a small fortune.

One man built a solid silver fountain out of which flowed a steady stream of wine for the refreshment of his guests. Silver was naturally the medium of exchange, but the people of Potosí could not wait for the coins to come from Spain to spend their wealth. Hence, in 1562, a mint was constructed of wood dragged overland from the faraway forests of Argentina. This Casa Nacional de Monedada still stands as a musty reminder of the silver glory that was Potosí.

The mines of Potosí, of course, were worked by Indians. It was a cruel system of forced labor and it took a dreadful toll of lives. The Indians were treated as slaves. In fact, in many ways, they were worse off and more harshly treated than Negro slaves in other colonies. Negro slaves had to be bought and paid for. Therefore, they represented an investment and received some degree of care. But Indian labor cost nothing. When Indians dropped dead in their tracks, others were drafted. In all fairness to Spain, it must be underscored that its laws did not allow this kind of treatment. As a matter of fact, the welfare of the Indians was very much on the mind of Spain at this period, and slavery was officially frowned upon. Dozens of laws were enacted to ensure humane treatment of the Indians in the colonies. But parallel with these laws came urgent and explicit instructions to send home more and more of the much-needed silver.

Officials of Peru and Bolivia were confronted with orders to be kindly in their treatment of the Indians and at the same time to speed up the production of the mines. If they relaxed their driving of the natives, they cut down the flow of silver to Spain. Such a slump, they knew, would not only lose them their lucrative posts but even, perhaps, their heads. The result was that in theory Spain protected the Indians, while in practice the Indians toiled and died in misery in the mines of Potosí.

Once an Indian was drafted for work in the mines, chances were that he would not live to see his home and family again. Many Indians were taken from the hot lowlands and transported to the high mountains of Bolivia, where the first blasts of the cold winter winds brought swift death to hundreds of men whose lives were adjusted to the heat of the jungle.

Potosí, from its earliest days, was worked by sinking shafts deep into the hillside. Rickety ladders, made of notched logs, led down to where the silver was being mined. Up and down these ladders crawled a never-ending line of Indians. There could be no letup, for day and night mule caravans waited to carry the silver over the mountains and down to the port of Arica where galleons were ready to take the silver to Panama for shipment to Spain in cargoes of solid silver.

Often these galleons and the silver-laden mule trains were attacked and robbed by pirates. Then back over the mountains would go the order to speed up production to make up for the loss. Whips lashed and the loads put on the lacerated backs of the Indians were made a little heavier. When one of the human cogs in the machine slipped to his death or dropped from exhaustion, another Indian was shoved into his place with hardly a moment's delay.

The Indians were not officially slaves, for that was forbidden by the law of Spain. They were paid for their work, but it was the very theory of payment that made them slaves in fact. The wages of the Indians were determined by Spanish officials called corregidors. These men were given great powers. It was their abuse of this authority that led to the great uprising among the Indians of Bolivia, the story of which will be told later in this chapter.

In return for labor in the mines, in basket weaving or pottery making, or in raising crops, the Indians were paid in trade goods imported from Spain. The nature of these goods and the prices charged for them was entirely in the hands of the corregidors. The first trick of the trade of a successful corregidor was to fix his prices so high that the first purchase would put an Indian so deeply in debt that he would find it next to impossible ever to work his way out. The next was to make sure that new debts were constantly incurred by the Indians. The reason: so long as an Indian owed for goods taken, the law forced him to work out that debt at any task assigned to him by the corregidor.

If the goods brought over from Spain for sale to the Indians had been articles they needed, the system would not have been quite so bad. But that was not the case. With no voice in the matter, Indians who never wore shoes were forced to accept silk stockings at high prices. Beardless Indians slaved for weeks in the Potosí mines to pay for Spanish razors they had no use for whatever.

There is one case on record of a merchant who imported a large quantity of spectacles, a rather useless item in a country where the eyesight of the average native is excellent even into extreme old age. The Indians did not want eyeglasses and the merchant, desperate to find some way of disposing of his spectacles, went to the corregidor for help. This worthy official solved the problem by issuing an order that Indians in his district would not be allowed to go to church unless they wore eyeglasses. In a very short time, the entire shipment of spectacles was sold at an enormous profit.

Time and again, the Indians appealed to Spanish authority for an easing of their burden. Here and there, in remote provinces, small groups of Indians rose in arms against their Spanish oppressors. But these uprisings were quickly put down. As the eighteenth century dawned, the Indians were more or less resigned to their hopeless fate. The glorious days of their great Inca leaders were gone forever—unless a great leader were to be born among them. That leader of the Indians was born in Tinta, in the Vilcamayu Valley, about 80 miles south of Cuzco, in 1742. He was baptized José Gabriel Condorcanqui, but he is better known and widely honored in Bolivia under his Inca name, Tupac Amaru.

Being the son of a chief, Tupac Amaru had the advantages of a good education. As a boy, he studied with Dr. Carlos Rodríguez, the Cura of Yanaoca. Next, he attended the Jesuit College of San Borja, in Cuzco, established by the viceroyalty especially for the education of Inca princes. Tupac Amaru was an apt scholar. He learned to speak Spanish with the precision of a native of Castile. But during this formative period, he never forgot the miserable existence of his own people or his own ancient Quechua language. When Tupac Amaru thought he had learned as much as he could from his Spanish instructors, he returned to Bolivia, where, before he was twenty years old, he succeeded his father as chief of Tungasuca and a number of other villages in the Vilcamayu Valley. Here the plans for revolt against Spain, that had formed in his young mind in Cuzco, extended in scope until they embraced the vast Inca kingdom of his ancestors. Tupac Amaru declared himself the heir to the nonexistent Inca throne. This move was approved by his people. Next, the young Inca set out to win Spanish recognition of his claim.

To this end, Tupac Amaru went to Lima in 1770. There he laid before the *Audiencia Real* his claim to the Marquisate of

Oropesa, which had been bestowed on his family by Philip II. After long debates, his right to the title was acknowledged, and Tupac Amaru was officially recognized as the direct descendant of the Inca Tupac Amaru, who had been executed by the Spanish in 1571.

Originally, it had been decreed that the Marquis of Oropesa should reside in Spain because it was feared that the wealth and power it bestowed upon an Indian might cause trouble in the colony. But that condition was not imposed upon Tupac Amaru. He returned to live among his own people, Also, it is doubtful if he received any benefits of the Marquisate. It is known that his main income was from ten *piaras*, or caravans of mules, that were employed in mountain transport service.

The chief advantage of the marquisate, however, was that it gave Tupac Amaru great dignity and authority among the Indians. It also made him more conscious of his responsibility to end the cruelties imposed upon his people. Wherever he went among the Spanish nobility and clergy, Tupac Amaru argued the cause of the Indians. The Spaniards listened politely. They made vague promises and promptly forgot them. When Tupac Amaru had exhausted every means of achieving his objective by peaceful methods, he finally decided to fight for the freedom of the Indians.

The immediate cause of open war was the cruelty of Corregidor Antonio Aliaga of Tupac Amaru's native village of Tinta. Several threats had been made against the corregidor's life, and only Tupac Amaru's sober advice had prevented bloodshed. But when the Inca, at last, realized that the only hope for his people lay in open rebellion, he did not hesitate. His first needs were guns and ammunition. As he had neither funds to buy them nor friends to get them from, the Inca hatched a scheme that stands out as one of the most brilliant coups in American history.

On November 4, 1780, Dr. Carlos Rodríguez, Tupac Amaru's boyhood teacher, gave a dinner party to celebrate his name day. Among the guests were the Corregidor Aliaga and the Inca chief. Early in the evening, Tupac Amaru excused himself, saying that he had some guests at his own house. But instead of going home, he hid with a few companions among the bushes outside Dr. Rodríguez' house. When the Corregidor Aliage started homeward a little later, he was captured by the Inca and his companions and taken to the Inca's house.

Long before this day, Tupac Amaru had decided that Aliaga had to die, not only as punishment for his misdeeds, but as a warning to others of his kind. But first, the corregidor, however unwillingly, was compelled to help the Indians by getting them Spanish money and arms. The Spanish official, after painful persuasion, signed an order on the local Spanish treasury and armory made out to Tupac Amaru. Through this trick, the Inca and his band of followers obtained $22,000 in coined money, some gold ingots, seventy-five muskets, and a few horses and baggage mules. Thus, the first army of Tupac Amaru was actually financed and armed by Spain.

Tupac Amaru next led his army against the province of Quispicanchi. His object was to capture Cabrera, corregidor of the district, but Cabrera had been warned and fled to Cuzco. The march upon Quispicanchi was fruitful in other respects, however. Tupac Amaru seized 18,000 yards of woolen and 20,000 yards of cotton cloth to make uniforms for his army. Some guns and ammunition and a few pieces of rusty artillery were also taken. By this time the Inca had a force of 6,000 men, but only 300 of them had firearms.

When the Corregidor Cabrera, who had fled from Quispicanchi before the Indian advance, reached Cuzco with news of the revolt, the city was thrown into a panic. An uprising of the Indians had never been regarded as a serious threat. The two regiments of Spanish soldiers stationed in Cuzco turned the Jesuit College into a fortress. Frantic pleas for help were sent by messengers to Lima.

A few days later, Tiburcio de Landa, governor of Paucartambo, and the Corregidor Cabrera, led a mixed Spanish and Indian army of a thousand men up the Vilcamayu Valley against Tupac Amaru. There Landa found himself surrounded by a superior rebel force. Moreover, his plan of attack was thwarted by a sudden snowstorm. As a result, Landa retired to the refuge of a church, from where he opened negotiations with the Inca. Tupac Amaru requested Landa to remove the women and children from his camp. The Spaniard refused and the two opposing forces prepared for battle. At the very beginning of the fight, the powder supply of the Spaniards exploded, blowing off the roof and one side of the church. There was nothing for Landa to do but order a charge against the Indians. The Spaniards fought heroically, but heavily outnumbered and not used to fighting in the cold and snow, they were badly beaten. All but twenty-eight of the Spanish troops were killed and and every one of those twenty-eight survivors was wounded. Both Governor Landa and Corregidor Cabrera were killed.

This Spanish defeat opened the gates of Cuzco to Tupac Amaru and his army. But the Inca was still unwilling to shed unnecessary blood of either his own people or of the Spaniards. Instead of following up his victory by taking possession of Cuzco, Tupac Amaru opened negotiations with the Spaniards for a peaceful settlement of the war. While waiting for a reply, he toured the Indian villages, explaining to his people that right was on their side. At every town, riding on a fine white charger covered with richly embroidered trappings, Tupac Amaru was received with enthusiastic acclaim. The dream of a reborn Inca Empire stirred in the heart of every Indian who heard the voice of the hero urging his people to have new hope and courage.

The Spaniards, of course, had no intention of dealing or making any concessions to the self-styled redeemer of his people, but they played for time while they built up their military strength. Complete victory was within the grasp of the

Inca at that time, if he had but known it. So desperate and weak was the situation at Cuzco that even the clergy was organized into a military unit. By the beginning of December, 1780, Cuzco had a force of 3,000 men under arms, but they were still afraid to face an Indian attack. More words, more proposals, and counterproposals, came from the Spaniards to gain precious time.

At last, in January, 1781, the Inca marched on Cuzco and camped on the heights overlooking the ancient city. Again he delayed attack while pleading with the authorities of Cuzco to avoid conflict. Again the Spanish brandished words. This time, Tupac Amaru attacked. The battle began on January 8. After 2 days of furious fighting, Tupac Amaru was forced to withdraw his forces to Tinta. There the Inca reorganized his army, and on February 11, attacked the Spanish stronghold at Paucartambo. In this engagement, the Indians numbered 60,000. But they were stronger in numbers than they were in discipline. Only a few hundred were armed with muskets. Defeat was inevitable against a Spanish army that had been given 3 months to prepare for battle. Tupac Amaru retired with his shattered army, determined to recoup his losses and gather an even bigger army for another attempt to win liberty for his enslaved people.

When the Spanish command saw the spirit of the revolt had not been broken, the viceroy in Lima sent a large army of veteran soldiers into the field. From the rear, the Indians were menaced by an army from Argentina, which had also become alarmed at the progress of the Indian revolution. The Inca forces were attacked near the village of Checacupe early in the spring. Tupac Amaru was determined to fight to the death. But before he had a chance really to match strength with the enemy, he was betrayed by one of his own leaders, Ventra Landaeta, who treacherously turned the Inca and his whole family over to the Spaniards.

With Tupac Amaru captured, the heart went out of the

revolt. Sentence was pronounced upon him on May 5, 1781, at Cuzco. He was condemned to death. But death did not come to him until he had been forced to watch his entire family killed before his eyes. Only then did the execution of the Inca take place. Tupac Amaru found the welcome freedom of Death—but a painful one. After torture, his body was torn to pieces by four horses pulling his limbs in different directions. It is told among the Indians that as this horrible scene was being enacted, a great wind arose, black clouds covered the heavens, and torrential rains came down in an effort to cleanse the earth of the blood of Tupac Amaru.

After the death of the Inca, the revolt smoldered for more than two years. There were occasional flare-ups here and there, but none of great importance. The most concerted effort was a long but fruitless siege of La Paz. The Indians were finally subdued, but they were neither beaten nor crushed. The descendants of the Incas remained hostile to Spain.

Their opportunity for revenge came some thirty years later when Bolivia's real fight for freedom began, in 1809. The patriots found in the Indians and in the living memory of Tupac Amaru, powerful and welcome allies.

The first uprising actually to overthrow Spanish authority in South America took place in La Paz, Bolivia, on July 16, 1809. A group of patriots, led by Pedro Domingo Murillo, overcame the royalist garrison. They captured the governor and proclaimed independence. The rebels were soon seized in a Spanish counterattack; Murillo was executed. It was the beginning of a long and desperate struggle for freedom. Not until 1821, with the great victories of Simon Bolivar and San Martín, did Bolivia see the dawn of her own independence.

Antonio José de Sucre's signal victory over the Spanish army at Ayacucho at the end of 1824 sounded the clarion of freedom for three South American countries, among them Bolivia. On January 29, 1825, the Spanish troops evacuated La Paz in favor of the patriot army led by General José Miguel Lanza. On the following day, the country's independence was proclaimed by authority of Simon Bolivar.

As an independent nation, the country was no longer satisfied with her name of Upper Peru, and to honor the Great Liberator, it was unanimously voted to adopt the name Bolivia. General Antonio José de Sucre was elected head of the government. The name of the official capital was changed to Sucre after Bolivia's national hero.

Today, Bolivia strangely enough owes her progress and prosperity in a large degree to the same Potosí Hill that was responsible for her days of horror, but instead of silver it is tin that is bringing wealth to the country from Potosí.

The presence of tin in the ancient Potosí mines had been known as far back as the Spanish operation of the mines, but the tin was discarded as worthless. Silver and gold were the only metals that interested the Spanish royal treasury. The commercial production of tin dates back only to around 1895, when a steadily growing canning industry created a demand for the metal. Since then, the wide use of tin cans for thousands of purposes has made tin the most important product of Bolivia.

In connection with Bolivian tin, the story of Simón I. Patiño cannot be omitted. Patiño was born of mixed Inca and Spanish blood, near Cochabamba, high among the Bolivian Andes. As a young man he was employed as a storekeeper near the town of Oruro, to which an Indian from the remote provinces came to trade one day. Everything was strange to the Indian; the people spoke a strange language and he was homesick. With shoulders drooping, he entered the store, dragging a sack that clanked along the floor. He mumbled the few Spanish words he knew, when to his amazement, the storekeeper spoke to him in his native Quechua. A broad smile took the place of his frown. Words came out fast and excitedly. The Indian continued the conversation in his mother tongue—

and indeed it was a tongue of riches, not of gold, or silver, but tin. The Indian opened his sack and showed Patiño some samples of high-grade tin ore. Then he leaned over and whispered into Patiño's ear that it came from near his village.

Perhaps no man has ever been more richly rewarded for a kindly act than Simón Patiño. He immediately realized the quality of the tin ore and quit his job at the store. Taking his wife with him, he set out for the Indian village, and with his own hands began digging out ore and rolling it downhill in a wheelbarrow.

Such were the humble beginnings of Simón Patiño, the Tin King of Bolivia, who changed the whispered tip of a lonely Indian into a fortune estimated at from 300 to 400 million dollars. But contrary to the way of the early Spaniards, Patiño did not take without giving. He is largely responsible for the present modern methods of mining in Bolivia and there are material evidences of his generous philanthropies from one end of the country to the other.

Bolivia is often called the Switzerland of South America. Once the country had outlets to the sea, but it ceded its harbors on the Pacific coast to Chile after a series of conflicts. Although Bolivia has no seaboard shore lines, it owns part of the largest lake in South America, Lake Titicaca, which lies among the Andes Mountains at an altitude of 12,500 feet. This lake has the distinction of being the highest steam-navigated lake in the world. Lake Titicaca is the traditional home of the ancient founders of the Inca Empire. The lake is closely interwoven with the history of Bolivia, although the northern half lies in Peru. About half the size of Lake Erie, its waters are icy cold and often swept by furious gales.

Although steamboats also ply its waters today, the strange balsas of the Indians are a familiar sight, as they were in the days of the Inca Empire. These boats are made of bundles of totora reeds that are found in the shallows along the shores. The boats are built of four bundles of these twisted reeds. Two are used for the bottom and two for the sides. The reed bundles are lashed securely together and bent upward in the front and rear; a most efficient and serviceable boat is the result.

These balsas are in use today by Indian fishermen who are descendants of the Incas. Many balsas have sails made of reeds plaited together and raised and lowered much like a slat blind. Although they become water-soaked after a time, the dry-docking of a balsa is simplicity itself. It is so light that it can be hauled up on the shore with one hand; the hot rays of the sun quickly dry out the reeds and make the craft seaworthy again.

There are many stories and legends in connection with Lake Titicaca. One is that an enormous chain of gold, heavier and larger than an anchor chain, was being carried to Peru in 1533 for the ransom of the Inca Atahualpa, who was held captive by Francisco Pizarro. When news reached the Indians that the Inca had been killed by Pizarro, they threw the golden chain into Lake Titicaca. If this story is true, then the Inca chain of gold still lies on the bottom of Lake Titicaca. The secret of its whereabouts and weight and value is as securely hidden as the secrets of the Big Stone people who once lived along the shores of the lake.

CHAPTER 15

Land on the Equator

Highlights of Ecuador

Discovered: By Francisco Pizarro and colonized by him for Spain in
   1533.

Population: 2,555,000.

Area: 337,395 square miles.

Language: Spanish.   *Capital:* Quito,

Government: Republic established in 1830.

Geographical Characteristics: A large plateau lies between the two
   ranges of Andean Mountains that run through the country
   from north to south.

Climatic Conditions: As the country ranges from jungle lowlands to
   mountain highlands, the climate is highly diversified.

Principal Products: Bananas, coffee, Panama hats, rubber, cattle
   products, cacao, balsa wood.

ALTHOUGH the name of the modern Republic of
Ecuador, meaning equator, is of comparatively recent
origin, the capital city, Quito, derives its name from
the Quitus, an ancient people who inhabited the land and
reached their height of power many centuries before the coming of the Spanish conquistadors.

In very ancient times, Ecuador was divided into many small
and independent kingdoms. Of these, the Kingdom of Quitu,
situated in the central Andean regions, was the most aggres-
sive. Little by little, by conquests or alliances, it extended its
influence throughout the entire country.

How long the Quitus were in power is not known. The story is that, toward the latter part of the eighth century, an unknown people, who called themselves Caras, came down the Pacific on large rafts and landed on the coast of Ecuador. They took possession from Cape San Francisco to Point Charapoto and built permanent towns. The Caras had an organized form of government, under the leadership of a monarch whom they called the Scyri, the Lord of All. They worshiped the Sun and the Moon, and one of their first acts was to raise temples to these gods.

The story told by the ruins of these temples and other structures indicate that the Caras had a high degree of civilization. They had a knowledge of astronomy and appear to have been skilled in other sciences and arts, although not to such a high degree as either the Mayas to the north or the Incas to the south.

It was not long before the Caras began to look for new fields of conquest. One by one, neighboring kingdoms were annexed to their domain. In the latter part of the tenth century, they subdued the Quitus and made Quito the capital of the Cara nation. Under the rule of the invaders, the country prospered. It remained at peace for some four and a half centuries, or until 1450. Then, during the reign of Hualcopo, an invasion of the armies of the Inca Tupac Yupanqui of the Empire of Peru began a long and bloody struggle for power between the two kingdoms.

It was the policy of the Incas that each ruler should add some new territory to the empire. Tupac Yupanqui, perhaps the greatest of the Inca conquerors, was determined to make the acquisition of Quito his contribution to the greatness of Peru. Before his death in 1460, Hualcopo had seen a great part of his kingdom conquered by the Inca, who was then making plans for the complete conquest of Ecuador. Hualcopo was succeeded by his son, Cacha, who announced his intention of resisting the invading Peruvians to the death.

At about that time, Tupac Yupanqui was dying. Hearing of the resistance being met by his armies, he instructed his son, Huayna Capac, to carry on the conquest of Ecuador. Then the Old Inca died. After a year of mourning, Huayna Capac set out with his armies for the north to add the kingdom of Quito to the already vast territory of the Inca Empire.

Cacha fought bravely to defend his land, but the Inca armies advanced slowly and surely into the heart of the nation, finally threatening Quito itself. Huayna Capac sent an ultimatum to the Quito chief, demanding his surrender. Cacha replied that the war was not of his making and that he would die before submitting. His proud and defiant challenge was the signal for a great Inca attack. Cacha, although gravely ill at the time, had himself carried in a chair to the battlefield, from where he directed his armies until he was killed.

In the face of a fierce Inca onslaught, the Caras threw down their arms and surrendered. Huayna Capac marched victoriously into Quito and the country was proclaimed a province of the Inca Empire. In many ways, Ecuador was the gainer by the conquest. But on one occasion a rebellious province learned to its sorrow that the Incas ruled their realm with an iron hand. When Huayna Capac learned of the revolt in that province, he punished the people by ordering 20,000 Ecuadorians drowned in a lake that to this day bears the name Yahuer Cocha, the Lake of Blood.

After the conquest and as a gesture of good will toward the newly conquered kingdom, Huayna Capac married a princess of Quito. Her name was Pacha and she became the mother of Atahualpa, whose tragic fate is told in the conquest of the Inca Empire by Francisco Pizarro.

It was along the coast of Ecuador that Francisco Pizarro first heard definite accounts of the Inca Empire and its wealth. But it was not until Peru had been conquered and its riches assured for Spain, that Pizarro turned his eyes to the Kingdom of

Quito to the north. In 1534, he sent Sebastián de Benalcázar to conquer Ecuador.

The Spaniards reached Quito on December 6, 1534. To their disappointment they found little treasure. Some returned to Peru, but Benalcázar remained to establish Spanish rule in Quito and to build settlements on the coast, including Guayaquil and Esmeraldas.

At about this time Pedro de Alvarado, governor of Guatemala, was carring out a project for the independent conquest of Ecuador. With 500 men and a well-equipped expedition he landed on the coast in March, 1534, and began the difficult journey over the mountains to Quito. That journey of Alvarado and his men is one of the most harrowing and futile in South American history. As the Spaniards, accustomed to the hot climate of Guatemala, climbed into the high mountains, they died by the score from exposure. The horses were eaten when food gave out. Even gold that had been taken from the Indians was discarded as the strength of the men was sapped by the hardships. The great volcano Cotopaxi erupted along the line of march, filling the air with ashes and terrorizing the already demoralized soldiers. When Alvarado led his men into Riobamba, with a handful of his original followers alive, came the final staggering blow. They saw the marks of horses' hoofs in the ground. This meant that other Spaniards had been there before them.

Alvarado soon heard that Benalcázar had already taken possession for Pizarro and that Quito was in Spanish hands. There was nothing for him to do but to turn back and head for the coast again. However, he did not return empty-handed. He gave up the "conquest" on payment by Francisco Pizarro of about $250,000.

While Benalcázar was in Quito, bewailing his fate in having been sent into a region where there was neither gold nor silver, a most exciting and welcome bit of news came to his ears. There were rumors of El Dorado, the Gilded Man, who bathed himself in gold dust. His home was reported to be along a lake in the north. The temptation was too much for Benalcázar to resist, and he set off with an expedition to find his promised land of gold.

During his absence, in 1538, Francisco Pizarro appointed his younger brother, Gonzalo, governor of Quito. Gonzalo too heard stories of the Gilded Man, as well as tales of a rich Land of Cinnamon, which was said to lie to the east over the mountains. To follow up these rumors, Gonzalo Pizarro in 1540 assembled the largest expedition that had ever been gotten together in that part of the world. He explored the Amazon highlands and although he found neither gold nor cinnamon, the venture led to the thrilling and dramatic journey down the Amazon River by Gonzalo's second in command, Francisco Orellana, whose story is told in the chapter on Brazil.

Gonzalo, believing that he had been deserted by Orellana, returned to Quito in 1541 with tales of disaster and hardships that made the hair of his listeners fairly stand on end. Of the 350 Spaniards who had started from Quito, only eighty returned, naked and emaciated, their bodies bruised and lacerated by the jungle, looking more like beasts than men.

In Quito another blow fell on Gonzalo: the news of the assassination of his brother Francisco Pizarro, in Lima, Peru. The Pizarros were no longer in favor and he was ordered by the Viceroy Vela to give up his post as governor of Quito. Gonzalo refused, and maintained his position in defiance of royal authority. When the troops of Lima, under the command of Viceroy Vela, marched on Quito, Gonzalo's forces defeated them and killed Vela. Pizarro was hailed as the victor and went to Lima in triumph. But his day of glory was brief. In 1548 he was arrested and executed for treason.

After the rebellion of Gonzalo Pizarro, Ecuador settled down as a province of the viceroyalty of Lima. Nothing of great importance occurred during the colonial period. It has been said that the country passed through a period of 250 years without history. Although there was peace, it was certainly no time of rejoicing for the people of Ecuador. Conditions of oppression and restrictions were even more unbearable than in other South American colonies.

The province was almost entirely cut off from the outside world, and even from the other colonies because of the high mountain ranges that hem it in. The governors ruled without check of any kind on their authority. When asked to account for his misdeeds, one Spanish governor is quoted as having replied: "God is very high; the King is very far away; I am here the only master!"

There were no rights of any kind in Ecuador under Spanish rule, according to the historian Cevallos. The orders of the king were disobeyed. Peace was maintained as the result of terror rather than the happiness of the people. Ignorance was imposed on the inhabitants as a weapon of tyranny. Printing was unknown. Justice was unheard of and no one was safe from the cruel and often fatal punishments that were ordered by the various governors at will. It is little wonder that under such conditions of slavery the people of Ecuador shouted with joy when they heard the battle cry of freedom being raised by their neighboring colonies.

There was an uprising against royal authority in Quito in 1809. It was quickly and drastically suppressed. Other attempts to overthrow the Spaniards followed. At last, on October 9, 1820, the city of Guayaquil on the coast obtained its freedom, and that brings into focus the days and deeds of General Sucre.

Antonio José de Sucre, the youngest and ablest general of the Great Liberator, Simon Bolivar, and the national hero of Ecuador, was born in Cumaná, Venezuela, on February 3, 1795. When the revolution broke out in Caracas, Venezuela, in 1810, Sucre was studying engineering. He immediately joined the patriot forces. At the age of fifteen he was made a lieutenant in the engineering corps.

The abilities of Sucre were quickly recognized. His rise in the Army of Independence was nothing short of meteoric. He was a lieutenant colonel in 1814. In 1817, Bolivar himself made the young officer a full colonel. Three years later, he was a brigadier general. When Simon Bolivar planned to liberate Ecuador and looked for a man in whom he "might place the greatest confidence," he turned to Sucre. In January, 1821, Sucre was made a full general and placed in supreme command of Bolivar's Armies of the South, with orders to sail immediately for Guayaquil. He was only twenty-six years old.

Sucre arrived at Guayaquil in May, and took up action against the royalist forces. Suffering several defeats, the Venezuelan general returned to Guayaquil and reorganized his army for a new campaign. Early in 1822, General Sucre again took up the fight against the Spaniards, and after a series of minor victories met the enemy at Pichincha, on May 24, 1822.

The battle of Pichincha is probably unique in military history, not because of the overwhelming victory Sucre won over far superior forces, but because of the location of the battlefield. This great drama of the struggle for independence was enacted on the slopes of a volcano, almost 12,000 feet above sea level, within sight of the city of Quito. As the battle waged, 50,000 sober-faced Ecuadorians watched from the city, their spirits rising and falling as one side or the other gained an advantage. They knew that on the outcome of the struggle hung their fate, and perhaps the fate of half of South America.

The day was almost over before a great shout arose. The battle of Pichincha had been won by General Sucre. Five days later, Ecuador proclaimed its freedom from Spain and joined with Venezuela and New Granada to form the Republic of Colombia.

Bolivar had freed Venezuela, Colombia, and Ecuador, and was extending his fight for the liberty of South American peoples southward. San Martín had liberated his native Argentina, and then marching across the Andes, had brought about the independence of Chile. As leader of the patriot army of Chile, San Martín had penetrated into the stronghold of Spain and secured the freedom of Peru. The two liberators were virtually facing each other in the field. Each had his own plan of campaign for completing the task of driving Spain out of South America forever. It was only natural that they should meet and discuss those plans.

San Martín landed in Guayaquil on July 26, 1822. He was met by Simon Bolivar. The two men embraced cordially. After an enthusiastic reception by the townspeople, they retired for preliminary conferences. On the following day the famous interview took place. The two men met alone. No one knows exactly what was said. But history was made, and also one of the noblest sacrifices in history.

From what happened, a shrewd guess can be made as to what was said when the two liberators met. Both men had the same ultimate objective in view: the liberation of South America from the oppressive yoke of Spain. But they had different ideas of how that should be accomplished to the best advantage of the people. Bolivar believed in a confederation under a strong central government. San Martín advocated the setting up of completely independent governments in each liberated country.

For either to abandon his plan and join forces with the other was out of the question. Bolivar and San Martín were both too sincere in their beliefs. No doubt there were moments during the interview when the fate of South America hung in the balance. One of them must give way to the other, that they knew. There could be no compromise between two such strong personalities. There was only one way to avoid a deadlock. San Martín, to his eternal honor and credit, gave way to Simon Bolivar, utterly and completely. When the two men emerged from the meeting, their faces were stern but their relations were extremely cordial.

That night there was a banquet and ball in honor of the two

great men. Some time during the festivities San Martín was missed. Not until the next day was it learned that he had quietly slipped off and boarded his ship in the harbor. During the night San Martín sailed away to self-imposed exile. In one of the greatest acts of self-sacrifice in history, San Martín gave up what was most precious to him in life so that his rival might carry out his fight for the liberty of South American people unhampered.

Left with a free field, Bolivar immediately began to put his plans for completing the victory of the patriots into action. General Sucre was left in charge in Quito. During 1823, Sucre combined his duties of administrator of Ecuador with those of a general. The Spaniards were still holding on in Peru, and under orders from Bolivar, an expedition was prepared to drive the royalists out of Peru once and for all.

The campaign began in the latter part of 1824, culminating in one of the most glorious and celebrated victories of the fight for South American independence, the battle of Ayacucho, in which the patriots under General Sucre wiped out the entire Spanish army. This Waterloo of South America was fought on December 9, 1824. In recognition for his brilliant accomplishment, Sucre was personally thanked and decorated by Bolivar who in the name of a free and grateful people bestowed on the young general the title of Grand Marshal of Ayacucho.

In 1825, as has been told in another chapter, Sucre was elected the first president of the new Republic of Bolivia, which also honored him by renaming its capital Sucre. But after a few years, Sucre resigned the office of president; in August, 1828, he returned to Quito, the "fair city of my heart."

Sucre tried to retire to private life, but at popular demand he was elected to the Ecuador congress in 1829. While he held this office, early in 1830, his native Venezuela broke away from the Colombian Federation and declared itself an independent republic. This action was soon followed by Ecuador.

As president of Bolivia, Sucre had become disgusted with the bickerings and petty jealousies that sprang up after the independence. Similar disillusionment also led him to resign from the Ecuador congress and retire to his country home.

Sucre was loved and honored by the people of Ecuador, but no man can achieve greatness, even in the service of others, without creating enemies. On June 4, 1830, while he was crossing the mountains of Berruecos, the bullet of such an enemy found its way into the kind and generous heart of Antonio José de Sucre. Today his remains lie in the Cathedral of Quito, and his name is venerated by the people of his adopted country.

The name Ecuador was adopted by the republic in 1830, on the suggestion of the first president, Juan Flores. The name is certainly appropriate, as the equator runs through the country, and the capital, Quito, lies only a few miles south of the line. Even as the imaginary line of the equator runs across from east to west, a very real formation of nature runs through the entire country from north to south, two parallel ranges of the Andes, known as the eastern and western cordillera.

At certain points these two ranges of mountains are connected by transverse ridges, known as *nudos*, or knots. They give this part of the country the appearance of a gigantic ladder, some 500 miles long, lying flat on the ground. It is between the "rungs" of this ladder that the greatest number of the inhabitants of Ecuador live.

The climate of this high valley, about 8,250 feet above sea level, is cool, even at the equator. On all sides are awe-inspiring peaks which rise to towering and snow-capped heights of more than 19,000 feet. Of volcanoes, active and inactive, Ecuador has more than its share. The nearest to Quito is Pichincha, the "boiling mountain," which has thrown the city into panic more than once by its eruptions. One outbreak, in 1575, is said to have covered Quito with 3 feet of stone and ashes.

To the south of Pichincha stretches a chain of volcanoes that are fortunately sleeping, but with fiery craters as a constant threat. The most famous of Ecuador's many volcanoes, and the highest active volcano in the world, is Cotopaxi. It stands 35 miles south of the capital. Rising 19,613 feet, menacing clouds of smoke always curl from its perpetually snow-covered summit.

Cotopaxi erupted in 1534, the year the Spaniards began their conquest of Ecuador, creating panic among the Indians and making easier the task of the conquistadors. Then the fiery monster was silent until 1741. For the next 26 years the fury of Cotopaxi spread terror and destruction in every direction. Large areas of land were completely ruined by constant rains of ashes and mud.

Despite the ever-present danger of death-dealing eruptions, Cotopaxi is pointed to with pride by Ecuadorians. They will tell you that it is 2,000 feet higher than the lofty Popocatepetl of Mexico, and that because of its much deeper snow line, it far surpasses in beauty the famed Fujiyama of Japan.

In the eastern part of Ecuador, known as the Oriente, are the vast jungles of the upper Amazon Basin, the home of the notorious head-hunting Jivaro Indians. It is through their horrible custom of shrinking human heads, examples of which can be seen in almost any museum, that the Jivaros have become so well known to the outside world. They are hunters and warriors and spend little time cultivating the soil. They are not really head-hunters, although they used to cut off the heads of their vanquished enemies, much as the North American Indians took scalps, as trophies of victory in battle.

For hunting, the Jivaros depend mostly on long blowguns from which are propelled small but deadly arrows. If these arrows are black at the tip, then they have been dipped in curare, the dreaded Flying Death of the jungle. While curare is manufactured and used by many different Indians in the Amazon Valley, this potent poison is probably more closely associated with Ecuador today. Through the cooperation of officials of the republic a recent expedition from the United States was able to obtain large quantities of curare for scientific study.

Strangely enough, curare, although a deadly poison and made by the Indians exclusively for the purpose of killing, has lately been found to have amazing medical properties. Spastic paralysis and certain other dreadful diseases have responded to curare when other treatments failed.

In the jungle, curare is manufactured under most primitive conditions, and to the accompaniment of weird rituals. Its effect is as quick as it is deadly. Apparently it paralyzes the voluntary muscular system of the body in a matter of minutes or seconds. Fortunately for the Indians, eating the meat of an animal killed with curare causes no ill effects.

The many strange drugs and medicines produced by the Indians of eastern Ecuador are only beginning to be studied by scientists in their laboratories. The cures that have already been effected with the proper and controlled use of curare give promise of more wonderful things yet to come from the mysterious jungles of the upper Amazon. Perhaps the head-shrinking Jivaros have done civilization a favor by calling attention to the still unexplored land of mystic medicines.

As the eastern jungles of Ecuador are of interest to science, so are the islands that form the westernmost extent of the republic, the Galápagos. They were discovered by Thomas de Berlanga, the Bishop of Panama, in 1535, while he was on his way to investigate the conduct of Pizarro in Peru. After the bishop's ship had been becalmed for several days, the group of islands were sighted just in time to save the bishop and crew from dying of thirst. The church dignitary was not much impressed by the islands, but in a report he wrote is found the first mention of the famous tortoises. These giant creatures are always associated with the Galápagos. They are found in no other place in the world.

These tortoises, some of which weigh almost 600 pounds,

proved a great attraction to the buccaneers in the seventeenth century. Not only did they find the meat good, but when carried along on the pirate ships as provisions for the voyage, it was found that the tortoises could go for long periods of time without food, thus supplying fresh meat at no cost. Every pirate who ever preyed on shipping in the Pacific visited the Galápagos, and many are the stories of buried treasure told about them. But there are also tales of cruelties and brutalities and maroonings that are hardly in keeping with the original Spanish name, the Isles of Enchantment, by which they were known before the group was called Galápagos, the Land of Tortoises.

After the buccaneers, the Galápagos were used by the whalers, who were also lured to the islands by tortoise steaks to be had for the taking. It is recorded that between 1831 and 1836, the peak years of Yankee whaling in the Pacific, more than 10,000 tortoises were taken off the islands. In addition to their delicious meat, these huge animals produce a clear and much-prized oil, for which they were also hunted and killed through the years. Wild dogs on the islands have killed no one knows how many thousand tortoises. The total result is that today there are hardly any of these interesting animals left.

The giant tortoise was but one of the many strange animals that caught the keen eyes of Charles Darwin, the world-famous naturalist, when he visited the Galápagos in 1835. He arrived on the *Beagle*, as a member of a party making a survey of the South American coast for the British government. When the *Beagle* sailed from England, Darwin was only twenty-two, but his brilliant and inquiring mind had already attracted the attention of leading naturalists. The *Beagle* remained only 5 weeks in the Galápagos, but that was long enough for young Darwin to make a complete study of the animal life on the islands. He also made observations that later were to form the basis of his sensational theory of evolution.

Among the animals that attracted Darwin's attention, besides the tortoises, were twenty-six species of land birds, gigantic marine lizards, albatross, penguins, and the curious flightless cormorant. Strange plants, strange fish, strange lizards, strange insects were eagerly noted by the young scientist.

The thing that Darwin found so unusual in these animals was that many of them showed a marked difference from those of the same species on the mainland. He wondered why. The Galápagos had evidently been cut off from the continent and outside influence of any kind from time immemorial. Could it be possible, he wondered, that these living creatures were adapting themselves to the peculiar conditions of the islands, and were on the way to becoming new species? Many years later Charles Darwin startled the world when in his great work, *The Origin of Species*, he gave his answer as: Yes!

One of the most interesting features of the Galápagos is the unique post office on Charles Island. This post office is under the control of no government and is maintained and operated purely on a basis of good fellowship among the sailors of passing ships. The establishment is simplicity itself. It consists of a cask, or small barrel, fastened to a tree near the anchorage known as Post Office Bay.

Although this barrel post office is in use today, its greatest popularity was in the days of whaling. Whalers who had rounded Cape Horn from the east on voyages that might take anywhere from two to five years, with no means of sending mail home by regular channels, eagerly looked forward to a stop-off at Post Office Bay. There they dropped their letters in the cask, knowing that they would be picked up by the first ship that passed by homeward bound.

CHAPTER 16

Paradise of the Pacific

❦

Highlights of Hawaii

Discovered: By Captain James Cook for England on January 20, 1778.

Population: 370,000.

Area: 6,407 square miles.

Language: English.   *Capital:* Honolulu.

Government: Territorial possession of United States.

Main Geographical Features: The eight inhabited islands of this chain of volcanic peaks stretch over a distance of about 400 miles. The islands are mountainous with intersecting valleys. The soil is ideal for agriculture.

Climatic Conditions: Probably the most ideal in the world. Never oppressively hot. Never chillingly cool.

Principal Products: Fruits such as pineapples and bananas, also sugar cane, coffee, tobacco, cotton, rice, and some meat products.

THE Hawaiian Islands were discovered about a thousand years ago by skillful Polynesian navigators. These fearless rovers of the seas came across the Pacific Ocean out of the west. They steered their huge seagoing canoes by the sun and the stars, and scanned the horizon for new island homes for themselves and their families. After a perilous journey of more than 2,000 miles, they sighted a series of green-clad islands whose towering mountains beckoned in a friendly way. There, giving thanks to their gods, they settled and began a new life that was to endure some eight hundred years.

The chain of islands known as Hawaii, extending for about 400 miles, is of volcanic origin. If the Pacific Ocean were ever to dry up, the islands would appear as a mountain range. Although there are countless small islands, the larger inhabited ones are: Hawaii, Maui, Lanai, Molokai, Oahu, and Kauai.

Just when, from where, and for what reason ancient Polynesians came to the Hawaiian Islands, is uncertain; but there is evidence that they came from the large groups of South Sea Islands below the equator. From the similarities in language, religion, customs, and legends, it is believed that the Hawaiians are a branch of the great Polynesian family. It includes the Maoris, Samoans, Tongans, and Tahitians.

The migration probably lasted over a period of hundreds of years, with new colonists arriving from time to time in small groups. It is thought that the first arrivals, the Menehunes of ancient Hawaiian legends, were driven out or conquered by latecomers from the Society Islands (Tahiti). Between six hundred and eight hundred years ago, it is believed, there was an established sea route between Hawaii and Tahiti used by these early navigators.

These voyages over thousands of miles of ocean in open canoes were an amazing feat of seamanship, but quite believable when it is considered that the Polynesians lived most of their lives on the water and knew how to use the stars to guide them. Water was the element of the Hawaiians more than land. Most of their food—fish, salt, and seaweed—was obtained from the sea. Swimming and surf riding were their favorite sports. They were expert in building and handling canoes. Some of their large double canoes used several sails and could carry dozens of people and heavy cargoes.

The Hawaiians were a simple people, with few needs. They brought no metals with them, and there were none on the islands. Therefore, to start with, their tools and utensils were made of stone. Beginning in the early part of the sixteenth century, soon after the Spaniards established their shipping routes from Panama to Peru and the Philippines, iron came to Hawaii. It came in the form of nails and other iron materials in the flotsam and jetsam of wrecked Spanish ships that were carried north on the ocean current and thrown on Hawaiian beaches by the waves. These bits of iron became the most precious possessions of the people—welcome gifts from the gods of the sea.

The society established on the Hawaiian Islands was made up of classes, or castes. At the top were the chiefs and priests, to whom all the wealth of the islands belonged. The common people did all the work. They were heavily taxed in produce and labor to support the aristocrats, who maintained their power by a fantastic system of tabus, or prohibitions. A tabu was that which was forbidden, to be avoided as dangerous and displeasing to the gods. This system of rules was oppressive. It regulated every detail of daily life and it served as a powerful weapon to ensure the subordination and obedience of the people to the rulers. Tabus were in the keeping of the priests, who took orders from the chiefs. There were many permanent tabus and also special tabus for every occasion or emergency. Penalties for violations were harsh, more often than not punishable by death, even if the guilty ones did not know they had violated a tabu.

A few of these tabus will make it evident how difficult life must have been for the Hawaiian man in the street. Among forbidden things were: for husband and wife to eat together; letting one's shadow fall on a chief; entering a tabu house; for a woman to eat bananas; wearing a garland while passing within the shadow of a chief. For such offenses, death was the penalty. If a chief wanted to fish in a certain inlet, he would order the priests to place a tabu on it for several weeks so that the fish would not be disturbed. Special tabus from time to time forbade launching a canoe, lighting a fire, producing tapa cloth, or making any noise.

Of course, some of these tabus were winked at, but the result was that if a chief, for any reason, wanted to get rid of an enemy, the tabus served more efficiently than poison or a stab in the back. The tabus applied to people of higher rank too, even to chiefs, but they were allowed to put a substitute of inferior rank in their place to suffer punishment or death for violations.

But despite these tabus, the Hawaiians were a cheerful, happy-go-lucky people. Their clothes were reduced to a minimum, consisting only of a tapa loincloth. The tapa cloth is made of fibrous material hammered from the bark of a tree. For battles and ceremonies, however, the chiefs wore magnificent and colorful feather cloaks, capes, and helmets. Sports and games played an important part in the lives of the Hawaiians. Surf riding, boxing, wrestling, foot races, and a form of bowling played with *ulumaika* stones were popular. To pass away their many leisure hours in their Pacific paradise, the natives played at darts and *konane*, a game much like our checkers; guessing games were among their favorites. On moonlit nights the entrancing songs of the islanders were carried out to sea by soft, cool breezes.

Of the gods of the Hawaiians, Pele, the volcano goddess, is perhaps the best known. Even today this feared goddess sometimes wreaks her vengeance, shaking the very earth and displaying her anger with roaring fire from her temple at the bottom of Kilauea, an active volcano in the southern part of the island of Hawaii.

The most important god in the history of Hawaii, however, is not Pele, but Lono, the god of Kealakeua. The story is told that Lono, in the dim days of ages past, killed his wife in a fit of jealousy. Then, struck with remorse, he left the islands, saying as he went, "I will return one day on a floating temple bearing coconuts, swine, and dogs."

This legendary promise of Lono was still alive in the minds of the islanders on January 20, 1778, when they saw two strange craft heading toward the village of Waimea on the

Island of Kauai. The Hawaiians had never seen the ships of Europeans, and it is little wonder they speculated on what and who these new arrivals could be.

"What are those floating rafts with branches?" asked a chief.

"Perhaps it is a great double canoe," answered a priest.

"More likely the sea monsters of Mana," replied another.

Then, as the ships came closer, and they could see the masts and riggings more distinctly, the priest spoke in an awed voice: "It is the floating temple of Lono! Lono has come back to us as he promised." Pointing to the masts and their rigging, he continued: "See, there are even ladders reaching up to his altar high in the sky."

The ships were not those of Lono, the long-absent god, but two ships of the British Navy, the *Resolution* and *Discovery*, commanded by Captain James Cook, one of the world's greatest maritime explorers. Captain Cook had already made a name for himself on two famous voyages of exploration and discovery into the Pacific. On this voyage, he had left England in July, 1776, for the primary purpose of exploring the northwestern coast of America in the hope of finding a water passage from the Pacific coast to Hudson Bay. For the discovery of such a passage, a prize of $100,000 had been offered by England.

In his time, Captain Cook surveyed and mapped a greater length of coast line than any other explorer. He drew the map of the Pacific with such accuracy that it is not much changed today. His explorations gave to England those great outposts of empire, Australia and New Zealand.

All this was behind Captain Cook when the pleasing sight of the Hawaiian Islands met his eyes, pleasing because they presented an ideal opportunity to rest and provision for the long and cold journey into Arctic regions in search of the northeast passage to the Atlantic.

Before the two English ships dropped anchor, they were surrounded by canoes filled with chattering natives. Captain Cook had his marines ready for action should the islanders prove to be hostile, as he suspected from the many stones they carried in the bottoms of their dugouts. But when the Hawaiians saw that there was nothing to fear, they threw the stones overboard in a gesture of friendship. The captain invited the natives aboard. They swarmed up over the sides, laughing and shouting. Some of the words were familiar to Cook. He had heard the natives of Tahiti and New Zealand speak in a similar dialect. Cook had only a slight knowledge of the language, but enough to understand that the Hawaiians wanted to trade their fish and yams for iron. As a matter of fact, so eager were the natives for iron that the British crew had a hard job to keep them from stripping the ship of every bit of the metal in sight.

This habit of the Hawaiians of taking whatever iron was lying around loose was the cause of the great tragedy that was to come about a year later. But, on this, his first visit, Cook accepted it philosophically. In his diary that first day, he wrote: "No people could trade with more honesty than these. Some, indeed, at first thought they had a right to anything they could lay their hands upon, but this conduct they soon laid aside."

An unfortunate incident occurred at the very beginning, however. Captain Cook sent Lieutenant Williamson ashore in a boat to find a suitable watering place. As the boat neared shore, a group of natives dashed out into the water and began pulling it up on the beach. One of the men grabbed the metal part of the boat hook. Williamson, perhaps excited and thinking trouble was in the offing, killed the man. On the surface, there seemed to be no deep resentment among the natives over this incident, but, as time proved, it was not forgotten.

After a short stay at Kauai, Captain Cook sailed on to the island of Niihau. There he obtained more salt and yams. On this island, the English were led to believe that the natives were cannibals. Thinking the reason might be that the people had nothing else to eat, Captain Cook left some goats, sheep, swine, and vegetable seeds. His good deed done, Cook, two weeks later, steered his course northward. He hated to leave the pleasant islands. On the other hand, he was eager to search for the passage to the Atlantic around the northern end of the American continent. Before he left, Captain Cook named the islands the Sandwich Islands, after his friend and patron, the Earl of Sandwich, first Lord of the Admiralty. The name, however, was never used except for a brief period in England when that country looked upon the Hawaiians as wards of the British crown.

For almost eleven months, Captain Cook sailed his two ships in a futile search for the eastern passage from the Pacific to the Atlantic. He explored the North American Pacific coast, sending parties into every bay and inlet. But each time the report was the same: "No passage." Most of these side expeditions were led by a young officer, William Bligh, who some years later played the leading role in one of the most famous mutinies of the sea—the Mutiny of the Bounty.

On this 1778 voyage into the waters of the northwest Captain Cook found the Russians active in the trade in furs. In his journal he wrote that a profitable fur trade should be established by the English in the North Pacific region. Toward the end of August, the expedition reached Cape North, and both officers and crew were tired of the futile search for a northeast passage. Food was running low. Day by day, the climate grew colder. Soon ice fields spread across the bleak seas. Navigation became dangerous. Still Cook pushed on northward until October 26, 1778, when he yielded to the pleadings of his crew that they return to the warmth and safety of the island paradise they had discovered. The men cheered when Cook set his course for Hawaii.

Meanwhile Captain Cook and his crew had not been forgotten in the island. There was much argument as to the origin of the white man and his ships. Some of the elders recalled Lono's promise to return on a floating temple. They argued that the English ships were indeed floating temples, therefore their white visitor must have been Lono and his sons. Others claimed that the actions of the white strangers were far from godlike, such as eating fire (smoking tobacco) and taking food from openings in their sides (pockets). The priests paraded their learning and said that they were sure that the white men were the same gods that had left their ancestors long before. The older chiefs were doubtful. The younger warriors proclaimed the British captain to be the god Lono.

The argument was still going on when the two English ships returned late in November, 1778. The chiefs of Kauai advised attacking. They wanted to avenge the murder of the warrior who had been shot while grabbing the boat hook. Such an attack, they argued, would also produce much of the treasured iron. The prospect of great quantities of iron was a pleasing one. But a woman chief recommended caution. If the stranger was Lono, she said, it would be better to make friends with him, at least until they were sure one way or the other.

It was fortunate for Captain Cook that, after sailing among the islands for more than a month, he put in at Kealakekua, which had been the home of the god Lono. There was no doubt in the village that their god had come home again. When Captain Cook went ashore the entire populace ran to meet him, and threw themselves on the beach before him. Wherever he went, the people dropped to the ground at his very sight. One writer, who was an eyewitness, says that after a time this getting up and down grew so tiresome that the whole population of 10,000 men and women on the island went around at all times on all fours, thus in an easy position to fall flat on the ground in proper reverence when the white god put in his appearance.

When Captain Cook dropped anchor in the bay of Kealakekua on January 17, 1779, his plans were innocent enough. He wanted only to repair his ships, take on provisions and water, make some astronomical observations, and then sail north for another try at finding the Pacific end of the westward passage through the Arctic regions. As the days drew into weeks, the natives grew tired of feeding the white men. Their own food supplies were dwindling. With every new demand upon the village by Captain Cook, the belief in his godlike qualities weakened. Various misunderstandings arose between the English and the Hawaiians. Then came a great blow to Cook's prestige with the islanders. A sailor, William Watman, died and was buried ashore. Surely, reasoned the natives, if a white man could die like any ordinary mortal, his leader could not be the immortal Lono. Time and again Cook's officers had advised him to play up more to the god role, but Cook refused to cater to what he dismissed as foolishness.

Another mistake Cook made was the setting up of an observatory within a sacred enclosure. The chief made no open objection to this violation of a sacred tabu, but the move was resented. A few days later, the ships needed firewood and Captain Cook, remembering a wooden fence around the sacred enclosure, offered to buy it for firewood in exchange for two hatchets. The chief told Cook he could have the fence as a gift. Cook accepted the offer, but native resentment grew deeper when the sailors not only took the precious fence, but also carried off a number of wooden idols for their cooking fires.

On January 25 the aged King Kalaniopuu visited Captain Cook aboard his vessel. He brought many presents of food and feathered capes. In return, he received some presents of iron. The king and his people maintained an outward show of friendship, but there was secret rejoicing when the two ships weighed anchor and sailed out of the harbor about ten days later. Things looked as quiet and serene as a cloudless sky, but a tempest of destiny was about to break.

Hardly had the ships sailed from the islands when a furious storm blew up, badly damaging the foremast of the *Resolution*. Captain Cook ordered the ships to put about, and on February 11, much to the disgust of the natives, the unwelcome visitors once more anchored in the bay of Kealakekua. This time, to the surprise of the Englishmen, the harbor was deserted. The chief had declared it tabu to rid it of the taint of the foreigners. But Captain Cook interpreted the lack of proper welcome as a sign of hostility. When the tabu was removed, the natives came out to the ships. They were not only in a decidedly unfriendly mood, but they also stole any iron they could lay their hands on. A group of natives attacked a small boat on shore. In the scuffle that followed a friendly chief was knocked down with an oar. Despite his injury, the chief saved the sailors from the infuriated Hawaiians, but he openly declared that he no longer believed Cook to be the god Lono. Secretly, the chief determined to avenge the act by stealing one of the small boats.

On the morning of February 13, the natives made trouble for a watering party of English sailors. The incident almost led to open hostilities. Later in the day some iron tongs and a chisel were stolen from the *Resolution* by a native who escaped in the ship's boat. The tongs and the chisel were recovered after a fight in which the sailors nearly got the worst of it. On the following morning it was found that the *Discovery's* cutter had been stolen during the night. Captain Cook decided to take strong action. With Lieutenant Phillip and a guard of armed marines he went to the Hawaiian village. Cook's plan was to get the chief, Kalaniopuu, aboard one of his ships and hold him prisoner until the boat was returned.

The old chief was willing enough. He met Captain Cook on the shore. But the chief's wife and several minor chiefs trailed along, begging their king not to trust the Englishman. Hundreds of natives swarmed around them. Their suspicions were aroused by the fact that Cook had come ashore with a heavily armed guard. The Hawaiians eyed the boats filled with sailors standing offshore, and armed themselves with daggers, spears, stones, and clubs. With each passing minute, the situation was increasingly tense. Yet, Captain Cook's plan almost worked. Kalaniopuu was about to step into an English boat when a runner told him that a Hawaiian warrior had been killed in a canoe out on the bay. On hearing this, the old chief hesitated. As Cook tried to pull him into the boat, a native struck at the English captain. Cook fired one barrel of his shotgun at the man, but because of a heavy mat the man was wearing over his chest, he was unhurt. When the Hawaiians saw their fellow uninjured by the white man's thunder weapon, they attacked Captain Cook. The marines and the sailors in the boat immediately opened fire. Captain Cook, horrified at what had happened, turned his back to the natives to order his men to cease firing. But before he could shout the command, he was struck down by a blow from behind. As he tried to rise, a warrior stabbed him in the back. Captain Cook fell headlong into the shallow water, dead. For a few furious minutes the battle continued, until the English were forced to retreat and made for the ships. Besides Captain Cook, four English sailors and thirty Hawaiians were killed. A week after Captain Cook's death, overtures of peace were made by the Hawaiians. Water and provisions were brought aboard the British ships. Late in the evening of February 22, 1779, the *Resolution* and the *Discovery* weighed anchor and sailed from the island.

Captain Cook, England's greatest explorer and navigator, was dead. Some of the powers of the gods of Hawaii had also died. From that time the old order changed in the paradise of the Pacific. News of Captain Cook's death quickly spread to shipping centers in Europe and America, with the result that for about seven years the Sandwich Islands were avoided by European ships. In 1786, white men returned to Hawaii when two French and two English ships called at the islands.

With the development of the northwest fur trade toward the end of the eighteenth century, Hawaii became a popular port of call for American and British ships. Traders came and stayed a few years or settled permanently. Sailors, either deserting or with the permission of their captains, left their ships and made the enchanting islands their homes. Little by little, with each passing year, new ideas changed the pattern of life on the islands, until finally the old pattern gave way to a new, in which European ideas and customs played major roles.

Another factor that speeded up the change in Hawaiian ways was that many youths left the islands for the outside world. These boys came back with new ideas and told stories that filled the stay-at-homes with a desire to copy the life of the white man. Hawaiians made good sailors because of their strength and willingness. It did not take long for English and American skippers to sign on the natives of the islands as members of their crews. Hawaiian men and women were engaged as servants by white settlers. With the ever-growing contact between the new world and the old, new wants and new desires arose that led to a slow but steady change in both thought and manners among the Hawaiians.

At the time of Captain Cook's visit, the islands were divided into several minor kingdoms, each ruled by an independent chief. A few years later, however, hostilities broke out among several of the more powerful chieftains, each of whom wanted to be recognized as the supreme ruler of the islands. The help of the white men was eagerly sought by these chiefs, and a lively trade developed in arms and ammunition.

The most important of the warring chieftains was Kamehameha, who eventually became the founder of a united Hawaiian kingdom. Many factors entered into his success in consolidating the islands, but chief among them was his own character and personality. There is no doubt but that he is the outstanding figure among all the Hawaiian chiefs, as a warrior as well as a statesman.

After many years of civil wars in Hawaii, peace of a sort was restored. Trade began to resume its normal course in 1796. By this time, Kamehameha had succeeded in consolidating all the islands under his rule except Kauai, which held out under Chief Kaumualii. Kamehameha was determined to achieve complete unity and made plans for war.

At this period, the foreign population of the islands began to grow by leaps and bounds. The ships of the foreigners needed a deep harbor. It was inevitable that the best natural harbor, at Honolulu, on the island of Oahu, should become the center of trade and activity. Honolulu grew as the natives followed the lead of the foreigners and slowly abandoned their picturesque and romantic beach town of Waikiki. By 1809, Honolulu was a village of several hundred houses, all shaded by tall coconut palms.

Meanwhile, King Kamehameha had kept steadily at his preparations to attack and conquer the island of Kauai. He bought large quantities of guns, ammunition, and cannons. Carpenters were busy day and night building a squadron of schooners. War canoes by the hundreds were assembled.

There is no doubt that the islands would have been plunged into a long and devastating war at that time, if it had not been for the good offices of an American trader, Captain Winship. In 1810, through Winship's influence, the two rival chiefs were brought together for a peace conference and a treaty of peace was signed. Kamehameha was recognized as the supreme ruler of all the islands except Kauai, which became a tributary state under the independent rule of Kaumualii.

With peace once again reigning over the islands, Kamehameha I retired to his native island of Hawaii, where he divided the time of his last years between sports and helping his people. In 1816 and 1817, the Russians from Bering Strait tried to establish a foothold in Hawaii, but Kamehameha drove them out. He died on May 8, 1819, mourned by everyone on the islands, Hawaiian and foreigner alike.

Kamehameha was succeeded by his son Liholiho, who, although he had the welfare of the islands and its people at heart, did not quite succeed in equaling his father's wise and intelligent rule. The most important event during his reign was the abolishing of the tabus. This was hailed by the people with loud acclaim. In 1824, Liholiho and his wife visited England, where both died the following year.

It was while Liholiho was still on the throne, in 1820, that the missionaries came to Hawaii, mostly from New England. The story is told that a Hawaiian youth, Opukahaia—who had been taken by a trader to New Haven, Connecticut—was found one morning sitting on the steps of Yale University, crying bitterly. The Reverend E. W. Dwight found him in his misery and asked the dusky lad what was wrong. Opukahaia replied that he was crying because of his ignorance and the ignorance of his people of the islands. Dwight, touched by the young Hawaiian's sincerity, not only had him sent to school, but took the first steps that led to the sending of missionaries to the islands.

When the first missionaries arrived in Hawaii, they were permitted to land only on condition that they depart at the end of the year. Instead, the missionaries remained and became a powerful force in shaping the destiny of Hawaii. Among the first were Hiram Bingham and Asa Thurston. Their teachings spread throughout the islands. They not only spread the gospel of Christianity, but established schools, reduced the Hawaiian language to a written form, introduced printing, and trained natives as teachers and interpreters. Early in 1822, the first Hawaiian reading and spelling books were printed.

At about the same time that the missionaries came, the commercial life of the islands received fresh impetus by the coming of the whalers. Up to then, the chief source of revenue, besides trading, had been in the fragrant sandalwood. It is believed that the commercial value of sandalwood was discovered by a Yankee sea captain who had followed his nose to the ship's galley where the cook was burning bits of the aromatic wood in his stove. The captain immediately realized that there would be a market for the sweet-smelling product in Canton, China. He was right. At the height of the trade, sandalwood was selling at $125 a ton. Hawaiians neglected farms and fields in the rush to cut sandalwood, with the result that by 1825, the wood was all but extinct.

Fortunately, however, rich whaling grounds were discovered off Alaska and Japan, bringing a rush of New England whalers into the Pacific. It is recorded that two whaling ships put in at Hawaii in October, 1819, the first of a vast fleet to bring new prosperity to the islands. The whaling captains made Hawaii their field headquarters because it was a long voyage back to New Bedford by way of Cape Horn. They found it easier to dump their cargoes of oil and whalebone at Hawaii for transshipment, and then set sail for more whales.

Between 1830 and 1870, the economic life of the islands was almost entirely tied in with whaling. It is estimated that in the top years of whaling more than 4,000 whaling ships put in at Hawaiian ports, with 18 million gallons of whale oil, more than 14 million pounds of whalebone, and nearly $1\frac{1}{2}$ million gallons of sperm oil.

In the late 1850's, however, the whaling industry began to decline in the islands. The reason was that the center of operations shifted to San Francisco. The final blow came in 1871 when most of the whaling ships that based at Hawaii were destroyed in a crush of Arctic ice.

The islands were lucky in never being wholly dependent on any one industry. After the establishing of the first sugar plantation in 1835, the sugar industry grew steadily and rapidly. Coffee and cattle contributed their share to the wealth of Hawaii. But strangely enough, the fruit that is most closely associated with Hawaii today, the pineapple, came quite late. It is true that the growing of pineapples had been introduced to the islands by a Spaniard, Don Francisco Marín, as early as 1813, but it was an inferior fruit of no commercial value. In 1882, Captain John Kidwell, the Burbank of Hawaii, began his experiments with the growing of commercial pine-apples. By 1892, he had selected the variety he considered best for the soil and climate, the delicious Cayenne. The first pineapple plantation was started at Manoa Valley, Honolulu.

As for the recent history of the islands, in 1839 King Kamehameha III issued his famous Declaration of Rights of the People. This was followed by the first constitution, signed in 1840. On October 8 of that year, a legislature was elected by popular vote.

During the years many claims had been made on the islands by various foreign powers, but between 1842 and 1844 the independence of the Hawaiian Islands was recognized by the United States, Great Britain, and France. This was after Hawaii had been under British rule from February to the end of July in 1843.

Although the monarchial form of government continued, talk of annexation by the United States began as early at 1849, especially as the commercial life of the islands and the west coast of the United States were so closely allied.

During the rule of Kamehameha V, the liberal constitution was revoked. His reign was a period of royal elegance and pomp, known as the golden age of the empire. Despite this reassertion of power, the monarchy was definitely on the way out.

In 1891, the famous and colorful Queen Liliuokalani ascended the throne. She was not satisfied with being a queen in name only, and dismissed the legislature. Public reaction following this drastic measure led to a visit of United States marines and the queen's removal from the throne.

On July 4, 1893, the first Hawaiian Republic was established with Sanford B. Dole as president. Five years later, at the request of the islanders themselves, Hawaii was annexed by the United States, and Sanford Dole was appointed governor. The Territory of Hawaii was created on July 14, 1900.

Queen Liliuokalani lived on into the new era. After she retired to her estate as a private citizen, her kindness won for her the love of her people. When she died in 1917, Hawaii saw the most elaborate funeral in its history. Even today, the people of the islands rise in respect when the familiar and beloved *Aloha Oe*, written by Queen Liliuokalani, is sung by Hawaiians to the softly vibrant notes of the native ukelele.

CHAPTER 17

Alaska, Land of Tomorrow

Highlights of Alaska

Discovered: By Vitus Bering for Russia in 1741.

Population: 75,000.

Area: 586,400 square miles.

Language: English.   *Capital:* Juneau.

Government: Territorial possession of the United States.

Geographical Characteristics: Major portion formed by the Aleutian peninsula, islands, and the narrow Alaskan Panhandle, crisscrossed by numerous mountain ranges.

Climatic Conditions: Owing to the close proximity of the warm Japan current, the Pacific coast region of Alaska has a mild climate. While farther north, winter temperatures are more severe, they are by no means excessively low.

Principal Products: Timber, minerals, such as gold and copper, food fish, coal, and a wide variety of agricultural products.

THERE are probably more false ideas current about Alaska per square mile than any other territory in the world—and that is a lot of misinformation when it is appreciated that Alaska covers an area of almost 590,000 square miles and has a coast line of 35,000 miles.

One of the most frequent errors concerns the size of Alaska. It is often thought of as a mere peninsula jutting out from the northwestern corner of the North American continent. The tremendous size of Alaska would be a startling revelation to most people if they should see a map of Alaska superimposed on a map of the United States. They would then realize that Alaska reaches from California to Georgia. In fact, the main body of Alaska would cover about one-fifth of the entire United States.

The climate is another surprising thing about Alaska. The popular notion is that the farther north one goes, the colder it gets. That is not true. Climate depends on three factors: distance from the equator; height above sea level; distance from warm ocean currents. Alaska, because of its vast size and geography, has many climates.

A climate very similar to that of New England prevails throughout the southeastern and southwestern sections of Alaska. Most of the harbors on the Pacific Ocean are open to navigation all year. In the southeastern part, the climate is so temperate that winter sports can be enjoyed only for a few weeks during the winter. It does get cold, really cold, in the Arctic regions, but even so the average temperature in Alaska is about on a par with that of Montana or the Dakotas.

Vilhjalmur Stefansson, the famous Arctic explorer, says that the average snowfall in the Arctic is less than it is in Pennsylvania. During his 10 years in the regions of the far north he never experienced any blizzards worse than those he knew as a boy in North Dakota.

The popular belief in a 6 months' night during the Arctic winter has done its share to give Alaska the reputation of being a bleak and desolate country. The truth is that even on the fringe of the Arctic Sea, where the sun is invisible for a little more than four months of the year, there is no long period of complete darkness. To make up for it, the sun is visible for almost eight months during the long summer day when Eskimos, at the farthest point north along the shores of the Polar Sea, do not see the sun set.

There are hundreds of thousands of square miles in Alaska where the summer temperatures range between 80 and 90°F. and even reach the 100 mark at times. In some regions, the huge Alaskan mosquitoes are an unfortunate accompaniment of summer. They fly in tremendous swarms and their bite is worse than that of any of the insects known in the United States. Even Alaskan animals beat a quick retreat for the timber line when these pests appear. There are reports of deer and moose actually having been bitten to death by huge swarms of mosquitoes.

As for vegetation, Alaska has more than 700 kinds of native flowering plants. The long period of daylight in the summer gives promise of a profitable agricultural future for the country. Experiments have shown that most ordinary farm products can be raised successfully in Alaska. Even in the Arctic north there is moss, lichen, and grass.

Alaska was discovered by Russians. To understand how that came about, it is necessary to go back to the middle of the sixteenth century, when Russian traders crossed the Ural Mountains. By the middle of the century, they had crossed Asia. The year 1713 found Russian pioneers exploring Kamchatka, in Siberia across the Bering Strait from Alaska, in one of the most rapid colonizing movements in the history of the world. The early conquest of the Alaskan Eskimos and kindred Indian tribes followed.

The story of Alaska begins with Vitus Bering, a Danish navigator who had gained a reputation in the Russian Navy. When, in 1725, Czar Peter the Great sought a man to lead an expedition to find a passage to India and China through the Arctic over the top of Europe and Siberia, he chose Bering for the task. On his first voyage in 1728, Bering came within a hundred miles of Alaska. The ice conditions forced him to turn back.

Because of the failure of this first voyage, Bering did not set out again until 12 years later to explore the Arctic and the Bering Sea. He sighted Alaska on July 16, 1741, at Mount St. Elias. Although Bering did not reach the mainland of the new country, that date marks the discovery of Alaska. Bering died when one of his two ships was wrecked on the Siberian coast before Christmas of that year. The other vessel, however, reached Russia in safety, and its crew brought back furs valued at $100,000. News of this rich fur country sent hordes of Russian adventurers into the Arctic to seek their fortunes, many of whom, instead, found death after horrible sufferings.

The exploration of Alaska proper, however, lagged. The Russians did not cross over to the mainland until 1761. Large-scale exploitation of the country for furs did not start until the beginning of the nineteenth century. Cutthroat competition among the early Russian fur traders led to a reign of terror and brutality in the north. The peaceful natives were enslaved, cheated, and murdered. Fur-bearing animals were killed in great numbers without any thought for the future.

These abuses led the Russian government to take matters in hand. In 1791, Alexander Baranof, a Russian drygoods salesman, was sent to take charge of the czar's North American interests. Baranof ruled his northern domain with an iron hand, but the ill treatment of the natives continued. Still, Baranof was a shrewd businessman. Under his management, the Russian American Company expanded and prospered. At one time Baranof was so powerful that he threatened to seize California and the Hawaiian Islands. Fortunately for the United States, he failed in these attempts. During this time other nations were trading in Alaskan waters, but in 1818 the Russian Navy took over, and all foreigners were barred from doing business in the north.

It is strange that in the earliest days, Spain, which was already in the Pacific, made no effort to explore or claim Alaska. Juan de Fuca sailed the North Pacific coast in 1592, with the only result that a strait was named after him. There is a record of a voyage to Alaska by a Spaniard, de Fonte, from Mexico in 1708. It was not until after the Russian discovery, from 1774 to 1794, that Spain conducted extensive explorations in the waters of southeastern Alaska. At that time, but too late for Spain, Bodega Quadra sailed to the present site of Sitka, in 1775, and mapped the coast line. By then, the English, too, were active in Alaskan waters. They clashed with the Russians over trading rights many times.

Captain James Cook was the most famous of the English navigators to investigate the northwestern regions of North America. On his last tragic voyage in 1778, told about in the chapter on Hawaii, Cook named Cape Prince of Wales and Icy Cape. He sailed into the Arctic Ocean until stopped by an ice barrier. Cook's surveys were so accurate that his charts serve today with but little change.

Other English navigators followed. George Vancouver, one of Cook's lieutenants, tried to complete the work of his former commander. He charted the entire north Pacific coast, and, despite the fact that he overlooked the Columbia River, his survey today forms an important basis of our maps of that region. His work is acknowledged as one of the most notable achievements in Alaskan exploration.

A colorful character of that era was an American, John Ledyard, who had also sailed with Captain Cook. He was a strange combination of dreamer and doer. When he found that he could buy furs for a few cents along the North Pacific coast and sell them for a hundred dollars in China, Ledyard had visions of a great commercial empire in the north. He failed to raise money in America, and also in France and England. His plan of breaking Russia's monopoly of the Alaskan fur trade met with no enthusiasm from capitalists. In 1786, he tried to interest Thomas Jefferson, who was then the minister of the United States in Paris.

Jefferson, advocate of this country's expansion, sold Ledyard on the idea of attempting to reach the Oregon Territory overland by way of Russia and Siberia, with the ultimate object of exploring North America eastward to the Mississippi. Ledyard accepted this tremendous assignment and set out for Alaska. He traveled across Europe and got as far as

Siberia, when he was arrested by order of Empress Catherine the Great. He was taken back to Russia and set free. He then went to Egypt where he died a few months later.

The United States first became seriously interested in the North Pacific as an outcome of the voyage of Captain Gray, who sailed around Cape Horn and discovered the Columbia River in 1792.

Russia, in the meantime, was taking furs out of the north in enormous lots. The Russians built a few sawmills and raised a few potatoes in Alaska. Ice became a commercial commodity, and during a period of several years the Russians sold 3,000 tons of ice at $7 a ton to an American concern in California. A few small iron foundries were operated, but the mineral wealth of the country was unknown. Aside from the fur trade, Russia completely failed to realize the potential wealth of Alaska.

As already mentioned, when the Russian Navy took control of Alaskan affairs in 1818, all foreigners were barred from trading. Both the United States and England protested strongly against this highhanded procedure. Russia was finally forced to give way. In 1824, a 10-year treaty granting equal trading rights was signed with the United States, followed by a similar agreement with England. With these rivals in the field, Russia strengthened her Alaskan defenses, and built Baranof Castle. A light in the tower of this castle served as a beacon for ships off the Alaskan coast for many years.

Our treaty with Russia lapsed in 1834. It was not renewed. Meanwhile, the United States became even more keenly interested in Alaska, especially as the British Hudson's Bay Company continued to enjoy trade privileges. Russia, on the other hand, was beginning to lose interest in Alaska, regarding it more as an investment than as a colony. There was always the danger that England might seize the country, and Russia could not afford to have an outpost of the British Empire right across from Siberia, separated only by the narrow Bering

Strait. It would be much better to have the United States as a friendly neighbor. When the question of selling Alaska came up in the administration of President Buchanan, Russia was most willing to listen.

In 1859, Senator Gwin of California, claiming that he spoke unofficially for President Buchanan, offered to buy Alaska for 5 million dollars. Russia was willing to sell, but wanted 10 million dollars. Negotiations were going on when the Civil War broke out, and the matter was dropped for the time being. During the war, Russia remained friendly toward the Federal government of the United States, in contrast with many European nations that favored the Confederacy of the South. In 1863, the Russian Navy visited American waters, greatly adding to the prestige of the government of the United States. The arrangements for this naval visit were made through Secretary of State Seward, who was also an advocate of the purchase of Alaska. When the Civil War ended, Secretary Seward renewed his efforts to get Alaska for the United States. In December, 1866, Baron Edward Stoeckl was sent to Washington by the Russian government to open negotiations. A deal for 5 million dollars was discussed, but it fell through. President Johnson was cool toward the proposition, but Seward was determined to carry out his plan. To everyone of importance and influence he argued in favor of the project, painting Alaska as a veritable paradise. It was worth many times the few millions involved, Seward insisted. Besides that, the United States owed Russia a debt for having sent the Imperial Navy into American waters when the Civil War had not been going any too well for the North.

Finally, a price of 7 million dollars was arrived at between Secretary Seward and Baron Stoeckl, with an additional $200,000 to settle the Russian American Company's obligations. On the night of March 29, 1867, the Russian ambassador called at Seward's house with a cablegram from the Russian government authorizing him to sell Alaska to the

United States for $7,200,000. The two men congratulated each other on the successful outcome of the negotiations, and the Russian diplomat suggested that they meet at the State Department the following day and go over the details of the sale.

But Seward was afraid to delay even one day. Congress was in special session and might adjourn at any moment. He wanted immediate ratification of the treaty. Although it was late at night, Seward dragged the bewildered Russian to his office in the State Department where the two men and a force of clerks worked all night. At 4:30 A.M. on March 30, 1867, the treaty for the sale of Alaska was signed by the authorized representatives of the United States and Russia.

Alaska was formally turned over to the United States at Sitka, on October 11, 1867, although the treaty had not been ratified by Congress and Russia had not been paid any money. The fight in Congress over the approval of Alaska's purchase was a bitter one. The administration of President Johnson was already under fire, and the cry that the buying of Alaska was just throwing 7 million dollars away echoed from coast to coast.

Secretary Seward was held up to scorn and ridicule on all sides. When he suggested that the new territory be called Alaska from the Eskimo name meaning Great Country, he was laughed at. Other names were suggested with ribald laughter: Seward's Ice Box, Johnson's Polar Bear Garden, Walrussia, and Seward's Folly.

But Seward stuck to his guns. The country is growing westward, he argued. He pointed to the transcontinental railroad that would soon be connecting the East with the west coast of the Pacific. A new era of expansion to California and Oregon and Washington Territory was inevitable. Under those circumstances, not to add Alaska to the new empire would indeed be folly said Seward. He won the battle. In the summer of 1878, the treaty was ratified and $7,200,000 was paid to Russia for one of the biggest bargains in world history. Yet, strangely enough, from the date of its purchase until 1884, the United States rather ignored the new territory of Alaska. The trade in furs, mostly seals, went on as before, but there was no law to regulate the industry. Alaska became a wild, lawless country, of which Kipling wrote: "And there's never a law of God nor man runs north of 53." The Army tried its hand at bringing law and order, but with no success. The job was taken over by the United States Navy in 1877, and until 1884 the seat of government for Alaska was the small but colorful United States ship *Jamestown*, with its home port at Sitka.

During this trying period, Congress argued about what form of government the new possession should have. Almost everyone seemed to know the solution but no two agreed. In 1884, a law was enacted for the northern territory, and a district court was established. Although the measure proved wholly inadequate for the vast territory, it was practically the only legislation for the government of Alaska enacted until the gold strike of 1898. But despite inadequate legislation, to the credit of its people, Alaska progressed and prospered.

Alaska played an important role in one of the principal industries of the United States long before its purchase from Russia. In 1848, the first Yankee whaler nosed its way through the Bering Strait. Such a wealth of whale oil did that pioneer of the United States whaling ship strike in Arctic waters, that it sailed home loaded to the gunwales with the precious liquid. The following year, 1849, about 130 American whalers made rich hauls in Alaskan waters. The fleet of New England whalers that yearly made its way through the Bering Strait into the whaling fields of the Arctic Ocean grew steadily, until, in 1857, some 400 ships spent the season in the vicinity of Alaska.

At the height of the whaling industry in the North Pacific, the Hawaiian port of Honolulu was an important field station for the whaling fleet. The Hawaiian Islands prospered through this activity for many years, until 1871, when a great whaling tragedy put an end to Hawaii as an important center of the industry.

In that year, a fleet of about forty-two whalers sailed from Honolulu through the Bering Strait for a summer of arctic whaling. The ships were mostly from New Bedford, and many of the captains had their wives and children on board. The prospect for a rich haul of oil and whalebone was excellent. It was with high hopes that the whaling men reached Alaskan waters in May. There they had the first disappointment. The ice was so heavy that it was not until the end of July that the ships could make their way to the Arctic waters between Icy Cape and Point Barrow, on the northern coast of Alaska. But once they got there, their spirits rose, for whales were plentiful. Better a late start than a bad start, said many of them as they filled the barrels in the holds of their ships with whale oil.

The whaling ships separated and went about their business, taking little heed that only narrow lanes of water were open between the ice. The smaller whaleboats made their way among the ice floes in pursuit of their game. The fogs were heavy almost every day, but that was the usual Arctic weather. The gales were of more than average severity, but then whaling men did not mind a little wind. Even when a few whaleboats were caught in a sudden ice crush and barely escaped, no one thought anything of it. The boats were hauled over the ice into open water and their crews went about their work.

The strips of water between the ice became smaller and smaller, until there was hardly room for the ships to swing at their anchors. Day after day, the captains hoped for a northeast wind to drive the ice pack back. Instead, a westerly wind made the situation worse. Several of the vessels barely escaped being crushed. Friendly Eskimos warned the whalers that there were signs of an early winter and that it would be wise to sail south. But as that would have meant a wasted voyage for the whole fleet, the crews continued to hunt for whales.

As the weeks passed the situation became more and more serious. Toward the end of August a fierce northeast gale drove the ice back. But instead of taking the opportunity to escape into safe and open water, the whalers sailed deeper among the ice floes where the whales were abundant.

Then the wind changed. The ice pack continued to press and threaten them. The first ship was caught on the second day of September. In the vicelike grip of the ice, her stout timbers snapped like kindling. The crew barely escaped with their lives. But even this warning was not heeded by the other skippers or their men. There were still plenty of whales about, and operations continued, although open water could be seen only from the mastheads.

A week later another ship was crushed. The following day a third vessel was the victim of the ice squeeze. The ships, all except seven, were now completely hemmed in by ice, with no chance of getting out until the following summer. The ships had neither food nor fuel for more than three months at the most. Therefore, the only salvation for those aboard was to try to make their way over the ice to the seven ships that were afloat in open water.

In the cold bitter morning of September 14, more than 1,200 whalemen with a few women and children took to the open boats from the icebound ships. It was hard pulling at the oars. The way through the ice floes was both difficult and dangerous. That night they spent on the ice, sleeping under overturned whaleboats as a protection against the biting cold and cutting wind. Before dawn, they were under way again, with the wind blowing a gale fury and threatening to swamp the boats at every pull of the oars. But New Bedford whaleboats were built to withstand any kind of weather and the oarsmen were strong and skillful. For a time, it looked as if they would never reach their goal. Then they suddenly found themselves in open water, clear of the ice, and within a short pull of the ships that were waiting to take them aboard.

Not a single life was lost, but thirty-three ships were abandoned in the ice. It was a great blow to the whaling industry. New Bedford whaling men alone lost more than a million dollars in the disaster. Honolulu, as a whaling center, never recovered from the setback.

Despite this disaster polar whaling in the waters north of Alaska was not completely abandoned. A smaller fleet sailed through the Bering Strait in 1872. The ice was merciful that year. No ships were lost. But, in 1876, twelve ships were caught in the ice. The vessels were abandoned by all but fifty men. They decided to remain with the ice-locked ships. Those who made their way across the ice were rescued after days of incredible hardships. Of the fifty men who stayed behind, nothing was ever heard again. A search the next year revealed no trace of the abandoned ships or their crews.

Almost from the time of its discovery, the fur seal was one of the most valuable resources of Alaskan waters. The most highly prized were those found off the Pribilof Islands in the Bering Sea. Under Russian rule, the seals had been hunted with no thought of conservation. Males and females were killed alike. This slaughter reduced the herds so rapidly that seal hunting had to be restricted to the young males of the herds. These were driven inland among the islands and then clubbed. This method allowed for a large kill each year without serious interference with the normal increase of the herds.

This policy was adopted by the United States, which had been active in the seal industry off the Pribilof Islands as early as 1868. In those days, the market price of a sealskin was $2.50. Sealskins became fashionable at about that time, and the price gradually increased. By 1890, a good skin sold for about $30. This rise in the value of sealskins led many hunters to kill the animals indiscriminately, and also to resort to pelagic or open-sea killing of seals.

Open-sea killing of seals had been practiced by the Pacific coast Indians from earliest times. The natives, paddling leisurely among the herds, would spear the seals (male or female) as they rested on the surface of the sea. Many pups were killed this way; besides, countless dead animals sank to the bottom and their skins were lost. Still, as practiced by the Indians for their limited needs, this method was not destructive. Soon commercial sea hunters, spurred on by the high price of skins, engaged in large-scale open-sea killing. In 1878, one ship engaged in this pelagic slaughter. In 1894, more than 140,000 skins were taken by ninety-four vessels.

The United States was strongly opposed to this method of seal hunting. In 1886 and 1887 the government seized seven Canadian ships engaged in pelagic killing, claiming that the waters of the Bering Sea, east of the Russian boundary, were under the complete jurisdiction of the United States. England protested. As the seizure of Canadian vessels continued, relations between the United States and England were strained almost to the point of war.

The question was submitted to arbitration in Paris in 1893. The exclusive rights of the United States were denied by the arbitration board. Although some degree of protection was given the seals, the valuable herds continued to decrease under the halfway measures of the decision. It was not until 1911 that the wasteful open-sea killing of seals was finally prohibited by agreement of all countries bordering on the Bering Sea.

The United States received its first big dividend from the Alaska investment in gold. The presence of pay dirt in the country had been a known fact since 1861, when a strike at Stikine River, later known as Cassiar, led to a mild gold rush. The gold fever then subsided, until Joe Juneau and Dick Harris found gold on Douglas Island in 1881. They sold their claims to John Treadwell of San Francisco. He formed four mines into the famous Treadwell group, which produced 20 million dollars in a generation. From 1885 to 1915 it was one of the world's largest and most profitable gold mines.

The Treadwell mines produced a low-grade ore, but by wholesale mining of as much as 250,000 tons a year, the venture showed tremendous profits. The real effect of these mines on Alaska was indirect. They employed from 200 to 300 men a year at about $2.50 and board a day. This gave independent prospectors a chance to gather a grubstake and go gold hunting on their own. It also served to spread the gold fever throughout Alaska.

The early Cassiar gold strike, although not rich, as gold strikes go, produced 5 million dollars by 1883, and attracted more than 2,000 prospectors. Then, in 1898, came the fabulous Klondike gold strike in the Yukon, in adjoining Canadian territory. The story of this fantastic gold rush is told in another chapter.

At the height of the Klondike stampede, gold was found on the Seward peninsula in Alaska near Cape Nome. It started a new gold rush. In 1896, Seward Peninsula was a barren waste with only a few hundred Eskimo inhabitants. Ten years later, it was crowded to overflowing with 10,000 eager gold seekers, whose annual "take" was about 8 million dollars.

The most remarkable chapter of the Alaska gold excitement was written in the sands of Nome Beach. A soldier and a miner were looking for driftwood along the sands when they found gold on the beach. The news spread like wildfire. Soon 2,000 miners were digging from $20 to $100 a day out of the sands. In 2 months, more than a million dollars was taken from the seashore.

Within a short time, the beach was literally black with humanity. It was easy to reach and the gold could be separated from the sands with the simplest sort of equipment. It was a poor man's gold mine. But, as it turned out, it was too poor to support the ill-advised thousands who flocked to Nome in the hope of raking a fortune from the sands. For every one who found gold, there were hundreds who found nothing. Disorders broke out among prospectors and immigrants who were stranded. The lax policy of the government in failing to provide adequate laws for Alaska came home to roost. The President of the United States hurriedly appointed a commission to report on a code of criminal administration. It was adopted in 1900. This code, the basis of the present-day judicial system of Alaska, was one of the most beneficial results of the Alaska gold strike.

The natives of Alaska, the Eskimos and other native tribes, took very little part in all these events that were happening in their country. Those who came into close contact with the centers of civilization gradually became part of the new way of life. Those in the more remote sections went on living as they always had.

To get back to popular misconceptions about Alaska, the belief that Eskimos live on oil and blubber is as widespread and false as any. The Eskimos are meat eaters, and their very name means eaters of raw flesh. Their own name for themselves is Inuit, meaning people. The Eskimos of Alaska are very much like the Eskimos of other parts of the Arctic, except that they have been more influenced by contact with white men. They are of medium height, with small hands and feet, Mongol eyes, and broad faces.

In the summer, they live in skin tents, which are covered with snow in the winter. Sometimes the tents are discarded for winter houses made entirely of ice and snow. The language of the Eskimos is difficult, and according to Dr. Stefansson, as hard to master as any four European languages. For purposes of trade, a jargon known as Chinook is employed. It is a mixture of English, French, and Indian.

The getting of food was probably always a serious problem with the Alaskan Eskimo. He is a hunter, living on the flesh of animals he kills. With his crude native weapons, he had to work hard for a living. Still, he killed no more than was necessary for food and to get furs for clothing. When he obtained the white man's guns and learned the value of furs, the Eskimo became a ruthless hunter. He did not realize that he was exterminating his food supply; that he was virtually shooting himself into starvation.

In 1891, Dr. Sheldon Jackson, a Presbyterian missionary decided to try to save the Eskimos from the ultimate starvation that faced them. As an experiment he imported sixteen reindeer from Lapland where the reindeer long had been the very source of human food and comfort. The reindeer were distributed among some Eskimos who soon became expert herdsmen. Since the experiment was successful, large-scale importation of reindeer into Alaska from Lapland was taken over by the United States government. By 1900 more than 1,200 had been brought in. So well did the animals thrive that by now Alaskan reindeer herds number more than 350,000.

The reindeer were strange to the Eskimo and he had to be taught to use them to meet his needs for food and clothing and even shelter, much as the American Plains Indian had depended on the buffalo. To solve this problem, the government established reindeer schools where young Eskimos were taught how to take care of the animals. The Eskimos, left to their own ways, would probably have exterminated the reindeer as they had their native deer and moose.

The success of the American reindeer experiment led Canada to adopt a similar measure many years later to save the Canadian Eskimos along the fringe of the Arctic Sea from slow but sure starvation. A herd of 3,000 reindeer was bought in Alaska from the Loman Brothers. Andrew Bahr, a short, stocky little Laplander who had come to Alaska with the original herd in the '90's, was commissioned to deliver the animals on the Mackenzie River, 1,000 miles away.

A drive of 1,000 miles may not seem very long in terms of the old cattle trails of southwestern United States. But with reindeer, through the uncharted wastes of the Arctic, it was another story. Andrew Bahr had to drive his herd of timid animals over mountains, across swamps, through howling hurricanes and blinding blizzards. It took him 5 years to cover that thousand miles. Although 90 per cent of the original herd of 3,000 was killed by wolves, eaten by the herders, or died, or strayed on the way, Bahr delivered 2,370 reindeer to the Canadian Eskimos at the Mackenzie delta. During those 5 years, there were five fawnings, one for each spring. Thus, not only Andrew Bahr, but the reindeer proved themselves tougher and more hardy than the Arctic at its worst.

The Eskimos are not the only ones who have been rescued by the timely arrival of a herd of reindeer. Perhaps the most thrilling and dramatic chapter in the drama of Alaska was the one enacted in 1898, when men of the Coast Guard, then the United States Revenue Cutter Service, drove a herd of reindeer north across Alaska to save a group of whaling men icebound at Point Barrow.

The news of eight whaling ships trapped in the Arctic ice near Point Barrow, Alaska, reached San Francisco early in November, 1897. As rescue ships would be unable to reach them until the following summer, nearly 500 whalemen faced starvation in the frozen north. President McKinley was told of their plight and turned the matter over to the Coast Guard as the only government agency that might be able to effect a rescue with the revenue cutter *Bear*, a sturdy icebreaker assigned to Alaskan patrol.

Captain Francis Tuttle of the *Bear* was a man of long experience in Alaskan waters. He knew that even his icebreaker could not get through the ice at that time of the year. There was only one solution: to drive food overland on the hoof. The only animals that would serve the purpose were the reindeer Uncle Sam had imported a few years before. It was a difficult assignment, and certainly an odd one for the Coast Guard. Those who undertook to perform this heroic task were all volunteers, inspired by the Coast Guard slogan: "You have to go; you don't have to come back!"

The plan was that an overland expedition set out for Point Barrow and on the way buy from Eskimos enough reindeer to provide food for the icebound whalemen to last until spring.

The overland party, under command of Lieutenant Jarvis, set out from the village of Tununak, Alaska, on December 18, 1897, with 1,300 pounds of equipment packed on four sleds pulled by forty-one half-wild huskies. Ahead of them stretched 1,500 miles of hostile and unknown country. It was winter, and almost from the first they ran into blizzards. Daily it grew colder and colder, but there was no time to stop and build fires during the short daytime rest periods. The thermometer kept dropping. By Christmas it was at 15° below zero. Fresh dogs were obtained from Eskimos as often as they could be found. Week by week, these seamen-become-dog-sled-drivers kept on the go through driving gales, not stopping for a single day's rest.

On January 1, 1898, they met one of the sailors who had left Point Barrow and the stranded ships 2½ months before to seek help. He was half dead. He told Lieutenant Jarvis that, when he left, his fellow sailors had been in bad shape both from cold and hunger. The rescuers pressed on. The snow became thicker and deeper, until the coastguardmen had to put on snowshoes, which were as strange to them as the dog sleds they were maneuvering. Deeper grew the blanket of snow, until some of the men had to go ahead and trample it down for the dogs. Golovin Bay was reached January 11. There the dogs were abandoned in favor of special Lapland freight sleds pulled by teams of reindeer. Jarvis had to master the technique of reindeer sledding overnight.

The house of Artisarlook, the Eskimo, who was to supply the first herd of reindeer, was reached on January 19. He was reluctant to give up his animals and leave his family, but he finally agreed to go along when Jarvis, in the name of Uncle

Sam, promised that the reindeer would be replaced. Then started the worst part of the journey, with Point Barrow still 800 miles away.

While Artisarlook's herd was being rounded up, Jarvis went ahead to collect more of the animals at Port Clarence. The cold was almost unbearable, with the mercury at 40° below. He picked up the reindeer and then headed for Cape Prince of Wales. There, on January 24, the various members of the expedition, including the Eskimo reindeer herders, met for the final lap of the northward dash.

Battling snow and wind and cold, they were able to make only from 8 to 12 miles a day, with both men and animals ready to collapse from exhaustion at the close of each day. The herd consisted of 438 reindeer. Clothing, equipment, and other supplies were carried in eighteen deer-drawn sleds. Eskimos were sent ahead to warn other Eskimos of their approach so that they would not shoot into the herd believing them to be wild reindeer. After a week it was found the sled deer were not fast enough as freight animals; Jarvis had to go back to dogs to pull the sleds.

It was the end of March when Lieutenant Jarvis and his men drove the herd of reindeer out on Point Barrow and into sight of the icebound whalers. They were greeted by wild shouts of joy. The half-starved, half-frozen sailors, many of them ill, had all but given up hope.

This dash of 1,500 miles across the snows of Alaska by a unit of Coast Guard sailors to deliver a herd of reindeer to starving whalers at Point Barrow is undoubtedly one of the greatest epics in the history of Coast Guard relief expeditions. It is a monument to the heroic qualities of the men and the animals who took part in it, and a never-dying tribute to the spirit of the Coast Guard service. It is an episode that men of land and sea in the far north will never forget.

The huskies, or Alaskan sled dogs, that proved so valuable to Lieutenant Jarvis, are a vital part of the north country's life. There are many stories of how these dogs have served man in times of emergency, but perhaps none greater than in 1925, when death and disaster threatened Nome.

It was winter when a diphtheria epidemic struck the snow-bound town. The lone doctor found himself without antitoxin, the lifesaving serum that would prevent widespread deaths by the dreaded disease. The doctor could only telegraph an appeal for serum to Seattle, the nearest point where it was available, and then pray and hope.

When the appeal for serum was flashed into Seattle, the antitoxin was immediately made available and started north with a speed that made history. The fastest steamer rushed the lifesaving cargo to Seward, Alaska. Then by fast train, it sped to Fairbanks. There, a waiting plane picked the serum up and flew it to Yukon, then the last northern outpost of the modern communications system. At Yukon, the first of a relay of the best dog teams in Alaska hauled the serum on the first lap across the snow to Nome. The last stage of the memorable journey was made by the famous dog-sled driver Seppala. He drove his animals for 340 miles without rest. With the temperature at 30° below zero, the dogs covered an average of 50 miles a day. On one day they ran 90 miles over the trackless snow. The serum reached Nome and the inhabitants were saved from a dreadful tragedy by Alaskan huskies. If it had not been for the great strength and courage of these dogs, the speed of steamer, train, and airplane would have availed nothing.

An interesting discovery, made in 1908 in Sitka, might have added a great deal more territory to the United States if it had been made earlier. In that year, Leo Nebokoff, going through some old Russian documents, came across an order from the Russian government requesting the governor of Alaska to bury tablets bearing the Russian coat of arms at various points along the Alaskan coast as a record of the empire's claim to that territory. An investigation revealed that the order had been faithfully complied with, and some of the tablets were located as far south as British Columbia. Technically, this made the entire Pacific coast of Canada a part of the Russian territory that the United States had bought as Alaska in 1867. If the discovery had been made prior to the boundary agreement with Canada in 1903, the United States could have claimed the entire North Pacific coast.

Still, the United States can never complain of not having received its money's worth when Seward bought Alaska for $7,200,000. Since March 30, 1867, Alaska has produced more than 450 million dollars' worth of gold, almost 200 million dollars' worth of copper, more than 80 million dollars' worth of furs.

In a single year, Alaska produced 30 million dollars' worth of fish for food. More than 21 million acres of forest lands, spruce, hemlock, and cedar stand ready for future needs. There is grazing land for herds of millions of reindeer and other domestic cattle. The rich loam of Alaska's valleys can grow enough grain and fruit and vegetables to feed a million people. Within Alaska's hardly opened treasure chest lie billions upon billions of dollars' worth of copper and gold and tin and coal and oil.

Hundreds of millions of dollars have already been added to America's wealth by Alaska. Billions upon billions of dollars of natural resources still await posterity. Yes, Alaska, is a Land of Tomorrow!

CHAPTER 18

Quest for the Northwest Passage

Highlights of the Dominion of Canada

Discovered: By John Cabot for England in 1497. First explored and claimed for France by Cartier, Champlain, and La Salle.

Population: 10,377,000.

Area: 3,684,463 square miles.

Language: English and French.   *Capital:* Ottawa.

Government: Self-governing dominion of the British Empire.

Main Geographical Features: Geographically, Canada divides itself into the following major regions from east to west: Circling Hudson Bay are the Laurentian Highlands, then the Lowlands of the Saint Lawrence, the Acadian Region, the Great Central Plains, the Pacific Mountain Area, and the Coastal Islands.

Climatic Conditions: Virtually the same as those of the United States above a line drawn across the country from New York to Northern California.

Principal Products: Canada is rich in natural resources such as lumber and minerals as well as fresh and salt-water food fish. Its fertile soil produces vast crops of wheat and other grains. Its manufacturing activities show steady increase with paper and pulp as the leading items.

Regions in This Chapter	Historical Data	Capital	Population	Area, Square Miles
Newfoundland and Labrador	British in 1497	Saint John's	293,951	155,134
Northwest Territories	Territory in 1869	Fort Smith	9,800	1,309,682

ARCTIC exploration in the Western Hemisphere began more than a thousand years before the long-sought-for northwest water passage around the top of North America was finally navigated by Roald Amundsen in 1905. In the latter part of the ninth century Otthar, a viking of Halgoland, told King Alfred of England about a land to the north where the sun shone either all the time or not at all. Around the year 890, this Scandinavian sailor had taken his small open boat round North Cape, along the coast of Lapland, and discovered the White Sea in the Arctic.

The Norsemen of that day, because of the barrenness of their land, were forced to depend on fishing expeditions for food. This led to the development of a race of hardy, courageous, and adventurous navigators. Without compass or maps they sailed westward across unknown seas and reached Iceland where they established a colony.

England had established trade relations with Iceland early in the fifteenth century, and the voyages of the Norsemen to Greenland and Vinland to the west may have been known to the British. It is certain, however, that English merchants followed the explorations of Columbus and Portuguese navigators for the sea road to the Spice Islands with keen interest. Even before Columbus sailed in 1492, some merchants in the city of Bristol had financed voyages to find land to the west across the Atlantic. These expeditions bore no fruit.

When Spain and Portugal, in the era of Columbus, divided the world between them for the purpose of exploring and claiming new lands, England was left completely out of the picture. In 1496, John Cabot, a Bristol merchant, induced King Henry VII of England to give him a ship to sail across the Atlantic where Columbus had discovered lands that everyone believed were Asia.

John Cabot, whose explorations formed the basis of all England's later claims to territory in North America, was born in Genoa, Italy. His real name was Giovanni Caboto.

He was the scion of a fine old merchant family. Cabot spent many years as a merchant in Mecca, the Holy City of the Moslems. There he traded with the caravans that came in from the East with rich cargoes of silks and spices from the Orient. Cabot was not only a good businessman, but he was interested in geography. Camel drivers and caravan merchants told him fascinating stories of Cathay and Cipango, the fabulous lands that Marco Polo had written about. From these merchants who came to Mecca, Cabot got the idea that Asia could be reached by sailing westward across the Atlantic Ocean from Europe.

It was to test this idea that John Cabot came to the bustling English seaport of Bristol. In March, 1496, he secured an audience with King Henry and convinced him that the discovery of a short westward water route to Asia would lead to a profitable trade in silks and spices.

The king was notoriously closefisted with money, so that Cabot's expedition was not a very grand one. It consisted of only one small ship, the *Matthew*, with a crew of eighteen men. A royal patent granted John Cabot permission to sail under the English flag "to all parts, regions and coasts of the eastern, western and northern seas, and to occupy them in the king's name." But Cabot was given strict instructions to remain within the latitude of England to keep from clashing with the Spaniards in the Caribbean.

The *Matthew* left Bristol on May 2, 1497, taking a northwest course. Cabot soon ran into a zone of icebergs and had to head south. On June 24, he saw land. Some authorities claim it was Newfoundland; others say it was Cape Breton Island. At any rate, as Cabot sailed southward along the coast he found rich codfish schools on the Grand Banks. Returning to England on August 6, Cabot reported to King Henry that he had found neither China nor Japan nor silks nor gold nor spices. All he had to show were a few berries his men had picked. Cabot had not seen a single human being in the land across the sea, but he knew it was inhabited because he had come upon snares to catch game and other traces of habitation. Cabot was sure that he had reached the outlying regions of China or Japan. Then he told enthusiastically of the great codfish runs, some so thick that they slowed down the ship. King Henry was not overenthusiastic, but he gave Cabot a bonus of $50 for his discoveries and made him an admiral.

The merchants of Bristol were more encouraged than the king. They felt that, with a better-equipped expedition, Cabot would be able to establish a profitable trade across the Atlantic. They fitted out five ships for Cabot, who sailed westward again the following year, with 300 men. Among them was young Sebastian Cabot, who later became famous as an explorer in his own right. One of the ships was damaged and had to turn back. The other four reached North America, where Cabot headed southward and discovered Cape Cod. The charts Cabot made on this voyage show the coast of North America running east and west instead of northeast to southwest. This falsification was deliberate. Cabot did not want to be accused of sailing south (as he did) of the latitude of England into Spanish-claimed waters.

There was great disappointment when Cabot returned to England with no further news of China or the Spice Islands. King Henry VII did nothing to follow up Cabot's discoveries. He was afraid of losing the friendship of the King and Queen of Spain, who frowned on the efforts of any other nation to extend its influence across the Atlantic. John Cabot was considered a failure by the men of his day, but the codfish banks he discovered have produced as much wealth as the gold mines of Mexico and Peru. Moreover, Cabot's explorations justified England's territorial claims in North America during the period of New World colonization in later years.

The French soon became interested in the codfish banks discovered by Cabot. Every year, large fleets of French fishermen set out from Saint Malo on voyages to the stormswept

Grand Bank. The blessing of the fishing fleet before it left Saint Malo for its dangerous journey across the Atlantic is a picturesque ceremony that has been carried down to this day. The interest of France in the New World quickly extended beyond mere fishing for cod.

By 1510, it was generally conceded that the lands and islands discovered by Christopher Columbus were not Asiatic. However, the belief that the Orient was not far off continued until Balboa discovered the Pacific Ocean in 1513. Then a frantic search began for a strait, or water passage across the new land to this western ocean. In 1520, Ferdinand Magellan discovered the strait that bears his name across the southern part of South America. This new waterway to the Spice Islands and the route eastward around the Cape of Good Hope at the tip of Africa were controlled by Spain and Portugal, respectively. That left France and England completely out of the race to the Orient unless a northwest passage could be found.

Since a southwest passage to the Pacific had been discovered, it was argued that a similar route must exist over the top of America. As a matter of fact, most of the map making in the early days along the coast of North America was done by explorers who sought a northwest gateway to the Pacific and the wealth of Asia. Over a period of more than two hundred years, French and English navigators probed into every bay and river mouth, hoping that some dent in the coast line would prove to be the elusive channel to the Pacific Ocean.

In 1524 Giovanni Verrazano, a Florentine navigator, sailing for France, explored the North American coast from North Carolina to Newfoundland. His was the first ship to sail into New York harbor. This was 85 years before the Hudson River was discovered by Henry Hudson. The voyage of Verrazano formed the basis for all New World claims made by France.

In 1534, the King of France ordered Jacques Cartier to make a search for the northwest passage. On his first voyage Cartier explored the coast of Newfoundland and discovered the Gulf of Saint Lawrence. On July 24, 1534, in Gaspé Harbor, he claimed the new land for France. Before this, Cartier had met some Indians at Paspebiac Point with whom he traded for furs. This was the first recorded fur transaction in Canada. The Frenchman tried to go up the Saint Lawrence River, but wind and current were so strong that he was forced to turn back.

In 1536, Cartier resumed where he had left off. He sailed up the Saint Lawrence to an Indian village called Stadacona (Quebec). There, a hostile chief refused to let Cartier proceed further westward. A salvo of twelve cannon shots made the chief change his mind. Early in October the Frenchmen came to a village the Indians called Hochelaga. It was situated on an island. Near it was a hill, which Cartier called Montreal (Mount Royal). An end was put to his inland journey by a series of impassable rapids which he named LaChine, thinking that beyond them lay China. By now, it was too late in the season to push farther west, so Cartier went down the river and spent the winter near Quebec. There, an epidemic of scurvy broke out among the men. The Indians showed the Frenchmen a native cure for the disease, a bark medicine; but even so, twenty-six Frenchmen died.

Up to this time, England had done nothing in New World explorations. Although it was believed that John Cabot had reached the outlying parts of Asia, it was almost eighty years before the British followed up his discoveries. In 1576, Sir Humphrey Gilbert published a treatise tending to prove that a strait must exist across the northern tip of the new continent. That very year, Martin Frobisher made the first of his three voyages into Arctic waters. After rediscovering Greenland, which had passed into oblivion with the death of the early Norse colony, Frobisher reached a point of land between

Baffin Island and Frobisher Bay. Hoping that he had found the coveted strait, the English navigator sailed up the narrow, rock-bound stretch of water. It proved to be landlocked, and inhabited by hostile Eskimos. These natives kidnaped five of Frobisher's men, who were never seen again. The English captain, in turn, captured an Eskimo, and took him back to England as a curiosity.

Martin Frobisher's explorations might have been more extensive if he had not discovered what he thought was gold. His men gathered tons of the goldlike ore. When news of gold reached the Queen, she was no longer interested in finding a northwest passage.

When Frobisher returned in 1577 with 200 tons more of the mineral, the discovery had already been made that it was only iron pyrite, known as "fools' gold." Despite this disappointment, and in the hope of finding real gold, Frobisher sailed again in 1578. On this third and last voyage he stumbled on what later became known as Hudson Strait. But Frobisher had orders to look for gold, so he continued on to Frobisher Bay. There he collected 1,300 tons of ore, which also proved to be "fools' gold," and worthless. After Frobisher came John Davis, who sailed along the western coast of Greenland in 1585, calling it the Land of Desolation. He crossed through Davis Strait and discovered Cumberland Sound, which he believed to be the opening of the northwest passage, even though he was unable to sail through it.

The Cabots probably sailed through Hudson Strait in 1498, as did later Elizabethan explorers, but Hudson Bay was not explored until 1610, when it was visited by Henry Hudson, after whom it was named.

The voyages of Henry Hudson between 1607 and 1611 were a continuous effort to find a northeast or northwest passage from Europe to the Orient. His first two voyages were made for the Muscovy Company and the English Trading Company in search of the northeast passage over the top of Europe.

When Hudson sailed in the *Half Moon* in April, 1609, under Dutch sponsorship, he planned to seek the northeast passage, but winds and waves were so rough that his crew induced him to steer westward instead. On this voyage Henry Hudson had a map he claimed Captain John Smith had sent him from Virginia. The map showed a westward water passage at the latitude of 40 degrees, which is the location of Philadelphia. Following the map, the *Half Moon* explored Delaware Bay and then sailed north to the Hudson River. Hudson sailed up the river that bears his name to a point between Albany and Troy. There he turned downstream again, convinced that he had discovered a river and not an ocean-to-ocean passage.

Hudson's fourth and last voyage was made for England in 1610 aboard the ill-fated *Discovery*. He sailed northwest, making his first landfall in the vicinity of Labrador; then he sailed north into Hudson Bay. James Bay, at the southern end, was reached in November. Here Hudson and his men spent a long, cold, and miserable winter. Many of the men were seriously ill. There was not enough food or fuel. The intense cold made for irritability and short tempers.

When the ice broke up in the spring, Hudson ordered the crew to get the ship ready to continue the search for the northwest passage. The men obeyed with reluctance, for many of them felt that it would be better for the captain to return to England instead of continuing the voyage into dreary and unknown Arctic regions. There was mutiny in the air as the *Discovery* worked its way through the ice in dense mist on June 12, 1611. The mutineers knew that Hudson was a stubborn man and would not listen to their pleas that the ship be sailed back home. They also knew that there was only about two weeks' supply of food on board.

The mutiny broke out on June 22, when Captain Hudson was captured and thrown into an open boat in which the mutineers had already placed Hudson's young son, the ship's carpenter, and a number of the sick men. The boat was cut adrift, and the last sight the mutineers had of Henry Hudson was as the little boat disappeared from view. The captain shook his fists toward the *Discovery* shouting defiantly that the wrath of heaven would descend on the heads of the mutineers. Henry Hudson and those cast adrift with him were never heard of again. Several of the leaders of the mutiny were killed by Indians when they landed a fortnight later near Hudson Strait. Others died of illness on the homeward journey. The remainder were arrested and tried for murder when the *Discovery* reached England.

Hudson Strait was explored by William Baffin in 1615. He decided to look for the northwest passage farther north. There he discovered Baffin Bay and named many of the inlets and peninsulas. Baffin failed to find the gateway to the Pacific but he headed in the right direction, and his explorations led to success more than two hundred years later when Amundsen sailed the strait.

By now discovery of a northern water passage to the Oriental markets was so important to England that an award of $100,000 was offered for the first man to find it. In 1778, Captain James Cook, one of England's greatest navigators, sailed through Bering Strait from the Pacific into the Arctic Sea looking for the western end of the northwest passage. Cook did not find it, but he made many discoveries. He named Norton Sound and Icy Cape, which remained the northernmost boundaries beyond which no navigator sailed for 50 years.

After the Napoleonic Wars, England assigned some of her ablest naval officers to the search for a northwest passage. The most famous of these were John Ross and Edward Perry. The latter reached Lancaster Sound in 1818. For crossing longitude 110 degrees west and proving that there was a water connection between the two oceans, he was awarded $25,000 prize money. After the discovery that a northwest passage did exist, voyages of exploration to the Arctic became almost an annual event for English navigators. In 1829, John Ross named Boothia. With the help of friendly Eskimos, who furnished dog sleds, Ross made a difficult overland journey to King William Island. In 1831, Captain Ross located the north magnetic pole on the west shore of Boothia peninsula.

Perhaps the greatest stimulant to Arctic exploration was the tragedy of Sir John Franklin. On his first voyage, in 1820, Franklin and his party were saved from starvation by friendly Eskimos. Five years later, in 1825, Franklin began his second voyage from New York, going overland to Great Slave Lake in northern Canada. He then followed the Mackenzie River until winter overtook him at Great Bear Lake. There he remained until spring, when he continued his explorations. At the same time Captain Beechey was carrying on the work begun by Captain Cook on the Pacific side. At one time the two parties were only 160 miles apart, although they were unaware of each other's presence.

Franklin sailed again in 1845, with 120 men in two ships, the *Erebus* and the *Terror*, to complete his explorations. He spent the winter of 1845 on Beechey Island; that of 1846 was weathered in the ice pack. In the spring of 1847, Franklin again continued his explorations until 1848, when the two ships had to be abandoned in the ice. The men started overland in a desperate dash for Bach's Fish River. None of them ever reached the world below the Arctic again.

When the years passed with no news of Franklin and his crew, relief expeditions were sent out to find them. In 1850 at least twelve ships were combing the Arctic for Franklin. Although the search was futile, some 7,000 miles of Arctic coast line were explored as the result of the search. In 1854 Dr. Rae of the Hudson's Bay Company, while surveying in Boothia, met some Eskimos who told of having seen thirty white men dragging a boat over the ice. Some time later they had come upon the party again, but by that time all the white men were dead. When notes written by Franklin and his officers, as they were dying, were found many years later, the *Erebus* and the *Terror* were eternal ghostly memories of the Arctic's greatest victory.

One of the most important discoveries that came about as a result of the search for Franklin, was made by Captain Robert McClure. He sailed his rescue ship, the *Investigator*, through Bering Strait from the Pacific. For many months McClure nosed in and out of the channels of the Arctic maze. In 1853, the captain and his men crossed the ice to Melville Sound in sleds, and then continued eastward to the Atlantic side. They thus completed the first northern passage, although they had not sailed through it. Robert McClure was knighted for his achievement and given half of the $100,000 award for finding the northwest passage. The other half was awarded to Dr. John Rae of the Hudson's Bay Company for his explorations in the Arctic.

One of the first American expeditions into the arctic was undertaken in 1879 aboard the schooner *Jeannette* under the command of Lieutenant Commander George W. De Long, a retired officer of the United States Navy. An interesting feature of this expedition was that it was financed by James Gordon Bennett, publisher of the *New York Herald*, who sent Henry M. Stanley into the heart of Africa to find Dr. David Livingstone. As we know, Stanley found the missing British missionary, but De Long did not find the North Pole. Instead, his ship was crushed by the ice of the Polar Sea. This happened near Bennett Island, several hundred miles north of the coast of Siberia. Commander De Long and most of his men froze to death.

However, it would be a mistake to say that the *Jeannette* sailed northward in vain. Its very destruction led to a significant discovery in connection with the currents of the Arctic Ocean.

In 1883, three years after the *Jeannette* had been abandoned by its crew at Bennett Island, a school teacher in a Danish colony on the east coast of Greenland found some wreckage on the shore near his home. On examining it, he discovered some papers that had been written by Commander De Long aboard the *Jeannette*. In other words, the wreckage on the coast of Greenland definitely established that the current of the Arctic Sea runs westward across the polar region. This was interesting news to one man in particular, namely, Fridtjof Nansen, a Norwegian who even then had begun the Arctic studies which in time, were to make him famous. It suggested to Nansen a novel but dangerous way of reaching the North Pole.

His idea was to go to Siberia and drift with the polar ice. With Nansen, to decide was to act. In 1893, he and thirteen companions sailed to Siberia, where they allowed their ship to be frozen in the ice north of Asia. Their vessel was specially constructed so that it would be lifted out of the water and on top of the frozen pack ice instead of being crushed by the pressure of the ice floes against the ship's sides. For 3 long years Nansen and his men slowly drifted across the Arctic Ocean but, unfortunately, the icy current did not carry them to the North Pole. Nansen and a companion made a dash over the ice in an effort to reach the Pole, but they were forced to turn back at 86 degrees 14 minutes north. Four years later, the Duke of Abruzzi tried to reach the North Pole from Fridtjof Nansen Land, but he got only a few miles farther than the Norwegian. That was in 1901.

The first aerial attempt to reach the North Pole was made in a frail balloon in 1897 by S. A. Andrée, a Swedish explorer. Andrée set out from Spitzbergen in his free balloon, carrying passenger pigeons to send back reports. A few messages were received. Then silence. The Andrée party floated out of human reach on the cold polar winds. Then in 1930, Dr. Gunnar Horn found the bodies of Andrée and his two companions on White Island in Fridtjof Nansen Land. A diary and some photographs that had been taken of the wrecked balloon 33 years before were mute evidence of the tragedy.

But returning to North America's role in arctic search, news of the destruction of the *Jeannette* did not reach the United States until 1881. In that same year Lieutenant A. W. Greely, of the United States Navy, led a scientific party into the Far North. Greely's work began on the eastern shore of Greenland and took him within 497 miles of the North Pole, the farthest north any explorer had been at that time. Meanwhile the Arctic took the expedition in its hostile grip and when relief ships failed to reach it at Cape Sabine, twenty-five of Greely's crew died of starvation. The survivors brought back much valuable data on polar conditions, which acted as a spur to further Arctic explorations by the United States.

Commodore Robert Edwin Peary, of the United States Navy, is the hero of the Arctic and the discoverer of the North Pole. Peary's message, dated September 6, 1909, reading: "Stars and Stripes nailed to the North Pole—Peary," thrilled the world. The American had actually reached the North Pole on April 6.

Peary's conquest of the North Pole was no lucky turn. He had prepared for the great moment for more than eighteen years. When he triumphed, it was his eighth attempt. Peary's outstanding characteristics were his infinite patience and his endless persistence. He did not know the meaning of the word defeat. His successful and carefully planned expeditions stand in sharp contrast to the long list of fatalities from disease, frost, shipwreck, and starvation that for almost three centuries were the lot of Arctic explorers. The main reason for his success was that Robert Peary realized that he could accomplish his cherished goal only by adopting the manner of life, the food, the sleds, the snowhouses, and the clothing of the Eskimos. He realized that through centuries of experience, the Eskimos had learned the most effective method of living in the Arctic. The dash that took him to his goal on April 6, 1909, covered 950 miles to the Pole and back by dog sled. It took 53 days. When Peary returned to the United States, a controversy was raging over his claim of reaching the Pole as against the claim of Dr. F. A. Cook, who said that he had reached the North Pole at an earlier date. Dr. Cook's claims were rejected by scientists. Credit for having been the first white man to reach the North Pole was officially given to Peary.

Roald Amundsen, the first man to sail through the northwest passage, was led to take up polar exploration by accounts of the tragedy of Sir John Franklin and by his admiration for his countryman, Fridtjof Nansen. Amundsen's parents wanted him to become a doctor. He studied medicine for a few years, until his parents died. Then he took up his chosen vocation in earnest. He toughened his body by strenuous exercise and inured it to stand the bitter cold of the winters of his native land. Next he took up the study of navigation, sailed as an ordinary seaman, and eventually joined an Antarctic expedition.

Meanwhile, his mind had constantly pressed for the solution of the mystery of the northwest passage. Shortly after the turn of the century, Amundsen and a few close friends began their preparations. Amundsen did not want the world to know that he was following the will-o'-the wisp of the westward passage. So he let it be known that his objective in the Arctic was to find the exact location of the north magnetic pole and to make scientific studies of variations that had been noticed in this powerful natural magnet.

In 1903, Amundsen had just outfitted a 70-foot, 30-year-old ship, the *Gjoa*, and was ready to leave when a merchant, to whom he owed money, threatened to take the vessel in payment for the bill. But Amundsen was not going to let an angry creditor stop him. On the night of June 16, the young Norwegian explorer and his crew of six slipped out of the harbor under cover of night. The Arctic, the unknown, adventure lay ahead of them. The *Gjoa* sailed northwest, to Greenland, and on to Baffin Bay and King William Island. There they observed the behavior of the north magnetic pole. One result of

Amundsen's observations was the important discovery that the magnetic pole is not stationary.

The King William Island camp had not been reached without difficulties. First the *Gjoa* ran aground on a submerged ledge of rocks, then a fire broke out and almost ended the venture. After that, a howling hurricane held the tiny craft in its grip for 4 anxious days. But at last they reached a little landlocked bay. There they built an observatory, which served as their headquarters for 19 months.

Not until August, 1905, did Amundsen head his vessel westward, slowly nosing out the northwest passage. He navigated Simpson Strait and sailed through waters so shallow that, time and again for weeks on end, the keel of the *Gjoa* barely cleared the bottom of the channel.

During the 3 weeks in the shallow, the crew of the *Gjoa*, whose draft was less than 8 feet, hardly ate or slept. Everlasting vigilance was necessary to prevent the ship from having its bottom torn open by submerged rocks. Then, on August 25, 1905, the lookout shouted that he had sighted a sail to the west. Amundsen ran on deck and climbed up the rigging of the stubby little mast. With a shout of joy he called the others. Straight ahead of them was a whaling ship. It turned out to be the *Charles Hansson* out of San Francisco riding at anchor in the Polar Sea about a mile west of the *Gjoa*. The northwest passage across the top of North America had been navigated at last.

But the discovery of the northwest passage was an anticlimax. Century after century, navigators had risked their lives hoping to find the northwest route to riches. Now, when it was found, it proved to have no commercial value whatever. Because of barriers of ice, reefs, and rocks, navigation through the narrow channel is necessarily slow, seasonal, and dangerous. Only ships of the shallowest draft can get through, and even then only at great risk.

When aviation came into its own some twenty years later,

Roald Amundsen was one of the first to realize that, by means of the airplane, man would at last be able to conquer the gap between east and west in the frozen north.

An unfortunate and almost fatal accident prevented Roald Amundsen and Lincoln Ellsworth, the famous American explorer, from being the first to reach the North Pole by airplane in 1925. Amundsen had had the idea of flying to the Pole for some time. During his expeditions to the north and south polar regions, he had studied weather and flying conditions. Then he began actual preparations, but for a time he was unable to carry them through for lack of funds. In 1925, Lincoln Ellsworth came to the Norwegian's assistance. The two men organized an expedition to fly from Norway to Alaska over the North Pole.

After several reconnaisance flights, they took off, on May 21, from Spitzbergen in two planes, one navigated by Amundsen and the other by Ellsworth. They roared north. Success was almost in sight when one of the planes developed engine trouble and had to make a forced landing on the ice. The other craft landed near by. Observations were taken. The polar fliers found that they were only 120 miles from the North Pole. So near, yet so far!

The disappointment in not reaching the Pole was forgotten in the task of getting off the ice before their limited food supply gave out and starvation got a chance to write a tragic end to their expedition. One of the planes was abandoned when Ellsworth's party crossed a dangerous stretch of ice floes to join Amundsen. Then the remaining plane had to be put in flying condition. A runway had to be built across the ice for the take-off. The latter task, according to Amundsen, necessitated moving, with their hands as their only tools, 500 tons of ice.

At last they were ready to try a take-off. One attempt after another ended in failure, until at last the plane soared into the air. After a few hours' flight, and as their gasoline was about to give out, motor trouble developed and forced Amundsen and Ellsworth to make a sea landing among icebergs. While Amundsen was taking observations of the sun to determine their position, a fishing boat was sighted. The plane was taxied across the water and the weary and exhausted explorers made the rest of the journey back to Norway by boat. There they received the acclaim of a world that had given them up for lost.

Various attempts to reach the North Pole by air failed until 1926. On May 9, Commander Richard E. Byrd, of the United States Navy, flew from Spitsbergen to the North Pole and back, in 15 hours. He covered a distance of 1,000 miles. Three days later Amundsen and Ellsworth achieved their ambition when they also flew over the North Pole. This time they used the dirigible *Norge* piloted by Colonel Umberto Nobile. Their flight, from Spitsbergen to Teller, Alaska, took 71 hours. This was the first aerial crossing of the northwest passage. In May, 1928, Nobile again flew to the Pole aboard his dirigible. It was wrecked and eight of the crew were killed. Amundsen joined in an airplane rescue party to search for the missing members of the crew. On that flight, Amundsen flew into eternity. His plane was wrecked. The Norwegian explorer and five companions were killed.

Following in the footsteps of Amundsen and Ellsworth and Byrd, four Russian aviators established a weather station at the North Pole in 1937, thus bringing to fulfillment the dreams of Nansen and other polar explorers who believed that one day man's conquest of the North Pole would have practical results. Experts believe that weather stations at the poles will enable observers to make long-range weather forecasts.

There is no way of estimating the potential wealth and future possibilities of the Arctic regions for there is still much for the explorer to do. The northwest passage eluded man for three centuries. It is not the boon to shipping that it was expected to be, but the fact that it served to draw brilliant and courageous explorers to the Arctic will some day pay higher dividends than the most optimistic seeker for the passage ever dreamed.

The various polar flights have called attention to the military and commercial possibilities of air routes across the polar regions. It is only a short flight across the Arctic from Canada to Norway or Russia with natural emergency landing fields on the ice. At certain seasons of the year, the longest stretch of open water is only 300 miles.

One of the most thorough Arctic explorers, Dr. Vilhjalmur Stefansson, spent more than ten years in the Arctic lands of North America that lie between the Arctic Circle and the Polar Sea. During that time he added more than 100,000 square miles to the maps of that region. Stefansson has no doubt done more than any man to clear up the fog of misconceptions about the Arctic.

Greenland

Discovered: By Gunnbjorn, Norwegian sea rover about 900.

Population: 17,000.

Area: 837,620 square miles.

Language: Danish.

Government: Danish crown colony.

Geographical Characteristics: Geologically, Greenland is part of Canada. It lies chiefly within the Arctic Circle and its major portion is covered by a mile-thick blanket of ice.

Climatic Conditions: Arctic and subarctic.

Principal Products: Whale oil, eiderdown, sealskins, and reindeer skins.

Greenland is the largest island in the world, but one of the least productive and least known. This is due to the fact that, while Greenland covers an area of 837,620 miles, only 132,000 square miles of coastland are free of the glacial blanket that spreads over the interior, covering whatever mountains and valleys there may be under its expanse of eternal ice.

A graphic picture of Greenland may be given by saying that its total area equals the square miles covered by Texas, New Mexico, Arizona, California, Oregon, and the state of Washington. Its ice-free region is about 10,000 square miles less than the area of Montana. But of this ice-free area, only 46,740 square miles are settled. This is about the size of Mississippi.

It may truly be said that Greenland was the New World steppingstone that led Europeans to the continent of North America more than a thousand years ago. After they discovered Iceland about 865, the Norsemen established regular sailing routes between Iceland and Norway. During one of these voyages, a Norseman known as Gunnbjorn the Sailor was blown off his course and landed on Greenland. He called the country Gunnbjorn's Rock. This name lasted until about 982 when Eric the Red decided to establish a Greenland colony. He thought the name Gunnbjorn's Rock was much too uninviting to attract settlers. So, to make this first land company in the New World successful, the crafty Norseman changed the name to Greenland. In line with his expectations, this promise of lush meadows attracted colonists. About 989, several hundred settlers sailed to Eric's Greenland colony aboard twenty-five ships. Eleven of these ships were lost at sea with all who were aboard.

The North American continent appeared on the white man's horizon for the first time in 986 when Bjarni Herlufsson, sailing from Iceland to Greenland, missed the southern point of Greenland and reached the northeastern coast of North America. Instead of investigating these new lands, Bjarni set course for Greenland. Spurred on by the stories told by Bjarni, Leif Ericson, son of Eric the Red, decided to explore the new lands to the west. He bought Bjarni's ship and hired Bjarni to serve as his navigator. Eric the Red was to join the expedition, but a few days before sailing, he was thrown from his pony. Although he was not hurt, the old Viking took this as a bad omen. He decided to remain in Greenland and the expedition sailed without him in the year 1001. It reached Newfoundland and cruised down past Nova Scotia to New England. Winter overtook the Vikings in Narragansett Bay. There they built huts and remained until the following spring. They returned to Greenland with enthusiastic accounts of the great forests and pleasant climate, fertile soil and green grass of the new country. They called it Vinland because of the wealth of wild grapes that grew there.

Leif Ericson may have had plans to return to Vinland, but instead he went back to Norway. There he was converted to Christianity. When he returned to Greenland a few years later, several priests were in his party. They were the first to carry the Cross to the Western Hemisphere. Members of the Greenland colony probably made trips to the North American mainland from time to time, but so far as is known, no colonies were ever established.

In 1261, Greenland came officially under Norwegian rule, which lasted until the fifteenth century. Then, sweeping pestilence in Norway, known as the Black Death, turned thought as well as memory from Greenland. The result was that the Greenland colony withered and died. About a hundred years later, in 1576, Martin Frobisher, in quest of the northwest passage for England, charted some of the coast of Greenland, as did John Davis, in 1585. From that time on, Greenland's icy mountains were frequently sighted by English and French navigators who braved the winds and blizzards of the north to find the waterway to the Orient around the top of North America. But colonization did not start again in Greenland until 1721 when the Danes led in the effort to establish settlements.

It is estimated that more than a million tons of Greenland ice are dropped into North Atlantic waters every year. The vast ice packs that cover Greenland do not stand still. The glaciers have a slow but steady flow toward the coast. During April,

May, and June, as the ice reaches the sea, it breaks off into chunks that range from small growlers to mighty icebergs. These latter drift with the current down upon the North Atlantic steamship lanes where they are deadly threats to shipping. One of the greatest lessons in man's mite against nature's might was given about midnight on April 14, 1912. Some 1,600 miles from New York, the then largest luxury liner in the world ran into an iceberg. In less than two hours, the liner sank. Of the 2,300 souls aboard, only 706 survived. The steamer was the *Titanic*, the pride of the sea; it was making its maiden journey from England to America. New York was its destination, but an iceberg sent it to the bottom of the sea. Since that time, with interruptions caused by wartime conditions, the United States Coast Guard has maintained an iceberg patrol during the danger months. By keeping watch on the slowly drifting and slowly melting icebergs and reporting their position by radio to ships or even by dynamiting the icebergs, the Coast Guard has removed one of the greatest dangers that face the men who sail the North Atlantic.

CHAPTER 19

Castles of Dreams in New France

Canadian Regions in This Chapter	Historical Data	Capital	Population	Area, Square Miles
Nova Scotia	French in 1604	Halifax	512,900	21,068
New Brunswick	French in 1639	Fredericton	408,000	27,985
Prince Edward Island	French in 1534	Charlottetown	88,100	2,184
Quebec	French in 1535	Quebec	2,875,000	494,534
Ontario	French in 1615	Toronto	3,500,000	412,582

U. S. Regions in This Chapter	Settled	Entered Union	Capital	Population	Area, Square Miles
Illinois	1720	1818	Springfield	7,874,155	56,665
Indiana	1733	1816	Indianapolis	3,416,152	36,354
Louisiana	1699	1812	Baton Rouge	2,355,821	48,506
Michigan	1650	1837	Lansing	5,245,012	57,980
Minnesota	1805	1858	Saint Paul	2,785,896	84,682
Mississippi	1716	1817	Jackson	2,181,763	46,865
Wisconsin	1670	1848	Madison	3,125,881	56,066

FOR more than a quarter of a century after Christopher Columbus made his great discovery, Spain and Portugal had virtually a monopoly on New World exploration. By the Treaty of Tordesillas, in 1494, a Line of Demarcation was drawn on a map from pole to pole, running 370 leagues west of the Azores. All lands to the west of this line were to go to Spain, while those to the east went to Portugal. It was a neat and simple arrangement for Portugal and Spain, but not a very satisfactory one for England and France.

England, as was shown in the chapter on the search for the northwest passage, sent John Cabot exploring in the forbidden waters as early as 1497, without any immediate result except the discovery of the rich codfish banks off New England. French fishermen made their way across the Atlantic to the Grand Bank a few years later, but it was not until 1524 that France officially moved to seek a foothold in the New World.

In that year, Francis I of France declared that neither Spain nor Portugal had exclusive rights in America. He sent Giovanni da Verrazano to explore and find new lands across the Atlantic to France. Verrazano reached land somewhere around North Carolina. He explored Chesapeake Bay, sailed into the mouth of the Hudson River, and then continued up the coast of New England. If France had not been so occupied with European wars at the time, and had been able to follow up Verrazano's explorations, history might have been different. As it was, 10 years passed before France again took an active part in the drama of New World exploration.

Jacques Cartier made his first voyage to America for France in 1534. His object was to find a water passage to the great western ocean that Balboa had discovered in 1513. Cartier touched at Newfoundland and landed at several points within the Gulf of Saint Lawrence. The Frenchman found the Indians friendly, although he did have to use some pressure to induce two Indian boys to return with him to France. When these young Indians learned some French, they told Cartier about a great river that led into a vast and rich inland territory.

In 1536, with the two Indians as guides and interpreters, Cartier returned to America. He discovered the Saint Lawrence River, on which he sailed up to an Indian village on the present site of Quebec. Farther up the river, he was forced to take to smaller boats to reach a large native village called Hochelaga. Cartier climbed a high hill which he named Montreal (Mount Royal). Being unable to proceed further because of rapids, which the Indians said were impassable, Cartier and his men returned to Quebec, where they spent the winter.

On this first contact between the Indians and the Frenchmen, Cartier laid the foundation for a lasting friendship between the French and the Indians of Canada by treating the natives not as savages, but as human beings. The Spaniards almost invariably had trouble with the Indians because their own attitude was hostile and unfriendly. The French, on the other hand, had very little difficulty with the Indians; they were clever enough to win the friendship of the redskins before penetrating into their country. As an example of how the Indians reacted to this sort of treatment, when Cartier's men fell ill with scurvy during the winter at Quebec, the natives gave the white men the medicine they prepared from the barks and leaves of a tree they called *Aneda*, or Tree of Life. But despite this medicine, which appears to have been made from the spruce tree, twenty-six of Cartier's men died.

Although Cartier had failed to find a westward passage, the King of France was delighted with his discoveries and decided to attempt colonizing along the Saint Lawrence River. In 1541, Cartier was sent with five ships to prepare the way for a colonizing expedition under Seigneur de Roberval, a close friend of the king, who was appointed viceroy of New France.

Cartier sailed up the Saint Lawrence and built a fort about 12 miles above Quebec. There he settled down to spend the winter and await Roberval and his colonists. When the expedition did not arrive by spring, Cartier sailed for home. Near Saint John's, Newfoundland, he met Roberval and three ships filled with colonists, but Cartier continued on his way to France. Roberval's settlers, gathered mostly from the jails of France, did not make a success of the colony. In 1543 Cartier sailed on his fourth and last voyage to the New World to bring home the luckless colonists.

Although these early efforts to plant a French colony in Canada failed, Cartier's explorations were, in time, to bear rich fruit. His discoveries gave France a legitimate claim on this vast territory, a claim that was strengthened by French fur traders who eventually extended its boundaries. The Saint

Lawrence became France's gateway to the New World. While England sent her explorers in quest of a northwest passage around the top of North America, the French were pushing their way up the Saint Lawrence and into the Great Lakes, also seeking a waterway across the continent.

Jacques Cartier opened the way, but Samuel Champlain was the real pathfinder, and the first successful colonizer of New France. Champlain was a veteran explorer before he took up his activities in Canada. Between 1599 and 1601 he made several voyages to the West Indies, during which he explored nearly the whole Caribbean Sea. In 1603, he visited Canada as the joint commander of an expedition. The rich cargo of furs brought back to France gave the king new interest in settling the country. In the following year, Champlain surveyed the Atlantic coast from Cape Breton Bay down to Boston Bay. There he discovered the Charles River and sighted Plymouth Rock in the harbor where the Pilgrims were to land 17 years later. On other voyages, this energetic Frenchman sailed up the Kennebec River. He also explored Cape Ann and Cape Cod.

These many preliminary exploring expeditions behind him, Samuel Champlain began his greatest work in 1608. In that year, he brought a group of colonists over from France and built a settlement at Quebec to trade in furs with the Indians. He chose Quebec as the site for the first permanent settlement in Canada because it offered several natural advantages. The lands along the shores of the Saint Lawrence were level; a steep wall of rock a short distance back from the river gave protection and the river itself provided an easy outlet to the sea for cargoes of furs. In selecting Quebec as the site of the first trading colony and the key to the Saint Lawrence Valley, Champlain proved his wisdom and foresight.

The Frenchman supervised the building of a fort and cabins for the settlers. Then he devoted himself to forming a friendly alliance with the Algonquin Indians. His success in this effort not only enabled him to expand his explorations, but gave New France faithful allies in later years of trouble with the English.

Champlain, to prove his friendship, agreed to help the Algonquins in their war against the fierce Iroquois. With only two French companions, he set out with a war party of fifty-eight Algonquins, heading south into Iroquois territory. While he was a member of this war party, Champlain discovered the lake that bears his name. When the Algonquins reached the fort of the Iroquois at Ticonderoga, they found that the enemy outnumbered them almost four to one. As more than 200 painted Iroquois warriors rushed the Algonquins, Champlain fired his musket and killed two Iroquois chiefs. When the Iroquois saw the magic of the white man's thunder weapon, they fled in wild disorder.

Champlain had saved his Algonquin friends from a massacre, but he had also made a bitter enemy for New France. From that day on, the Iroquois hated the French as much as they did their traditional enemy, the Algonquins. French trappers, traders, and settlers who valued their scalps had to make long detours to avoid Iroquois territory. Some historians believe that this skirmish between Champlain and the Iroquois at Fort Ticonderoga, in the summer of 1608, was what led these hostile Indians to become the allies of the English in their wars upon the French later on.

In line with the French policy of close relationship with the Indians, Champlain developed an exchange plan whereby young Frenchmen were sent to live among the Indians to learn their language and their ways while young Indians were sent to France to become acquainted with the language and customs of the white man. Champlain's star pupil in this wilderness training school was Étienne Brule, who, as a mere boy, went to live among the Hurons and Algonquins.

Young Brule became an accomplished woodsman, and his knowledge of the Indians made him an invaluable pioneer in the early days of New France. He lived almost constantly in Indian territory for about eighteen years. Brule was actually the first white man to live in country that was not known to the whites until many years later. In 1615, Brule crossed Lake Ontario and made his way to the Susquehanna River, which he followed down to Chesapeake Bay. While returning to Canada, Brule was attacked and seized by Iroquois warriors, who relished an opportunity to practice their art of torture on a Frenchman. According to his own story, Brule was tied to the stake. Dry brush was placed at his feet ready to be lighted. He was resigned to death by torture and fire, when an Indian tried to rip a cross from around his neck. That was too much for Brule. He cried out: "If you take that cross and kill me, you and all your relatives will die!"

So fierce and unafraid was the Frenchman's look that the Indians backed away. Fortunately Brule's threats were just then impressively backed up by a clap of thunder and a flash of lightning as the heavens grew black and a storm broke. In the face of such magic, the Iroquois let their prisoner go.

During his years in the wilderness, this young Frenchman served his compatriots in many ways, as a trader, guide, and adviser. Unfortunately he could not read and write so that he was unable to make accurate maps of the places he visited. It is known that he explored Lake Huron. He may also have visited Lake Superior and reached the present site of Duluth and other regions years before they were placed on the map. Brule's life suddenly came to a painful end in 1533. While living among the Hurons, he was attacked and killed by some of his supposed Indian friends.

If Étienne Brule had been trained in surveying and map making, it might very well be that today he would be recognized as one of the greatest explorers of the New World, ranking alongside Cartier and Champlain.

In recognition for his services, Champlain was made governor of New France, in which capacity he was forced to surrender Quebec to the English in 1629. For the three years of British occupation of New France, Champlain was a prisoner in England. When peace was made between the two nations and Canada was returned to the French in 1632, Champlain again assumed the governorship. He held that post until his death in Quebec in 1635.

The year of Champlain's death marked the introduction of the French seignorial system into Canada. This system was a modification of the medieval feudal system in Europe. Under it, large landed estates were granted to nobles or other men of importance. These seigniors, in turn, divided their lands into small farms which were worked by tenant farmers who paid tribute to the local lord and master. As practiced in New France, this paternal system was successful and, in most cases, not a heavy burden on the peasants. Rent was paid to the seignior in a small share of the produce of the land, and only 6 days' work a year were required by the landlord. In return, the seignior built a fort and gave protection to his tenants. It was a time-tried system in France and, on the whole, it worked for the mutual benefit of both classes.

New France prospered. The French were excellent colonizers, able hunters, industrious farmers, clever traders, good woodsmen, and skillful trappers. Their ability to make friends with the Indians has been mentioned. A great deal of credit for this must go to the French priests and missionaries who were a vital part of the colony almost from its inception.

The sandaled feet of the missionary priests followed close upon the moccasin-made path of the trail-blazing traders and trappers. Champlain invited the Franciscans to come to New France. They were followed by the Jesuits and the Carmelites. The first mission was established by the Jesuits at Port Royal, in 1611. French priests and lay brothers worked alongside the rough and ready fur traders, penetrating into the wilderness, sharing their dangers and hardships. While the traders exchanged powder, cloth, and trinkets for the precious skins of fur-bearing animals, the friars, clad in coarse gowns and hoods, tended to the physical and spiritual welfare of the Indians.

The Black Robes, as the missionary priests were called by the Indians, often went into the unknown where even the hardy traders feared to go. Many of them lived among the most hostile tribes, accepting privations, dangers, tortures, and even horrible death as all in the line of duty. During the first half of the seventeenth century, thirty-two Jesuit priests were tortured and met the death of martyrs among the Indians of North America. Many of these humble friars were keen explorers, and it is from their carefully kept writings that we have our most detailed, and in many cases, only knowledge of the history of that day. Almost on the heels of the friars came the sisters of the church to minister to the needs of both the French and the Indians. Among these courageous and self-sacrificing women were the Ursuline sisters, who served as teachers, and the Hospitalières, who devoted their lives to nursing.

One of the most important actors in the story of New France is the Father of Waters, the Mississippi River. This river was new to the men of Europe who first saw it, but it was old, very old to nature. In its early days, this mighty waterway saw the downfall of the Empire of Dinosaurs. In its youth, it saw the birth of the Age of Mammals. In its middle years, it saw the Ice Age spread its chilly blanket of solid ice over much of the land and disappear. In its old age, it saw bearded, white-skinned men come to its banks.

The Mississippi was first seen by a European in 1519, when the Spaniard, de Pineda, sailed past its yawning mouth, while searching the Gulf of Mexico for a passage to the Spice Islands of the East. Next the unhappy Cabeza de Vaca and his companions sailed through the Mississippi Delta before they were shipwrecked on the coast of Texas in 1528. Then came Hernando de Soto, who, in 1541, crossed the wide river just south of where Memphis stands today. De Soto is known

as the discoverer of the Mississippi. After de Soto died of fever
in 1542, his harried companions hurriedly built a few ships and
sailed down the river to its mouth, frantically seeking a Spanish settlement. But none of these adventurers thought the
Mississippi important enough to warrant exploration. That
was left for the French-Canadian priests and fur traders to
accomplish a hundred years later.

Two of the greatest pioneers of New France were Pierre
Radisson and Medard Grosseilliers, fur traders and explorers
extraordinary. Their story is told in the chapter entitled
"Wealth in the Wilderness." Among their many accomplishments, these two pioneers, between 1658 and 1660, were the
first white men to see the great plains and the upper stretches of
the Mississippi River.

The first to explore the Father of Waters were Father
Jacques Marquette, a Jesuit priest, and Louis Joliet, a fur
trader. While at his mission on Lake Superior, Father Marquette heard the Indians talk about a great river that apparently flowed west into the Pacific Ocean. Being adventurous
of spirit, the priest longed to find out if this river really was the
waterway to the west so many men had been seeking. In the
spring of 1673, his opportunity came. With Joliet as his companion, Marquette set out from the Straits of Mackinac. It was
a strange party that paddled its way across Lake Michigan:
five naked but friendly Indians, a priest inspired to carry the
word of God into the wilderness, and a shrewd trader hoping
to expand the fur trade into new territory.

Marquette and Joliet guided their canoes across the lake and
into the Fox River, which they followed until it was too narrow for navigation. Then they crossed a short portage to the
Wisconsin River. They rode its current down to the Mississippi. At last they were in the Father of Waters, and their
hearts were light with joy. Their birch-bark canoes sped
swiftly down the mighty river. They passed the Ohio and
reached the junction of the Mississippi and the Arkansas

River. There, friendly Indians warned them that it would be wise to stop. Ahead of them lay bad Indian country, they were told. By that time, the two Frenchmen realized that the river could not possibly run into the Pacific as its course was not westward but almost due south. They concluded that instead it probably emptied its waters into the Gulf of Mexico to the south. Since they had accomplished their mission, they turned back and began the difficult and arduous journey upstream.

When they neared Lake Michigan, Father Marquette was taken ill. It was agreed that Joliet should go ahead and carry the news of their discovery to the governor of Quebec. Marquette and his faithful Indians continued slowly, but the priest grew worse. One day he died on the bank of the river that bears his name. Father Marquette was only thirty-eight, but he had accomplished his great ambition, to travel down the swiftly flowing current of the Father of Waters.

The news Joliet brought of their explorations excited the colonists of New France. A whole vast new territory was opened up to the traders and trappers. The journey of Marquette and Joliet formed the basis on which France laid her claim to the entire Mississippi Valley, from the Greak Lakes to the Gulf of Mexico. Also, it set the scene for La Salle, the leading character in the drama of New France to make his heroic entrance on the stage of New World exploration.

René Robert Cavelier Sieur de La Salle was born in Rouen, France, on November 21, 1643, of wealthy parents. His father, a prominent merchant, planned a career as a priest for his son, a fair-haired, gentle, and none-too-sturdy youth. When he was entered in a Jesuit college at the age of fifteen, the good fathers little dreamed that their pupil was to become one of the most daring and adventurous characters in history. La Salle, the boy, was a dreamer. As he grew up, he became a dreamer who made history.

As a part of his studies, La Salle learned about the lands across the ocean in New France. His restless spirit was not satisfied just to read and hear about the things that were being accomplished in the wilderness; he wanted to take part in the accomplishing, to explore the mysterious unknown forests and rivers and lakes of America. When he was twenty-three years old, La Salle resigned from the Jesuit order and announced his intention of going to New France. To establish himself in the New World, he sold his annual income for a pittance of two or three thousand dollars, and sailed for Quebec early in 1666. He reached Montreal, which was little more than a missionary post held by the Seminary of Saint Sulpice. There La Salle settled on a farm a few miles outside the town.

The life of a farmer suited La Salle as little as that of a priest. Again he grew restless. Like Father Marquette, he heard Indian tales about a great river that ran into a distant sea. Could it be the coveted waterway to the Orient? La Salle made up his mind to find out, and to finance an exploring expedition he sold his farm. In July, 1669, he left Montreal with seven canoes and twenty men, making his way up the Saint Lawrence River and into Lake Ontario.

Not much is known about this first voyage of La Salle, except that he discovered the Ohio River and sailed down its course, probably as far as the present city of Louisville, Kentucky. He took possession for France of the lands of the Ohio Valley, a claim that was many years later to form the basis of a bitter and bloody controversy between the French and the English. There is evidence that La Salle's men rebelled against going further and that he had to make his way overland back to Montreal. There he arrived in 1671.

Even at this early time, La Salle had in his mind great plans for the expansion of France in America. He saw an overseas empire that ran from the Saint Lawrence to the westernmost of the Great Lakes; from the Great Lakes to the mouth of the Mississippi. Fortunately, Count Frontenac assumed office as governor in 1672. He was in sympathy with La Salle's ambitious dreams of empire. On the governor's recommendation,

La Salle went to Paris in 1674 to get approval of their plans from King Louis XIV.

La Salle was well received at the court of France, for the king was anxious to expand and strengthen his Canadian possessions. Louis XIV was pleased with the young adventurer and what he had to say. He not only raised La Salle to the nobility, but gave him the right to govern his estate in New France, Fort Frontenac, as a seignior.

When La Salle returned to Canada, Father Marquette was dead and Joliet's story of their discovery that the Mississippi ran its course into the Gulf of Mexico was the talk of the colony. The Father of Waters had figured prominently in La Salle's plan ever since he had first heard of the great river, but now it became even more important. He determined not only to sail down its current to the sea, but to explore and colonize the valley. All that would take time, preparations, and money —a great deal of money. Also, Count Frontenac and La Salle had many powerful enemies both in New France and at home, and these enemies did everything they could to make things difficult for them.

Rumors were spread in Paris that La Salle was living a wicked and wasteful life at his seignioralty, Fort Frontenac. This was untrue. La Salle's estate prospered, and he could very well have continued living as a land proprietor, dealing in furs, and amassed a great fortune without risk or hardships. But La Salle's heart was in exploration and not in trade. In 1677, he once again journeyed to France, this time to lay definite plans before the king. On November 5, 1678, he was granted a royal patent to explore lands to the west and to build forts, at his own cost, wherever he thought it necessary for the defense of newly opened territory. To compensate La Salle for the expense of erecting forts, he was given a 5 year monopoly on buffalo hides in the new regions.

In New France, Count Frontenac had been paving the way for La Salle's venture and thus incurring the even greater enmity of factions that resented his power as well as the privileges the king had given La Salle. When the latter returned to Canada, he found himself accused, along with the governor, of having taken large and illegal profits from the fur trade. This must have been a grim joke to La Salle. He had borrowed up to the hilt and even mortgaged his estate and possessions to finance the expeditions. But some of the opposition were not satisfied with merely slandering. Before his departure, La Salle narrowly escaped death from poison that had been placed in his food.

The first step in La Salle's plan of empire was to construct a ship for navigation on the Great Lakes. After that he proposed to build another vessel on the Illinois River. This ship was to carry trade between the great Lakes and the mouth of the Mississippi River, where La Salle planned to establish a French settlement. All along the line were to be strong forts and trading posts. It was an ambitious plan. But if carried out, it would make France a great power in the New World.

On January 22, 1679, the building of the first ship, the *Griffon*, got under way not far from Niagara Falls. La Salle had imported the rigging, anchors, and iron fittings from Europe. The work was left in charge of a young Italian, Lieutenant Henry de Tonty, whom La Salle had brought with him from France. The building of the vessel involved many problems. Delays were caused by hostile Indians and incompetent and untrustworthy workmen. But early in August, the ship was completed, and on August 7, 1679, it was launched on Lake Erie. It was the first sailing ship on that body of water. The *Griffon* was sent across the Great Lakes to Green Bay. There it picked up a large cargo of furs for Niagara. La Salle anxiously awaited news of the ship's arrival. He needed the furs to satisfy the clamoring demands of his creditors in Quebec and Montreal. But the *Griffon* was never heard of again. Whether it was wrecked in a storm or whether the sailors stole the furs and sank the ship, or whether Indians destroyed it and killed the crew remains to this day one of the unsolved mysteries of the Great Lakes.

When the *Griffon* failed to arrive, La Salle continued his journey toward the Mississippi to start the next stage of his grand venture. With him at this time was a mixed crew. Some of the men were faithful and competent. Others were scoundrels and worthless. Among the most faithful must be counted Henry de Tonty, who was now La Salle's right-hand man. Tonty was a picturesque character, and a veteran of many European campaigns. His left hand had been blown off by a grenade. He had had an iron hand fitted onto the stump. Over it he always wore a velvet glove, so that it was difficult to tell that it did not cover a normal hand. But when that left hand of iron descended on the skulls of hostile Indians, the victim knew that Tonty indeed had a hand of iron. It is said that many cracked Indian skulls were evidence of Tonty's metal fist.

Another of La Salle's stout companions at that time was Father Hennepin, who is credited with the discovery of Niagara Falls. There were two other friars, Gabriel Ribourde and Zenobe Membre; also a Mohican guide and hunter named White Beaver, whose knowledge of the wilderness saved the expedition from disaster and starvation more than once. Besides these, there were twenty-seven others. Many of them had no doubt been deliberately placed with the expedition by La Salle's enemies with orders to try to wreck it. One of those, Nicholas du Plessis, even tried to shoot La Salle in the back as they were crossing the portage at Saint Joseph-Kankakee.

This portage was the turning point in the voyage. Up to that time, La Salle had been going upstream. Once across this portage and on the Kankakee, his course went downstream. From this river, the party entered the Illinois River. There La Salle set his men to building Fort Crèvecoeur (Heartbreak), which was to be one of the line of proposed forts and the base for further exploration. At this point Father Hennepin was sent by La Salle to explore the upper Mississippi. For 3 years Father Hennepin was lost in the wooded wilderness. When he returned to New France he had explored the upper Mississippi from the mouth of the Illinois to the Falls of Saint Anthony, at the present site of Minneapolis.

On March 1, 1680, the day after Father Hennepin left him, La Salle set out for a quick overland dash to Quebec to arrange for further credit to buy supplies and equipment. This journey from Fort Crèvecoeur to Quebec, through more than a thousand miles of trailless country, La Salle made in 65 days. Before the end of the trip, only La Salle was able to go on. His four companions, all hardened, veteran woodsmen, fell one by one by the wayside, exhausted by the grueling pace set by their leader.

When La Salle reached Fort Frontenac he found that his creditors had taken his most valued possessions; his canoes and ships had been wrecked by his enemies. Still, La Salle's indomitable spirit and unflinching courage renewed the faith of certain merchants in Montreal who extended him additional credit. As he was ready to return to Fort Crèvecoeur, a message came from Tonty telling La Salle that his men had destroyed the fort and thrown his trade goods into the river. Next they had raided the other forts La Salle had erected, Miami and Saint Joseph, and stolen all his furs. Some of the traitors, La Salle learned, were in ambush on the far shore of Lake Frontenac, waiting to kill him as he passed by on his way back to the Illinois River.

The news of the disaster failed to discourage La Salle and the threat of ambush did not frighten him. He made a surprise attack upon his would-be assassins and turned them over to Governor Frontenac for punishment. Then La Salle pushed on with twenty-five new men, all carefully selected for loyalty and ability. But before he rejoined Tonty and the few men who had remained faithful, many months passed. Not until February, 1682, did La Salle reach the Mississippi and start his history-making journey down the unexplored reaches of the Father of Waters.

La Salle proceeded slowly, exploring the country as he went. Finally on April 9, 1682, he and his small group of followers stood at the mouth of the Mississippi. A column was erected and on it was placed the coat of arms of the king. Near it, from a tall pole, fluttered the flag of France. Then, as muskets were fired, Sieur de La Salle, with his plumed hat in his hand and his sword glittering in the sunlight, solemnly took possession for the King of France of all the lands and tributaries and people of the Mississippi River and its valley. There was wild cheering after La Salle spoke the final words of his proclamation! "I name thee Louisiana!"

On his way north back to Canada, La Salle left Tonty and a small garrison at Fort Saint Louis on top of Starved Rock on the Illinois River, and then continued to Quebec. His enthusiasm for colonizing and establishing a regular trade route between the Great Lakes and the Gulf of Mexico along the Mississippi River met with little response in New France, where Count Frontenac had fallen from power. La Salle's enemies shouted ridicule and his creditors demanded money. There was only one place for La Salle to go—the court of Louis XIV. The fall of 1683 saw La Salle once more on his way to France, to place his dream in the hands of the king.

Despite the efforts of La Salle's enemies, the king was favorable to the plan for colonizing the Mississippi. On April 14, 1684, La Salle was given a royal commission to explore further, to build forts, and to establish a French settlement at the mouth of the Mississippi River. It was decided that La Salle should return to America by ship, sailing directly to the mouth of the great river. The expedition consisted of four ships and 400 men. Trouble arose almost immediately between La Salle, who was commander in chief of the land expedition, and the admiral of the little fleet, Beaujeau.

One of the vessels was captured in the Caribbean by

Spaniards. The three remaining ships entered the Gulf of Mexico toward the end of 1684, but by some mischance they sailed past the mouth of the Mississippi. Despite frequent attempts, they could not find the Mississippi Delta. The reason was that in those days navigators had no accurate means of determining longitude. La Salle did not know his exact position east and west. At last, in January, 1685, the ships landed in Matagorda Bay, Texas, some 400 miles west of the mouth of the Mississippi, and in Spanish territory. One of the ships was wrecked by a careless and disobedient pilot.

From this point on La Salle's story is one of tragic reverses and bitter disappointments. Beaujeau sailed back to France, leaving one ship, which ran on a reef and was wrecked. The fort La Salle built at Matagorda Bay was repeatedly attacked by Indians. Starvation and disease reduced the numbers of the garrison with appalling swiftness. La Salle's frequent and frantic journeys up and down the coast to locate the Mississippi all ended in failure. At last, in 1687, he decided to lead a small party overland north to Canada for help. But before he could carry out his plan, La Salle was betrayed by his followers for the last time. On March 19, near Trinity River, Texas, he was shot and killed from ambush by one of his own men. Just about this same time, the small fort at Matagorda Bay was attacked by Indians who killed most of the Frenchmen and carried the rest off as captives. When a group of Spanish soldiers reached the fort two years later, in 1689, it was in ruins. La Salle's dream of a French empire in the Mississippi Valley had ended in a nightmare.

When news of the tragic end of La Salle's venture reached Canada, his enemies gloated. In Paris, the king was busy with wars and consigned La Salle to oblivion. It was not until many years later that France realized the true importance of La Salle's scheme and sent an expedition to found a colony at the mouth of the Mississippi River.

That was in 1699, when Pierre d'Iberville, a veteran in the

service of colonial France, built Fort Maurepas on an island in Biloxi Bay and established a trading post. A short time later, his brother, Bienville, founded New Orleans, which was to become the Queen City of the South and the gateway to the entire Mississippi Valley. Thus began the days of French Louisiana.

The great promises held out for the rich harvest to be reaped in the new colony proved a deep disappointment. From the first, Louisiana was looked upon more as a speculation than as a colonizing scheme. "Go to Louisiana and get rich quick," was the slogan of the enthusiastic promoters of this vast new realm of France. But there was more promise than payment. Antoine Crozat held Louisiana under royal grant from 1712 to 1717, when John Law's notorious Mississippi Company took over. The Paris promoters of this land boom painted rosy pictures of easy money to be made in Louisiana. They promised to pay the entire public debt of France out of revenue from the exploitation of the colony. The French people were sold on the scheme and millions of francs were invested. John Law found that raising money was one thing, but making it pay dividends in Louisiana was quite something else. After a series of pitiful failures, the Mississippi Bubble burst, creating a dreadful scandal in Paris. In 1732 the crown took over the colony, with no better success in putting it on a paying basis.

Meanwhile, in Canada and in the Ohio Valley claimed for France by La Salle, the French were clashing with the English. Both demanded the same territory by right of prior discovery. This period of conflict, known as the French and Indian Wars, lasted from 1689 to 1748, when the stage was being set for the final act in the battles between France and England in North America.

The story of the French and Indian Wars is too long and complicated to be told here, but out of that long and bitter conflict rose many heroes. One of the most courageous of these was not a soldier, but a fourteen-year-old Canadian-French girl, Madeleine de Vercheres. In the fall of 1692, the Iroquois, allies of the English, attacked and wiped out many of the Carignan forts along the Canadian border.

In October, the commander of one of the forts, Captain de Vercheres, was on military duty in Quebec and his wife was visiting in Montreal. The captain's young daughter, Madeleine, and a younger son had been left at the fort in charge of three field hands. One morning a band of fifty painted and yelling Iroquois braves attacked the fort. The field hands started to run for the woods. The fort would have fallen easy prey to the attackers if the girl had not taken command of the situation. Barring the gate, she put on a soldier's hat and gave orders to the pathetic little army of three terrified men and a boy. With her own hands she fired the single cannon. Inspired by her heroism, the men defended the fort. Day after day, the siege lasted. None of the whites dared to sleep for more than a few minutes at a time, hardly leaving their posts to eat. When, on the seventh day, Lieutenant de la Monnierie came to the relief of the fort with forty men from Montreal, Madeleine saluted the officer and asked in a trembling but grave voice: "Sir, can you relieve the guard now? We've been on duty for a week without rest." Then she fell to the ground in a dead faint.

Madeleine was typical of the patriotic spirit of the French that made it possible for the people of New France to hold out against superior British forces as long as they did. Another example of fearless loyalty is that of the Acadians. French colonists settled in Acadia, or Nova Scotia, as it is known today, as early as 1603, but England claimed it on the ground of John Cabot's exploration in 1497. In 1713 Acadia was ceded to England. The French inhabitants, however, clung to their French habits, speech, and traditions despite every effort to Anglicize them. Their sympathies in the struggle between France and England over colonial territory were all with

France. In King George's War, between 1744 and 1748, many Acadians fought with the French against the English. When, in 1755, England made ready to oust the French from North America, it was deemed unwise to leave French sympathizers in Acadia to give aid and comfort to the enemy.

All Acadians who refused to take an oath of allegiance to England were deported and distributed among the English colonies from Massachusetts to Georgia. About 6,000 men, women, and children were embarked on ships bound for new homes in the south. Families were broken up. In some cases, children were separated from their parents. But these brave people preferred even exile and tragic parting from their families to disloyalty to France. In his famous poem, "Evangeline," Henry Wadsworth Longfellow tells the story of two sweethearts who were separated in exile and their heart-rending search for each other in strange lands.

King George's War was the last of three long and bitter wars. It ended in 1748 without settling the quarrel between France and England. There was a period of armed truce until 1754, when hostilities were resumed. At first, the French were victorious, but in 1758, the tide of war turned in favor of England. The French line of forts in the Ohio Valley fell one by one; and the following year the northern strongholds of New France, Forts Niagara, Duquesne, Ticonderoga, and Crown Point, surrendered to the British. There remained only Quebec, the key to the Saint Lawrence Valley and the strongest citadel of New France in Canada.

The brilliant English General, James Wolfe, sailed up the Saint Lawrence River in June, 1759. For more than three months he laid siege to Quebec, which stood secure and defiant on its lofty height on top of a cliff more than 200 feet above the river. Finally General Wolfe decided to risk everything in a bold attack. During the night of September 13, 1759, his army overwhelmed the French forces at the river and then began the precarious climb up the side of the cliff. By dawn the whole

English army of 4,500 men had reached the heights and were arrayed in battle formation on the Plains of Abraham.

News of the surprise attack reached the French commander, Marquis Montcalm, at his headquarters 10 miles away. He immediately ordered a counterattack. That day, the Plains of Abraham was the scene of one of the epic battles in history. General Wolfe was wounded and died before he knew that victory was his. Marquis Montcalm was also mortally wounded. When he was told that he would not live, he replied: "Thank God! I shall not live to see the surrender of Quebec."

Quebec surrendered a few days later. This was the blow that sealed the doom of the French empire in America. By the treaty of 1763, England gained Canada and all French possessions east of the Mississippi River except New Orleans. But the British were cheated out of the vast lands that had been claimed by France west of the Mississippi. France had turned these lands over to Spain in a secret pact in 1762, a year before signing of the treaty.

News that New Orleans and the territory west of the Mississippi had been ceded to Spain did not reach New Orleans until 2 years later. When the first Spanish governor, Juan de Ulloa, arrived in Louisiana, the people rose in arms and drove him out. They were afraid that, under Spain, they would be deprived of their liberties and lose their profitable trade with France. The rebellion was short-lived, and Ulloa's successor restored order.

When the American colonies won their independence from England and set up the Republic of the United States, a movement of westward expansion created a bustling inland trade. The only outlet for commerce in the fast-growing area between the Alleghenies and the Mississippi was down the great river to New Orleans. But New Orleans was Spanish, and the Spaniards imposed heavy and restrictive duties on American goods, which the settlers in the Mississippi and Ohio Valleys resented bitterly. Threats of seizing New Orleans and even of seceding from the new nation caused alarm both to Spain and the United States.

Napoleon, through another secret treaty with Spain, regained control of New Orleans and all Louisiana for France. Then, fearing that in his war against the British, the enemy might seize Louisiana, Napoleon decided to get rid of the territory. In addition, France needed money. Thomas Jefferson, who was elected President of the United States at that time, realized this. He evolved a plan of settling the problem of a free port at the mouth of the Mississippi by purchasing New Orleans from France.

James Monroe was sent to Paris in 1803 to cooperate with the American minister to the French capital, Robert Livingston, in making arrangements to buy New Orleans. While the two Americans were negotiating with the French minister, Talleyrand, for the purchase of New Orleans, the Frenchmen asked them how much they were willing to pay for the entire Louisiana Territory. Monroe and Livingston were amazed at this suggestion. They had authority only to make a deal for New Orleans, but the offer was too important to be endangered by long delays in communicating with the President and Congress. Acting purely on their own initiative, they signed a treaty on April 30, 1803, whereby the whole Louisiana Territory was purchased by the United States for 15 million dollars.

President Jefferson, Monroe, and Livingston were severely criticized for having "squandered" 15 million dollars of the new nation's money on a vast wilderness, but time has amply justified their foresight. In the purchase of the French province of Louisiana, the United States secured territory that today comprises the states of Louisiana, Arkansas, Missouri, Kansas, Iowa, North Dakota, South Dakota, Wyoming, Montana, Oklahoma, and parts of Minnesota, Idaho, and Colorado. The Louisiana purchase covered about half a billion acres, much of it the richest farm land in the United

States. The price: about 3 cents an acre. With the Louisiana purchase, President Jefferson also introduced a new note in international relations, the acquisition of territory by purchase instead of conquest.

During the War of 1812, fought between the United States and England over the freedom of the seas for commerce, New Orleans became a battleground and the scene of General Andrew Jackson's celebrated victory.

Andrew Jackson, Old Hickory, was a frontier statesman-soldier. He was born of Scotch-Irish parents who had settled in the wilderness of the Carolinas. His education was haphazard, and as a youth he showed his greatest interest in fighting. Despite his lack of "book learning," Andrew Jackson became a United States senator and a supreme court judge in Tennessee. When the war of 1812 broke out, he eagerly seized the opportunity to return to his avocation of fighting. His offer of the services of himself and a band of rough frontiersmen was gladly accepted by the government.

Old Hickory's first big victory was not over the English, but in a battle against the Creek Indians at Horseshoe Bend, Alabama, on March 27, 1814. Then, when the British threatened New Orleans, Andrew Jackson and his band of frontiersmen marched south and prepared to hold the Queen City against the English or die at their posts.

Andrew Jackson was a leader of irregulars, but in the defense of New Orleans he received the support of even more irregular soldiers, the pirate crew of Jean Lafitte, the notorious buccaneer. Lafitte and his brother had once been imprisoned in a Spanish dungeon. In revenge for their tortures they set themselves up as pirates, preying on Spanish ships. They operated in the Caribbean and the Gulf of Mexico and had their headquarters in Barataria Bay, just west of New Orleans. There Jean Lafitte ruled as king of his pirate band, openly defying Governor Claiborne of Louisiana. When Lafitte brought a stolen Spanish ship to Barataria Bay and openly advertised the sale of its cargo in New Orleans, the governor fumed and fretted. But for all his objections, the good citizens of New Orleans flocked to Barataria Bay to buy pirate plunder at bargain prices. Claiborne offered a reward of $500 for the capture of the pirate; Lafitte roared with laughter and came back with an offer of $30,000 for the governor's capture. All New Orleans smiled. They knew Lafitte was a pirate, but since he preyed only on Spanish vessels and never molested American shipping, the people of New Orleans encouraged him to remain.

In the fall of 1814, the British sought to enlist the aid of Lafitte and his band of pirates for an attack on New Orleans. The pirate, although his brother was held a prisoner by the United States at the time, held off the English with excuses. Meanwhile he got in touch with Governor Claiborne and told him about the enemy's plans.

When Old Hickory was busily preparing for the inevitable battle with the British, Lafitte sent word to General Jackson offering the services of himself and his men. Jackson scorned the offer of assistance from pirates, despite the fact that his army needed all the help it could get. Lafitte also knew that it would take every fighting man available to defeat the British. When his offers to join the forces of the United States had been repeatedly refused, Jean Lafitte, risking arrest, walked boldly into New Orleans and called in person on Andrew Jackson. What was said behind the closed doors in the general's headquarters is not known, but the two rough and ready fighters evidently came to a quick understanding. At any rate, Old Hickory's frontiersmen and Lafitte's pirates joined forces. On January 8, 1815, their combined armies defeated the British veterans and saved New Orleans.

The victory aroused great enthusiasm throughout the country. Then came the anticlimax: news that peace had been declared between the United States and England on December 24, 1814, and the war had been over when the frontiersmen irregulars of Andrew Jackson and the pirate patriots of Jean Lafitte saved New Orleans. Yet, the battle had not been fought in vain. The complete victory over superior English forces gave tremendous confidence to the people in the strength of the young republic. It calmed any fears that the Louisiana Territory and the great northwest would ever again be threatened by a foreign power.

CHAPTER 20

Wealth in the Wilderness

Regions in This Chapter	Historical Data	Capital	Population	Area, Square Miles
Manitoba	French in 1731	Winnipeg	700,139	246,512
Saskatchewan	Province in 1905	Regina	921,785	251,700
Alberta	Province in 1905	Edmonton	731,605	255,285
British Columbia	Province in 1871	Victoria	694,300	366,255
Yukon	Territory in 1898	Dawson	4,230	207,076

THE saga of fur trading and trapping in the New World is the story of the making of North America's map. For it was the tireless quest for the wealth of furs deep in the wilderness of the interior that opened up the doors of new frontiers—new frontiers for settlers who seldom were far behind the trail-blazing fur traders.

Next to codfishing, the trade in furs is the oldest and one of the most profitable industries of Europeans in North America. A few years after John Cabot discovered the rich codfish banks off New England, in 1497, English, French, and Portuguese fishermen sailed their fleets of small boats across the Atlantic to the codfish grounds on the Grand Bank. When these fishermen landed on the North American coast to clean and dry their catch, they came in contact with the Indians, whom they found eager and ready to trade.

The fishermen were disappointed when they found that about all the Indians had to give in exchange for knives, fishhooks, and trinkets, were furs, mostly beaver pelts. Furs were used very little in Europe in those days, for they were a luxury that few could afford. At first, the fishermen failed to realize that the furs they scorned offered greater profits than the codfish.

The fishermen, however, slowly built up a side line in fur trading. But it was a minor side line for a good many years. In 1611, when Henry Hudson's mutinous crew put that famous navigator adrift in Hudson Bay, there were some beaver pelts aboard the ship. The men regarded the furs as worthless. It was not until the Europeans learned how to process beaver skins that the fur trade began to boom. When it got under way, the fur industry developed into a rich and far-flung enterprise.

The pioneer explorers of the vast unknown interior of North America from the Arctic Ocean to Texas, from the western slopes of the Appalachians to the Sierras and the Pacific, were the fur traders and trappers. They were the true path makers of the North American wilderness.

From the first, France was the leader in the fur trade. New France in Canada was built on a foundation of furs. Other nations were also interested in the newly discovered wealth. English ships set up a trade in beaver pelts with the Indians along the coast. The Dutch built trading posts all along the Hudson River to Albany.

Because the French first saw the great possibilities of the fur trade, by the beginning of the seventeenth century, they had virtually a monopoly on the business. Fur trading was strictly regulated by the French government from the very first. Exclusive monopolies were granted by the king. The settlers were allowed to engage in the trade only by licenses, which were expensive. Heavy tolls and taxes were imposed on all furs brought into the royal trading posts, and the prices paid for skins were fixed, regardless of supply and demand. Privileges of all sorts could be bought by bribing officials. Favoritism held wide sway. Taxes and fines were imposed at every turn.

As conditions grew worse in the colonies, many settlers

escaped from the burdens of government taxes by leaving the settlements. They made their homes in the wilderness where they joined the Indians, adopting their habits and ways of dress. These voluntary exiles into the wilderness were known as *coureurs de bois*, or wood rangers, and later as *voyageurs*. They were a reckless, adventursome lot but they played an important role in the development of the fur trade. They penetrated deeper into the interior than the regular traders and thus opened up new territories. Many of them made valuable discoveries.

One of the best known of the *coureurs de bois* was Jean Nicolet of Three Rivers. In 1634, Nicolet, guided by Indians, penetrated as far inland as the shores of Lake Michigan. A few years later he heard descriptions of a tribe far to the northwest that answered his notion as to what the Chinese looked like. The discovery of the northwest water passage to Asia was still the dream of every explorer. Nicolet set out to visit this tribe. He entered its village dressed in an elaborate Chinese mandarin robe, gaily embroidered with figures of flowers and birds. The robe was worn in case the people really were Chinese and he had found China. But practical Nicolet held a pistol in each hand—just in case. He discovered that he had been put on a false trail. The village was a poor Indian huddle of shelters near what is today Green Bay, Wisconsin.

Three Rivers was also the home town of two of the greatest pioneers in the fur country, Pierre Esprit Radisson and Medard Grosseilliers. The adventures and exploits of these two Frenchmen are without a rival in the history of their time.

In 1652, young Pierre Radisson and three boy companions were hunting outside the village of Three Rivers when they were attacked by a band of Indians. Radisson was about fifteen at the time. His companions were killed and scalped on the spot. He was taken captive. For more than two years he was enslaved by the Indians. Once, when he tried to escape, he was caught and tortured. But at last he managed to elude his captors and make his way back home to Canada by way of New York. The years he had spent in the wilderness with the Indians had made Radisson a man of the forests, with the skill and cunning of an Indian in the craft and lore of the woods. He had learned the ways and the language of many of the Indian tribes. His wilderness school had been a hard one, but he made good use of the training.

On his return to Three Rivers, Radisson found his sister married to Medard Grosseilliers, also an expert woodsman and as keen on a life of adventure as Radisson, but less hotheaded and a shrewd trader. They formed a partnership and, in June, 1658, they went west on their first major expedition, joining up with a group of Algonquin Indians and French *voyageurs*. They had gone only a few miles when the party was attacked by a band of Iroquois. At the very first Indian war whoop most of the Frenchmen took to their heels, but not Radisson and Grosseilliers. They stood their ground with the Algonquins and came through the fight with their scalps intact.

They continued westward until winter overtook them near Green Bay. In the spring they crossed over into what is today Wisconsin. There they found a great river, which Radisson described as "a mighty river, great, rushing, profound and comparable to the St. Lawrence." There is very little doubt that they had reached the upper Mississippi. Thus Radisson and Grosseilliers may have been the first white men to see the Father of Waters in its northern course.

Father Marquette, who saw the Mississippi 10 years later, is generally credited with the discovery. But Radisson's written description of the river they reached in 1659 makes it almost certain that they were there first. The truth is that the discoveries and explorations of Radisson and Grosseilliers were neglected for a long time, and little credit was given them for their many remarkable accomplishments as explorers. Radisson kept a journal which came to light several generations after his death. To be sure, this journal of the exploits of the partners was happily rescued from oblivion, but by the time it was discovered, the territories they explored had been mapped by other men.

During the 1659 journey, Radisson and Grosseilliers probably penetrated as far west as the country of the Mandan Indians on the Missouri, where the Lewis and Clark expedition wintered almost 150 years later. Radisson wrote of towering mountains, which leads to the belief that they came close to the Rockies.

While in the west, Indians told them about a great sea or bay of salt water far to the north. This was Hudson Bay, which was known as the Great Salt Bay among the Indians. After its discovery by Henry Hudson, the bay had been explored by Thomas Button in 1612, who visited Baffin Land and the Nelson River; in 1619 the mouth of the Churchill River was discovered by Munck, a Danish navigator. In all, some seven separate expeditions had explored the Hudson Bay region, but no permanent settlements had been made.

In New France, neither the exact location nor the overland distance to the Great Salt Bay or Bay of the North was known. But Radisson was sure that he could get Indians to guide him and his partner to it.

Early in the summer of 1661, Radisson and Grosseilliers went to the governor of New France and asked for a license to explore and trade for furs in the Hudson Bay region. The governor said he would grant the license if the two partners would share half the profits with him. Radisson hotly spurned the offer and declared they would go north without a license. The governor then reminded the two traders of the penalties of bartering in furs without a license: imprisonment, the galleys for life, even death. To prevent them from going, the governor issued orders that they were not to be allowed to leave Three Rivers without his permission. Radisson and Grosseilliers were not stopped so easily. The merchants of Three Rivers, knowing that the two partners always brought back more and better furs than other traders, secretly supplied them with provisions and trade goods to barter for furs. Then, one moonless night, the two adventurers stole out of Three Rivers and silently paddled their canoes into the night. They had already arranged for a group of Indian guides to meet them a short distance upcountry.

By November, 1661, Radisson and his brother-in-law reached a point somewhere north and west of the site of Duluth; there they decided to spend the winter. They built a small fort, or stockade, the first trading post in the northwest.

News of the white men's arrival spread like wildfire among the redskins. Indians came to the fort by the hundreds, laden with rich furs to trade for beads and trinkets. Not satisfied with waiting for the Indians to come in with their furs, Radisson visited the tribes in the surrounding country and induced them to collect furs and bring them to the trading post. In the meantime, Grosseilliers, whose enormous black beard fascinated the Indians, remained at the fort to take care of the trading.

The two partners were well aware that they were in bad Indian country, and that they would be unable to meet a concerted Indian attack with their few rifles if trouble were to start. So they resorted to cunning, and constructed a highly efficient and original system of protection. Radisson surrounded the fort with a network of strings that were attached to bells inside the fort. Night-prowling Indians, stumbling against a string, would ring a bell inside the fort and raise an alarm. In addition to this automatic burglar alarm, Radisson made long, thin tubes of birch bark and filled them with gunpowder. These explosive tubes he arranged in a circle outside the stockade. They were connected by a fuse to the fort.

The idea was that, in case of attack, the master fuse would be set off. In a few seconds the first powder-filled tube would explode. The flare would jump to the next tube, and so on, until there was a circle of fire around the stockade. The hope was that this would scare the redskins away. As events turned out, the two Frenchmen were attacked by Indians, and their highly original protective devices served them well.

There is some uncertainty about the exact itinerary of Radisson and Grosseilliers when they continued on their way north to the Great Salt Bay that was their objective. From the writings of Radisson, it appears that they crossed the divide and journeyed down a river that emptied into a large bay of salt water. If that is the case, that Salt Water Bay could be nothing but Hudson Bay.

One thing about which there is no question is that Radisson and Grosseilliers had found a country fabulously rich in furs. When they returned to Quebec in the spring of 1663, they headed a fleet of 360 canoes, each canoe so loaded with furs that it could hardly keep afloat. The cargo was valued at $300,000. It should have made the two partners rich, but when taxes, the king's share, the governor's share, and various fines for trading without a license, had been deducted, there was only $20,000 left for the two traders.

Radisson and his partner raged and ranted. They went to Paris and placed their case before the King of France, but in vain. Grosseilliers was even imprisoned for a while. Both were told that they would never be given a license to go on another fur-trading expedition. Righteously indignant, the two men decided to go elsewhere to seek their fortunes and to carry on their project of establishing a trading post at Hudson Bay. They returned to North America, and at Port Royal, Nova Scotia, they chartered two vessels for an expedition to the Bay. While they were getting ready, one of the ships sailed on a fishing voyage and was wrecked. Before the two Frenchmen could go north, they were forced to go to Boston to answer a lawsuit in connection with the wrecked vessel. They were acquitted, but the trial had cost them all the money they had.

An Englishman of position and influence, Sir George Cartwright, happened to be in Boston at the time. He became interested in the tale the two picturesque adventurers told about the wealth of furs at Hudson Bay. He invited the two Frenchmen to go to England with him and tell their story to King Charles II. Feeling that they owed no loyalty to the France that had treated them so shabbily, they accepted the offer, and sailed from Boston in the late summer of 1665.

On the way to England their ship was attacked by a Dutch raider. Radisson barely had time to destroy his precious notes and maps of the fur country before they were taken prisoners. The Dutch ship, after seizing the cargo of the Englishmen, and with Sir George and the two Frenchmen aboard, sailed for Spain where the three prisoners were put ashore. In due time, they made their way to England. There they found King Charles a ready listener to their glowing tales of fabulous profits to be had by organizing a fur-trading expedition to Hudson Bay. The king endorsed the proposed venture and in 1668 two ships sailed from England, bound for Hudson Bay. The vessel carrying Radisson was forced to turn back because of storms, but the other, the *Nonsuch*, with Grosseilliers aboard, made an uneventful voyage and landed the adventurer at Hudson Bay on August 4. A small trading post was built, and after a winter's trading the ship sailed back to England loaded with furs.

The cargo brought back by Grosseilliers far exceeded the expectations of the men who backed the venture. The king, whose treasury needed a new and steady source of revenue, was delighted. The outcome was that in 1670, a royal charter was granted to "Adventurers of England trading into Hudson Bay." That was the beginning of the famous and far-flung empire of the Hudson's Bay Company. Prince Rupert was made governor, to remain in England, while Charles Bayley was appointed resident governor at Hudson Bay. Radisson and Grosseilliers were both rewarded and given employment by the company. An expedition sailed for Hudson Bay and a series of forts and trading posts was erected: Fort Nelson, Fort Albany, Fort Hayes, and Fort Rupert.

Shortly after the company was founded, the French heard of the venture and sent a force under Charles Abanel against the English in Hudson Bay. The English accused Radisson and Grosseilliers of instigating this attack. The two Frenchmen, disgusted at this unjust charge, quit the Hudson's Bay people and returned to New France.

Meanwhile, a company had been formed in Quebec to trade in Hudson Bay. This company hired the two partners to head an expedition to build a fort and trading post in the territory they had helped open for the English company. The expedition sailed aboard two French ships. When it reached the bay early in the year, an English party was already there, and shortly an illicit trading ship from Boston arrived. By cleverly playing one against the other during the fur-trading season, Radisson managed to capture both the English and the Bostonians and to take all their furs. These he shipped back to Quebec in addition to his own collection of furs.

When the partners returned to Quebec expecting acclaim and rewards, they were surprised to find themselves practically ignored. Grosseilliers took this setback rather calmly and decided to retire from the fur-trading business, but Radisson demanded his share in the profits of the pelts he had sent back. When his demands were denied, he returned to the service of the English Hudson's Bay Company, and hurried north to seize a large collection of furs his nephew had gotten together at Hudson Bay.

Radisson continued in the service of the Hudson's Bay Company for many years. One of his greatest contributions to the trade was a treaty he negotiated between the English and the Indians in the bay region. The treaty has endured to this day. Despite his excellent work, the company grew distrustful of him when war broke out between England and France. He was removed from active duty. With the years, he was forgotten, and in his old age Radisson had to sue the governors of the Hudson's Bay Company to secure a pittance to live on.

Meanwhile France cast hungry eyes on Hudson Bay and in 1697, while France was at war with England, a French naval expedition under Pierre d'Iberville attacked and forced the surrender of the English at Hudson Bay. But it was wasted effort. When the war ended, England's rights in the bay were acknowledged, and the Hudson's Bay employees moved back into their battered forts and began rebuilding. As the eighteenth century dawned, the French in Canada became seriously worried about the spread of the Hudson's Bay Company trade westward into territory they considered their own. With a view to reestablishing contacts and opening up new fields, Count Verendrye undertook a combined exploring and fur-trading expedition in 1731. The count, a soldier of France who had distinguished himself in the service of Louis XIV, had come to America to take up the fur trade. In 1728, he was in charge of a small post at Lake Nipigon. There an Indian chief told him about a great western ocean and a river that flowed into a sea of salt water.

In June, 1731, Count Verendrye, his three sons, and his nephew, Jemerais, set out from Montreal with a party of *voyageurs* and Indians to find an overland route to the western ocean. Verendrye was unable to get the support of the government, but the merchants of New France promised to underwrite the expedition, pay all expenses, and furnish supplies. Troubles beset Count Verendrye almost from the start. The merchants failed to keep their promises. His nephew died. The heaviest blow came when his eldest son and twenty of his men were killed by a Sioux raiding party. Delay followed delay and kept the Frenchman running back and forth between Montreal and his wilderness advance camp at Fort La Reine.

It was October, 1738, before he was able to set out for the Mandan country on the Missouri River. There he learned from the Indians of white men with black beards living on the shores of the great ocean to the west. They meant the Spanish colonists in California. Verendrye wanted to cross the continent to the Pacific, but once again the broken promises of the merchants to send supplies forced him to go back to Montreal. Count Verendrye was thoroughly discouraged by that time. Instead of setting out again himself, he sent his two sons to carry on the explorations.

The two young Frenchmen reached the Black Hills in the spring of 1742 and crossed the Bad Lands, where they saw great herds of elk. In June, they reached the Big Horn range of the Rockies. The Verendryes made plans to cross the Rockies but an Indian war was brewing and the party had to turn back.

The accomplishments of Count Verendrye and his sons over a period of more than twelve years may at first glance look like so much wasted effort. But closer scrutiny reveals that a great deal of new territory was explored and opened up for the French fur trade. During the years a line of trading posts had been established, which did much to stop the flow of furs to the English at Hudson Bay.

In 1763, France lost all her North American colonies. After the battle on the Plains of Abraham, Canada became an English possession, and the Hudson's Bay Company found itself for the time being the undisputed master of the Canadian fur trade. But soon many of the French reestablished themselves as independent traders, and with the *coureurs de bois* they rapidly became serious rivals of the English. Then, too, the Russians were making themselves felt in Alaska. Bering Strait had been discovered in 1741 by Vitus Bering, and by 1761 the Russians were active in the fur trade in Alaska. At first, the Russians did not give serious competition to the English. Their Alaskan harvest in furs came from the sea otter. The Hudson Bay trade was practically all in beaver pelts. In Canada, beaver skins were, as a matter of fact, the coin of the realm. Throughout Hudson's Bay Company territory the value of all trade goods was reckoned in beaver skins.

The Hudson's Bay Company had been sitting back and taking in the profits without trying to build up the trade or to extend its operations into new territory. England was dissatisfied with this policy. The government let it be known that in return for its liberal charter, the Hudson's Bay Company was expected to explore and extend the British domain in Canada and to become active in the search for a northwest water passage to the Pacific Ocean.

Roused from his sleep of prosperous contentment by orders from England to get busy, the company's Governor Moses Norton, at Fort Prince of Wales, sent Samuel Hearne on an expedition to find the Coppermine River and open up new trade territory. According to Indian stories, this river ran straight to the Pacific. Hearne, who had resigned from the British navy to join the Hudson's Bay Company, started on his first expedition in November, 1769. He went overland by dog sled. The Indians were hostile. Even his Indian guides deserted him. To make the going even more difficult for Hearne, these red rascals traveled ahead of him, out of sight, scaring away the game he depended on for food. When Hearne persisted in pushing on, the Indians wrecked his supply sleds, and he was forced to turn back.

Early in 1770, Samuel Hearne set out again, this time on snowshoes. On this trip he managed to get far within the Arctic Circle. Then the Indians stole his surveying instruments. Unable to take observations, the Englishman had to retrace his steps for the second time. He reached Fort Prince of Wales in November. Toward the latter part of the same month he started out for the third time, with Chief Mantonabee as his guide. He found the Coppermine River, but soon learned that it was not the westward water passage. He kept on, far into the Arctic regions, until he was satisfied that there was no passage to the western ocean from Hudson Bay.

When Herne returned to Fort Prince of Wales in June, 1772, Governor Norton had died. Hearne succeeded him as governor. Ten years later, in August, 1782, three French warships commanded by Captain La Pérouse anchored in the harbor and trained their guns on Fort Prince of Wales. Governor Hearne, caught unawares, surrendered. But the flag of France flew over Hudson's Bay posts only for a brief time. Instructions came from Paris ordering the French commander to give up the fort and evacuate Hudson Bay.

With peace restored and the French gone, the Hudson's Bay Company again relaxed and settled back to rest on its laurels. But a new source of irritation was about to spring up. Scotch fur traders and independent English fur men got together in 1783 and organized a rival organization. It was called the Northwest Company. They made friends with the French *voyageurs*. Before the English were aware of what was happening, Northwest Company fur-trading posts paralleled those of the Hudson's Bay Company. With a warehouse in Montreal and posts extending far into the west, this new company was soon cutting into the profits of the Hudson's Bay people.

Every year there was a meeting of the Northwest Company members at the grand portage of Fort William on Lake Superior. To this gathering, the fur lords came in style, expensively dressed in gaudy costumes, their canoes laden with fine wines and exotic imported foods. The object of the conference was to discuss plans and explorations for the coming year, but the meeting also served as a colorful pageant to impress the Indians, whose liking for pomp and finery was a great asset to these Nor'westers, as the men of the Northwest Company were called.

The Nor'westers went into the wilderness, direct to the Indians, instead of waiting for the furs to come to them. Because of this policy, many of them became famous as explorers: David Thompson, Alexander Mackenzie, Simon Fraser, Hugh Monroe, and Alexander Henry the younger, to mention a few.

David Thompson had worked for the Hudson's Bay Company as an astronomer and mathematician in connection with map-making surveys. In the employ of the Northwest Company, he made many valuable observations along the south shore of Lake Superior, the upper Missisippi, and Lake Winnepeg. Briefly, Thompson became the greatest map maker of Canada. His explorations took him up north to Saskatchewan and as far as Lake Winnepegosis. In later years, he explored the Rockies. He also built Kootenai House, the first fur-trading post in the Columbia River region.

Perhaps the greatest of all the Nor'westers was Alexander Mackenzie. He came to North America at an early age and entered the fur trade. When the Northwest Company was formed, he entered its service. While in charge of the far north post at Fort Chippewan, he had come upon a great river that he thought might be the elusive northwest passage. He decided to find out, and also to have a try at the $100,000 award offered by the British government to the discoverer of a northwest waterway connecting the Atlantic and Pacific Oceans.

In June, 1789, Mackenzie embarked from Fort William on Lake Superior with four French *voyageurs*. He traded for furs as he headed north to the great river he had seen. For many weary months he followed the course of the river. At every bend he expected to catch a glimpse of the western ocean. At last he reached an Eskimo village on an island in a large lake. Mackenzie, his hopes high, climbed the highest point in the island. There were only mountains to the west, but spread before him to the north, he saw a vast sea. It was, however, a sea of frozen water; instead of a water route to the Pacific he had reached the Arctic Ocean. Mackenzie was not the first European to set eyes on the Polar Sea. That honor belongs to Samuel Hearne.

Mackenzie returned to the Northwest trading post of Fort William, after having followed the great river that bears his

name almost from its headwaters to its mouth where it empties
into the Arctic Ocean. But the intrepid explorer was not ready
to end his search for a waterway to the Pacific. In October,
1792, he embarked on another expedition. This time he went
westward. After spending the winter trading, he continued
in May, 1793, and followed the Peace River to its source.
Then he made a short portage to the Fraser River (discovered
by Simon Fraser) which he followed until he was halted by
impassable rapids. Refusing to be stopped, Mackenzie
abandoned his canoes and went on overland. He crossed the
Rockies, and pushed westward, until he reached the Pacific.
To mark the achievement of his goal, the Nor'wester painted
a legend in large letters on a rock: "Alexander Mackenzie,
from Canada, by land, the 22nd of July, 1793."

The energy and initiative of the Nor'westers made them not
only brilliant explorers, but costly rivals for the Hudson's Bay
Company. The two companies were bitter enemies for many
years. Finally in 1821 they were combined, after open warfare
had threatened to disrupt the entire industry.

News of the enormous profits being made by the Russians
in sea otters off Alaska interested England. In 1776, the famous
British navigator and explorer, Captain James Cook, sailed
on the last of his many notable voyages. One of the objectives
of this expedition was to look for a northeast water passage
between the Pacific and Atlantic Oceans around the north
coast of North America. He was also to investigate the possibilities of the fur trade. His expedition reached Alaskan water
in 1778, passed through the Bering Strait, and pushed on
until forced to turn back by an ice barrier. Captain Cook was
killed by natives on a Hawaiian Island, but when his ships
returned to Europe, news of his discoveries in the North
Pacific created considerable interest in England and in the
United States.

Boston merchants, whose fast ships were already engaged
in the China trade, decided to investigate the possibilities of

the North Pacific fur trade. In 1787 two ships, the *Washington*, under Captain Robert Gray, and the *Columbia*, commanded by Captain John Hendrick, sailed from Boston, their holds full of knives, kettles, blankets, and beads for the Indian fur trade. They were the first Yankee ships to round Cape Horn.

In September, 1788, Captain Gray was at Nootka Sound, on the Pacific coast. There he met an English expedition of two ships under Captain Meares, who had sailed with Cook on his last voyage. The English were building a third ship, the *Northwest American*. This vessel was the first real ship to be built on the North Pacific coast.

The relationship between Captain Gray and Captain Meares was friendly enough, but the Englishman tried to discourage the American. He complained of the small profits to be made in furs and painted an exaggerated picture of the ferocity and hostility of the Indians. But Meares made no headway with the shrewd Yankee captain. Gray went right ahead with his fur trade. With a full cargo of furs, he set sail for Canton, China, in the *Columbia*. There he traded his furs for tea and again set sail, reaching Boston on August 10, 1790, via Cape Good Hope. He was the first American captain and his was the first American ship to sail around the globe.

So enormous were the profits of Captain Gray's voyage that he was sent out to the Pacific again almost immediately. The idea of buying furs from Pacific coast Alaska Indians for a few cents and selling them for hundreds of dollars in China, appealed to the Yankee merchants. On his second voyage in the ship *Columbia*, Captain Gray investigated reports of a great river on the North Pacific coast. He entered what is today Grays Harbor. On May 11, 1792, he sailed his ship across a bar of raging breakers and entered a great river, which he named the Columbia in honor of his ship.

A short time later, Captain Gray met the English explorer, Captain George Vancouver. He told Gray that he had heard the sound of the breakers where the rushing river joined the sea, and that he had intended to investigate. If Vancouver had done so, he would have discovered the Columbia River ahead of Captain Gray. That would have changed the course of North American history. It was on the grounds of Gray's discovery of the Columbia that the United States won its claim upon the Oregon Territory.

The fur profits of the Hudson's Bay and the Northwest Companies led to the formation of other fur-trading companies. None of them was conspicuously successful. These early independent ventures were mostly British. The United States did not really enter into the competition until John Jacob Astor, in 1808, conceived the idea of cornering the fur trade in American territory by establishing a fur monopoly.

John Jacob Astor came to the United States in 1784 from Walldorf, Germany. On the way over he met a fur trader who induced him to invest his money in furs. Astor bought a lot of beaver skins. These he sold in London at such a handsome profit that he decided to devote his life to the fur business. Astor was a clever merchant, but he was essentially a businessman, not an actual trader in furs, or an explorer.

At first, Astor bought his furs from the Northwest Company, and over the years built up a great fortune. While sitting in with the members of the Northwest Company in Montreal, he began to realize that there was no reason why he should share his profits with them. Why not start a company of his own? Slowly his plan crystallized. In 1809, together with a number of independent traders, he formed the American Fur Company, with a capital of a million dollars. He bought the old Mackinaw Company that traded along the upper Mississippi and the Great Lakes, and proceeded to put his plan into operation.

Astor's idea was to establish posts along the Missouri and Columbia Rivers with a warehouse at the mouth of the Columbia. Ships were to be sent to the Pacific coast around Cape Horn each year to pick up the furs, carry them to China to be traded for tea and other oriental merchandise, and then return to New York by way of the Cape of Good Hope. Two expeditions were fitted out. One went overland through the Missouri Valley to the Columbia River. The other went by ship with supplies and materials and sailed around Cape Horn.

The sea expedition left in September, 1810, aboard the *Tonquin*, commanded by Captain Thorn, a former naval officer. The voyage was far from pleasant. Ill will developed between Captain Thorn and Duncan McDougal, the leader of the traders, almost from the start. The *Tonquin* reached the Columbia River in March, 1811. There, after harsh words between McDougal and Thorn, the traders and their supplies were put ashore to begin building a trading post a short distance up the river, at a place that was named Fort Astoria.

The post had hardly been completed when David Thompson of the Northwest Company arrived with a party of traders. To the consternation of the Americans in the party, McDougal, who had been a Nor'wester himself, greeted the Canadians with open arms. Thompson made no trouble at that time. After looking over the setup of his rivals, he proceeded up the Columbia River to establish a post, only to find that the Americans had gotten there before him.

In the meantime, Captain Thorn, who had gone up the coast to trade with the Indians, sailed himself into trouble. Ignoring the warnings of men more experienced with the natives, he allowed the Indians to come aboard the ship in large numbers. One morning the Indians were unusually quiet, concentrating all their trading on knives and other weapons. The white traders who were on board grew alarmed and appealed to Captain Thorn to order the natives ashore. The warning came too late. With shrill war whoops, the Indians suddenly sprang into action, setting to work with knives and tomahawks. The Americans fell bleeding and dying by the score, Captain Thorn among them. Four of the men managed to barricade themselves in the cabin. They kept up such a steady fire that the Indians fled from the ship.

As night fell, three of the white men took to a small boat. They left behind the company's clerk, Lewis, who said that he was too badly wounded to join them. Unfortunately for them, they did not travel far enough down the river before going ashore. The moment they set foot on land they were attacked by Indians and killed. During the night, Lewis, the clerk, planned his revenge upon the Indians and prayed he would live long enough to put it into execution. At dawn the dying man propped himself up against the ship's railing and shouted to the Indians to come aboard. Soon the redskins were swarming over the side. When the ship's deck was thick with Indians, Lewis dragged himself into the cabin and lit a fuse that ran down into the powder magazines. With a terrific explosion the vessel was blown to bits, killing more than 200 Indians and seriously injuring many more. Lewis also died, but that was part of his plan.

When news of the *Tonquin* disaster reached Fort Astoria, the traders were both shocked and alarmed. An attack from their rivals of the Northwest Company was expected momentarily. The relations between the United States and England were seriously strained at that time. War loomed on the horizon. The Indians in the neighborhood were hostile. McDougal managed to keep them peaceful only by threatening to give them smallpox, which he told them he carried in a corked bottle. In spite of these troubles, the Americans continued their work, strengthening their fortifications and building more posts along the Columbia River.

At about this time Astor's long-delayed overland expedition reached Astoria, under command of W. P. Hunt. Trapping and exploring expeditions were organized. Hunt was sent to Alaska on the supply ship *Beaver*. Nearly all the men were out buying furs. Just when Astoria was at its weakest in man power, the war which had broken out between the United

States and England made itself felt on the Pacific coast. An English expedition attacked Fort Astoria and took it with hardly a struggle. The American flag was hauled down, and the fort was renamed Fort George.

The fall of Astoria put an end to John Jacob Astor's fur venture on the Pacific coast. However, the peace of 1814 restored the territory to the United States and in 1815 a law was passed by the government expelling British fur traders from the United States. All the English posts south of Canada and east of the Rockies fell into Astor's hands, and before long he virtually had a monopoly of the American fur trade.

In 1821, General William H. Ashley and a group of Mountain Men organized the Rocky Mountain Fur Company, which did a profitable business in furs despite the powerful forces of the Astor interests. One of the chief explorers for this company was Jed Smith. He was the first white man to reach California overland from the East. He also carried his activities north into the Oregon Territory. In 1823, a party of Rocky Mountain Men discovered South Pass, the easiest gateway through the Rockies. The most interesting thing about the Rocky Mountain Fur Company was its personnel, the keen-eyed, sharpshooting Mountain Men.

As early as 1806, at the time of the Lewis and Clark expedition, the mountains of the northwest and southwest were an open book to the Mountain men, who had penetrated into the wilderness in search of beaver. The typical Mountain Man was a picturesque fellow with his fur cap, fringed deerskin hunting shirt, leather leggings, and moccasins. When he set out on the trail, his outfit consisted of a rifle, a powder horn, 4 pounds of lead, a bullet mold, seven traps, a blanket roll, 7 pounds of flour, and a long-bladed hunting knife. Where the French *voyageurs* depended on canoes for locomotion, the Mountain Men relied on horses. While the Mountain Men traded with the Indians for furs, all of them were expert trappers.

Most of the Mountain Men were ignorant of everything but wilderness lore. As they did not record their journeyings on paper, they never got credit for the tremendous part they played in unfolding North America's map. The sum total of their knowledge of the wilds, which passed from mouth to mouth, eventually proved of great value to later scientific exploring expeditions. A large part of the territory covered by Lewis and Clark had been known to these trappers for years. That holds true also with respect to nearly all the map-making explorations conducted by the United States Army in the West during the first half of the nineteenth century. Some of the Mountain Men, such as Colter, Beckwourth, and Bridger, kept journals of a sort, but their reputations as tellers of tall and fanciful stories were so great that few of their discoveries were taken seriously.

Jim Bridger was the King of the Mountain Men. He was a born "prevaricator" and could spin yarns without end at the drop of a hat—and Jim never hesitated to drop his own hat. His nickname, even as a young man, was Old Gabe because he was such a "gabber." Bridger was also a born explorer. He liked nothing better than to nose out new territory. This nose for nature led him to make many new and startling discoveries. He is believed to have been the first white man at Salt Lake, in what is now Utah, in 1824. Two years later Bridger discovered the scenic wonders of Yellowstone Park. But few of his fellows believed Jim Bridger's accounts of the many marvels he had seen, because of his reputation as a prevaricator. No one would believe that he had found a great salt lake or a place where great fountains of steam shot high into the air.

One of Bridger's favorite stories was about the Big Horn Mountains. He told of one place where it took so long for the echo to come back that he used it as an alarm clock. He would shout, "Git up, Jim Bridger, git up!" when he bedded down at night. And, he would go on with a sober face, "So help me, Hannah, just about sunrise that echo would be a-coming back, sure as daylight, and shout right into my ear, 'Git up, Jim Bridger, git up!'"

Another of his stories relates how he and a companion were attacked by a whole tribe of Indians, under conditions that made escape impossible. When the gullible listener asked how they got away, Bridger said that they didn't. "Both of us was killed!" Then there was the story of how he saved a whole Indian nation from starvation during a bad year by the simple means of driving a herd of buffalo into the Great Salt Lake, where the salt preserved the meat in nature's own brine. It was Bridger's facility for making up tall stories that made people doubt accounts of his genuine discoveries, many of which sounded as fantastic as his prevarications.

Although the Mountain Men liked their jokes, life on the whole was a serious business with them. On one occasion Jim Bridger and his partner Fitzpatrick discovered that they were being followed through rich beaver country by two men from the American Fur Company who were spying out the land. When they could not throw their rivals off the track, they deliberately led them into dangerous Blackfeet territory, where their competitors were attacked by the Indians and one of them scalped.

It was as a member of the famous Bridger Beaver Brigade that Kit Carson, the most celebrated of the Mountain Men, got his start. As a boy, Carson was apprenticed to Dave Workman, a saddler in Franklin, Missouri, then an outpost on the very edge of the western frontier. His daily contact with the Mountain Men made Kit dissatisfied with his tame work and he longed for the rough and ready life of a frontiersman. In 1826 he met Jim Bridger, who filled Kit's ears and mind and heart with stories of the wild. Finally Kit Carson could resist the lure of adventure no longer and ran away to become a trapper in the wild mountain country. David Workman posted a notice offering a reward of 1 cent for the return of his runaway apprentice. Evidently the lad who was to become the greatest scout of the West and one of the foremost trail blazers in the United States, was not a very valuable harness maker.

If Kit Carson had not followed the call of adventure and joined the Mountain Men, the United States would have lost one of its greatest pioneers. It was mainly Carson's knowledge of the unmapped West that enabled Fremont to survey the Oregon Trail and blaze a new route into California—trails over which the first hardy immigrants traveled in covered wagons to settle the West.

The Mountain Men clung to their wilderness ways of life until the fur trade died with the thinning out of the beaver population. Then they drifted into other occupations. Some became guides for immigrant trains and government expeditions. Some took up the life of professional hunters. Others settled on farms, as did Jim Bridger, who died in 1881.

Although the United States got Oregon by the treaty of 1814, the fur traders of the Canadian Northwest Company continued to maintain their hold on the country. During the War of 1812, most of the American traders had been driven out or were killed by Indians. With the opening of the West to settlers, Americans flocked to Oregon Territory by the thousands. When the Hudson's Bay Company continued trying to hold sway in that part of the West, the settlers rebelled. They raised the war cry: "Fifty-four forty or fight!" This meant that they wanted the United States to claim possession of the entire Pacific coast region up to Alaska, based on Captain Gray's discoveries.

The English based their claim on the explorations of George Vancouver. War threatened between the settlers and the Canadian fur traders, but fortunately it was averted by treaty, signed on June 15, 1846. Great Britain and the United States agreed to fix the boundary at 49 degrees north latitude, the present international boundary between this country and Canada.

While the American Fur Company was putting down roots and extending its activities in the United States, the rivalry between the two Canadian companies was rapidly reaching a point of open warfare. Traders of the Hudson's Bay Company and groups of Nor'westers clashed more and more frequently. On June 14, 1816, a company of twenty-seven Hudson's Bay men encountered a group of sixty half-breeds in the employ of the Northwest Company. When Semple of the Hudson's Bay Company ordered the half-breeds to leave the territory, they opened fire. The leaders of both detachments tried to restore order, but it was too late. Before the battle, known as the Massacre of Seven Oaks, was over, all but six of the Hudson's Bay Company men were killed.

More violence followed, until Lord Selkirk, the influential head of the Hudson's Bay Company, secured arms and ammunition from the government. With a reinforcement of British soldiers he marched on the stronghold of the Nor'westers at Fort William on Lake Superior. Unable to resist an organized force, the leader of the Northwest Company surrendered the fort without a struggle. Peace did not come until the government finally took a hand and ordered hostilities to cease. The rivals were instructed to take their difficulties to the courts of law in England, but as neither of the organizations could afford to have its highhanded methods aired in the open, they grudgingly joined forces. In March, 1821, the two companies were united. The name of the Hudson's Bay Company was retained. So far as history is concerned, the story of the new Hudson's Bay Company can best be read on the map of Canada. Even today there are large areas throughout northern Canada where the only place names are those of Hudson's Bay Company posts, and where the only permanent inhabitants are the factors, their assistants, and a few scattered Eskimos who are totally dependent on the company for their livelihood.

It was to one of these remote trading posts of the Hudson's

Bay Company on the Yukon River that George Carmack came one day in August, 1896, with a cartridge shell full of gold he and his two Indian "boys" had found in the bottom of the Klondike River, just above where it empties into the Yukon. When Carmack told of his find and how rich the pay dirt was, the little community of Forty Mile hardly waited for him to finish. Within 3 days every person who had the means of locomotion was on his way to the Klondike. The great Yukon gold rush was on!

The real discoverer of gold on the Klondike was a prospector named Bob Henderson. While panning gold in a creek bottom, he injured his leg. On his way to a settlement to have it treated, Henderson met Carmack and told him about his find. Carmack decided to investigate. He found pay dirt just as he was about to give up. The result was that Carmack became rich, the King of the Yukon, while poor Henderson lost out. While the real discoverer of the strike was laid up with a bad leg, another prospector jumped his original claim. When Henderson was well enough to get around, he staked a new claim, which he was unable to work. He sold it for $3,000. Almost half a million dollars was taken out of Henderson's second claim, before the owner sold it for more than $200,000 to a mining syndicate.

News from the isolated north traveled slowly in those days. A year went by before the news of the gold strike reached the outside world. On July 15, 1897, the ship *Excelsior* reached San Francisco with the first party of gold-lined prospectors. Within the hour of the ship's arrival, telegraph keys were clicking, sending the exciting news all over the world. "Gold in the Yukon!" Those were the magic words that electrified the entire nation. Young and old, rich and poor, men and women, left their homes, closed their shops, quit their jobs, and headed for the Klondike by the thousands. But out of every hundred who started for the gold strike, fewer than ten reached Dawson, the heart of the Klondike gold rush.

The hardships and sufferings and obstacles that faced the gold seekers defy description. The going was easy up to Juneau, Alaska. From Juneau they went to Skagway or Dyea, depending on which trail they planned to follow over the mountains, White Pass or Chilkoot. Chilkoot Pass became famous, principally because of the section where the fortune hunters had to make their laborious way up a long series of steps cut out of solid ice.

In the heart of the winter of 1897, when the gold stampede was at its height and the mercury at its lowest, men who knew nothing about the north fought their way through snow and ice, over mountains, along narrow, dangerous trails. In order to survive, each man had to carry a year's supply of food. The end of this 600-mile path of pain was Dawson, the boom town that sprang up almost overnight. Tons of gold worth millions upon millions of dollars were taken out of creek beds in the Yukon. But the Klondike strike, rich as it was, eventually ran its course. Prospectors still roam the Yukon and the wilderness of the Canadian northwest, always hoping that some day another strike as rich as the Klondike bonanza will be found. Many of these gold seekers earn grubstakes by trapping and trading furs, which are today the coin of the realm in those regions of the north where the standard of the Hudson's Bay Company still flutters over trading posts as it has for hundreds of years.

CHAPTER 21

People of the Morning Light

Highlights of the United States

Discovered: Atlantic coast line discovered in 986 by Bjarni Herlufs-son and explored by English, French, Dutch, Spanish, and Portuguese navigators starting with John Cabot, for England, in 1497.

Population: 131,669,275 (Continental United States, 1940 census).

Area: 3,026,789 square miles (Continental United States).

Language: English.　　　　*Capital:* Washington, D. C.

Government: Independence declared in 1776.

Geographical Characteristics: Geographically the United States divides itself into the following major regions from east to west: Atlantic Coastal Plains, Appalachian Highlands, Gulf Coastal Plains, Central Plains, Laurentian Plateau, Ozark Plateau, Great Plains, Rocky Mountain Region, Western Plateau, Pacific Ranges, and Coastal Plains.

Climatic Conditions: Extremely diverse, with temperatures inter-mediate between those of the Arctic regions on the one hand and those of the torrid zone on the other. In some parts of the country, summer maximum temperatures equal those of the tropics. In other parts, winter temperatures equal those of the Arctic.

Principal Products

Leading Agricultural States: South Atlantic states, Mississippi Valley states, Kansas, Nebraska, Iowa, North Dakota, South Dakota, also Pacific states: Corn, cotton, grain, sugar, and tobacco are the leading crops.

Leading Mineral States: Michigan, Pennsylvania, Arizona, Utah, Montana, West Virginia, Rocky Mountain states. Many

428

metals are found in bountiful quantities with iron, copper, lead, gold, and silver in the lead. Also in the ground are vast resources of coal and petroleum.

Leading Manufacturing States: New York, Massachusetts, Connecticut, New Jersey, Pennsylvania, Michigan, Illinois, Indiana, Wisconsin, Missouri, and California.

Leading Fisheries States: Main sources of food fish are the waters of New York, New England, and the North Pacific. The Great Lakes also provide a huge supply of food fish.

Leading Lumber States: States in the region of the Appalachian Highlands, Michigan, Wisconsin, Georgia, Oregon, California, and Washington.

State	Settled	Entered Union	Capital	Population	Area, square miles
Connecticut*	1635	1788	Hartford	1,710,112	4,965
Delaware*	1726	1787	Dover	264,603	2,370
Maine	1624	1820	Augusta	845,139	33,040
Maryland*	1634	1788	Annapolis	1,811,546	12,327
Massachusetts*	1620	1788	Boston	4,312,332	8,266
New Hampshire*	1623	1788	Concord	489,716	9,341
New Jersey*	1664	1787	Trenton	4,148,562	8,224
New York*	1614	1788	Albany	13,379,622	49,204
Pennsylvania*	1682	1787	Harrisburg	9,891,709	45,126
Rhode Island*	1636	1790	Providence	711,699	1,248
Vermont	1724	1791	Montpelier	357,598	9,564

* Original colonies.

WHEN the Indians of the New England coast first saw white-skinned and fair-haired strangers come to their shores from the east, the direction of the rising sun, they called them People of the Morning Light. Who the first Europeans were to hear themselves called by that picturesque name, we do not know. They may have been the Vikings. Perhaps they were some of the French and English fishermen who followed in their small boats close upon John Cabot's discovery of the codfish banks off Newfoundland in 1497. We do know that white men touched the mainland at an early unknown date, and that when the first English settlers reached New England in 1620, they were greeted as People of the Morning Light. In time, this came to be the name given by the Indians to all the early settlers along the greater part of the North Atlantic coast of America.

The first attempt to settle New England was made by Sir Walter Raleigh who, in 1602, sent Bartholomew Gosnold to America to establish a trade in furs and fish and to found a colony. The colonists were landed on Cuttyhunk Island, off Cape Cod. While Captain Gosnold sailed in search of fish and furs, the colonists built a fort and a storehouse. But the would-be settlers did not like the island, and one summer was enough for them. When Gosnold appeared in the fall, they abandoned the colony and returned to England.

In 1606, King James chartered the London and Plymouth Companies for the purpose of colonizing in the New World. In the following year, came the Virginia venture. The early misfortunes of that colony discouraged further attempts for some years. Captain John Smith, after his misadventures in Virginia, was employed by the Plymouth Company to explore New England; he made his first voyage in 1614. In 1616, as a reward for his work in mapping the New England coast, Captain Smith was made Admiral of New England. He established no settlements, although he did land at Plymouth, which later was to become the home of the colonists aboard the *Mayflower*.

In England a group of people called Separatists—who became known as the Pilgrims—were persecuted because of their religious beliefs. Although they found a haven of refuge in Holland, where they were allowed to worship as they pleased, they were not satisfied to raise their children upon foreign soil. The unsettled lands of the New World presented a solution. The leaders of the Pilgrims sought a charter to colonize across the ocean. This was granted. On September 6, 1620, the *Mayflower* sailed from Plymouth, England.

After a long voyage, the ship reached Cape Cod where it remained at anchor near Provincetown, while the leaders looked for a better and safer anchorage. They found it at Plymouth Rock. Here the *Mayflower* dropped anchor in Plymouth harbor, New England, on December 16, 1620. While looking for a likely site for their settlement, the Pilgrims lived aboard the ship. By common agreement they had made a compact setting forth the form of their government, which they all solemnly promised to obey. John Carver was elected governor of the Plymouth Colony, with Captain Miles Standish as the military leader.

The first winter of the Pilgrims was a hard one. Many died of hunger, cold, and disease. When spring came, there were only about fifty survivors. Luckily the Indians were friendly, and the colonists were especially fortunate in finding an Indian who had been in England and spoke English. This Indian, Squanto, had been captured years before by European fishermen and taken to Spain and England, from where he had been able to return to his native land. Squanto proved a friend in need to the Pilgrims. He showed them how to plant corn, trap, hunt, and fish.

Although the first winter was one of untold suffering, no one wanted to return to England in the spring. The Pilgrims had found the home they sought, where they could build according to their ideas and worship according to their beliefs. A treaty of peace was made with the Indians. This pact lasted for 50 years. Once clouds of war appeared on the horizon when Chief Canonicus of Narragansett sent Governor Bradford a snakeskin full of arrows as a threat of war. But the war clouds quickly vanished when the governor sent the snakeskin back filled with gunpowder.

That fall, when the first crop was harvested, the Pilgrims invited their Indian friends to join them in a feast of thanksgiving. It lasted the better part of a week. The following winter proved less severe, for the Pilgrims were beginning to learn the ways of the new land. But the colony grew slowly and few new settlers arrived. From a population of 180 in 1624, the colony had increased to only 300 by 1626. The problem of growing enough food was solved by allotting each colonist a piece of land, instead of planting as a community project. As the colony grew, some of the settlers began looking for better farm land, and new settlements were founded to the north of Plymouth.

John Endicott and a group of colonists settled in Salem in 1628. In the following year, the Massachusetts Bay Colony charter was granted. The area of this colony ran 3 miles north of the Merrimac River to 3 miles south of the Charles River. To the west it reached all the way to the Pacific Ocean. This was due to the belief that the land mass between the Atlantic and the Pacific was narrow. Immediately upon the granting of the Massachusetts Bay Colony charter, the Puritans arrived in New England under the leadership of their governor, John Winthrop. Landing first at Salem, the Puritans went on to Charlestown, where bad drinking water forced them to move on to Boston.

With the Puritans came trouble to New England. The very thing the Pilgrims had come to seek, religious liberty, was not tolerated in the Puritan towns. No one was allowed to have any voice in the government unless he was a member of the Puritan Church. Attendance at church was compulsory.

In 1636, a young minister, Roger Williams, took the Puritans to task for their intolerance. His recommendation that the church and the government should be separate, was considered dangerous to the colony. Williams was tried and banished from the colony. With the help of Narragansett Indians, he planted a colony on the Mohassuck River, which he called Providence. In this colony, in 1647, the first New England laws guaranteeing religious liberty were passed. Providence, chartered as the Rhode Island Colony in 1663, soon became a haven of refuge for colonists banished by the intolerant policy of the Massachusetts Bay Colony.

The first written constitution in America was adopted by the colonists of Connecticut in 1639, when they found that they were outside the jurisdiction of the Massachusetts Bay Colony. In 1662 a charter was granted, making Connecticut an independent colony. New settlements and new colonies were also being founded to the north. New Hampshire was settled by a band of colonists under Captain John Mason, and Maine was opened up to settlers by Sir Ferdinando Gorges.

In one way the intolerance of the Puritan colonists served a useful purpose. It led to the exploration of new lands and the establishment of new colonies by those who left the Puritans or were sent into exile. The towns grew and became known as the United Colonies of New England. They consisted of the Massachusetts Bay Colony, Connecticut, Plymouth, and New Haven. So jealous were these colonies of their rights that, in 1686, when the English governor, Andros, demanded that the colonists of Connecticut surrender their charter, the document, according to tradition, was removed from the files and safely hidden in the hollow of an oak. This tree became famous as the Charter Oak. The charter remained in its hiding place until Andros was recalled to England. When the thirteen colonies proclaimed their independence in 1776, the Connecticut charter became the state constitution of Connecticut.

The most tragic chapter in the history of New England is the persecution of so-called witches. Salem was the center of the witchcraft trials, and eighteen "witches" were condemned to death during the reign of terror. Persons afflicted with nervous disorders were accused of being witches and practicing witchcraft. Their trials were a cruel parody on justice. Confessions were obtained through whippings and tortures. Anyone could bring an accusation of witchcraft against a fellow citizen and verdicts of guilty were often given on the testimony of imaginative children and the false testimony of enemies. Fortunately this madness, which reached its height in 1692, did not last long. The people came to their senses and the persecution of witches came to an end.

In the meantime, other colonies were being formed along the Atlantic coast south of New England. In 1614, on the grounds of Henry Hudson's discoveries for Holland, the Dutch claimed the land of the Hudson Valley, from Staten Island to Fort Orange, now Albany, and called it New Netherland. In 1623, a Dutch settlement was made on Manhattan Island. In 1626, Peter Minuit, the Dutch governor of New Netherland, bought Manhattan Island from the Indians for the equivalent of $24 in red cloth, beads, and trinkets. At that time there were about thirty houses clustered near the tip of the island. England also claimed New Netherland, based on the explorations of John Cabot, and said that it had been included in the charter granted to the Plymouth Company in 1606 by King James. But nothing was done by England until 1664, when three British ships, laden with soldiers, sailed into New Amsterdam and summoned the Dutch to surrender.

The governor of New Amsterdam at the time was Peter Stuyvesant. He was called Old Silver Leg, because he wore an artificial leg to replace one he had lost while fighting in the West Indies. This wooden leg was banded and tipped with solid silver. Peter Stuyvesant defied the English commander and said that he would die rather than surrender. To show his anger he tore up a letter that offered the Dutch very liberal terms. The people of New Amsterdam were not so ready to fight. When some of them put the pieces of the English letter together and learned the easy terms of the British, they forced Old Silver Leg to surrender without a fight. The name of New Amsterdam was changed to New York, in honor of the Duke of York, brother of the English king.

In the same year that New Amsterdam fell to the English, the Duke of York granted the territory between the Hudson and the Delaware Rivers to his friends, Lord John Berkeley and Sir George Carteret. As Carteret had once been governor of the English island of Jersey, the colony was called New Jersey. The section that is today Delaware was settled by fifty Swedish colonists in 1638. It was called New Sweden. In 1655, Peter Stuyvesant gained control over the little colony. After the defeat of the Dutch in New York, New Sweden became English. In 1704 it became the separate colony of Delaware.

Maryland, so-called after Queen Mary, was settled by Cecilius Calvert, second Lord Baltimore, under a grant by King James I to his father in 1632. Calvert bought the land for his colony from the Indians, an unusual procedure in those days. Pennsylvania was granted to William Penn in payment of an unpaid debt owed by the King of England to Penn's father. William Penn, with a hundred colonists, mostly Quakers seeking religious freedom, came over in 1682. He landed at what is today Chester, Pennsylvania. In the Quaker spirit, Penn founded and laid out Philadelphia, the City of Brotherly Love.

The Pilgrims and the Puritans and those who followed in their wake, soon learned that there was only one direction they could turn for a livelihood. That was to the sea. New England today has a high place in agriculture and industry, but the early settlers had to live close to the coast where the land was not too fertile and the wilderness was thick. It took time to get a foothold. In Virginia and the Carolinas, tobacco proved the magic wand to wealth, but in New England, the colonists could not raise ready marketable crops. In order to get goods and tools and other things from Europe, the New Englanders turned to the sea for fish. There was some early trade in fur and lumber, but fish was the main item of trade, and Boston and Salem soon became thriving seaports.

The American merchant marine got its start in New England on a community basis. Individual colonists did not have enough capital to build ships, so shipbuilding was entered into by groups of people who formed ship syndicates. A ship had been built on the Kennebec, in Maine, in 1607, 13 years before the landing of the Pilgrims. It was a 30-ton boat called the *Virginia*. The first truly New England ship, however, was the Blessing of the Bay. Its keel was laid at Medford, Massachusetts, in 1631. It was well named, for the *Blessing of the Bay* opened up new channels of trade down the Atlantic coast as far as New York. It proved that the way to prosperity for the New England colonies was by building up a sea trade. The commercial success of this first ship was so great that shipyards sprang up almost overnight all along the New England coast.

Shipbuilding was a cooperative venture. The people of a locality would pool their ready cash to buy lumber, rope, iron, and other materials. Those who had no cash could earn a share in the project by putting in time on the building of the ship. On the same basis of sharing in the profits of the voyage, merchants would provide provisions for the ship's crew. The members of the crew, from the captain down, were paid very little in wages, but each man was allowed to bring along his personal stock of trade goods. This arrangement was the keystone to the success of the colonial merchant marine, and of early whaling as well. It gave every man a close and personal interest in the success of the voyage. Paul Revere, who is most famous for his midnight ride and the part he played in the War for Independence, made a very valuable contribution to the American merchant marine in its early days. Revere discovered that copper sheets along the bottoms of ships not only prevented fouling but also put a stop to the costly damage done by barnacles and other parasites of the ocean that bore through the unprotected bottoms of wooden ships.

The policy of England to curb the expanding trade and industry of the colonies soon began to create friction. That, and heavy taxes and the curtailment of personal liberties that the colonists had come to regard as sacred, tended to increase the rift between the colonies and the mother country. England passed laws to force the colonies to trade in a way that would be all to the advantage of English merchants. These laws, known as the Acts of Trade, were disobeyed by the colonial shipowners. They felt that it was their right to sail their ships to whatever ports they wanted, carrying whatever goods would yield the best profit. Various other laws acted in restraint of trade; the manufacture of steel and the cutting of lumber was prohibited. One of the most objectionable of the laws was one that permitted English soldiers to break into any home and search for smuggled goods on which taxes had not been paid.

The French and Indian Wars, fought between England and France in North America from the end of the seventeenth century almost to the eve of the War for Independence, had a definite influence on the future of the colonies. For the first time the colonists, fighting with British regulars against the French and Indians, met each other and were able to exchange ideas.

Also, as fighters they found themselves equal, if not superior, to the British regulars. Most important of all, the French and Indian Wars served as a training school for American officers and soldiers, the greatest of whom was George Washington. On the other hand, the French and Indian Wars cost England large sums of money. The English parliament thought that the colonies should pay the major part of the bill.

Grenville, then prime minister of England, suggested in 1764 that the colonies should be more heavily taxed. In that year came the Sugar Act, imposing a heavy duty on sugar, which was one of the colonies' principal items of trade with the West Indies. This act led to large-scale sugar smuggling which added fuel to the fire of discontent. Closely following the Sugar Act was the notorious Stamp Act. This law demanded that government tax stamps should be placed on all public documents, such as wills, deeds, mortgages, checks, pamphlets, and even newspapers. Although this tax was not particularly large, the colonists refused to buy the stamps. Taxation had become a matter of principle. There was a growing demand for colonial assemblies that alone should have the power to impose taxes. The clamor against taxation without representation gained momentum rapidly. Sons of Liberty societies were formed almost everywhere and a boycott on English goods was put in effect. The colonists demanded the rights of British subjects: legislative assemblies and trial by jury.

Patrick Henry and James Otis led the people in their resistance to the Stamp Act and other taxes they considered unjust. After less than a year, England repealed the Stamp Act, mainly owing to the efforts in behalf of the colonies by Benjamin Franklin, who lived in London at the time.

Of all the American patriots of the colonial and early independence period, Benjamin Franklin and his work have the greatest influence on our everyday lives today. He was an outstanding representative of a people who demanded the right to think and speak for themselves as free Americans. Although Franklin is most closely connected with Philadelphia, he was born in Boston. He was the fifteenth child of a poor candle molder and soap boiler. Young Benjamin was destined for the ministry, but lack of money forced him into the printing trade instead. At seventeen he ran away from home and made his way to Philadelphia. There, within a few years, he owned his own print shop, published a magazine, and wrote his famous *Poor Richard's Almanac*.

Throughout his life, Benjamin Franklin always served the people. His brilliant but simple writings helped the cause of the colonies, and he had a share in preparing the Declaration of Independence. His many inventions, from the Franklin stove to improved eyeglasses, made life better for the average citizen. Franklin refused to take out patents on these inventions. He gave them all to the world. His research into physics, especially the nature of electricity, gained him international fame

Franklin was typical of the patriots who gave their time, their money, and risked their lives to serve the cause of freedom and independence in North America.

The good done by the repeal of the Stamp Act was canceled by the Townshend Acts of 1767, putting a tax on tea, glass, paper, lead, and other common articles of commerce. Again the colonists protested the injustice of taxation without representation. They refused to pay the taxes. The protest was so loud that England repealed the Townshend Acts in 1770, all except the tax on tea. This duty was retained as evidence that England still held to her right to impose taxes when and how she pleased. The colonists were equally defiant. They refused to buy tea and used a substitute made from leaves and roots of plants. Large cargoes of English-owned tea rotted in warehouses for want of buyers. On December 16, 1773, a group of patriots disguised as Indians, boarded a British ship anchored in Boston harbor and dumped its cargo of tea into the water.

In reprisal for the Boston Tea Party, King George III induced parliament to pass harsh laws punishing the city. These laws, known as the Intolerable Acts, were aimed at Boston, but all the other colonies came to that city's help. As a result, the First Continental Congress was held in Philadelphia in September 5, 1774. A petition was addressed to the king, asking for the immediate repeal of the laws.

King George III replied to the colonists by instructing General Gage, the royal governor of Massachusetts, to arrest John Hancock and Samuel Adams, two prominent patriots, and send them to England for trial. On the night of April 18, 1775, General Gage marched with 800 men to Lexington where Hancock and Adams were reported to be in hiding. Somehow the news of the British advance leaked out. Two Sons of Liberty, William Dawes and Paul Revere, rode through the countryside shouting, "The Redcoats are coming!" and calling the minutemen, or colonial militiamen, to arms.

When the British troops reached Lexington they found fifty minutemen drawn up in a square on the common. The British commander commanded the rebels to disperse. When they stood their ground, he ordered his soldiers to fire. Eight minutemen were killed and ten wounded. Meanwhile Hancock and Adams had escaped from Lexington. The British marched on Concord where the commander had orders to seize some military supplies the patriots had hidden there. At North Bridge over the Concord River, the British troops again encountered the minutemen, this time in a larger force of some 400. The British opened fire and their fire was returned by the Americans. After a brief skirmish, the patriots swarmed over the bridge and forced the redcoats to retire. The war for American independence had begun. At Concord Bridge today stands a sculptured figure of a colonial Minuteman bearing the immortal words of Emerson:

> By the rude bridge that arched the flood,
> Their flag to April's breeze unfurled,
> Here once the embattled farmers stood
> And fired the shot heard round the world.

After the War for Independence was won, the thirteen colonies became the thirteen states of the young republic. When peace came, the merchant marine proved of vital importance in putting the United States on its feet. In 1787, some merchants of Boston decided to make a bid for the rich fur trade of the Pacific coast and sent two ships filled with trade goods around Cape Horn to the Pacific. Captain Gray, in the *Columbia*, sailed with a cargo of furs from the Pacific coast to China, where he traded the furs for tea and sailed back to Boston by way of the Cape of Good Hope. Captain Gray, as told in detail in a preceding chapter, was the first American to sail around the world, and the enormous profits of his voyage stimulated a shipping boom.

Then followed a great era for American shipping and commerce with China and other parts of the Far East. The new nation learned that its furs and other native products were wanted in the East. On the journey back to home port in Boston, Salem, or Philadelphia, the graceful, full-rigged Yankee ships rounded the stormy Horn or the Cape of Good Hope, laden with exotic cargoes of silks, spices, teakwood, and tea.

It was no longer necessary for the United States to depend on English shipping for the luxuries demanded by a rapidly growing nation. For the first time in more than a hundred years, since the decline of Spain as a maritime nation, another nation threatened England's supremacy on the seven seas. The War of 1812 saw the emergence of a maritime North America whose captains were as adept in battling English men-of-war as they were in braving the elements.

The history of New England, and to a great extent the history of the United States, has been written by the men who went down to the sea in ships. Of these, perhaps the most romantic and colorful are the Yankee whaling men. With sturdy arms and stout heart, the Yankee whaleman battled the elements and wrested from the depths of the sea a livelihood that grew into a great industry.

He had the character and courage to renounce, sometimes for years at a time, the foods and comforts of shore life. He had the stamina to endure hardships and labor against overwhelming odds until the purpose of the voyage was accomplished: a holdful of whale oil and whalebone. Whaling began with shore whaling off the Long Island and New England coasts. As the whales close to shore grew scarcer, whaling boats grew larger and went farther to sea, until at last Yankee whalemen sailed the seven seas from the Arctic Ocean to the waters of the South Pole.

The history of American whaling dates back to the earliest days of colonization. When Captain John Smith sailed to explore the coast of New England, in 1614, he carried a permit to fish for whales. The charter of the Massachusetts Bay Colony granted the same privilege to the colonists. In those early days, whales were so plentiful along the coast that they could be taken in small boats rowed from shore. The way to whaling as a big industry was opened by Christopher Hussey of Nantucket and five companions who were blown far offshore in their small boat in 1712.

It was shortly after New Year's. For several weeks not a single whale had been sighted off the south shore of Nantucket. Day after day, Hussey and his crew had rowed up and down the shore looking for whales. One bitter cold January day, the six men rowed farther from shore than usual in their desperate hope to get a whale. Then, like a shot out of a cannon, a heavy wind came howling out of the north and swept the little boat out to sea. Hussey tried to head into shore, but the wind was too strong. No matter how hard the men rowed they kept moving seaward. At last they gave up, headed the boat into the wind, and bailed for their lives. None of them ever thought he would see Nantucket again. Then the cry, "Whale Ho!" came from Christopher Hussey. Standing at the steering oar in the stern of the wave-tossed boat, he had seen a school of whales. He got out the harpoon and told his crew to get ready to "tie on to" a whale. Whaling in deep water in a heavy sea was something unheard of in those days, but Hussey would not be stopped. As the men pulled at the oars a whale came to the surface a boat's length away. Hussey hurled the harpoon through the air and made a strike. After a brief but hectic fight, the whale was dead. The men were jubilant because their victim was a sperm whale, whose forehead is filled with the pure and precious sperm oil.

The sperm whale was and still is a floating fortune, richer than any other whale in precious oil. The only sperm whale that had been found up to that time on Nantucket was a dead one that had drifted ashore. It had not even been suspected by the Nantucket men that living sperm whales were in New

England waters until the lucky accident of Christopher Hussey and his companions in 1712. The catching of that huge sperm whale actually saved their lives. They made the boat fast to the whale's lee side, where oil oozed out on the storm-tossed waters and made the sea smooth as glass.

From that time on, it did not take whalemen long to figure that there was more profit in building larger boats and going out to sea for sperm and other whales than in sticking to small-boat offshore whaling. That was the beginning of a mighty industry. For more than 150 years, whaling was one of the leading factors in American commerce. The courage and enterprise of Christopher Hussey and his companions in "saving" a sperm whale at sea, was the first step toward making Nantucket the capital of the whaling industry.

The earliest records of organized shore whaling come from Sag Harbor on eastern Long Island, but Nantucket took the lead at an early date. When whaling ships began to exceed 200 or 300 tons, the Nantucket harbor entrance was too shallow for ships of such big draft. The government refused to supply funds to deepen the harbor; about a hundred years ago it was the subject of heated controversy in Congress. The Nantucket whalemen lost, and the defeat of the project was the death knell of Nantucket as a whaling port. New Bedford gradually took the lead in the rapidly growing industry. From a tiny village of 700 in 1790, it grew into a city of more than 20,000 in the early 1800's. The city became a self-sustaining hub of the whaling industry. The ships that went down to the sea were built in its yards, outfitted at its wharves, and manned by New Bedford men. Practically everything in the nature of stores and gear that went into a whaleship was made in or near New Bedford: boats, sails, rigging, casks, biscuits, salt beef, and clothes. The manufacture of ready-made clothes arose from the need of whaling men to outfit themselves for a voyage of several years' duration.

The prosperity of New Bedford and many other New

England towns and cities was founded on sperm oil and whale-bone. During the heyday of whaling, from 1833 to 1863, as many as 329 ships were operating out of New Bedford at the same time. Twelve to fifteen ships a day cleared for deep water. The docks and wharves were the center of business activity. The whole water front was alive with people, cluttered with gear and stores, with ships clearing and making port.

At sea, the thrilling cry that roused the whalemen to action was, "Thar she blows!" Whaling was not just a matter of sighting and taking the whale. Often a dangerous struggle ensued in which the men pitted their brawn and cunning against the brute strength of the whale. The battle did not always go to the whalemen. The sperm whale is a fighter, courageous, quickwitted, and a formidable enemy. It usually directs its attack against the small boats. On occasion, how-ever, the sperm whale has been known to attack whaling ships with startling and disastrous results, when he has sub-stituted his forehead for his usual fighting weapon, his jaw. There are at least five instances where huge sperm whales rammed whaling ships head on and sank them.

Whaling was usually done from small boats. The harpooner would sink his lance into the whale then the whale usually dove for the bottom. As it "sounded," rope fastened to the harpoon in the whale ran red-hot over the side of the boat. Next, the whale would make a horizontal dash and drag the boat behind it at a furious pace. This was the famous Nan-tucket sleigh ride. It might last for hours until the whale, worn out, was dealt its death's blow with a lance. Next the whale was brought alongside the ship and the work of trying, or boiling off the oil began. A fire was built in the brick ovens on deck under the big try pots. While the fires were getting the vats good and hot, the whale blubber was cut into strips, or blankets. This blubber was thrown into the vats and the oil boiled or tried out of it. Next the oil was poured into coolers and then stored in casks in the hold.

With whalebone at $6 a pound and sperm oil bringing $1 a gallon, New England whalers at the height of the industry often made comfortable fortunes. In 1846, America had 736 whaling ships with a total tonnage of 230,000 tons. These ships disposed of some 10,000 whales, representing 160,000 barrels of sperm oil, about 328,000 barrels of whale oil, and more than 5 million pounds of whalebone. The average yearly value of these products was from 7 to 8 million dollars. Today, whaling in the style of the Yankee sailormen of New Bedford and Nantucket is only a memory. The introduction of coal oil and petroleum spelled the doom of whale oil for general use.

New Bedford was the world's whaling center until the discovery of oil in the earth. Today there is probably not a single old-time whaling man living in New England. Whales are still being hunted, but by different methods. Today whales are being taken by a highly organized system of huge factory ships, small whaling steamers, and speedy airplanes that fly over the ocean. The pilots of these planes keep sharp lookout for whales and radio their location to the factory ship at the whaling base. Small, fast steamers armed with harpoon guns go after the whale, kill it, and tow it back to the factory ship. There the whale is cut up, boiled, and turned into its main by-products, its blubber for oil and its meat for food sold in the Orient, while the bones are ground up for fertilizer.

Ambergris was the foundation of many a New England whaling fortune. Whenever a sperm whale was caught, the whalers always looked eagerly for ambergris. Now and then the search was rewarded. Back in 1859, the *Boston Ledger* told how a Nantucket whaling crew killed a whale that contained a lump of ambergris that weighed 750 pounds, worth close to half a million dollars.

Ambergris is an interesting by-product of the sperm whale. It is believed to be a secretion caused by diseases of the liver or intestine of the sperm whale. This creature lives almost entirely on squid, and squids have sharp and horny beaks.

The belief is that ambergris may result from irritations caused by these beaks in the whale's intestines. Chemically, ambergris resembles gallstones. Ambergris is very rare and that is why it is so valuable. It is used in making fine perfume because of its unusual ability to hold the perfume scent, and a little goes a long way.

Floating ambergris has been found at sea or on the beach. According to one report, a few years ago a sailor on the Gloucester schooner *Mary Ann*, picked up a lump of ambergris with a boat hook. It weighed 28 pounds and was valued at $12,000.

The early settlers in New England went down to the sea in ships for smaller fry than whales—smaller fry such as the rich harvest of codfish on the Grand Bank. During their first winter in Plymouth, fish was the mainstay of the Pilgrims. As time went on, fish became the principal article of New England commerce. Gloucester, just north of Boston, soon became the earliest and most important fishing port in the United States. The city was founded in 1623, only 3 years after the *Mayflower* landed. For more than 300 years the men of Gloucester have faced the terrors of the deep on the fishing grounds of the Grand Bank and the Georges Banks, known throughout the world as the graveyards of the Atlantic. In the past 100 years alone, almost 1,000 Gloucester ships and more than 5,000 Gloucester fishermen have been lost at sea. The winter is the time of greatest danger. It takes almost superhuman skill and courage to climb over the slippery ice-covered deck of a fishing schooner that is being tossed up and down on the choppy waves over the banks. Storms sweep out over the banks from nowhere. They usually bring sleet, snow, rain, and fog with them, depending on the seasons. Many fishing schooners have been run down by steamships in the dense fog. These are but few of the many risks the Gloucestermen take to bring in their catch of fish.

Most of the fishing, especially for codfish and halibut, was done in the old days from rowboats, called dories. A schooner would carry from six to twelve dories. Each dory would be from 15 to 20 feet long. For the actual fishing, two men would go in each dory, fishing with 300-foot lines. At 4-foot intervals along the main line would be many short lines, each with a hook on it and baited for action. With several of these lines neatly coiled up in tubs in the bottom of their dory, two fishermen would have 12,000 feet of line and about 3,200 hooks to look after at one time. When the cod were running strong, a dory man might make a haul of anywhere from $1\frac{1}{2}$ to 2 tons of fish a day. And at the end of a long, hard day's fishing, he would have to help clean the catch and pack it in ice. Today steam trawlers do most of the Grand Bank's fishing but still, here and there among them, there will be schooners whose dory men are hauling in the cod from bobbing "nutshells."

Dory men, then as now, often were lost for days in their small open boats. Some were picked up. Some just disappeared into the fog. Some sailed close to Davy Jones's locker and yet lived to tell the tale. One of those was Howard Blackburn, whose life is one of the epics of Gloucester dory men.

Of February 25, 1883, Blackburn and Tom Welch were working their lines in a dory when a gale sprang up from the southeast. They pulled in their lines and rowed for the ship. But the wind, dead against them, was so strong they could not make any headway. Then snow began to fall so thick that they could not see the ship. The two men did not know where they were headed, but they continued rowing to keep their blood circulating. All day, the storm lashed them with its icy whip and the snow fell like a curtain. As night came, the snow stopped and they could see the ship's light far in the distance. Throughout the whole night they strained at the oars in a desperate effort to reach their vessel, but the head wind was too strong, the waves too high. Toward dawn, a fog swept over the sea and once more the ship was hidden from view. Blackburn decided that their only chance was to try rowing their dory to Newfoundland, more than a hundred miles away.

To protect their hands against the freezing spray from the winter seas, all Gloucester men wear thick woolen mittens. If they do not, their hands will freeze. In the course of the night Blackburn had to take off his mittens to fix the sea anchor that kept their frail craft headed into the onrushing waves. At that very moment a wave swept into the boat. While baling the water out, Tom Welch accidentally threw Blackburn's mittens into the sea. Tom offered Blackburn his own wool mittens, but Howard refused to take them. It grew colder toward dawn and a thick coating of ice formed over the little boat. Heavy seas threatened to swamp them. Time and again the boat came close to foundering. It was bail and row. Bail and row. The two men had neither food nor water. Their brine-soaked clothes were frozen to their bodies.

On the second day, Blackburn's hands began to freeze, but he refused to release his grip on the oars. He insisted that by keeping his tortured hands around the oar handles they would freeze that way. Instead of sitting with rigid useless hands he could keep on rowing. During the third night Tom Welch froze to death. After that, for 5 days and 5 nights, his hands frozen to the oars, with a dead man as his cargo, Howard Blackburn rowed on, and finally won. More dead than alive, he reached Newfoundland. As a result of this journey Howard Blackburn lost all his fingers and toes and part of one foot. His days as a fisherman were over. But he did not grumble or growl—Gloucesterman's Luck.

The greatest thrill in the lives of Gloucestermen in the days of the sail was the homeward run from the fishing banks with cargo holds full of fish for market. It was always a race to land a cargo first. Often several Gloucestermen would leave the banks for the home run at about the same time. Then it was a game of seamanship, skill, and daring. It was driving all the way, with every foot of canvas the ship could carry, with every sail set no matter how hard the wind, how high the waves.

There was an object in this racing. The price of fish would often slump in an hour or two after the first ship came in with a heavy load and filled the immediate demand. Old-timers along the Gloucester water front still tell of the days they would all set sail on the banks and then head home in a living gale of wind on a raw January day. Today the Gloucester fishermen do not depend on sail alone. Most of the schooners are equipped with Diesel engines and many are steam trawlers. In a few days, these can catch more fish than the old-time vessels could take aboard in several weeks. But the work of the Gloucester fisherman has not been made much safer. In the last 10 years some sixty fishing boats out of Gloucester were lost on the banks.

What happened to them? The same fate that has always awaited the men whose daily bread comes from the salty deep: victims of the forces of storm and stress, leaks, collisions, reefs, and ice.

CHAPTER 22

Settlers of the Southern Seaboard

State	Settled	Entered Union	Capital	Population	Area, square miles
Alabama	1702	1819	Montgomery	2,830,285	51,998
District of Columbia				663,153	70
Florida	1559	1845	Tallahassee	1,877,791	58,666
Georgia*	1733	1788	Atlanta	3,119,953	59,265
Maryland*	1631	1788	Annapolis	1,811,546	12,327
North Carolina*	1650	1789	Raleigh	3,563,174	52,426
South Carolina*	1670	1788	Columbia	1,905,815	30,989
Virginia*	1607	1788	Richmond	2,664,847	42,627

* Original colonies.

NEAR the spot where the Saint Johns River empties into the waters of the Atlantic Ocean on the northern coast of Florida, Ponce de León, who had sailed with Christopher Columbus, landed on Palm Sunday in the year 1513 and claimed the country for Spain. Because of its luxurious vegetation and its multitude of flowers and the thousands of birds that sang in the sunlight, de León called the land, Florida. At that time, de León was governor of the Spanish island of Puerto Rico. He had sailed north to seek the fabled Fountain of Youth. When he landed in Florida, he believed that he had reached his goal.

That Ponce de León failed in his quest on this, his first visit, and that he failed to find the Fountain of Youth on his second journey in 1521, comprise the most familiar episode of North America's early history. Instead of perpetual youth, de León found eternal rest as the result of his second trip to Florida. He was fatally wounded by an Indian arrow.

On at least two occasions, Florida was used as a springboard by Spanish expeditions sent overseas to explore North America. As mentioned in previous chapters, these expeditions, under Pánfilo de Narváez in 1528, and Hernando de Soto in 1539, came to grief. From that time on, Spain lost interest in Florida and the lands northward along the Atlantic coast, until news came to Castile that French Huguenots were colonizing on the coast of Florida.

In 1562, Jean Ribault attempted to establish a French colony on Paris Island, near Beaufort, Georgia. This colony failed. Two years later, René de Laudonnière, with seven ships of French settlers, succeeded in establishing a colony on the Saint Johns River, Florida. He called it Fort Caroline. Furious over this trespassing upon Spanish domain, the King of Spain, in 1565, dispatched a fleet of nineteen ships and 1,500 men under the command of Pedro Menéndez de Avilés. Coming as a complete surprise upon the unsuspecting Frenchmen, de Avilés won an easy victory. He razed Fort Caroline and built, instead, a Spanish city which he called Saint Augustine. This oldest Spanish citadel in North America is also the oldest city in the United States.

From then on, Spain kept a more vigilant eye on the long Atlantic coast line, the lands of which she claimed by virtue of discovery, as far north as Virginia. As a matter of fact, the first settlement ever planted in Virginia was established by Spaniards in 1570. This colony did not take root, as the Indians killed the colonizers. Almost a decade went by before the next attempt of colonization was made in Virginia. It was in 1578 that England began its stirring and dramatic efforts to establish colonies on the southern seaboard of the Atlantic coast. Colonization of Virginia is a story full of stress, strife, and starvation. It is a story of struggle against hostile nature and hostile Indians, but it is also a tribute to man's persistence and courage in the face of adversity and repeated failures. It is a story with a happy and glorious ending, for out of tragic and unfortunate beginnings emerged a liberty-loving colony that gave birth to great patriots who bequeathed to Virginia its justly deserved name as the cradle of American liberty.

The first threads in the tapestry of Virginia start with the great age of expansion and exploration in England during the rule of Queen Elizabeth. Not to be outdone by the empire ambitions of other nations, Elizabeth decided that England should sink colonial roots in the New World, not only as a source of new wealth but to secure territories claimed on the grounds of discoveries made by early English explorers. In 1578, the Queen sent Sir Humphrey Gilbert, a brother-in-law of the brave and gallant Sir Walter Raleigh, to seek out a likely location for a colony. This first effort failed completely. In 1583, Gilbert sailed again, combining his colonizing endeavor with a search for the northwest passage. On the return voyage, the heroic Sir Humphrey lost his life in a storm.

In the following year, 1584, Sir Walter Raleigh continued his brother-in-law's work. He sent Philip Amidas and Arthur Barlowe to sea with instructions to sail south of Newfoundland and to locate a site suitable for an English settlement on the North American coast. The expedition reached what is today North Carolina. The captains were impressed both by the hospitable climate of Roanoke Island and the friendliness of the Indian chief they met there. After trading some beads and trinkets for furs, the two Englishmen sailed home. They submitted a favorable report to Raleigh and the queen, who approved a plan for colonization. The place was called Virginia, in honor of the Virgin Queen, as Elizabeth was known.

The first English colonizing expedition was sent to North America in 1585 under the leadership of Sir Richard Grenville and Ralph Lane. The colonists were unsuited for the rigors of pioneering and the whole venture was poorly managed. Disaster faced the little group. Fortunately, Sir Francis Drake arrived from a series of successful raids against Spanish colonies in Santo Domingo, Colombia, and Florida, in time to save the colonists. They were only too glad to return to England with Drake. Just as they departed, a relief ship arrived from the mother country, but the settlers had had enough of the New World and could not get back home quickly enough.

Walter Raleigh was not a man to be easily discouraged. He financed another colonizing venture the next year, with John White as governor. Among the 150 settlers who sailed to Roanoke Island were about a score of women and children. They included Governor White's daughter, Eleanor, and her husband, Ananias Dare. The building of a colony was begun with high hopes. In the fall, a daughter was born to the Dares. She was named Virginia and she was the first white child of English parents born in America.

When Governor White realized that it would take time for the colonists to grow enough crops to feed themselves, he returned to England for supplies. When he came back in 1591 he found Roanoke Island deserted. It had been agreed that if the settlers had to abandon the colony for any reason during his absence, they would leave a marker indicating where they had gone. Governor White found the word Croatan carved on a tree. It had also been agreed that if some serious mishap forced the colonists to abandon the settlement, a cross would be carved above the message. As there was no such cross, Governor White concluded that the settlers had left of their own free will. Many attempts were made to locate a place called Croatan, but no sign of the colonists was ever found.

The tragedy of the lost colony put an end to further efforts to colonize Virginia until 1605 when the idea of establishing a settlement in Virginia again created much interest in London. Under charter from the king, the Company of Merchants of London and Gentlemen Adventurers to Virginia was promoting the sale of shares to raise money for a new colonizing venture. While the promoters painted rosy prospects of gold and glory to be gained in Virginia, the public asked embarrassing questions about the fate of the lost colony and the reasons for the previous failures. Still, sufficient adventurers and money were found to send out a colonizing expedition of three ships in the early part of 1607.

It was a motley crew that sailed for Virginia aboard the *Susan Constant*, the *Discovery*, and the *Goodspeed*. There were adventuring nobles and hard-bitten soldiers of fortune aboard, but only a scattering of men who knew the priceless arts of carpentry or farming or blacksmithing. The captains were Christopher Newport, Bartholomew Gosnold, and John Ratcliffe. Among this oddly assorted group was one young adventurer who was to make history in Virginia. His name was Captain John Smith.

Captain John Smith is one of the most glamorous actors in the drama of North American colonization. Few men have lived lives so romantic, so full of dynamic action. Although very young, he was one of the ablest soldiers and leaders in the company. Without his tireless energy and courage, there can be no question but that the third attempt at founding an English colony in Virginia would have ended in failure. Captain Smith won his spurs and coat of arms and other military glory on battlefields in Europe, Asia, and Africa before he was twenty-one years old. When he joined the Virginia Company, he was only twenty-six, but his experience and wisdom made up for what he lacked in years.

Many of the colonists were jealous of Captain Smith's reputation. They accused him of planning to set himself up as supreme authority when they landed in Virginia. The arch-enemy of Smith was Captain Ratcliffe, a man of poor ability and a mean nature, as history depicts him. Even while the ships plowed their way across the Atlantic, Captain Ratcliffe plotted against John Smith. One day he demanded that Smith be arrested and tried for treason.

Edward Wingfield, one of the more influential members of

the Virginia Company, defended Captain Smith. He said that Smith had saved the expedition from disaster more than once. He recalled how Smith repeatedly had set the ships on their course when the navigators were not sure of the way; how he had supervised the mending of a dangerous leak; how he had succeeded in making peace among the men when trouble broke out on shipboard. Wingfield added that no one had the authority to place Smith under arrest as the officers of the colony would not be known until the ships reached Virginia. This was because, by the king's orders, the names of the men chosen to govern the colony had been placed in a box which was not to be opened until the party landed.

Ratcliffe was insistent, and matters went so far that the ships put in at an island where preparations were made to hang Captain Smith. Fortunately, the plot was not carried out; but Smith was placed under technical arrest. On the morning of April 26, 1607, after 4 days of heavy storms, the sight of land was greeted with shouts of joy. Later in the day, the ships sailed into Chesapeake Bay and a small party was sent ashore. These first visitors found spring in Virginia very pleasant. But as darkness fell, Indian war whoops rang out followed by showers of arrows. Several of the whites were wounded before the roar of their muskets sent the Indians flying into the woods. The joy of the morning was changed to gloom and misgivings by this hostile reception from the natives.

The settlers explored the coast of the bay in small boats for several days, looking for a suitable location for a settlement. At last it was decided to sail the ships up a river to a small peninsula about 50 miles inland that seemed to offer good protection both from storms and Indians. The river was called the James, and the town the colonists began to build in May was named Jamestown, in honor of King James.

One of the first acts of the colonists on landing was to open the sealed box containing the names of the men who were to serve as a governing council. Captain Smith's enemies, much to their surprise and discomfiture, found that he was one of the seven councilmen. Wingfield was elected president. Ratcliffe and his followers tried to prevail on the others to void Smith's appointment. In answer, Captain Smith demanded a jury trial on the charges that had been made against him. As a result of the trial, the first trial by jury in America, Captain Smith was cleared of all charges and assumed his rightful place in the governing council.

It is true that John Smith was headstrong and impulsive, but those very qualities were to save the colony from disaster. The settlers, for the most part, were as lazy and shiftless as the Spanish adventurers who settled in Santo Domingo in the days of Columbus. Many of them even refused to help in building houses. They were insulted at the very suggestion that they work with their hands. As for planting crops? They pointed to the abundance of berries, game, and fish, and sneered at Captain Smith's warnings that nature would be less kind when winter set in.

If it had not been for Captain Smith's resourcefulness and industry, the entire colony would have died of starvation and disease that first terrible winter from 1607 to 1608. When harvest time came, there was nothing to harvest. Then the colonists at last realized their foolishness. As the food situation grew desperate, Captain Smith made several journeys up the cames and other Virginia rivers and creeks to exchange Jopper, beads, and various trade goods with the Indians for corn and other food. When the Indians discovered that the white men's constant demands for food threatened their own limited food supply, they became hostile. From then on, Smith took his life in his hands on every foraging expedition into the wilderness. But the courageous captain threw caution to the winds. The welfare of the pathetic Virginia Colony was his main concern.

On one of his trips to the Indians, a band of warriors killed Smith's two English companions. Before he was taken captive,

Smith shot two Indians. The Englishman was brought before Powhatan, paramount chief of the Virginia Indians. A council found Smith guilty of killing the two warriors, and ordered him executed. This trial took place early in January, 1608.

Just as Smith knelt down to place his head on the execution stone, Pocahontas, daughter of Powhatan, flung herself over Captain Smith's head to protect him. The warriors stormed and raged. When Powhatan finally restored order and asked Pocahontas the meaning of her action, she said that it was her right as a woman of the tribe to save the life of a captured warrior by claiming him as a brother. After long and loud arguments, Powhatan declared that his daughter was within her rights, and Captain Smith's life was saved.

That was the beginning of a long friendship between Captain Smith and Pocahontas. It also helped to improve the relationship between Smith and the Indians. But, despite this help, things were going from bad to worse with the colonists. In the summer of 1608, disease ran rampant in the colony. The site on which they had built Jamestown was unhealthful, swampy, and infested with mosquitoes. The water was bad. Relief ships came but the food they brought was moldy and unfit to eat. There were constant flare-ups among the settlers due to jealousies and dissension. Hotheaded colonists, time and again, disrupted the friendly relationship Captain Smith had established with the Indians through his association with Powhatan and Pocahontas.

The situation in January, 1609, was much the same as it had been the year before. The colonists faced starvation. The Indians were short of food themselves, and their patience with the ever-insistent white men was about at an end. When Smith pleaded with Powhatan to sell some food to the starving colonists, the chief spurned his offer of copper in payment. He said that his people needed corn badly themselves. The crops had been poor that year, but he might sell 30 bushels of corn for thirty British swords and muskets.

Captain Smith was not only afraid to sell firearms and swords to the Indians, but Powhatan's attitude warned him that the days of friendly cooperation had come to an end. How right Smith was in this appraisal was demonstrated shortly afterward when Pocahontas warned Smith that her father was planning to waylay and kill him. Smith and his companions barely escaped Powhatan's trap by capturing, at pistol point, the very Indians who were sent to take them prisoners.

Despite the hostility of the Indians, Captain Smith managed to scrape together enough food here and there to carry the colony through the winter. With the coming of spring he took a firm attitude with the colonists in Jamestown. He set up a "no work, no eat" policy. By means of grudging labor, crops were planted at last; game and fish were killed and caught in large numbers and salted for storage against the next winter. The prospects of the colony looked brighter, but with the coming of the fall of 1609, John Smith's role in the drama of Jamestown came to an abrupt end.

Captain Smith was seriously injured in a gunpowder explosion and had to return to England after spending several months in bed, dangerously ill. During the months of his illness, nine ships with 400 new colonists came to Virginia. Big plans were made for the future of the colony. But the prevailing notion was that in some mysterious way the colonists would be able to eat without planting crops and get rich without soiling their hands. During the winter of 1609–1610, the settlers found out how right Captain Smith had been. He was a hard taskmaster, a merciless driver, but his true worth was not appreciated until he was gone. It was then that the horror and the hunger of the terrible "starving time" struck the Virginia Colony.

The storehouses were empty. The Indians flatly refused to part with food of any kind. Starvation and death strode down the muddy streets of Jamestown with heavy strides. Relief ships that had been expected did not arrive, and when they did, in May, 1610, there were only sixty colonists left—sixty crawling skeletons.

The relief ship, the *Sea Adventurer*, carrying Sir Thomas Gates, Sir George Somers, and Captain Christopher Newport, together with colonists and food, had been wrecked on the Bermuda reefs. There the survivors were forced to remain until they could build two small ships to carry them to Virginia, where they expected to find the colonists in a position to feed them. Instead, the colonists needed food. There was one consolation. The ships, small as they were, offered a means for the unhappy pioneers to return to England. What little food that could be scraped together was taken aboard the ships. The colony was abandoned. As the vessels, with their pathetic cargo of starving humanity, sailed out of the James River, they met three well-provisioned ships under Lord de la Warre. But for that last-minute meeting, Virginia would have ended in another failure. Instead, the colonists sailed back and gave Jamestown a new lease on life.

The colonists probably would have gone back to their idle ways if Sir Thomas Dale had not come out as governor in 1611. He ran the colony with an iron hand. Work was the order of the day. Discipline was restored and the Indians were brought to terms.

The relationship between the Indians and the English were vastly improved in 1614 when John Rolfe, a successful young planter, married Pocahontas. This union was very pleasing to Powhatan, who now threw the full weight of his influence into the scales in favor of the colonists. Through his associations with the Indians, John Rolfe learned how to grow tobacco. Up to that time, all tobacco used in England had been grown by Indians, but owing to the great market for the product in England and other parts of Europe, the crops produced by the red men were not sufficient to meet the demand.

Soon other planters followed Rolfe's example. In a very short time, tobacco became the leading crop of Virginia, and a most profitable one. The only obstacle in the way of the tobacco boom was that there was no labor supply available to work the plantations. This had become a pressing problem by 1619, when it was solved through the arrival at Jamestown of a Dutch ship with a small cargo of eighteen Negro slaves. The captain said that he had been forced to seek port in Virginia because his supply of food was almost exhausted. He also explained that he had been planning to throw his cargo of slaves overboard. He was saved that unpleasant duty when the Virginia planters were only too glad to buy the Negroes for their tobacco plantations. This introduction of tobacco growing and slave labor was the beginning of the plantation system in the South. The year that brought the first Negro slave shipment to the colonies also witnessed the inauguration of the House of Burgesses in Jamestown, the first representative assembly in America.

Eventually, slavery became a problem that threatened the harmony of the Union. As the situation grew increasingly critical toward the middle of the nineteenth century, one of the world's greatest humanitarians, Abraham Lincoln, stepped to the fore. In 1862, he issued his famous Emancipation Proclamation which set 3 million slaves free. But it was not until the Civil War had been fought, from 1861 to 1865, that slavery in North America actually came to an end.

But, returning to 1619. As the years went by, the Virginia colony continued to grow. So did the tobacco crops. In fact, by 1622, tobacco was the only crop grown in Virginia. It was said that tobacco grew everywhere, being planted even in the streets of Jamestown. Tobacco brought prosperity, and prosperity made the colonists careless. They let the Indians come into Jamestown in large numbers without taking any defense precautions.

The price of this carelessness was paid in 1622 when Opechancanough, who had succeeded his brother Powhatan as ruling chief, made a savage attack on the unsuspecting colonists. Three hundred and seventy men, women, and children were killed by the Indians, who themselves suffered heavy losses in the revenge raids staged by the Virginians. Although the Indians never again attacked Jamestown, raids on outlying settlements continued for more than half a century.

When Sir William Berkeley, governor of Virginia, neglected to take action against the Indians as late as 1676, Nathaniel Bacon, a young planter, roused his neighbors and took matters into his own hands. The governor moved to stop the colonists, but the revolt spread. Soon Bacon and his army of planters marched on Jamestown and burned the city. They forced Berkeley to take refuge on an English ship lying at anchor in the harbor. The uprising ended quickly through Bacon's sudden death. Berkeley returned to Jamestown where he meted out heavy punishment to the rebels. Berkeley's conduct was strongly resented by the colonists and he was finally recalled by the king.

Although the Bacon revolt failed, it did serve notice on the English crown that the colonies would stand for just so much abuse.

Despite its many setbacks, the Virginia Colony grew and prospered and was more than ready when called upon to face its next crisis a hundred years later. As one of the thirteen colonies that fought the American War of Independence, Virginia perhaps contributed more than any other single colony, at least in outstanding patriots who made possible the birth of a free United States of America.

Of the War for Independence it has been said that George Washington was its sword; Patrick Henry its tongue; and Thomas Jefferson its pen. All three were sons of Virginia.

Patrick Henry, four years younger than George Washington, was born in 1736. A brilliant orator, Patrick Henry became a great success as a member of the Virginia House of Burgesses, making his thrilling and dramatic debut as a denouncer of the Stamp Act. When he condemned the actions of the English parliament and the king, some more conservative members shouted cries of "Treason!" To which Patrick Henry shouted back, "If this be treason, make the most of it!" He was an early advocate of independence from England, saying on many occasions that he was not a Virginian, but an American.

At the famous meeting of Virginia patriots in Old Saint John's Church in Richmond, on March 23, 1775, Patrick Henry warned his fellow countrymen that they must arm against oppression, and fight if necessary. His closing words on that occasion rank among the greatest utterances in American history: "I know not what course others may take," he cried out, "but as for me: Give me liberty or give me death!" Patrick Henry lives in history as one of the leaders in the fight for freedom from England.

Thomas Jefferson, the father of American democracy, was a man of many interests: a statesman, diplomat, administrator, scientific farmer, and philosopher. Jefferson was the leading figure in the Continental Congress, and in 1776, he won immortal fame as the draftsman of the Declaration of Independence. All through the war and to his death in 1826, Thomas Jefferson served his nation. In his latter years, he retired to his beautiful plantation where, as the Sage of Monticello, he gained a reputation as a wise philosopher, kindly friend, and magnificent host, loved by everyone who came in contact with him.

George Washington, the Father of his country, was born at Bridges Creek, Virginia, on February 22, 1732. After giving up a boyhood dream of becoming a sailor, young Washington took up the study of surveying. The wealth of Virginians was in land. Few of them knew the extent of their property to the west, and there was plenty of work for a competent young surveyor.

When he was only sixteen years old, George Washington was employed as a surveyor by Lord Fairfax, the greatest landowner in Virginia, whose vast holdings extended into the blue Ridge Mountains. Washington did his work so well that Lord Fairfax secured for him a position as public surveyor. This job young Washington held for 3 years.

At the age of twenty-one Washington was made a major in the Virginia militia. When trouble broke out between the English and French over possession of the Ohio Territory, Governor Robert Dinwiddie of Virginia sent Major Washington to warn the French commander that the Ohio Valley was British territory, and to ask him to surrender the French forts to the English. Washington covered the 500 miles of wilderness and back in record time. He had been received by the French with courtesy, but the reply he brought back to Dinwiddie proved unsatisfactory. The French claimed the Ohio Valley. This claim became one of the causes of the French and Indian War in which Washington fought and gained the military training that was to prove so valuable later against the British.

In 1754, when war broke out between the English and French, Washington was sent to seize a French position at the head of the Ohio River. There he met a force of French and Indians in the battle of Great Meadows. When the French erected Fort Duquesne, young Washington countered by building Fort Necessity near by, where he was forced to surrender to the French on July 4, 1754.

Later General Braddock, commander in chief of English forces in North America, was ordered to proceed against Fort Duquesne. His army consisted of 1,400 British regulars and 700 provincial troops. As this force moved toward Fort Duquesne, Washington, whom Braddock had chosen as one of his aides, warned the British general of a French and Indian surprise attack in the woods. While an excellent soldier, Braddock was not familiar with frontier warfare and was too confident of his own fighting methods. He disregarded Washington's advice.

When only 8 miles from its objective, Braddock's army was

surprised by 900 French soldiers and Indian warriors and suffered a terrible defeat. General Braddock was among those who died. Only Washington's able leadership in organizing an orderly retreat prevented a complete massacre.

When the colonies finally took arms against the British to win their independence, George Washington was ready to serve the cause of freedom. On July 2, 1775, he assumed command of the Continental Army at Cambridge, Massachusetts. For 6 years he led the American forces of the War of Independence, until he accepted the surrender of General Cornwallis at Yorktown, on October 19, 1781. This was the end of the revolution and the real beginning of the United States.

For many years after the founding of Jamestown, Maryland was part of the Virginia Colony. It was first settled in 1631 by William Claybourne, who established a trading post near the spot where the Potomac River enters Chesapeake Bay.

When Lord Baltimore established the Maryland Colony in 1634, Claybourne and his associates objected vigorously. It is believed that they were guilty of sending the Susquehanna Indians on the warpath against the Maryland colonizers. These Indians established themselves in an old fort on the Piscatawa River, and it took the combined forces of an army of colonists from Maryland and Virginia to dislodge them. Aside from this conflict, the early settlers in Maryland had little trouble with the Indians and prospered in peace.

In 1775, 2 years after the Boston Tea Party, Maryland staged a tea party of its own. This happened in Annapolis when a group of irate Marylanders fought their way aboard the *Peggy Stewart*, a British ship, and threw its cargo of tea overboard. October 9 is still celebrated in Maryland as Peggy Stewart Day.

The story of North Carolina begins in the days when Sir Walter Raleigh attempted to establish a colony on Roanoke Island. Actually, no settlements were established in North Carolina until 1670, when eight British noblemen, friends of

King Charles I, were granted a vast tract of land known as Carolina. They formed a company known as the Lords Proprietors. The colony got off to a bad start owing to troubles with Indians and the Spaniards in Florida. Disputes followed when French Protestants settled in the southern part of Carolina which, in 1711, separated from North Carolina.

In the early part of the eighteenth century, the buccaneer Edward Teach, better known as Blackbeard, ruled the pirate roost. He made his winter headquarters in an inlet on the North Carolina coast. Blackbeard was never molested by law-abiding citizens because he was protected by the governor of the colony, despite the fact that the pirate, time and again, raided peaceful settlements along the Virginia, Carolina, and Georgia coast. Finally, the governor of Virginia had enough of Blackbeard's raids. In 1718, he went over the head of the governor of Carolina and sent Lieutenant Maynard with two small ships to Blackbeard's headquarters. After a desperate fight, the pirates were defeated. Blackbeard was killed.

A great historic event was enacted in North Carolina in 1775 when the famous Mecklenburg Declaration of Independence was written on May 20 in the city of Charlotte. It was subscribed to by members of the Mecklenburg militia when they heard about the battle of Lexington.

The first English South Carolina settlement came into being in 1670 when the Lords Proprietors planted a colony on the Ashley River and called it Charles Town.

Angered by this invasion of lands that they considered part of their Florida domain, the Spaniards incited the Indians to make war on the British. In 1686, the Spaniards made a quick march upon South Carolina from Saint Augustine and wiped Stewart Town, a Scottish colony, out of existence. Six years later, the English tried to destroy Saint Augustine, but were defeated. A brave and successful show of courage was made by Colonel William Rhett in Charles Town in 1706. A large French fleet sailed proudly into Charles Town harbor to capture the city. The French soon sailed out again, but not so proudly, with an ill-assorted fleet of armed merchant vessels shooting at their heels. Incidentally, 12 years later, Colonel Rhett dealt a decisive blow to the pirates who had been interfering with Carolina ships and colonies.

The Carolina laws under the Lords Proprietors caused everlasting conflict and strife. These laws virtually established a feudal system and encouraged the development of large plantations similar to the estates acquired by the conquistadors in South and Central America. In 1719, the colonists prevailed upon England to cancel the charter and create a royal government instead.

What with Indians and pirates and Spaniards besetting them, the Carolinians sought to establish a buffer state between their colony and the Spaniards in Florida. A plan for the founding of such a colony, in 1717, by Robert Montgomery, failed to bear fruit. But in 1732, the land rights to what is today Georgia were granted to General James Oglethorpe. The Georgia colony was to serve a threefold purpose: as a military buffer state; to experiment with the growing of silk and wine grapes; and to give people owing money in England a chance to work out their debts instead of rotting in English jails. Savannah was settled in 1733. Although Georgia progressed slowly at first, prosperity came in a small degree with the planting of rice and cotton after silks and grapes had failed. Georgia was the last of the thirteen American colonies established by the British.

General Oglethorpe's colony was threatened by a force of 3,000 Spanish soldiers in July, 1742. With only a thousand men under arms, he was in no position to meet the Spaniards in battle. When one of his colonists deserted to the Spaniards, Oglethorpe resorted to a clever ruse. He started a report among the Spanish that the deserter was really an Oglethorpe spy. Then he sent the deserter "secret orders" to try to keep the Spaniards in Georgia three days longer as a British fleet with

2,000 men was on its way to sack Saint Augustine in Florida. Of course, crafty old Oglethorpe made sure that the message fell into the hands of the Spanish commander, who immediately hurried back to Saint Augustine, where he learned that he had been hoodwinked.

How Florida was discovered by Ponce de León in 1513 and how Saint Augustine was founded by Pedro Menéndez de Avilés in 1565 has been told. Although Spanish Florida was a thorn in the side of the southern colonies, the Spaniards did not have a peaceful existence by any means. After being burned to ashes by Francis Drake in 1586, Saint Augustine rose again only to be destroyed four-score years later by the English buccaneer, John Davis. In 1763, Spain surrendered Florida to England in return for Havana. After 20 years of British rule, Florida was recaptured by Spain in 1783. After the creation of the United States, frequent friction with the Spanish in Florida made the absorption of Florida necessary. It was ceded to the United States in 1819 in settlement of damage claims of 5 million dollars by the United States against Spain for injury to American shipping during the Napoleonic Wars. Florida became American territory in 1822, with Andrew Jackson as its first governor.

Today people often arbitrarily lump the southern seaboard states together as those south of Mason and Dixon's line without knowing either the exact location or the origin of that famous boundary line. The story goes back to colonial days, when a dispute arose between William Penn and Lord Baltimore about the boundary lines of their two colonies. It was not until many years later, in 1763, that two English surveyors, Charles Mason and Jeremiah Dixon, came over from England and settled these boundary differences. A part of their work was the surveying of a line between Maryland and Pennsylvania, known as Mason and Dixon's line, which was to become important during the Civil War period as the dividing line between slave states in the South and "free" states in the North.

CHAPTER 23

Red Men and Blue Grass

State	Settled	Entered Union	Capital	Population	Area, square miles
Kentucky	1765	1792	Frankfort	2,839,927	40,598
Ohio	1788	1803	Columbus	6,889,623	41,040
Tennessee	1757	1796	Nashville	2,910,992	42,022
West Virginia	1727	1863	Charleston	1,900,217	24,170

WHEN the early explorers for England and France probed along the North American shore line and penetrated inland claiming vast territories for their respective nations, they were sowing the seeds of future strife. This taking possession of huge slices of continent with the flourish of a sword and the waving of a flag was all very well in the beginning. As the years passed, however, and the explorers were followed by traders and then by settlers, there came confusion and conflict.

La Salle's dream of a French empire in the Mississippi Valley became a nightmare to English colonists as they slowly began to filter westward across the mountains from the Atlantic coast. When, in 1670, La Salle discovered La Belle Rivière and took possession of the fertile Ohio Valley for France, he was unknowingly staking claim to one of the bloodiest battle-grounds in North America. If England and France had been at peace in Europe, all would probably have been well in North America, but the two nations were almost continuously at war. This European hatred and rivalry bred conflict in the New World colonies.

When the English and French came to blows, each side made use of its Indian allies as the most destructive wilderness weapon. The French made friends with the Indians of Canada and the Great Lakes. The English sought and won the cooperation of the powerful Iroquois nation.

The French and Indian Wars began in 1689, as a direct result of European hostilities. They lasted until 1748, with brief periods of armed truce. The cause of the conflict was the migration of English colonists into the Ohio Valley, which was discovered and claimed for France by La Salle. As early as 1669, John Lederer of Virginia had crossed the Blue Ridge Mountains, the first white man to conquer this eastern barrier between the coast and the interior. During that year and the next, he led three expeditions across the mountains. By 1675, English explorers had penetrated into the Roanoke River Valley and into the Cherokee country of Kentucky and Tennessee.

Slowly, but surely, the English pioneers pressed westward along the Ohio River and the Great Lakes. To meet this threat, the French built more and stronger forts. There were many bitter local battles, but by the middle of the eighteenth century, both the French and English realized that the days of frontier skirmishes were over and that only a real fight to the finish could establish permanent ownership of these new, rich lands.

In 1753, Governor Dinwiddie of Virginia sent word to the French to evacuate the Ohio Valley. His demands were based on the claim that the territory belonged to the Virginia Colony, as part of the colony's royal ocean-to-ocean grant. The bearer of the governor's message was twenty-one-year-old Major George Washington of the Virginia Militia. His guide was Christopher Gist, from whom Washington learned many tricks of the wilderness that were to come in handy later. The outcome of Washington's mission was unsuccessful and led to the outbreak of war, as has been told in the chapter on

Virginia. When Washington was returning to Virginia, some French Indian allies ambushed him. If an Indian's rifle had not missed fire, the Father of his country would probably have been buried under the snowdrifts of the Alleghenies in 1753.

Hostilities broke out between the French and English in 1754. The English suffered reverses at first and the proud red-coated regulars of General Braddock, with drums beating and banners flying, were all but wiped out when they came up against the Indian method of fighting from behind trees and rocks. Then the fortunes of war changed, and after a series of victories, Quebec fell in 1759, ending the rule of New France in North America. But the troubles of the English were not over. Powerful Indian enemies of the British were not bound by the peace between the European factions, and they still fought the English. The redskins would, no doubt, have been easily subdued if it had not been for Pontiac, chief of the Ottawas and a brilliant leader and organizer of his people.

Early in November, 1760, Major Robert Rogers, commander of the celebrated Rogers' Rangers, received orders from Sir Jeffrey Amherst to take possession of Fort Detroit with a detachment of his Rangers. After delivering dispatches at Fort Pitt, Major Rogers proceeded along the shores of Lake Erie to the mouth of the Chogage River. One cold and rainy day, Rogers ordered his men to encamp until the weather cleared. Hardly were they settled in the forest when a party of Indian warriors arrived. They said that they were emissaries of Chief Pontiac and commanded Rogers not to advance any further into their lands before he had an interview with their chief. Major Rogers, who knew he was in territory that had never seen the British flag, replied that he would be glad to meet the chief.

Before the day was over, Pontiac appeared and demanded to know by whose permission Rogers was crossing his domain. The Englishman then informed Pontiac that the French had been defeated and that he was on his way to Fort Detroit to take command. He further told Pontiac that it was the desire of the British to restore peace among whites and Indians alike. The news of the French surrender came as an unpleasant surprise to Pontiac. He told Rogers that the French were his allies and that it was not easy to make new friends. Then he left, warning Rogers and his men to remain where they were until the next morning, when he would let Rogers know whether or not he could go on to Fort Detroit.

Major Rogers and his Rangers spent an uneasy night, expecting an attack at any moment. But the dark hours passed peacefully. In the morning, Pontiac returned and said that he had thought the matter over. If the English desired to live in peace with the Indians, it was good. His people did not want war, but they did want their rights respected. Rogers repeated his assurances of the previous day. After smoking a pipe of peace, the two chiefs, white and red, parted on a final pledge of friendship. The Rangers marched to Fort Detroit, where, a few years later, the dramatic climax of Pontiac's great conspiracy against the English was to be enacted.

Major Rogers, a native of New Hampshire, was at this time at the height of his fame. The spectacular exploits and hairbreadth escapes of his band of Rangers had made them the heroes of the New England colonies. These Rogers' Rangers, half hunters and half woodsmen, were trained in wilderness fighting that made them dangerous enemies. They went armed like the Indians, with knife, hatchet, and rifle.

The early arena of operations of the Rangers was chiefly around Lake George, between Forts Ticonderoga and William Henry. There they rendered distinguished service in the fight between the English and French colonies, intercepting French dispatches between fort commanders and beating back enemy scouting parties. In the summertime, they traveled mostly over the rivers and lakes in canoes and whaleboats. When winter came, they put on snowshoes or skated across the frozen lakes and camped at night among snowdrifts.

The leader of this fearless band of backwoods fighters, Major Rogers, was tall, with rough features and a strong body. He was a skilled woodsman, and the match for any Indian. But he was also cautious, so much so that he was at times accused of cowardice. During the unsettled period after the defeat of the French at Quebec, Major Rogers and his Rangers proved themselves invaluable in handling Indian difficulties.

Pontiac's pledge of friendship to Major Rogers may or may not have been sincere, but events during the next 2 years stirred up among the Indians an even deeper hatred against the English than had existed before. The shortsighted British policy of underestimating the redskins as enemies was paving the way for trouble. If the Indians had expected the English to accord them the friendly treatment they had received from the French, they were disappointed.

The French had been good friends of the Indians in deeds as well as words. They had not only looked after their redskin brothers when they were sick and hungry, but had supplied them with guns, and powder, and bullets. Over a period of years, hundreds upon hundreds of Indians had learned to depend on French rifles to hunt their food and had lost their cunning and skill with bow and arrow. When the English abruptly stopped issuing powder and bullets to the Indians, many tribes were faced with actual starvation. Having learned to rely so heavily on their French allies in times of want, they suffered great hardships. All these factors, singly and together, combined to stir up the trouble that was brewing among the Indian confederacy dominated by Pontiac.

Without the driving force of Pontiac, the Napoleon of the redskins, the Indians might have accepted their fate in silence. But Pontiac had plans to regain the lands and the freedom of his people. He hated the English, a hate he kept well hidden from the whites, but a hate eloquently expressed when he urged the tribal chiefs to unite in driving the British out of the

Great Lakes region and to reestablish the power of France in Canada.

Pontiac was a military leader of unusual ability. His plan of campaign went beyond the usual brief and scattered raids of Indian warfare. It was the Indian warrior's lack of staying powers that cost him defeat so often in fighting the white man. Pontiac's plan was a real campaign, discussed in council and carefully thought out. In the spring of 1763, after long preparations, Pontiac was ready. At a given signal there was to be a systematic attack on the British line of forts along the lakes. The red Napoleon reserved for himself the stronghold of the enemy, Fort Detroit. At that time the Fort was commanded by Major Henry Gladwyn, one of the ablest officers of the British colonial army.

Pontiac was clever. He maintained his outward show of friendship toward the English, and established several Indian villages almost within arrow shot of Fort Detroit. So well did the Indian chief conceal his real feelings that none of the English suspected the impending Pontiac revolt.

In 1763, Fort Detroit consisted of a hundred or so small log buildings surrounded by a stockade about 25 feet high. Built within the walls of the stockade were blockhouses for the use of soldiers in case of attack. Outside the stockade was a large village in which lived approximately 2,000 French-Canadian settlers who had remained when the British took over. Beyond lay the Indian encampments of Pontiac and his Ottawa Indians.

Late in April, Major Gladwyn began to notice unusual activity among Pontiac's Indians. Then, on May 5, Madame St. Aubin, wife of a French trader, went to the Ottawa village to buy venison and maple sugar. While there, she noticed some of the warriors busily sawing and filing off the barrels of their rifles until the guns were only about a yard long. On returning she told her neighbors about this strange activity. A blacksmith recalled that several Indians had come to his shop offering to purchase saws and files. He had refused to sell them when the Indians would not explain why they wanted the tools. Meanwhile St. Aubin went to Major Gladwyn with the news and warned him to be on his guard. Although his suspicions were aroused, the Major took no action.

It is probably true that Major Gladwyn received additional information from a spy the following night, but the more romantic story is that a young Ojibwa girl revealed the Pontiac conspiracy to the British commander. According to this story, the Indian girl came to the fort on the afternoon of May 6, bringing a pair of elk-skin moccasins the major had ordered from her. After the moccasins had been delivered, the guards noticed her lingering inside the stockade until it was almost time for the gates to be closed for the night. Major Gladwyn was informed and had the girl brought in for questioning.

The Indian girl was reluctant to speak at first, but, under coaxing, she revealed Pontiac's plot. On the following day, she told the Major, Pontiac and sixty of his chiefs would come to the fort and ask for a council. Each of the chiefs would be hiding a sawed-off rifle under his blanket. After delivering a speech, Pontiac would offer a wampum belt as an indication of peace. That was to be the signal for attack. Every Englishman would be killed, but the French, whom Pontiac still regarded as his friends, were to be spared.

The guards at Fort Detroit were doubled that night, and Major Gladwyn mounted the wooden ramparts from time to time to peer into the darkness. The night passed without incident. Early in the morning, Pontiac and his sixty blanketed chiefs approached the fort and Major Gladwyn allowed them to enter. Although he knew of their plot, he did not want to let the Indians know that he had any fear of them. The whole garrison, however, had been ordered under arms.

Pontiac and his chiefs marched across the open square of the fort in single file, looking right and left, and with signs of surprise on their faces as they noticed how many of the English soldiers were up and about, those not on guard being drilled. Then the Indians entered Major Gladwyn's headquarters. The commander and his officers wore their swords and pistols in their belts. All this the crafty Pontiac noticed. "Why," he demanded of Gladwyn, "do I see so many of my father's young men standing outside with their guns?" Gladwyn replied that his soldiers always were ready for battle.

Both eyed each other like foxes. Pontiac was no longer quite sure of his ground, but he delivered his speech, professing friendship for the English and telling, at length, how he and his chiefs had come to smoke the pipe of peace. When he had finished, he held the wampum belt toward Gladwyn. There was a motion of blankets among the Indians. But at the same time, Major Gladwyn made a prearranged sign with his hand. There was a rattling of arms from the passage as a squad of soldiers got ready for action. From the yard came the sound of trumpets calling the troops to assembly. Pontiac's face fell. The blankets of the chiefs once more were tightly wrapped around them, hiding the sawed-off rifles.

When the tension was lessened, Major Gladwyn, giving no indication that he knew he had forestalled an attack by his strategic show of force, returned Pontiac's sentiments of friendship and the group of chiefs left the fort. In view of what followed, Major Gladwyn has been criticized for not holding Pontiac and the chiefs as hostages, but the commander could not have known how serious and widespread the conspiracy was.

A few days later Pontiac and a large number of braves were refused admittance to the fort. The Indians retired in a hostile mood, and the soldiers from the blockhouses saw a group of them run to the house of an old English woman who lived outside the stockade with her family. Almost immediately the air was filled with pitiful screams, and there was no doubt that the first white scalps had been taken. From then on it was open war between Pontiac and the British garrison. Major Gladwyn, realizing that his small force was outnumbered more than twenty to one by armed Indians, decided to defend the stockade instead of attacking. The siege of Fort Detroit was on. For more than five terrible months the defenders beat off one furious attack after another.

During this period, Gladwyn expected ships to arrive from Fort Niagara with supplies and reinforcements. When at last the expected boats were sighted coming down the lake, the British set up a shout of welcome. Answering shouts came from the ships, but they were the war whoops of Indians who had captured the vessels and scalped or captured the English soldiers and sailors. In July another ship appeared. Again the Detroit garrison feared a trick as no one was visible above the decks. But as the boat sailed up the river under fire from Indians along the banks, the decks came to life with soldiers who answered the redskin fire. This time the besieged soldiers shouted themselves hoarse. Aboard the ship were two detachments of regular soldiers and Major Rogers with twenty of his Rangers. The plan was for the British to embark on the boats and give up the defense of Fort Detroit, but the ever-increasing force of Indians under Pontiac and other chiefs made it impossible for the English to attempt an escape.

Then came the end of September. For more than five months, the Indians had made almost daily attacks. It was an extraordinary feat for a race of warriors who had never been known to maintain any sort of united action over a period of more than a few days at a time. But some of the braves began to grow tired of the siege. One day several chiefs came to the fort under a flag of truce. They told Major Gladwyn that they wanted peace. Gladwyn took their words with a grain of salt, suspecting rather that they had heard news of the large army that was coming to the relief of Fort Detroit from Fort Niagara.

A truce was agreed upon by all but Pontiac, who continued to lead his warriors in fierce attacks on the garrison. At last

Pontiac, too, abandoned the siege of Detroit, but only when the French settlers sent word to him that under no circumstances could he expect any aid from his former allies, the French. When Pontiac heard from the mouths of the French themselves that they were the allies of the English in the fight, he was thunderstruck; he retired, troubled and confused.

Although Pontiac withdrew from Fort Detroit toward the close of 1763, the chief of the Ottawas did not sign a treaty of peace with the English until 1765. Even then he did so with hatred in his heart. To his dying day, Pontiac held the belief that his White Father in France would send ships and men to drive the English out of the Great Lakes region. That futile dream ended in 1769, when Pontiac was treacherously murdered in his sleep by a Kaskaskia Indian at Cahokia, Illinois.

The Pontiac Conspiracy was more than just a local Indian uprising. It had spread terror throughout the colonies bordering on Indian lands, although the colonies along the frontiers more or less accepted Indian fighting as a part of their daily lives. The thirteen colonies were beginning to have troubles and problems more serious than marauding redskins. The rumblings of liberty were beginning to be heard from Georgia to Maine. While James Otis was denouncing the Writs of Assistance in Boston and Patrick Henry, in Virginia, was raising his voice in the cause of freedom, a frontier drama of equal importance to the future United States was being played in North Carolina.

The leading actor in this drama of the backwoods was Daniel Boone, one of the most important and colorful figures in America's pageant of pioneers.

In 1769 Daniel Boone was living on a frontier farm in the Yadkin River Valley in North Carolina. One spring day a traveling peddler stopped with his pack horse at the Boone cabin. Daniel Boone recognized the peddler as John Finley, who had served with him under Major George Washington during General Braddock's tragic march against the French and Indians some fifteen years before. Boone told his friend about his life of farming and hunting, mostly hunting. He complained bitterly that it was getting overcrowded in North Carolina, with a house and family every mile or two. "I feel the need of elbowroom," he told Finley.

Finley, the peddler, had the answer on the tip of his glib tongue. He had just come from the mountains over west, from the country the Indians called Ken-ta-kee (Kentucky) or Meadow Land—the Land of Blue Grass. "If it's huntin' you're looking' for," said Finley, "you'll find a powerful lot over them thar mountains. There's deer at every lick, birds in every bush, an' herds of buffalo run so thick the ground trembles when they're on the move." But Finley also warned Boone that it was bad Indian country, Indian fighting and hunting ground.

Savage Indians and unknown wilderness held no terror for Daniel Boone. Finley's enthusiastic description of the untouched, uninhabited lands to the west over the mountains fascinated Boone, who was a born pioneer and adventurer. The lure of elbowroom was too strong for him. There were two ways to get to this Meadow Land of Blue Grass: the fairly easy way along the Ohio River and the difficult way through the Appalachian Mountain wilderness by way of the Cumberland Gap. Boone took the hard road and blazed the trail for the famous Wilderness Road through Cumberland Gap that was to become one of the most important early highways of the westward migrations. The wilderness road lay through swamps and streams and thick forests, uphill and downdale. There were no trails of any kind. The woods were filled with hostile Indians who regarded white men as rank intruders in their Ken-ta-kee.

Only a man like Daniel Boone could have penetrated that wilderness and lived to bring back the story. He was superior even to the Indians in woodcraft, and he could outsmart the redskins at their own game of stalking and covering up his trail. He was able to find his way through hundreds of miles of wilderness and maintain himself for months on end with the aid of only a tomahawk and hunting knife. He was a dead shot with his long rifle, and he had an everlasting passion to set his feet on new pastures.

Daniel Boone was tall and thin, but strong as a steel cable. He was usually clad in deerskin shirt and trousers, with elk-skin moccasins on his feet. He is generally pictured as wearing a coonskin cap; as a matter of fact he habitually wore a decrepit old cloth hat. When he reached the bad Indian country, Boone's preparations for the night camp usually began in the afternoon when he set up a decoy camp to fool prowling Indians. Then he would make his way through the wilderness with the cunning of a stalked animal, covering up his tracks, walking in streams and on rocks, jumping from tree stump to tree stump, swinging from wild grapevines like a monkey, using every means his quick mind could think of to break his trail.

After hunting in the Kentucky country and exploring the wilderness for more than a year, Daniel Boone returned to North Carolina to tell his neighbors wonderful tales about the new region to the west. In 1773 he started out for the wilderness with a small group of hardy settlers. This first attempt to found a settlement in Kentucky failed because of repeated and murderous Indian attacks. Not discouraged, Daniel Boone continued to work toward the realization of his dream to carve a new settlement out of the wilderness.

At the same time another man was dreaming dreams very much like those of Boone, but along different lines. This man was Judge Richard Henderson, whose dream was of promoting a fantastic real estate boom in Kentucky and the fertile Ohio Valley. Judge Henderson's scheme was to buy some 20 million acres of land from the Indians, break this land up into subdivisions, and sell the subdivisions to the immigrants who were coming to America by the thousands. Henderson formed the Transylvania Company, and he hired Daniel Boone as explorer and advance man.

When Governor Martin of North Carolina attacked the scheme as illegal and fantastic, Judge Henderson pointed to the land grants that had been given to the Hudson's Bay Company, the London Company, and many others. He insisted that his land company was a boon to the colonies as, in a short time, there would not be room enough for everybody along the coast. Henderson's most prophetic argument was that in case the colonies decided to break away from England and fight for their independence, his settlers in the Ohio Valley would provide a ready-made army to protect the western frontier of the colonies.

On March 17, 1775, at Sycamore Shoals on the Watauga River, Henderson and his partners bought 20 million acres of Ohio Valley land from the Indians for $50,000 worth of trade goods. More than a thousand Cherokee Indians were there as an escort for the Great Chief Oconostota. When the chief accepted the goods in payment, he warned the white men that he and his chiefs would keep their part of the bargain, but that he could not speak for the young braves who might still look upon Ken-ta-kee as sacred Indian hunting ground. He warned them in solemn words: "The land beyond the mountains is a dark ground, a bloody ground, and there is a black cloud hanging over it."

A short time later Daniel Boone and a group of settlers reached the site selected for Fort Boonesboro, which was to open up the back door to Kentucky. They reached it on April 19, 1775, the day after the first shots of the American fight for independence had been fired at Concord.

As the Cherokee chief had predicted, Kentucky did become a dark and bloody ground for the settlers who followed Daniel Boone across the mountains. Henderson's colossal land scheme was forgotten in the more important events of the Revolutionary War, but the settlers continued to pour into Kentucky and they remained despite obstacles, hardships, and frequent Indian attacks.

At one time Daniel Boone was captured by a band of Shawnees. His fame as a hunter, fighter, and woodsman had spread among the Indians, who greatly admired him. Boone took advantage of this feeling and pretended to enjoy his captivity. So well did he play his part and so thoroughly did he flatter the redskins, that they adopted him into the tribe. The ceremony was something of an ordeal for Daniel Boone, including as it did, having all his hair but a scalp lock pulled out by the roots. After a time, the Indians allowed their white brother to go hunting a short distance from their encampment. They gave him ammunition but kept close track of the amount of powder and lead he used. The idea was that the Indians had no fear that Boone would try to escape if he had no ammunition and powder with which to kill game. But Daniel Boone fooled the Indians by using only half charges of powder and half a ball for each shot. Over a period of time he was able to accumulate a good supply of ammunition. As time passed, the Indians let Boone go farther and farther afield to hunt, until one day he did not return. A party of warriors immediately set out to bring him back, but when they found his trail, Daniel Boone was well on his way to Boonesboro.

The Wilderness Road of Daniel Boone saw a great westward flow of settlers into the land of Red Men and Blue Grass, where Boonesboro stood as a brave citadel of pioneers in their battle against the wilderness and hostile Indians. Often, when streams were flooded, the wagons overturned. Every kind of hardship lined the way, yet the pioneers did not turn back. When they reached their destination, the settlers had to begin at the very bottom; they had to start by clearing the ground for a cabin site. They had to be jacks-of-all-trades working with the simplest of tools. To build their cabins and make their furniture, they had to cut their own lumber from logs. Every bit of food they ate, they had to raise themselves or take from the forest.

The women had plenty of work besides just keeping house.

They had to make their own candles if they wanted light at night; to spin and weave if they wanted clothes; to make soap; to cure hams; and to churn butter. The wives of the pioneers had to be experts in molding bullets, in loading the heavy Kentucky rifles, and even in shooting them when their menfolk fell from the redskins' arrows or musket balls.

The Kentucky rifle became famous chiefly because of its great accuracy, and because of the marksmanship of men like Daniel Boone. Once, with a Kentucky rifle, Daniel Boone shot an Indian sniper dead in his treetop perch at a distance of 200 yards. The Kentucky rifle was long, 5 feet as against the modern rifle's 3½ feet, and it weighed about 11 pounds. Another remarkable feature of the Kentucky rifle was the speed with which it could be loaded and shot. The frontiersmen could pour in powder, wad down paper and ball, prime the lock, aim, and fire, all in less than 30 seconds.

The pioneers who came over the Wilderness Road fought not only to defend their homes from Indians, but during the latter years of the War of Independence they formed the rear guard of the newborn republic. In fact, warfare of this type brought into action one of the heroes of the American Revolution, George Rogers Clark.

Before he assumed his role in the war, Clark was a well-known frontiersman, hunter, and Indian fighter. A native Virginian, he studied surveying, coming to Kentucky in 1776 on the heels of Daniel Boone. He was convinced that the Indian raids against the American settlements were being engineered by the British. In 1778, he set a plan before Patrick Henry, governor of Virginia, for putting an end to the Indian raids. The governor endorsed his proposition to ask for volunteers for an expedition to attack the English strongholds in the Ohio Valley, principally the former French forts of Kaskaskia and Vincennes. Patrick Henry made the young patriot a lieutenant colonel and wished him luck.

Indeed, George Rogers Clark needed luck for what he

proposed to do. To attack the Ohio forts of the English was a bold undertaking with a small and poorly armed force operating far from the nearest source of supplies. Clark enlisted 200 recruits. Without telling them the objective of their journey, he took them down the Ohio River in flatboats to Corn Island (Louisville, Kentucky). There he ordered the men to make a clearing for a settlement. Ignorant of the real purpose of the expedition, Clark's followers thought it was simply a colonizing venture. Then Clark began putting his makeshift soldiers through stiff drills. Little by little, he revealed his plans. When he broke the news of his planned attack on Fort Kaskaskia, many of the men deserted. That was all right with Colonel Clark, who wanted only fighters of unquestioned courage in his little army.

It was midsummer when Clark felt that his men were ready. They embarked in flatboats and continued down the Ohio River until they reached the overland trail to Kaskaskia. There the boats were well hidden in the thick brush. Carefully, Clark led his men on foot through the wilderness, marching only by night as they neared the fort. Colonel Clark's plan was to have a surprise attack make up for his lack of numbers. On the night of July 4, 1778, he advanced on Kaskaskia. The British, having no idea that an American force was near, were holding a dance, with practically all the officers in attendance. The French settlers and neighboring Indians looked on as the red-coated officers and their ladies danced to lilting music. Suddenly, the buckskin-clad figure of Colonel Clark stepped into the room where the dance was in progress. The music stopped abruptly. Clark told the dancers to carry on as before, except that their festivities would go on under the protection of the flag of Virginia instead of the British flag. Thus Clark took Fort Kaskaskia to the tune of a dance without firing a shot.

Governor Rocheblave was arrested in his bedroom, awakened from a deep sleep, and was greatly embarrassed as he faced his

American captors in a nightshirt. In the morning, the French pastor of the church, Father Gabault, assured Colonel Clark of his friendship and sympathy. He proved a great help in calming the French residents who had been led by the British to believe that the Americans were murderous bandits who would kill them on the spot. When the French saw how considerate Clark and his men were of their rights, they welcomed them with open arms, especially when they were told that the French government had offered help to the colonies in their fight for independence. Father Gabault went to Vincennes near Fort Sackville on the Wabash and induced the people of that British-held town to surrender to the Americans. When the news of these startling events reached Governor Hamilton in Detroit, he immediately marched on Vincennes with 500 men, recaptured it, and established headquarters in near-by Fort Sackville.

The winter of 1778–1779 was one of watchful waiting for the two opposing commanders: Clark on the Mississippi and Hamilton on the Wabash. Hamilton was known to the Americans as "the hair buyer," owing to his habit of buying the scalps of the colonists from the Indians to encourage the red men to raid American settlements. In Vincennes, Hamilton felt secure until spring, for he did not dream that Clark would try to march through the wilderness in the winter. He underestimated the determination of Colonel Clark.

In February, 1779, during the worst part of the winter, Clark, with 170 men, set out to give battle to Hamilton and the British at Fort Sackville. It was a heroic march. For 15 days the Americans struggled through swamps, flooded streams, and heavy snow, eating sparsely of what buffalo meat and rabbit they managed to kill. At the Wabash, Clark constructed rafts and managed to ferry his valiant band across the swollen river. On the other side, they continued their march, through miles of ice-cold water reaching up to their waists. Clark was always in the front, urging his men on by jokes or tongue lashings, depending on the circumstances. Again, as at Kaskaskia, surprise was the factor that brought Clark victory. Hamilton, most hated of the British generals in North America, surrendered after a brief and ineffectual defense.

Other British strongholds in the Ohio Valley fell to Clark in quick succession. They remained in his hands until the close of the Revolutionary War. Then the entire region was ceded to the United States by England. For his accomplishments, George Rogers Clark has been called the George Washington of the West. If Clark had not captured and held the Ohio Valley against the British and if Daniel Boone had not opened up the Wilderness Road to settlers, chances are that the territory that was then known as the Northwest would today be part of Canada, and a British possession, thus losing to the United States five states: Ohio, Indiana, Illinois, Michigan, and Wisconsin.

When the tidal wave of immigration from the Old World to the New really swept over the Allegheny Mountains at the end of the War of Independence, the Ohio River, starting at Pittsburgh, became a water highway for men and materials westward bound. In its day, the Ohio has probably carried more traffic and freight than any other river in America. As the years went by, the river carried many different kinds of craft on its swift current, from Indian canoes to rowboats, from rafts to flatboats, from sturdy keelboats to fragile vessels made from skins, from boats propelled by horsepower to streamlined steamers.

The most famed of all these vessels was the Ohio keelboat. It was about 50 feet long and from 10 to 12 feet wide. Its hold was boarded over, and it could carry several wagonloads of freight. Along its sides were catwalks for the rivermen to walk as they pushed the clumsy craft along with long poles. Keelboats were the first vessels, except canoes, that were able to make their way upstream on the Ohio.

The flatboat, or broadhorn, of the pioneer years was just what its name indicates. It was flat, and might be anything from a floating barn door with a packing case as a shelter to an elaborate raft with a house and barn on its deck.

During the early days of Ohio travel, attack from red men was a common occurrence. Often Indians would force white or renegade captives to run along the river bank shouting frantically for help. The idea was to lure the flatboat men to shore. If they landed to rescue the apparently hysterical white person, likely as not, a band of whooping redskins would jump out of the bushes, scalping knives ready for the kill. This ruse was so common that there are many instances on record where rivermen refused to stop to rescue white captives who had really escaped and were being pursued by redskins.

After the Indian menace on the Ohio, came the outlaws and pirates. These early forerunners of modern gangs made the lives of the flatboat and keelboat men both exciting and dangerous. One of the most notorious of the river pirates was Bully Wilson, who ran a place in a cave near Hurricane Bars, on the Mississippi. To draw thirsty rivermen into his deadly parlor, he put up a sign reading: "Wilson's Liquor Vault." But this cave inn soon became known as Cave-in-Rock, the hiding place of the most desperate river ruffians who worked for Bully Wilson. His agents were stationed upstream, where they offered to help pilot boats through the treacherous bars. Once aboard, the fake pilots ran the boats on the beach of Cave-in-Rock where a gang of cutthroats ran out to kill and plunder. The stolen cargo was then floated down to New Orleans and sold.

There were so many riverside taverns of the Bully Wilson type that travelers were at a loss to know where it was safe to put up. The standard advice was to pass by any tavern where the landlord was missing a nose or an ear. When keelboat passenger packets came into service, they advertised safety from pirate and Indian attack as an inducement to promote trade. One such announcement stated that the passengers were protected under cover made proof against arrows and musket balls and provided with portholes for returning fire in case of attack.

The rivermen themselves were picturesque, if rough, individuals. Their favorite sport was rough-and-tumble fighting with no holds barred. The riverman described himself proudly as "half horse, half alligator." Brute strength was part of his job, and if the alligator referred to the toughness of his hide, it was an apt description. The most notorious rowdy on the Ohio was Mike Fink, who through the years grew into a legend. It was the boast of this Paul Bunyan of the River that he "could outrun, outhop, outjump, throw down, drag out, and lick any man in the country." And he made good his boast all too often.

The steamboat came to the Ohio not long after Fulton's *Clermont* made its sensational run up the Hudson from New York to Albany in 1807. The Ohio Steamboat Navigation Company was formed in December, 1810, and the first steamboat, the *New Orleans*, navigated down the Ohio in March, 1811. It covered 8 miles in an hour. As on other rivers, steamboat travel progressed by leaps and bounds on the Ohio. The period from 1830 to 1840 saw the Gingerbread Era, when gilded, floating palaces sailed the river. It was also the period of racing, resulting in many disasters. The most tragic was that of the *Moselle*, which exploded at Cincinnati on April 25, 1838, with 250 men, women, and children aboard. The four boilers of the *Moselle* were being forced to beat a previous record. Without warning, all four blew up at once. More than eighty persons were known to have been killed, and of the fifty-five missing, many were never found. This and other disasters eventually led to strict regulations against racing and to careful steamboat inspection.

The Ohio Valley today is rich in apple orchards, principally because of one man, John Chapman, better known as Johnny

Appleseed. This strange character came to the Ohio Valley in about 1806. For some forty years, he distributed and planted appleseeds all over Ohio, and in parts of Indiana and Illinois. He always went barefooted, and dressed in gunny sacks, wearing a metal cooking pot for a hat. In the wildest Indian country he never carried a gun, for the Indians were his friends, and he distributed medicinal herbs among them. If any settler gave him money for his appleseeds, Johnny gave the money to the poor. That he was a queer person cannot be denied, but even today many an Ohio Valley farmer looks out on his fine apple orchard and gives thanks to Johnny Appleseed.

The Ohio River and its broad valley have played a vital role in the history of the United States. Shrewd Andrew Carnegie once called the Ohio basin the workshop of the world. It is a descriptive name, for the "Beautiful River" discovered by La Salle in 1670 today serves many great industrial and commercial centers such as Pittsburgh, Cincinnati, Wheeling, and Louisville. It is also an outlet for the great oil and coal regions in Pennsylvania and West Virginia. On its waters ply barges and steamboats laden with oil, grain, lumber, iron, and steel products from the land of Red Men and Blue Grass. Today, the dark and bloody ground of the Indians is bright and rich with all the things that help to make life in the New World worth living.

CHAPTER 24

The Lone Star Rises

State	Settled	Entered Union	Capital	Population	Area, square miles
Arizona	1580	1912	Phoenix	497,798	113,956
Colorado	1858	1876	Denver	1,118,820	103,948
New Mexico	1537	1912	Santa Fe	528,687	122,634
Texas	1686	1845	Austin	6,418,321	265,896

THE early history of discovery and exploration in Texas is one of great ambitions and great disappointments. It is almost as if the land of the Tejas Indians had resented the intrusion of the white conquerors. For 200 years, disaster and defeat were the lot of those who followed their guiding stars into the vastness of Texas.

While exploring the north shore of the Gulf of Mexico in 1519, Alonso Pineda sailed along the coast of Texas, but as he did not land, the country's first actual contact with Spaniards was delayed 10 years, until 1529, when Alvar Núñez Cabeza de Vaca started his remarkable and heroic trek across Texas to the Pacific.

The story of Cabeza de Vaca began at the port of San Lúcar, Spain, from where he sailed as an officer in the expedition of Pánfilo de Narváez to explore and conquer Florida. In those days, Florida included all North American lands known to the Spaniards. The expedition was an ambitious one, consisting of 600 men aboard five ships. Among those who sailed were three other men who were to play important parts in the dramatic chapter of exploration that was about to be

489

written: Alonso Castillo and André Dorantes, both captains in the Spanish Army, and Dorantes' Negro slave, Estevan.

The ships made a swift and uneventful passage across the Atlantic, but in Santo Domingo troubles began. To begin with, more than a hundred sailors and soldiers deserted. Sixty men and twenty horses were drowned when two of the ships were wrecked in a hurricane off Cuba. At last, on Friday, April 14, 1528, the expedition landed in Tampa Bay on the west coast of Florida. General Narváez sent the ships up along the coast and led his men inland. With the ships gone, retreat was cut off.

Hopes were high as they started their overland journey into the unknown country. But as they put miles behind them, the going became more and more difficult. Lakes, swamps, and great dense forests that had at first excited wonder and admiration soon loomed as never-ending obstacles. The Indians were hostile and made continual war on the invaders. Months after months of misery and suffering took their toll of men and horses. The land was far from hospitable in the way of food. After a year of aimless and fruitless wandering, General Narváez called a halt at a bay near the sea. He named it the Bay of Horses. This was in the region of Appalachee Bay in the western part of Florida.

He summoned his captains, Cabeza de Vaca, Castillo, and Dorantes, for consultation. Their minds were no longer fired with the spirit of conquest. Their only thought was how to escape with their lives. There was only one way: by sea. The only way to get ships was to build them. A quick inventory was taken; there was not a single boatbuilder in the outfit, and only one carpenter. They had no nails, no hammers, no anvils, no saws, no tools of any sort except their swords. Still they built, not one ship, but five.

It was a herculean task. They melted their stirrups and spurs and armor, even the scabbards of their swords and the metal parts of the crossbows. Out of the metal, they forged saws, axes, hammers, and nails. Slowly the boats began to take shape. The horses were killed, and from the tails and manes, ropes were woven for the rigging. Sails were made from shirts, coats, and breeches. To carry water on the voyage, they made water bags from the skins of the legs of the slaughtered horses. When, at last, the miserable little fleet was ready to put to sea, these determined Spaniards were as proud of it as any grand admiral of his flotilla.

On September 23, 1529, the five vessels were headed into a turbulent sea. The Spaniards made a fair start, although none of them had the slightest knowledge of navigation. Then storms overtook them. One by one the crude ships were wrecked. Many of the men were drowned. The survivors of the mass shipwreck were washed ashore on an island which they appropriately called the Island of Ill Fortune. The Indians were friendly enough, but the only food they had to offer were a few roots and berries. During the winter, many of the Spaniards died of exposure and starvation. As spring came, the few who were still alive escaped to the mainland. De Vaca was one of them. They were pitiful sights, naked skeletons, hardly able to walk.

Cabeza de Vaca was more dead than alive. When he was unable to keep up with his companions, they deserted him. But de Vaca did not die. He recovered his strength and, far from beaten by the many trials he had suffered, he started out into the wilderness on foot, hoping against hope that he would eventually reach a Spanish settlement.

Unable to live off the harsh land, he joined up with bands of Indians he encountered, traveling from tribe to tribe the best he could, sometimes as a slave of the Indians, always an outcast. The Indians had little respect for this strange man who did not know how to hunt or to fish. He asked to be allowed to earn his keep by carrying wood and water, but that was squaw's work, and could not be performed by a man, not even a slave, according to Indian tradition.

Then, when his fortunes were at their lowest, opportunity came to Cabeza de Vaca. An Indian had injured himself and was dying. The Spaniard, taking his life in his hands, treated the wound. The Indian, whose life had been despaired of, lived. It was a miracle. From that day on, de Vaca was esteemed as a medicine man and his services were in constant demand. The Spaniard hated the deception, but it was that or starvation. As time passed on, de Vaca also won the good will of the Indians as a trader. On the coast he picked up shells and traded them to inland Indians for flakes of flint, for arrow reeds, or for red clay to make war paints. As the months passed, de Vaca kept his eyes and ears open. Bit by bit, listening to the Indians whose language he had mastered, he came to the decision that the only way to freedom lay toward the west, toward the Pacific.

Although his condition had improved, there was never enough to eat, for the Indians themselves were able to get only a meager living from the land, eating roots and tasteless prickly pears. He had no clothes to protect him from the wind and sun, rain and cold. Still the days made their slow and painful journey into weeks; the weeks into months; the months into years. Keeping track of time was impossible for Cabeza de Vaca, so that he never knew exactly when he met up with Captain Castillo, Captain Dorantes, and the Negro slave, Estevan.

These three had also been enslaved by the Indians. They told de Vaca of their hardships and of their many futile attempts to escape. After they had compared notes, the three Spaniards agreed that nothing short of a miracle would save them from a lifetime of slavery among the Indians. The thought of a miracle inspired de Vaca. The cures he had been able to effect among the natives had been regarded as miracles. He told his companions about how, because the Indians had faith in his powers, he had been able to heal many of them only by a touch of the hand. It was out-and-out deception, of course, but it suggested a solution to their problem.

Without delay, Cabeza de Vaca put his proposition up to the Indian chiefs. He impressed upon them that he and his companions were great and powerful medicine men, but that they would lose their powers to heal if they were not allowed to travel westward, toward the setting sun. The Indians, whose lives were cloaked in superstitious tradition, saw nothing strange in this. If the great medicine men must travel toward the west, then it could be arranged, for they knew that to anger anyone with such powers was to invite the wrath of the gods.

Not since the day when the Pied Piper led the rodents out of Hamlin into the waters of the Weser River had there been a procession such as that which followed de Vaca and his companions across Texas, into New Mexico and Arizona. Month after month, different groups of Indians escorted the Spaniards from village to village. But it was a serious affair, this traveling medicine show, both to the Indians and the Spaniards. Many cures were made by applying the simplest treatment to infected wounds; others were the result of applied psychology. In return for their services as healers, the Indians gave the Spaniards food and clothing and escorted them to the next village, always toward the west, toward the setting sun. They were treated as gods, and were called the Children of the Sun, much to the amusement of the Negro slave, Estevan, who also practiced the arts of a medicine man.

This stopping at every village made progress slow, and the seasons passed from winter to summer and back to winter again many times. Then, one day, Cabeza de Vaca saw an Indian wearing some odd pieces of metal on a string around his neck. He examined them closer. To his joy, he saw that they were the buckle of a Spanish sword belt and the nail from a horseshoe. The Spaniards could hardly contain their wild elation as they questioned the Indian. He told them of men like themselves, with heavy beards, who had come to that country many moons before, from the west.

Hope gave wings to the feet of the Spaniards. Hardly stopping to rest or eat, they pressed on, convinced that at last they were near a Spanish settlement. A few days later, they came upon four Spanish horsemen, soldiers in the service of Melchor Díaz, governor of the Spanish province on the Gulf of California. It is hard to say which party was the more amazed to see the other. One of the first questions de Vaca asked was the date. He was told that it was March, 1536. Eight years had passed since they had first landed in Florida, and seven since the shipwreck.

As a guest of Governor Díaz, Cabeza de Vaca was grieved to learn that it was the custom of the Spaniards in that part of Mexico to enslave the Indians to work the mines. De Vaca, who had a brotherly feeling for the Indians, remonstrated with the governor, pointing out that slave raiding among the Indians was not only inhuman but illegal according to the laws of Spain. Díaz only laughed and told him to take his complaints to Mexico City where they were glad enough to get the gold mined by Indian slaves.

After a brief stay, de Vaca and his companions went to Mexico City. There Cabeza laid charges against the slave-raiding governor before the Viceroy of Mexico. He was told to mind his own business. De Vaca sailed back to Spain, his heart set on returning as governor of Florida. He was doomed to disappointment. Hernando de Soto had already been given that position by the King of Spain.

While in Mexico City, sensing the hostility of his fellow countrymen, Cabeza de Vaca had been very closemouthed about his experiences during the trek across Texas and the Southwest. The Negro slave, Estevan, however, made up for his leader's reticence. The Negro not only boasted of his powers as a medicine man, but letting his imagination run away with him, he spoke of gold he had seen. Flattered by the attention he received at the very mention of gold, Estevan hinted that he knew where to find the Seven Cities of Cibola, with roofs of gold and walls studded with emeralds.

Antonio de Mendoza, Viceroy of Mexico, believed Estevan's story. He bought the slave from his master, Captain Dorantes, considering him to be literally worth his weight in gold. The viceroy then placed the Negro in the services of Father Marcos de Nizza, a Franciscan monk and veteran explorer, and sent the two on a scouting expedition to locate the Seven Cities of Cibola.

Estevan again played the part of medicine man. But where with de Vaca he had been a miserable bundle of naked skin and rattling bone, he was now decked out in fantastic finery. On his arms and legs he wore shiny rattles and jingling bells. His head was adorned with an elaborate feathered headdress, his body covered with robes of velvet, silk, and satin. Estevan's escort was made up of a large group of Indians.

When the expedition reached the Valley of Sonora, Father Marcos sent Estevan ahead to look for the Seven Cities. If he found them, he was to send a messenger back with a wooden cross. The size of the cross the Negro sent back would indicate the wealth and magnificence of the golden cities he had found; the larger the cross, the bigger and richer the city.

This arrangement was made in March, 1539, and continued for about two months, with Estevan being several days' march ahead of Father Marcos. Ever so often, the Negro sent back wooden crosses, small ones, to indicate that they were approaching the Seven Cities of Cibola. One day in May, Father Marcos received a huge cross, 6 feet high. Greatly excited, the priest spurred his horse on, only to learn the next day that the Negro had met his death in the Indian village of Havikuh. The Indian guides urged Father Marcos to turn back, but he rode ahead. It was late in the afternoon. Just as the sun was setting, the priest looked down upon the pubelo village of Havikuh from the top of a hill. To his deluded eyes, it looked like a great golden city, surely the capital of the fabulous Seven Cities of Cibola.

As Father Marcos hurried back to Mexico, the wonder of the

sight he had seen grew in his mind. When he described it to Viceroy Mendoza, he told of having seen a city greater than Mexico City, and all of gold. On the strength of this news, the viceroy lost no time in organizing a large and expensive expedition under the command of Francisco Vásquez de Coronado, who had come to Mexico with the ambition of serving his king by expanding the realm of New Spain.

When Coronado set out with a large army, including 250 horsemen, there was no doubt in his mind that the march would end at the Seven Cities, and that their enormous wealth would be his for the taking. Day after day, the army marched northward. The hot sun beat down on the soldiers' armor, making them like ovens. But what did heat and dust and weariness matter when the greatest treasure on earth was near at hand?

One day, Coronado, also from a hill, saw one of the Seven Cities of Cibola bathed in the glow of the setting sun. After a night of joyous anticipation, came the cold, gray light of day. The golden city had vanished, and in its place was a group of yellow-white Indian adobe buildings. The Golden City was all a trick, a trick played by the brilliant reflection of the desert sunlight and sunset. It was a hard blow for the Spaniards to take. There must have been tears shed and oaths uttered that morning when they were so rudely awakened from the dream of golden castles to find only an Indian village. This rude end of the Cibola mirage occurred just south of the present site of Gallup, New Mexico.

Hope dies hard. Coronado refused to believe even the evidence of his eyes. He pushed on in search of riches and headed eastward into Texas. There an Indian told him of the rich land of Quivira to the north. Ever ready to follow any gold-tinted will-o'-the-wisp, Coronado marched on to Quivira, and another bitter disappointment. Quivira turned out to be a poor Pawnee Indian village which stood about 11 miles northeast of where Great Bend, Kansas, is today. To reach it, Coronado had to march through Texas, north through

Oklahoma into Kansas. He was the first white man to see the Indians of the plains and the great herds of buffalo. While on the march, one of Coronado's officers, Captain García de Cárdenas, discovered the Grand Canyon, in 1540. When Captain Cárdenas reported his discovery to Coronado and described its awe-inspiring magnificence, the general was not a bit interested.

Coronado found and saw many strange and wonderful things on his search for the Seven Cities of Cibola, but still, because he did not discover golden wealth, he considered his quest a complete failure. That he was the first white man to see the culture and wealth of the Plains Indians meant nothing to him. That he was the first to see the herds of countless buffalo browsing on the prairies was of no value. That one of his men discovered the Grand Canyon, one of the greatest works and wonders of nature, he gave no passing thought. That his travels gave white men knowledge of thousands of square miles of new country was not considered. In brief, despite this amazing wealth of discovery, Coronado returned to Mexico City sad and weary and bitter, a failure and the laughingstock of his countrymen.

At about the same time that Coronado was searching for the elusive Seven Cities of Cibola, Hernando de Soto and his expedition landed in Florida. From the Indians, de Soto also heard of rich golden cities, and he lost no time setting out for this El Dorado in the wilderness beyond. A short distance inland, after they got under way, the party met a lone and strange-looking Spaniard, Ortiz by name. He had been one of the companions of the ill-fated Narváez expedition. Like Cabeza de Vaca, he had escaped and gone to live among the Indians, whose language he had learned. He also told de Soto about a land of gold of which the Indians spoke. Ortiz was engaged as a guide, and a party of 550 horsemen disappeared over the western horizon, most of them never to be seen again by their companions who stayed behind.

Hernando de Soto, like Coronado, saw many strange and

wonderful things, including the mighty Father of Waters, the Mississippi River, which he discovered. The party crossed the river in rafts and continued the search for gold into Arkansas, but was finally forced to turn back. It was a small and sad and embittered group of men that reached the banks of the Mississippi again, in 1542. The Indians regarded de Soto as a god. When Hernando de Soto died, his men were afraid to let the Indians know that their leader was a mere mortal who bowed to Death like other men, so they secretly weighted the body and lowered it into the great river he had discovered.

The small group of Spaniards who survived the hardships of the wilderness then marched toward Mexico. They were stopped by the flood waters at the mouth of the Brazos river and by the hostile Indians who had even then seen enough of white men to regard them as their enemies. The Spaniards were forced to turn back to the Mississippi where they laboriously built seven small boats. While they were busy at that task, the Mississippi rose in angry flood. Its raging torrent almost wiped out the tiny settlement. When the flood subsided, the Spaniards launched their crude boats and sailed down to the Gulf of Mexico. Following the coast, they finally reached a Spanish colony at the mouth of the Panuco River, near Tampico, Mexico.

In 1581, three missionary priests set out to build missions along the route of Coronado. When they did not return within a year, a relief party, under Antonio de Espejo, was sent to find them. Espejo was too late. The monks had been killed by the Indians. But Espejo did find a new river, now called the Pecos, and he is believed to have been the first to call the country he had explored, New Mexico.

Other Spaniards made their sporadic way into New Mexico and Texas in those early years, but the first who brought colonists and founded a settlement, was Juan de Oñate. His party consisted of more than a hundred men who drove 7,000 head of horses, cattle, and sheep. There were eighty wagons loaded with food and tools and trade goods for the Indians. On reaching the Rio Grande, Oñate founded a settlement. He called it El Paso. Having done this, Oñate went on to conquer the Indians farther west. In 1605, he scratched a crude record of his accomplishments on Inscription Rock in the western part of New Mexico.

Other Spaniards crossed the Rio Grande into Texas during the seventeenth century, but the first white men to come in force after Oñate were Frenchmen, under the leadership of Robert Cavelier Sieur de La Salle, whose dreams of a French empire along the valley of the Mississippi were to end in tragedy on the soil of Texas.

La Salle had descended the whole course of the Mississippi River from the Great Lakes to the Gulf of Mexico. On that amazing journey was born his dream of empire, the story of which is told in the chapter, "Castles of Dreams in New France." The end of the story is part of the history of Texas.

In 1685, La Salle sailed into the Gulf of Mexico with plans to found a French colony at the mouth of the Mississippi. Owing to miscalculations, he missed the mouth of the great river. He was forced to put in at what was probably Matagorda Bay, Texas, a few hundred miles to the southwest of the Mississippi Delta. There one of his ships was wrecked by an insubordinate captain. Another ship left and returned to France.

La Salle, determined to find the mouth of the Mississippi River, set out overland, leaving some of his men to construct a fort. The Frenchman found the La Vaca River. As it was a better site for a settlement than Matagorda, he ordered the stockade moved there, and named it Fort Saint Louis in honor of the King of France.

For almost two years, La Salle continued his search for the mouth of the Mississippi without finding it. Finally he decided to make the journey overland to Canada, only to be treacherously killed by his own men on March 19, 1687. The exact place where La Salle was killed is not known, but it is believed to have been on the banks of one of the branches of the Trinity River, in Texas. Meanwhile Fort Saint Louis did not last long. The Indians lured the Frenchmen into a feeling of false security and massacred all but a few, whom they took as prisoners.

Meanwhile, news of La Salle's colony in Texas reached the Spaniards in Mexico. Captain Alonso de León with a small army was ordered to cross the Rio Grande and drive the French intruders out. But even as La Salle had been unable to find the mouth of the Mississippi, the Spaniards had trouble in locating the French settlement. For almost four years Captain de León combed the country. At last, in 1689, he came across some of the French survivors of the disaster at Fort Saint Louis. They were held in captivity by the Indians. The Spanish captain secured the release of the Frenchmen and had them guide him to Fort Saint Louis, which was in ruins. Captain de León discovered a few half-burned books and some other articles which he took back to Mexico City as evidence that La Salle and France were no longer to be feared in the lands above New Spain.

But the Viceroy of Mexico was not satisfied with this report. To prevent the French once and for all from making new attempts to settle in Texas, he again sent Captain de León, accompanied by Father Massanet, to establish missions and garrisons at strategic points along the Texas frontier. The first mission was established in 1690, and was called San Francisco de las Tejas. It was short-lived. Almost as soon as the soldiers left, the Indians started to harass the missions. Then followed drought, disease, and starvation. At last the fathers were forced to abandon the mission.

A quarter of a century later, the Spaniards made another effort to establish permanent missions in Texas. Once more, fear of a French invasion was the reason. By this time, New Orleans had been established at the mouth of the Mississippi River by the French, and their traders were pushing into the Red River region of Texas.

Hopes of profit led one French trader, St. Denis, to cross into Texas territory with a small trading party in 1715. But instead of Spaniards with gold in their pockets, they found abandoned missions and sheep and cattle running wild. St. Denis pushed down to the Rio Grande. At Eagle Pass, he came upon a Spanish outpost under the command of Captain Ramón. The Spanish officer promptly arrested the Frenchmen and seized their goods. The story is told that while he was in jail, St. Denis fell in love with the captain's daughter, Marie. The girl returned the feeling and pleaded with her father, Captain Ramón, to release the trader.

When St. Denis explained that he and his fellow traders had no interest in conquest, but only in making an honest profit, Captain Ramón set St. Denis free and gave his consent for the Frenchman to marry his daughter. After the wedding, St. Denis offered to guide the Spaniards through their own country for the purpose of establishing missions. The offer was accepted. The French trader and his bride set out along what was to become the famous old Spanish Trail. They were accompanied by Spanish soldiers and a group of mission-building fathers. At the end of the trail, at Natchitoches, on the Red River in Louisiana, St. Denis and his wife made their home. Here they set up a trading post, and, for any evidence to the contrary, lived happily ever after, at peace with both the Spaniards of Texas and the French of Louisiana.

Mission building by the Spaniards in Texas was now carried on in earnest. San Francisco de las Tejas was restored. Another establishment, built near the site where San Antonio stands today, became the center of activity. From 1715 until nearly the close of the century, the mission fathers continued their work in Texas. The most famous mission was the pine-log establishment of San Antonio de Valera, better known to history as the Alamo.

After the French and Indian Wars, France transferred Louisiana to Spain, closing it to American colonists who already were beginning to move beyond the confines of the thirteen colonies. Even in those early days, many North American eyes looked upon Texas as a land of opportunity. With the peace that came after the War of Independence, this was even more true.

In 1805, shortly after the Louisiana Purchase, a young United States Army officer, Zebulon Montgomery Pike, began a series of explorations and surveys from the Rio Grande to the Canadian border. He traveled south, in 1806, to the Rio Grande and into Spanish territory, where he was held a prisoner for a short time. The most outstanding result of Pike's activities, except giving his name to Pikes Peak, which he discovered, was the establishing of the Santa Fe Trail, the great artery of trade into the Southwest.

After the Louisiana Purchase, disputes arose between the United States and Spanish Texas over boundaries. The United States gave up claims to parts of Texas when it bought Florida from Spain in 1819. Some people in the Southwest were indignant at what they called the highhanded action of the government in giving Texas to Spain.

The true foundation of Texas was created by the home-building settlers and colonists who drifted into Texas from the United States in large numbers, beginning about 1820. The way for this southward migration was paved by Moses Austin, a Connecticut Yankee who had migrated to Louisiana Territory. In 1820, Austin went to Texas on horseback and asked the Spanish governor at San Antonio for a land grant on which to settle a colony of American pioneers. Governor Martíne said he would think the matter over. Moses Austin returned to Missouri, where he died shortly before word came that the land had been granted.

His son, Stephen Austin, then only twenty-eight years old, carried on with the plan to colonize Texas for Americans. He hurried to San Antonio, and was told to choose the land he wanted for his colony. The American selected the rich region between the Brazos and Colorado Rivers. He accepted Spanish citizenship and sent word for his colonists to join him at the new capital, San Felipe, the town he established on the Brazos River.

The easy terms on which land was offered in the Austin colony drew thousands of North Americans into Texas. Single men over twenty-three years of age were given 640 acres, with an extra 320 acres when they married. Land cost 12½ cents an acre, payable on easy terms. Moreover, the land was tax free.

Austin and his pioneers had been in Texas less than a year when the revolution in Mexico ousted Spanish rule. When the news reached Austin, he set out for Mexico City to get his land grant confirmed by the new government of Mexico. He remained in Mexico for a year. When he returned, Austin brought guarantees of the colony's rights from the Mexican government. The American venture was beginning to prosper. What gold had been for the Spaniards and furs for the French, rich free lands were for the Americans. Immigrants kept pouring into Texas as they did into other newly opened parts of the country.

The Americans in Texas, however, did not get along any too well with the Mexicans. Rumors reached Mexico City that the Americans were planning to set up an independent state in Texas. While the Mexicans were beginning to look upon them as a menace to the state, the Americans, in turn, grew more and more resentful of the restrictions that were imposed upon them by Mexico.

A clash was inevitable. The spirit of democracy had come with the Americans into Texas. It had infected many of the Spaniards and Mexicans who had not forgotten their sufferings under the iron heel of Spain. The new administration in Mexico failed to live up to the expectations of a democratic form of government. It was no secret that the United States sympathized with the American settlers in Texas. In 1825,

President Adams tried to extend the Florida Treaty with Spain to include a part of Texas. Failing in this, he tried unsuccessfully to purchase Texas from Mexico.

The background to the Texas Revolution was basically the same as that which had brought on the American War of Independence. Liberties were curtailed. High and arbitrary taxes were imposed. Mexican soldiers were garrisoned in the towns to enforce laws which Texans considered unjust and unreasonable. In 1830, the territory was closed to all outsiders. This last decree, enacted under the rule of President Bustamente of Mexico, was deeply resented in Texas. When the protests of the Texans went unheaded, open revolt broke out. General Santa Anna, a rival of Bustamente, sided with the Texans, and lent his aid in driving Mexican soldiers out of Texas.

On October 1, 1832, delegates from all provinces in Texas met at San Antonio. It was the first meeting of its kind in the history of Texas. Stephen Austin was elected chairman. A resolution calling for the province to become a separate and self-governing state was drafted. Although the Texans announced that their intentions were peaceful and that they remained loyal to the Mexican constitution of 1824, they also provided for a militia. The plan called for the enrollment of all men between the ages of sixteen and fifty for military duty. This act was regarded by the Mexican government as treasonable. Austin, who was already being called the father of Texas, replied that "if Texas does nothing for herself, she is lost."

Petitions of the Texans were ignored. Even harsher regulations were imposed upon them. Another convention was called in April, 1833. Sam Houston and David Burnet were appointed to draw up a constitution. Then a committee of three men, including Austin, was selected to take the Texas constitution to Mexico City to get the approval of the Mexican government. For some reason, the two other members of the delegation found it inconvenient to go. Stephen Austin went to Mexico City alone.

General Santa Anna, who had sympathized with the Texans and aided them against President Bustamente, changed his attitude when he became president of Mexico. Then followed new severe restrictions against Texans on orders from Santa Anna. When Stephen Austin arrived in Mexico City, he was treated with open hostility. At an interview with Vice-President Farias, something said by Austin was interpreted by Farias as treasonable. Austin was arrested and thrown into prison, where he was kept incommunicado for 3 months. For the next year he was held a prisoner in Mexico.

The news of Austin's arrest incensed the Texas patriots. However, they were afraid to take direct action while Austin was in the hands of Santa Anna. Finally, in 1834, Santa Anna set Stephen Austin free, and let him return to Texas with vague promises of improved conditions. Back in Texas, Austin found his countrymen determined to fight for their freedom. The crisis came in 1835. A group of patriots under Colonel William B. Travis drove a company of Mexican soldiers and tax collectors out of Anahuac. Santa Anna ordered the Texans to lay down their arms. When they refused, he gave orders to crush the revolt without mercy.

The war was on. The Texans banded together under Sam Houston as commander of the east. Stephen Austin commanded a force that attacked the Mexicans at Gonzalez, where he gained a victory. Then Goliad was taken, and the Texans prepared to march on San Antonio. In October, 1835, San Antonio fell to the patriots. General Cos, brother-in-law of Santa Anna, was allowed to leave Texas with his army on the promise that he would not return. Cos agreed. He returned to Mexico to meet the wrath of his brother-in-law, Santa Anna, who was not going to let Texas go that easily.

The Texans grew overconfident as the result of their victories. They were unprepared when General Santa Anna appeared before San Antonio with a large and well-equipped army late in February, 1836. There were only 150 Texans in San Antonio, under Colonel James Bowie, who was desperately ill. Colonel Travis, second in command, supervised the removal of the small garrison to the old Alamo mission, which he believed could be better defended.

As the defense of the Alamo was getting under way, the famous frontiersman and trapper, Davy Crockett, carrying his trusty rifle, Betsey, in his arms, arrived and offered his services to the Texans. On February 22, the Mexicans, under Santa Anna, 1,600 strong, advanced on the Texans. In defiance, they raised the Lone Star flag. It had thirteen stripes, alternate red and white on a blue ground; on the blue background was a large five-pointed star and between the points were the letters T-E-X-A-S.

Santa Anna, before opening hostilities, sent an ultimatum to Colonel Travis. He said that, unless they surrendered, every man, woman, and child in the Alamo would be put to death. Colonel Travis answered with a cannon shot. That was on February 23. All day and all night the Texans withstood the steady fire of the Mexicans. The next day, February 24, Travis realizing that the situation was desperate, smuggled out a letter asking that relief be sent to the defenders of the Alamo. This letter is one of the most courageous and stirring documents in the history of the United States, and is therefore given here in full:

> Commander of the Alamo
> Bejar, February 24, 1836.

To the People of Texas and
All Americans in the World,

Fellow citizens and compatriots: I am besieged, by a thousand or more of Mexicans under Santa Anna. I have sustained a continual bombardment and cannonade for twenty-four hours and have not lost a man. The enemy has demanded a surrender at discretion, otherwise the garrison are to be put to the sword if the fort is taken. I have answered the demand with a cannon shot, and our flag still waves proudly from the walls. *I shall never surrender or retreat.* Then, I call on you in the name of Liberty, of patriotism and everything dear to the American character, to come to our aid, with all dispatch. The enemy is receiving reinforcements daily and will no doubt increase to three or four thousand in four or five days. If this is neglected, I am determined to sustain myself as long as possible and die like a soldier who never forgets what is due his own honor and that of his country.

Victory or Death
William Barret Travis
Lt. Col. Comdt.

P. S. The Lord is on our side. When the enemy appeared in sight we had not three bushels of corn. We have since found in a deserted house eighty or ninety bushels and got into the walls twenty or thirty head of beeves.

Travis

Days passed, but help did not come. The night of March 5 was very quiet in the mission. The exhausted patriots knew that the end was near; relief could never reach them in time. Death came the next morning, on March 6, when Santa Anna ordered a final furious attack. Even then, the Alamo did not fall until every fighting man of the defenders had given his life. Not satisfied with this brutal victory, Santa Anna ordered the bodies of the Texans burned.

Santa Anna then led his army in a march of terror and destruction throughout that part of Texas. But while their torches could burn and their bullets could kill, the Mexicans had no weapon that could silence the newborn Texas battle cry that was ringing out louder and stronger: "Remember the Alamo!"

A provisional Texan government was formed. Sam Houston was the commander in chief. His task was to rally the Texas patriot army to stop the advance of Santa Anna. Houston, instead of rushing to meet the Mexicans, led Santa Anna a chase over the country, waiting for an opportune moment to strike back. The opportunity came on April 20, 1836, on the banks of the San Jacinto River. This time it was the Mexicans who were overconfident. Toward sunset on April 21, Sam

Houston gave the order to attack. The cry of "Remember the Alamo!" rang out. When the battle was over, only about thirty of Santa Anna's 600 Mexican soldiers were alive. Among the living, but captured, was Santa Anna. He successfully pleaded with Houston for his life. The Alamo had been avenged. With the capture of Santa Anna, Texas was free. The Lone Star Republic was founded, and in September, 1836, Sam Houston was elected the first president. Stephen Austin was made secretary of state, an office he held but briefly, until his death in December that year.

Following this victory came the growth of Texas. Settlers poured across the border by the thousands. The Mexicans continued to make trouble, refusing to recognize the independence of the Texas Republic. On top of that question was another problem: the annexation of Texas as a part of the United States.

Finally in 1845, Texas joined the United States. The admittance of Texas to the Union as a state was declared by Mexico to be an unfriendly act. The Mexican War was fought to secure the southern border of the United States along the Rio Grande. Old Rough and Ready Zachary Taylor led the forces of the United States to victory. By the Treaty of Guadalupe Hidalgo in 1848, the question of Texas' status was settled. The United States gained a great deal of territory. It included New Mexico, California, and territory that later became the states of Colorado, Utah, Nevada, and Arizona. A payment of 15 million dollars was made to Mexico.

But the end of the war did not settle the problem of Texas. There was still a thousand miles of southern frontier to guard against marauding Mexicans and Indians. Outlaws and bad men from other parts of the country flocked to Texas. They had to be held in check. The challenge of maintaining law and order through the vast state of Texas was taken up by a group of mounted scouts whose fame, as the Texas Rangers, soon spread throughout the country.

The Texas Rangers were organized in 1835, while Texas was still fighting for her freedom. When that job was done, the Rangers accepted the responsibility of maintaining law, preserving order, and promoting peace. From 1835 and for a hundred years, until the Rangers were absorbed by a larger agency in 1935, these fearless and gallant fighting men carried on the tradition of a service that has made the Texas Rangers synonymous with courage and daring, honesty and straight shooting.

There is an old Texas saying to the effect that where you find grass and water, you will find a cattle ranch. It was the open range, free grass and free water, that made Texas the greatest cattle country in the world. It was all free. There was only the Indian and the buffalo to dispute the claims of the cattlemen.

The factors that led to the rapid growth of the Texas cattle empire in the latter half of the eighteenth century were the great cattle drives to northern markets after the Civil War; the extension of railroads into the West; the subduing of the Indians, and the extermination of the buffalo. The elimination of the buffalo was thought to be important, for these native animals, in herds of millions, ate the grass that was needed for the cattle.

Cattle, however, were nothing new to Texas. Two years after Hernando Cortez conquered Mexico, Gregorio de Villalobos brought some fine Spanish calves to Mexico. These calves were the beginnings of the cattle industry in North America. Coronado took 500 cows along on his quest for the Seven Cities of Cibola. His men were poor herders, and the animals escaped by the score. Running wild and with no natural enemies to curb the increase of their herds, these Spanish cattle developed during the years into the "ornery" Texas longhorns. Horses are as important to the cattle business as the cattle themselves. They, too, were the gift of Spanish conquistadors. Descendants of runaway highly bred Spanish horses ran wild by the thousands.

Thus, in the course of the centuries, we find cattle and horses growing wild and running wild in the Southwest. Before the Civil War started, Texas was rich in cows; rich in horses. After the Civil War, owing to the loss of a market for more than five years, Texas had so many cattle that it was cattle poor. When Texans who had fought in the war returned home, they had more cattle than they knew what to do with, but no money and no credit. The Texans had cattle by the millions of heads, which they couldn't find a market for at any price; but up north beef was bringing high prices.

The reason for this state of affairs was that there was no way of getting Texas cattle to market; no way of joining supply and demand. Then, in 1866, some Texans got the bright idea of driving cattle north to Kansas, in the hope of finding a market there. The idea was not very well thought out. About a quarter of a million head were driven north that year, and most of the cattlemen who had a part in the drive lost all they had. The Texas longhorns died by the thousands on the drive, and those that did reach Kansas found no buyers. The reason was that there was no way of bringing the beef product east.

To remedy that situation, Joseph McCoy, an enterprising businessman, induced the Kansas-Pacific railroad to extend its tracks into Abilene, Kansas, at the northern end of the old Chisholm Trail from southern Texas. While the railroad was being brought into Abilene, McCoy built a stockyard and sent word down to Texas that he was ready to buy cattle and pay good money.

Texas cattlemen took up McCoy's proposition. In 1868, the longhorns started moving north to Abilene in huge herds. In 1869, some 350,000 head were sold in Abilene, and the number rose to a million within 3 years. With steers bringing from $30 to $40 a head in Chicago, Texas cattlemen became rich. Cattle was king in Texas.

The period of the great cattle drives is one of the most colorful and romantic in the history of Texas. The Chisholm

Trail, for instance, was a thousand miles long, from San Antonio, Texas, up to the Red River and then north into Abilene, Kansas. Every mile of the way had its dangers and hazards and hardships, from blizzards to bandits; from floods to stampedes.

Flooded rivers were the greatest barriers. When the spring rains swelled narrow streams to raging torrents, a mile or more across, the cow herders faced a real problem, especially with stubborn Texas longhorns that more often than not refused even to enter the water.

As for the cow waddies, or herders, their life on the trail was one of hardships. They got little pay, little sleep, and a lot of hard work. The cowboy was in the saddle from dawn to dark, and on a drive there was herd riding at night to prevent stampedes.

Of all the dangers on the trail, the stampede was probably the worst. Texas longhorns are not like ordinary cattle, placid and peaceful. They are dynamite on legs, jittery, nervous, and temperamental, ready to stampede with or without cause. At night, any unexpected noise, from a clap of thunder to the rustling of a leaf, might stampede a herd into mad, furious panic. It was this peculiarity of Texas cattle that led the cowboys to sing their soft songs at night. They found that music had a soothing effect on the cattle. Hence, at night on cattle drives were heard the soft, slow, sad cowboy songs called Longhorn Lullabies.

Cattle towns sprang up along the northern terminals of the cattle trails. They were loud, rip-roaring, and wicked. Besides Abilene, there were Dodge City, Ellsworth, and Cheyenne, just to mention a few. But the great cattle drives lasted only 20 years. Then the days of the free and open range were over. Someone invented barbed wire to fence in range land. The battles for range water ended when windmill pumps brought water from below the ground, Cowboys, instead of wearing six-shooters in their belts, carried pliers for mending barbed wire and a can of machine oil to keep the water pumps in smooth running order. Throughout the story of strife and struggle in the West, there runs the thread of the battle for water.

The water problem, which was solved by the Texas ranchmen in their own way, has been solved for other, less fortunate parts of the Southwest by harnessing the Colorado River. This wild stallion of rivers runs its furious and headlong course through the Grand Canyon of the Colorado. If Coronado, the conquistador, had been told that the ribbon of a river at the bottom of the mighty canyon, discovered by one of his captains, would some day produce more wealth than the mines of Mexico and Peru combined, he would have laughed with scorn. And yet, that is what came to pass.

The Grand Canyon of the Colorado River is one of the most spectacular sights in the world. Its steep walls are pages in which one can read the history of Mother Earth for the past several million years. The most generally accepted theory is that the Grand Canyon dates back about 8 million years. During this time, the Colorado River, with the help of winds, torrential rains, and shattering frosts, carved that mighty spectacle, the Grand Canyon.

The vastness of the Grand Canyon can best be appreciated when it is realized that if the whole Manhattan sky line could be placed on the bottom of the canyon, an observer from even the tallest building would be unable to look over the top of the canyon. The tallest building in the world would have to be five times as tall as it is to reach from the bottom of the Grand Canyon to the edge of the rim on top.

The river that snakes its way along the canyon bottom for 1,000 miles is a series of more than 500 rushing falls, boiling rapids, and seething whirlpools. The Grand Canyon, as was mentioned before, was first seen by Captain Cárdenas of the Coronado expedition, in 1540. The first white man known to have crossed from one side to the other over the Colorado

River, was Father Escalante, a Spanish missionary, in 1776. The first American to make the trip through the Grand Canyon was James O. Pattie, a beaver trapper, who worked his traps along the Colorado River in 1825.

There was no serious or scientific exploration of the Colorado River until 1869, when Major John Wesley Powell, soldier, engineer, naturalist, and explorer, tackled a job that everyone considered foolhardy and impossible. Powell made up his mind to map the river and canyon and to study rock formations and animal and plant life along the course of the Colorado, from its starting point in Wyoming to the end of its run in Arizona.

The Powell expedition left Green River City, Wyoming, on May 24, 1869, in specially constructed boats, strong enough to withstand the punishment of being pounded against rocks by the strong river current, yet light enough so that they could be carried around waterfalls and rapids. The party consisted of ten men. They had food for 10 months. At first the going was smooth and easy. But, as the party got deeper and deeper into the canyon, troubles and dangers increased. Soon it became an almost continuous fight for life against the raging river and its deadly crushing power. Some days the party made 30 miles or more, other days saw progress of only a few hundred yards. Through June, July, and into August, Powell and his men fought against heavy odds.

By that time, they were three-quarters of a mile in the depths of the earth, with steep walls of the canyon rising skyward on each side. Roaring rapids and tumbling falls came almost one on top of the other. Then, to add to their torture, it began to rain—cold, icy rain driven by sharp, cutting winds. On August 27, three of the men had enough and deserted, taking their chances on climbing the wall of the canyon and finding friendly Indians to help them. On the very next day, Major Powell and his remaining companions sailed out of the Grand Canyon, completing one of the most daring and difficult expeditions in the history of exploration. The ironic twist of fate is that the three men who deserted because they were afraid to die, were the only members of Major Powell's expedition who lost their lives. They were killed by Indians.

Major Powell's expedition was an important survey that placed many rivers, mountains, valleys, and canyons on the map. So accurate were his surveys, that very few changes had to be made when modern engineers began the work of taming the lower part of the Colorado River to put it to work at Boulder Dam.

The people in the southwestern part of the United States, in California, and in northwest Mexico, used to tremble in fear whenever the Colorado River burst into flood. At other times, the river would all but dry up, bringing with it parching droughts. It was beyond man's wildest dreams to hope that the wild river could be tamed and taught to provide a steady flow of water from the great reservoir back of Boulder Dam at Black Canyon. Yet it was done, through the magic of modern engineering.

This engineering feat cost Uncle Sam about 165 million dollars, but for that money a vast region that was once barren desert now grows rich and green with essential crops. If Boulder Dam had been in operation in 1934, at the height of the great drought, much of the distress and destruction in the Imperial Valley of California could have been avoided. While the chief function of Boulder Dam is to feed water to thirsty lands, its second important service is to provide cheap electric power and lighting to farms and towns over a large area.

And thus, although the Seven Cities of Cibola were but an illusion in the minds of Estevan and Father Marcos and Coronado, the wealth was there had they not been blinded by wishful dreaming, a wealth of new green pastures for modern conquerors of the soil.

CHAPTER 25

Gateway to the Setting Sun

~~~

State	Settled	Entered Union	Capital	Population	Area, square miles
California	1769	1850	Sacramento	6,873,688	158,297
Idaho	1842	1890	Boise	523,440	83,888
Nevada	1850	1864	Carson City	110,014	110,690
Oregon	1838	1859	Salem	1,087,717	96,699
Utah	1847	1896	Salt Lake City	548,393	84,990
Washington	1811	1889	Olympia	1,721,376	69,127

THE chronicle of California—from discovery to state-hood—is one of swiftly changing dramatic scenes. The leading actors in the mighty cast range from the haughty, swashbuckling conquistadors to humble but energetic priests; from fearless trail blazers to covered-wagon pioneers; from spendthrift gold miners to farsighted empire builders.

First on California's stage appears Juan Cabrillo. He is credited with the discovery of California in 1542. But in the prologue, staged 2 years earlier, Hernando de Alarcón sailed into the Gulf of California and reached the mouth of the Colorado River. Don Alarcón had come up from Mexico with two ships as part of Coronado's expedition in quest of the Seven Cities of Cibola. He landed on the shores of the gulf, and was the first white man to set foot on the soil of the Golden State.

This early visit was without consequence. It left the honor of real discovery to Juan Rodriguez Cabrillo, a Portuguese navigator sailing for Spain. He entered a bay he named San Miguel (San Diego) on September 28, 1542. With some of his men, he went ashore. They met with a hostile reception from the Indians. With three of his crew wounded, Cabrillo weighed anchor and continued up the coast. On October 10, they landed at an Indian village on the mainland of the Santa Barbara Channel. There Cabrillo took formal possession in the name of the King of Spain.

On January 3, 1543, after having explored the coast of California for 3 months, Cabrillo died as the result of an accident at La Posesión (Cuyler's Harbor). Before his death, Cabrillo transferred the command of the expedition to his chief pilot, Bartolomé Ferrelo, who sailed northward as far as Rogue River, Oregon, and then returned to Mexico.

The reports of the discovery of California evidently did not excite Spain very much. No colonies were started and the next visitor was the English adventurer, Francis Drake, who, on June 15, 1579, sailed his famous *Golden Hind* into Drake's Bay, north of San Francisco. Drake claimed the country for England, held a religious service for his crew, and then nailed a sixpence to a post to remind future callers that the land he had named New Albion was the property of England. This claim was to be brought up by England more than 250 years later, at a very critical point in the history of California.

In 1595, Sebastián Cermeno, looking for harbors that might serve as havens of refuge for the Spanish galleons to Manila, was wrecked near Drake's Bay, at a place he called San Francisco Bay. Taking a small boat, Cermeno headed southward, missing the Golden Gate. He did, however, sight and make a note of the excellent Bay of Monterey. There is a record of another Spanish explorer's visiting the coast in 1603, but no settlements were established. California remained ignored and forgotten for more than a hundred years.

The conquest and subsequent colonization of California is unique in New World history. It was brought about not by the swords of conquistadors in shining armor, but by humble Franciscan monks armed only with the Cross and kind words. It was this peaceful invasion by Spanish priests that laid the foundation for the colonial realm that grew into California in the course of the years. These early missionaries were not only servants of the Church, but tireless explorers, able colonizers, and excellent map makers. Spain made a very wise decision when, in 1769, she sent a "sacred expedition," under Father Junípero Serra, to colonize California.

Russia was the cause of Spain's sudden interest in California. The Russians were well established in Alaska by that time and were beginning to extend themselves too far south for Spain's comfort.

The first permanent settlement in California was made on May 17, 1769, at San Diego, near the foot of the present Presidio Hill. On July 1, Father Junípero Serra, father-president of the missions, arrived. Before his death, in 1784, he had established nine missions in California. Year by year, the Franciscan fathers founded new missions, establishing twenty-one in all, the one farthest north being at San Francisco. These missions were about a day's journey apart on the Royal Road constructed by the priests, from San Diego to Sonoma. They were surrounded by fields and orchards that were worked by the Franciscan fathers and the Indians.

Life in California went its peaceful way, in sharp contrast to the violent course of events in other Spanish colonies. In October, 1784, the first great land grant to a private family was made. It was the Rancho San Rafael, granted by Governor Pedro Fages to José Verdugo. It covered parts of where the cities of Glendale and Burbank stand today.

The first American to reach California, John Graham, arrived in the fall of 1791, as a member of a Spanish exploring expedition. From existing records, he appears to have died and been buried on the very day he landed at Monterey. In October, 1796, the first American vessel, the *Otter*, with Captain Ebenezer Door in command, anchored at Monterey. Seven years later, in 1803, the first commercial otter-hunting expedition reached California when the American ship *Lelia Bird* put in at San Diego. Otter hunting was against the Spanish law and there was a brief artillery battle between the Spaniards and the Americans. There were no casualties, however, and the *Lelia Bird* departed on March 22, with a poor cargo.

California history of this period was rather somnolent, but in 1806, a romantic episode that has been celebrated in novel and in poem took place in San Francisco. In April of that year, the Imperial Inspector of Alaska for Russia, Chamberlain Nikolai Petrovitch Rezanof, arrived in San Francisco to secure food for the starving Russian colonists at Sitka. The Russian commander fell in love with the daughter of the Spanish governor of San Francisco, Concepción Arguello.

When the Russian had accomplished his mission in California, he returned to Alaska and started off across Siberia to get the consent of the Czar for his marriage to the Spanish señorita. Before he reached his destination, Rezanof died. When the news reached the girl in San Francisco years later, she was grief-stricken and entered a convent.

While the Franciscan missionaries went their simple, quiet way in California, events of tremendous significance for the future of the Pacific country were taking place in the United States. Thomas Jefferson, in 1800, was elected the third President of the United States. He was not alone a brilliant statesman, a fervent patriot, and an able executive, but he was also an amateur scientist with a deep-rooted interest in exploration.

In 1803, the Louisiana Territory was purchased from France at the instigation of Jefferson. But for 20 years before that momentous transaction, Jefferson had been beset with the idea of an exploring expedition to survey the vast regions between the Mississippi River and the Pacific coast. In 1783, and again in 1793, Jefferson advocated an expedition to probe into the great unknown Northwest. Both projects failed. But, in 1803, as President of the United States, he managed to persuade Congress to appropriate $2,500 for an expedition to trace the Missouri River to its source, find the eastern end of the Columbia River, and follow it down to its mouth at the Pacific Ocean.

It was easy for Congress to define the objectives of the proposed expedition. To find men to achieve them was another matter. President Jefferson, after much deliberation, chose his young friend and former secretary, Meriwether Lewis, to head the party. Lewis, in turn, recommended his friend, William Clark, as second in command. The appointments were approved and preparations for the Lewis and Clark expedition got under way.

Meriwether Lewis was especially fitted for his great command. Army training and knowledge of the out-of-doors combined to give him the necessary qualifications. Born in 1774 of a distinguished Virginia family, he was a close friend of Thomas Jefferson. Yet this friendship was by no means the sole reason for the President's appointment of the young captain to such an important and responsible post.

The young officer had, from an early age, shown an interest in natural history. That interest had been backed by years of practical experience. Lewis knew how to hew paths through the untrodden wilderness. What was even more important, he was trained to see with eyes of mature wisdom and judgment what lay along the paths he walked.

In addition to these special abilities, Meriwether Lewis possessed other qualifications. Young as he was, he knew men and how to lead them. This he had proved while serving in the militia during the Whiskey Insurrection. Later he had joined the regular army and been commissioned a captain at the age of twenty-three. President Jefferson was well aware of the young officer's background and qualifications when he gave him his great chance as the leader of the first major exploring expedition sponsored by the young government of the United States.

William Clark also possessed a background of army and pioneering experience. A brother of the famous General George Rogers Clark, he was a Virginian by birth and a Kentuckian by upbringing. He had seen service under Mad Anthony Wayne in the wars of the Northwest Territory, where he had been a comrade in arms of Lewis. A firm bond of friendship had sprung up between the two men. Lewis was so impressed by Clark's brains and character that, when the time came, he chose Clark as his lieutenant. The choice was wise.

The two young men received explicit instructions from President Jefferson. They were to trace the Missouri River to its source, cross the highlands, and follow the best waterway they could find to the Pacific Ocean. They were told to keep their eyes open, to see and study everything—the soil and the face of the country, the weather and the climate. Reports were to be made of animal life and the presence of minerals. Above all, they were to find out if the furs from the Pacific regions could be transported east and carried down the Missouri instead of being shipped west to the Pacific coast. If this could be done, the United States would control the fur market and Saint Louis would become the fur capital of the world.

An important objective of the expedition was to establish friendly contacts with the red men and to make them realize the strength and integrity of the government of the United States. In May, 1804, the Lewis and Clark expedition began its journey up the Missouri River in three boats. One was a large craft, 55 feet long, with a sail and places for twenty-two oars; the two others were smaller, with places for six or seven oars. Mindful of President Jefferson's orders to cultivate the good will of the Indians, the party did not hurry. Slowly, throughout the summer, they made their way up the Missouri, battling the swift and muddy current. Summer faded into bleak autumn, until, on October 27, after a journey of 1,600 miles, they went into winter camp among the Mandan Indians.

The site for their winter encampment had been carefully chosen by Captain Lewis, not far from Bismarck, North Dakota. While at Fort Mandan, Lewis and Clark gained an invaluable recruit. This new member of the party was an Indian squaw, Sacajawea, or Bird Woman, whose knowledge of the Rocky Mountain region was eagerly welcomed by Captain Lewis and his men.

In the whole list of Indian heroines, from Pocahontas to Ramona, there is not one that rises above Sacajawea. She was the daughter of a chief of the Shoshone Indians, a tribe that made its home on the western side of the Rockies. As a young girl, in 1799, Sacajawea went with her people to spend the fall and winter on the banks of the Missouri River. There she was captured by a group of Minnetaree warriors, traditional enemies of the Shoshones. She was kept a prisoner for about five years. Then her captors sold her to a French-Canadian fur trader, Toussaint Charboneau, who married her. Charboneau and Sacajawea happened to be among Mandan Indians when Lewis and Clark arrived. When the explorers said that they needed an interpreter, Sacajawea and her husband volunteered.

Sacajawea had a tiny baby, only a few months old, when she joined the expedition. The wilderness they had to face was enough to make hardened men falter. Yet the Indian woman was eager and ready to push on into the mountains, carrying a papoose in a basket on her back. Without her knowledge of the way through the Rockies, Lewis and Clark might never have found Lehmi Pass, the door to the Pacific. More than that, her presence opened the way for the full cooperation of the Shoshones, through Sacajawea's brother, who, at that time, was chief of the tribe. In their journals, Lewis and Clark are generous in their praise of this brave and courageous Indian woman.

The first winter in the wilds was one of preparation for

hardships yet to come. In the spring of 1805, the party pushed upstream once more. The heavy boats proved too clumsy and were abandoned for six large canoes made of green cottonwood planks. Then came months of wearying effort. The canoes were unmanageable, the navigation difficult, and progress all too slow. There was mile upon footsore mile when there was nothing to do but to disembark and haul the canoes from the shore. The deep river, with its rapid currents of wild, white water rushed over stones as sharp as razors. On each side rose high rock walls.

Then came the Yellowstone River, pouring its flood into the Missouri; Mari's River, named by Lewis. Next, the thunder of the great falls of the Missouri. There was hope in the roaring sound of those falls, a hope that became a reality when they knew they were near the crystal spring that was the mighty river's source. The canoes were abandoned. Footsore and weary, the explorers continued on their way into the wilderness. Westward! Always westward!

Sacajawea led the men over Indian trails they would never have been able to find. At last they crossed the Continental Divide. They reached the Shoshone country where Sacajawea's brother did all within his power to help the expedition. This not only meant food and rest for them all, but also Indian ponies to make the last stage of the journey easier. But the struggle with the towering snowy crags of the Pacific range proved far from easy. At last they found water again, navigable water. The Indian ponies were exchanged for canoes which carried them safely through the dangerous rapids of the Clearwater River. The end of October came, and with it their arrival at their destination down the Columbia River to the shores of the Pacific. Victory! A trail had been blazed clear across the country to the ocean. Thomas Jefferson's orders had been carried out.

After a miserable winter, the Lewis and Clark expedition began its return journey on March 23, 1806. On September

23, they reached Saint Louis, to receive the acclaim of the whole nation. They had covered 8,000 miles of unexplored territory and made history. The success of the project was a triumph of military discipline and the coordination of practical and technical knowledge.

Meriweather Lewis and William Clark were hailed as the pathfinders of the Far West. They opened the way that Pike, Fremont, and other intrepid explorers were to follow. The records they brought back, their day-by-day journals, are evidence that they carried out their orders with keen vision and true scientific spirit. But of all the information brought back by the Lewis and Clark expedition, that which had the most immediate and material results was the complete data on the location and distribution of fur-bearing animals, the story of which was told in the chapter, "Wealth in the Wilderness."

The Lewis and Clark expedition was actually the key that opened the door to the West. As a result, the Oregon Trail was established, although at first it was known and used only by traders and the Mountain Men. The same was true of the famous Santa Fe Trail, from Independence, Missouri, across the plains to the old town of Santa Fe, New Mexico. Regular use of the Santa Fe Trail began around 1821, but very few immigrants passed over it. It went only halfway to the Pacific, and it was not until the time of the gold rush that it was extended to Los Angeles.

In 1842, great masses of colonists were ready to move westward. Only one thing held them back: the lack of proved surveyed routes across the unknown country beyond the Mississippi. The route surveyed by Lewis and Clark was too far north. The land beyond the western terminal of the Santa Fe Trail was known only to veteran scouts, or the fur-trapping Mountain Men.

Old-time trappers, such as Étienne Provost, Jim Bridger, Kit Carson, and Old Bill Williams, knew every path and trail, but the knowledge was in their heads. With the Indians as hostile as they were, the taking of a scalp might mean the loss of one of these walking maps, and tragedy for the expedition he was guiding. The Mountain Men were explorers, and good ones, but they could not make surveys or even accurately describe the country they knew so well. Maps put together from their knowledge resulted in many fantastic and often serious errors. Entire mountain ranges were often left out and lakes put where none existed.

The crying need was for an accurate survey of the Northwest, especially for a practical and central route for immigrant caravans. In 1842, that cry was answered and the need filled by John Charles Fremont, later known as the Pathfinder of the West.

Fremont, poor and without family connections, had become an officer in the United States Army by the rear door, through the influence of a friend. He soon proved himself to be the equal of the finest West Pointer. Being just a soldier did not satisfy young Fremont. He studied astronomy and became an expert surveyor, geographer, and map maker. He trained his body to withstand hardships and the buffeting of the elements. To top off his qualifications as a promising young officer, he married—against the wishes of her father—the beautiful daughter of the wealthy and powerful Senator Benton of Saint Louis.

When the call came for a man to survey a route to the Northwest, Fremont, then twenty-nine years old, was ready and accepted the assignment. He set out on the first of his three expeditions into the West on May 2, 1842, just six months after his runaway marriage. He got off to a lucky start, for shortly after leaving Saint Louis for the Missouri, Fremont ran into Kit Carson, the ablest and most picturesque scout of that day. Kit Carson agreed to guide the Fremont party for $100 a month.

Kit Carson had been an apprentice of the wilderness since

he was fifteen. He was a master woodcraftsman who knew every trick of the trail. He not only spoke Spanish and French in addition to his native tongue, but he understood several Indian dialects. Carson was adept at the Indian sign language, and, as were all the Mountain Men, he was a walking map and encyclopedia of plains and mountain lore. Originally, these Mountain Men, like Kit Carson, had been trappers, but when the beaver began to give out and trapping for furs was no longer profitable, they turned to scouting for a living. They hired themselves out to parties such as Fremont's and supplied army posts and immigrant trains with buffalo meat.

In the middle of June, 1842, the Fremont expedition really set out. When, 3½ months later, they came down the Missouri again, Fremont had accomplished all his objectives and explored and mapped the country between the Missouri and the base of the Rockies. Only one incident marred the journey —the upsetting of one of the boats with the loss of most of Fremont's instruments and records. Fortunately, his observations had been kept in duplicate and all his journals but one were recovered.

The tangible results of the expedition were proof that the route he had surveyed could be traveled by eight-mule dray carts; that there were herds of buffalo to feed the immigrants; that there was plenty of grass and water for the mules and horses. A twelve-year-old boy had accompanied the Fremont expedition, which showed that entire families could make the journey without risk. The publication of Fremont's findings were, to a great extent, responsible for the surge to the Oregon Territory that followed.

Fremont's second expedition, in 1843, was larger and better equipped. Kit Carson joined the outfit at Pueblo, Colorado. From there the party headed for the Great Salt Lake. On the way, Fremont overtook the great trains of lumbering wagons of the first great migration to Oregon. He and his men were cheered as they rode by, for both Fremont and Kit Carson were well-known figures.

At that time, the Oregon country was claimed by both the United States and England. Although there were few settlements, a treaty gave both countries the right to send settlers there. As a result of the Lewis and Clark expedition and the first Fremont journey, reports had spread regarding the fertile soil, fine climate, and abundance of fish, game, and fur-bearing animals in Oregon. People from all over the East got the "Oregon fever." The first large migration started from Independence, Missouri, in 1843.

When large numbers of Americans began to settle in the lower part of Oregon, the United States claimed exclusive rights to this territory. England protested. A long and bitter quarrel began. "Fifty-four forty or fight!" became the battle cry of the American settlers. This meant that they wanted American territory to extend up to 54 degrees 40 minutes of latitude north. Fortunately war was averted. An agreement was reached in 1846, which divided the Oregon Territory between the two nations at the forty-ninth degree latitude north. The line runs straight west from the Lake-of-the-Woods to the Pacific coast.

But to return to Fremont, after he and his party headed west in 1843, they reached Salt Lake, in Utah, without mishap. The unique lake had been discovered by Jim Bridger some years before, but Fremont was the first to submit its waters to a scientific examination. For days he paddled around the lake with Kit Carson. He boiled 5 gallons of the water and obtained several quarts of fine white salt.

From Salt Lake, Fremont continued to the Columbia River, which he reached in the beginning of November, 1843. There he decided not to retrace his steps, but to follow a return route that would take him through the Sierra Nevadas. It was a bold plan to tackle the towering and unknown mountains with winter approaching. In January, 1844, he announced to his amazed men his decision to cross the Sierras into California. His reason was that, in case the quarrel over Texas should result in war between the United States and Mexico, the government would need accurate information about California, then a province of Mexico. Fremont also wanted to map the shortest and most direct route to California for the United States Army.

It was a herculean task crossing the mountains which rise to 14,000 feet. The entire country was a frozen waste, with the passes choked with snow 5 feet deep. In places, where only treetops showed, the snow was more than 20 feet deep. Day after day they struggled up slippery ice-covered mountainsides, where men and animals often lost their footing. But at last, on February 20, the party reached the summit of a pass to which Kit Carson had guided them. Below them stretched the fertile Sacramento Valley. This pass, which they had come a thousand miles from the Columbia River to find, is today known as Carson Pass, at Woodford, California.

On their way down into the Sacramento Valley they met Spanish-speaking Indians who told them of the vast ranch of John Augustus Sutter. In March they arrived at Sutter's Fort, ragged and exhausted. They were made welcome by Sutter, who ruled the rich valley in the manner of a benevolent but despotic medieval baron. During his stay at Sutter's Fort, Fremont learned of the discontent of many Californians with the rule of Mexico and of the hostility between American settlers and the Mexicans. Fremont filed all this in his head for future reference. He started on his return journey in the spring, arriving in Saint Louis in August, 1844.

Fremont's third expedition, in 1845, was even more ambitious than his previous two. With sixty-two men, well armed, Fremont headed straight for California. There is no doubt that he suspected that war between the United States and Mexico might overtake him in Mexican territory across the Rockies. Kit Carson again was chief scout.

The route followed this time was through central Nevada and then southwest to California. Fremont reached Sutter's Fort, in the Sacramento Valley in December, 1845. Although Fremont's objective was Oregon, he delayed his departure from California, awaiting events that, when they came, were to change the course both of the country and his life.

Meanwhile, things had been happening in California. To understand them, it is necessary to go back over the track of time to the second decade of the nineteenth century. News of the 1821 revolt that secured Mexican independence from Spain reached Monterey, California, on April 11, 1822. Governor Pablo Sola immediately replaced the Spanish flag with the new standard of the Mexican Republic. Santa Barbara followed suit on April 13, and California passed from Spanish rule to become a part of Mexico.

On November 27, 1826, a trapper, Jedediah Smith, arrived at the San Gabriel Mission, near Los Angeles, the first American to reach California overland, from the East. After a very short stay, Smith headed north for some 300 miles into the mountains. There he spent the winter and rejoined his partners in the fur trade at Salt Lake in the summer of the following year.

The year 1839 was an important one for California, for it marked the arrival of John Augustus Sutter in San Francisco, from Honolulu. He had come from Switzerland to New York as an immigrant in 1834. Since that time he had followed the Santa Fe and the Oregon Trails; he had worked for the Hudson's Bay Company in Canada and for the Russian American Company in Sitka, Alaska. Attracted by stories of the rich soil, Sutter came to California with dreams of building up an agricultural and cattle empire.

A year after his arrival, Sutter was authorized by Governor Juan Alvarado to build Sutter's Fort on the site where the city of Sacramento stands today. The following year he bought out the interests of the Russian American Company at Fort

Ross, California. In January, 1842, the Russians withdrew completely from California and confined their activities to Alaska.

Commodore Thomas Jones, commander of the United States Pacific Squadron, added a comic opera touch to California history in 1842. On October 19, receiving an erroneous report that his country and Mexico were at war, Jones seized Monterey. The bewildered citizens surrendered without a fight. The flag of the United States was raised over the city. Two days later, the hasty and overzealous commodore learned of his mistake. He returned Monterey to Mexico with profuse apologies, lowered the American flag, and raised the Mexican standard, which he saluted.

The first wagon train from the east (Missouri) to reach California arrived at Fort Sutter in December, 1844, carrying Elisha Stevens and a party of fifty men, women, and children in twelve wagons.

Despite the hostility toward Americans and the frank attitude that they were not welcome in California, immigrants gradually drifted in, attracted by the climate, soil, abundance of grazing land for cattle, and the many fur-bearing animals. By 1845, there were more Americans than Spanish Californians in many sections of the state.

In 1845, Thomas Larkin, then consular agent for the United States in Monterey, California, made overtures for the purchase of California. His offers were abruptly rejected. Feeling between Mexico and the United States over the Texas question was tense. In September, an order was issued that no more Americans would be allowed to enter California and that those already there would be required to leave by the following spring.

American pioneer farmers and trappers in Sacramento Valley, who already disliked and mistrusted the Mexican officials, were highly indignant. They talked freely of taking action. There were rumors that the Mexican government intended to massacre them. On June 14, 1846, a group of twenty-four Americans in Sonoma took General Vallejos prisoner. They hauled down the Mexican flag, and raised their own standard. It was a homemade flag made of a piece of light cloth with the figure of a bear painted on it with berry juice, as no paint was available. There was great cheering as the Bear Flag of the Independent California Republic went up.

Just before these events occurred, Fremont traveled up and down California getting firsthand information. He asked the Mexican authorities for permission to purchase supplies for an extended stay. His request was grudgingly granted. A short time after, in March, 1846, while Fremont was camped on the Hartnell Ranch, 25 miles from Salinas, a company of Mexican cavalry rode up and the Americans were ordered to leave California on instructions from General José Castro. Fremont was indignant. He told the officer that he had been offered the protection of Castro and that he would leave when he was ready, and not before.

Not satisfied with verbal defiance, Fremont erected a small fort at Gavilan Peak. There he raised the American flag and prepared to resist the expulsion order of General Castro. Three days later, he abandoned the fort and retired to Sutter's Fort on the American River.

After a while, Fremont thought it wise to lead his small army outside California territory. But he did not go far—just north of the border into Oregon Territory. He kept a sharp watch on the trend of events, fearing that serious trouble would break out at any time. If it did, he knew that England would be only too eager to declare California a protectorate of the British Empire. This action would be based on the 250-year-old claim of Sir Francis Drake. Fremont had no authority to act. He felt, however, that since he was on the scene with a semimilitary force, it was his duty to protect American citizens living in California.

Early in May, 1846, Lieutenant Gillespie of the United States Marines arrived with dispatches for Fremont. Whether among those dispatches were secret verbal orders authorizing Fremont to look out for the interests of the United States, is not known. Lieutenant Gillespie, after a long and arduous journey climaxed by an Indian attack at night, found Fremont camped on the edge of Lake Klamath. Gillespie had left Washington early in November, 1845, and gone by way of Vera Cruz, Mexico City, then across Mexico to the Pacific port of Mazatlán; from there by boat to Honolulu, and from Honolulu to Monterey, a journey of more than six months.

It has been said that Lieutenant Gillespie may have had verbal instructions for Fremont to take action in California. That he painted a grave picture of the strained relations between the United States and Mexico over the Texas question, there can be no doubt. But whatever the reason, Fremont gathered his men and retraced his steps into California. At Sutter's Fort he heard of the Bear Flag revolt in Sonoma. With a force of 160 men he went to the aid of the Californian patriots. That was in the latter part of June, 1846. Although a state of war actually did exist, neither Fremont nor anyone in California knew of it. Fremont gave as his reason for taking military action that British men-of-war were lying off San Francisco, awaiting the first opportunity to take control of California. Fremont took a great gamble. If he was wrong, it meant disgrace and the end of his career.

On July 2, 1846, Fremont and a small party of men crossed San Francisco Bay to Fort Point. They seized El Castillo de San Joaquin, spiked the guns, and took supplies and ammunition. On the return trip, Fremont took time from more weighty matters to give the name Golden Gate to the magnificent entrance to San Francisco Bay.

From this action of Fremont's was born his California Battalion. It was a strange army composed of an odd assortment of trappers, scouts, sailors, farmers, and ranchers, willing fighters and expert marksmen. As Fremont was about to march south against the Mexican forces, the long-awaited news reached him that war had been declared and that United States warships were in California waters. Actually, President Polk had declared that a state of war between the United States and Mexico existed on May 13, 1846, but even such exciting news was many months in reaching California.

On the day when Fremont and his men crossed San Francisco Bay, Commodore Sloat of the United States Pacific Squadron reached Monterey and took possession, raising the American flag and sending instructions that San Francisco also be seized. Sloat, who had acted so quickly because he had heard of Fremont's actions, was amazed to hear that Fremont had received no direct orders to take military steps in California. Sloat retired from the scene of action, leaving Commodore R. F. Stockton in charge. Stockton and Fremont joined forces and made ready for a concerted attack on General Castro, who was at Los Angeles with 500 Mexican soldiers.

To accomplish this plan, Fremont's battalion was taken into naval service and went to sea in the sloop *Cyane*. During the voyage to San Diego, Kit Carson and most of the other Mountain Men suffered terribly from seasickness. Landing at San Diego, they marched on General Castro and easily defeated his army. On August 13, 1846, the Americans entered Los Angeles, and with a brass band at their head, paraded through the streets to receive the acclaim of the people.

About the same time, General Stephen W. Kearny was marching toward California with 2,000 men of his Army of the West, to take California from Mexico. At Sante Fe, during the latter part of August, General Kearny met Kit Carson, who was on his way to Washington with news of the defeat of Mexican forces in California. Carson told the general that the conquest had been accomplished by Stockton and Fremont. As a result, General Kearny released all his army except 100 dragoons and commanded Carson to guide him from

Santa Fe to Los Angeles. In reducing his forces, Kearny made a mistake. He had no way of knowing it, but after Carson left California for the East, the Mexicans gained the upper hand over the small American forces. When Kearny reached California territory in December, 1846, he was attacked by Mexicans at San Pasqual, some 40 miles from San Diego. His small force of dragoons were beaten by the Mexicans and surrounded. The plan of the Mexicans was to starve Kearny's outfit into surrender. Fortunately, a young American, Edward Beale, and an Indian boy managed to slip through the enemy lines to San Diego, where they told Stockton about Kearny's plight. Stockton sent immediate relief.

On January, 10, 1847, Los Angeles was reconquered by the United States forces and the American flag raised. From that day on, the war to all intents and purposes was over in California, although the Treaty of Guadalupe Hidalgo, ending the conflict between the United States and Mexico, was not signed until February 2, 1848. By this treaty, New Mexico, California, Nevada, Utah, most of Arizona, and part of Colorado were ceded to the United States on the payment of 15 million dollars. When California was admitted to the Union as a state in 1850, Fremont was elected one of the first two United States Senators, the other being William Gwin.

Although not directly connected with the story being told here, a drama that was played in the Mormon colony at Salt Lake in Utah is so unusual and interesting that it deserves mention. The Mormons had come from Nauvoo, on the Mississippi River, in Illinois, through Iowa, Nebraska, and Wyoming to settle on the shores of the Great Salt Lake in the summer of 1847, under the leadership of Brigham Young.

The first winter for the Mormons was a hard one, and the coming of spring saw their food supply all but exhausted. There was no flour for bread, and the grains and roots they had were needed for the planting of crops. The Mormons lived on a not-too-nourishing diet of beef, milk, pigweeds, segoes, and thistles, with not very much of any one of the items. But they worked the fields, cleared away the sagebrush, and planted their crops. Irrigation ditches were dug to bring water to the thirsty land. As the months passed, the grain grew.

Then came the crickets. They came swarming down from the hills by the millions. Like a big, black river, they flooded the land, crawling, jumping, leaping. They spread over the fields of grain, and ate everything in sight. For weeks, every man, woman, and child in the Mormon colony fought the insect invasion. They turned water into irrigation ditches and drowned them. They built bonfires and burned them. They fought with clubs and brooms. The Mormons prayed as they fought, but it looked as if nothing could save their crops— crops that meant life—from destruction.

It was when they were about to give up hope that ocean birds came to the rescue, sea gulls, flying in by the thousands from the Pacific coast. Like a great cloud they came, casting vast moving shadows over the fields. For miles the sea gulls settled on the ground around the colony and ate the crickets. Every morning for 3 weeks the gulls came flying in to feed on the destructive insects. When these unexpected allies left, the insect plague had been conquered and most of the crops of the Mormons were saved. In Salt Lake City there now stands one of the most unusual monuments in the world. It was erected by Mahonri Young, and is dedicated to the sea gulls that so miraculously delivered the Mormon pioneers from starvation and saved the Salt Lake colony from extinction.

While the Mormons in Utah were recovering from their battle with the crickets, fate was working out the next move of the many pawns on the chessboard of California. The first move was made in the Sacramento Valley, where John Augustus Sutter had received a grant of more than a million acres of land. Through his energy and intelligence, Sutter had developed a settlement with a population of almost 30,000 people. His dream of a great empire of the soil was rudely shattered on Friday, January 28, 1848, when Jim

Marshall came down from Sutter's sawmill with the news that he had found gold.

Sutter told Jim Marshall that he thought it best to keep the discovery quiet. No one knew how much gold there was, he reasoned. If the news leaked out, the whole community would become gold crazy, leaving the crops and orchards to go to waste. It was much better to forget about the gold, Sutter said, and continue as they were, taking the wealth from the soil in the form of crops.

Jim Marshall looked at Sutter in unbelieving amazement. "No," he shouted, "you can't shut the doors on gold!"

Gold! The word spread. Gold! Gold at Sutter's Mill! Gold in the Sacramento Valley. When the news reached San Francisco and Pacific coast towns, the gold rush was on. Sutter had been right when he said that men would abandon crops and orchards for the lure of gold. They left homes and farms, stores and families. Crews deserted their ships. Before the end of the year, there were 600 crewless boats in San Francisco harbor. It took 7 months for the news to reach New York, where it was not believed at first. Not until December 5, 1848, when President Polk confirmed the news of a California gold strike in his message to Congress, did the gold rush really start.

Gold! Gold at Sacramento! Gold in California! The cry rang out through the nation. By ship and prairie schooner the gold seekers came. By horse and mule. On foot. The voyage around Cape Horn of many months was too slow for the impatient gold seekers. They swarmed across the Isthmus of Panama. Across Nicaragua. In the first year of the rush, 1849, more than 42,000 prospectors poured into Sacramento Valley.

Some of the forty-niners struck it rich, fabulously rich. But more were lucky if they made a living. The average income for a Sacramento prospector was only $8 a day. Many of them never made even that much, and a man needed money to live—much money. There were no bargain prices during the gold-rush days. Eggs cost $6 a dozen; shirts $40 a piece; milk $1 a quart; and flour $2 a pound.

Then the gold began to thin out. Some of those who had struck it rich stayed rich, but most of them lost or spent their sudden wealth. Large numbers of people were stranded, luck-less souls who had not even cash enough to get home.

Among those who were ruined by the gold rush was Sutter. One would have thought that with all that gold on his lands, Sutter would have become a multimillionaire. Instead, ruin descended upon him when the thousands upon thousands of gold-hungry forty-niners poured into the valley, and swept away his dream. At the very beginning, his farm hands, carpenters, trappers, and shopkeepers quit their jobs. Why work for wages, they asked, when there was gold to be had for the taking?

When the gold rush really got under way, Sutter faced a greater battle against the swarms of gold diggers that invaded his realm than the Mormons ever had against the crickets. And there were no sea gulls to save Sutter. Among those who looked for gold were men of all sorts, including thieves and bandits. From Sutter they stole 10,000 horses, 12,000 head of cattle, and 15,000 sheep and hogs. There was no one to stop the lawlessness. There was no police protection of any kind. Even the soldiers of the United States Army in California deserted to join the gold rush. Eventually the miners them-selves united to establish a rough system of law and order of their own, but by that time, Sutter had been ruined.

Sutter began to hate gold. It seemed to bring him only bad luck. He financed gold diggers who cheated him. Gold lost him everything he had. Sutter was one of the foremost pioneers in California and he played an important role in the early growth and development of the state. He was generous, help-ful, and honest. Yet he died a poor old man in Washington, in 1880. It has been said that he died of a broken heart.

The great Comstock Lode, one of the richest streaks of pay

dirt in the world, was discovered on Sun Mountain in Nevada, in 1859. In the course of 16 years, more than 300 million dollars' worth of silver was taken out of that one vein alone. The Comstock Lode had really been discovered several years before by two brothers, Allen and Hosea Grosch, from Utica, New York. They came out to Sun Mountain in 1851 to prospect for gold. Year after year they kept up their search. They found little gold but a lot of "blue stuff" that looked like petrified clay. They tested this peculiar ore with chemicals they had brought along from the East. Settlers told them that there was no gold in Sun Mountain, and that the "blue stuff" was just a lot of worthless junk. The two young men did not give up. They kept on looking and in 1857 they struck what they were after, but they kept their secret. They wanted to make sure that their find was what they thought it was. But they kept their secret too well. Both died, one from blood poisoning and the other in a blizzard. Their secret died with them.

What the Grosch brothers had learned was that the worthless "blue stuff" was rich silver. Their great discovery, which they did not live to enjoy, was the fabulous Comstock Lode.

With the Comstock strike, came the wonder days of Virginia City, where miners worked hard and played harder. Virginia City gave birth to such powerful financiers as Mackay, Flood, Hearst, and Sutro. It also gave birth to many colorful characters such as Eilley Orru, whose meteoric career from poverty to riches and back to poverty makes her one of the most interesting women of the early days of the West. Lastly, but far from least, Virginia City gave birth to the famous *Enterprise* newspaper and the journalistic career of Samuel Clemens, who later on was to be known wherever the words of men are read as Mark Twain.

For a while, Virginia City boomed with all the boisterous clamor of a mining town. Then the metal output diminished. Soon Virginia City became a ghost city and the brilliant days of Sun Mountain ended in the twilight of obscurity.

After the Nevada bonanza days, came Colorado's turn, where both gold and silver were discovered at about the same time, giving rise to a brief but lusty boom.

Next came the cry of gold in Montana, in 1861, drawing miners from the other diggings that were beginning to give out. A few more became rich, while others either settled down to ranching or went on to new fields. Then there was the Adler Gulch mine, which yielded 25 million dollars' worth of gold in 3 years. But again it was the same story; for every man who struck it rich, dozens found nothing. As a result of the Adler Gulch strike, hundreds of disappointed miners settled down as farmers in Idaho and near-by localities.

The powerful magnet of gold and silver is what drew people to the West to seek their fortunes. Some came back East as rich as Moguls. But most of them stayed, by the tens of thousands, to live their lives in the West. The settling of the West was well under way before the Civil War was over. When the country returned to normal at the end of the war, the call of the West was heard and heeded by thousands more who wanted opportunity rather than the glittering and often false promises of gold.

CHAPTER 26

Wheels Roll Westward

State	Settled	Entered Union	Capital	Population	Area, square miles
Arkansas	1685	1836	Little Rock	1,948,268	53,335
Iowa	1778	1846	Des Moines	2,535,430	56,147
Kansas	1727	1861	Topeka	1,799,137	82,158
Missouri	1764	1821	Jefferson City	3,775,737	69,420
Montana	1809	1889	Helena	554,136	146,997
Nebraska	1847	1867	Lincoln	1,313,468	77,520
North Dakota	1780	1889	Bismarck	639,690	70,837
Oklahoma	1889	1907	Oklahoma City	2,329,808	70,057
South Dakota	1794	1889	Pierre	641,134	77,615
Wyoming	1834	1890	Cheyenne	246,763	97,914

IT has been said that the greatest single contribution to the progress of man was the invention of the wheel. Certainly there is ample evidence that the swift development, expansion, and growth of North America was largely made possible through rapidly improving means of transportation and quick communication.

The earliest permanent settlers on the Atlantic coast were at first confined along the coast because there was no way for them to penetrate the wilderness of the vast and unknown continent on whose eastern edge they clung. Couriers of the woods, brave missionaries, and hardy men who ventured upon unchartered trails and waterways by foot or in primitive canoes, served only to increase the impatience of the coast-bound groups. As time passed and the Indian trails widened and took the form of roads, the urge to go west began to find an outlet, however small.

In this New World, amid hostile red men, the business of keeping alive occupied most of the time of the early settlers; but as they became accustomed to their surroundings, they found time to extend the roads and copy the coaches of Europe. The roads were rough and rutted and the carriages were crude and uncomfortable, but they marked the beginning of North American transportation. Soon roads and coach routes connected several coastal communities.

New westward avenues of travel by land and water began to open up. There was the Mohawk Trail westward through New York and the Wilderness Trail pioneered by Daniel Boone through Cumberland Gap into the Ohio Valley. Flatboats and barges soon carried freight and settlers down the Ohio and into the Mississippi. But nature does not always design her waterways to meet the needs of man's urge to seek new horizons. Therefore to supplement nature's waterways, the construction of man-made waterways, canals, was begun.

Canal projects took form in many sections of the country, but most of them were of purely local interest until George Washington made a definite campaign for a canal to link the Ohio Valley with the Atlantic seaboard. Washington appreciated the enormous potential value of western territory. He had begun his travels, horseback and afoot, at the age of sixteen, as a surveyor on Lord Fairfax's vast Appalachian Mountain domain in Virginia. Washington was one of those rare men who actually see what they look at; who observe, analyze, and remember.

As he journeyed up the Potomac, down the Monongahela, and over the trails, Washington's photographic eye saw the great wealth of these far places. He tried to convince Governor Dinwiddie of Virginia of the importance to England of westward expansion and the need of transportation facilities to bring it about. But the governor paid no heed to what he termed the visionary ideas of an enthusiastic boy of twenty-two. Washington kept trying. Even his arduous labors in the Revolution did not make him forget the project. On his return to Virginia after the Revolutionary War, he again took up his work in favor of transportation facilities to the west.

About 1785, Washington's efforts bore fruit. He saw work begin on a canal, just above the city of Washington, at Great Falls, marking the first corporate work in America on an improvement of navigation for public use.

From then on slow transportation progress was made in the United States; but it was progress, despite floods, inexperience, lack of money, and insufficient public interest in canals or in transportation in general. The history of American canal projects would fill several volumes. Before canals really came into their own, steamboats made their appearance, revolutionizing water travel as their churning paddle wheels rapidly cut both the time and cost of travel. The paddle wheels of river boats were important among the wheels by which migration moved westward.

Although Robert Fulton is generally associated with the first steamboat in the United States, a watchmaker by the name of John Fitch was experimenting with steamboats as early as 1785 in Pennsylvania. By 1790, Fitch had established a regular passenger service on the Delaware River, but owing to the lack of financial backing, this first steamship line was a failure. It was Robert Fulton's *Clermont* that proved the practicability of steamboat travel when, on August 17, 1807, it puffed its way from New York to Albany, a distance of about 150 miles, in 32 hours. That was the beginning of the steam era, not only on the Hudson, but on other rivers in America. The paddle wheels were pushing toward western horizons.

In the days before steam there was much transportation on the Ohio, Mississippi, and other inland waterways, but it was nearly all one-way traffic. The flatboats, barges, and scows then in use could float downstream, but it was a slow, almost superhuman task to pole or tow the heavy boats upstream against the current. In most cases, the flatboats and barges were broken up and sold for lumber at the end of the voyage, while the boatmen walked back home.

With the coming of the steamboat, all that was changed. From one-way avenues, the inland waterways changed into arterial highways that stimulated the expansion and growth of the Middle West. The first quarter of the nineteenth century saw the tide of westward travel swell at an amazing rate. The Great Migration began after the War of 1812. Waves of settlers flooded the Ohio Basin. Covered wagons and coaches and freight wagons rolled over rutty trails farther west. Caravans of settlers streamed across the country in all sorts and types of conveyances. The most famous vehicle of that day was the Conestoga wagon. It was built almost like a boat on wheels and was pulled by a six-horse team.

It was not until 1825, when steamships already sailed the large inland rivers, that the completion of the Erie Canal furnished the most important link of that era between the East and the West. Men of New York [state] had long dreamed of a water connection between the Hudson River and the Great Lakes. They knew that such a link would not only serve the state, but the growing new nation. In 1807, Jesse Hawley proposed a canal from the Hudson River to Lake Erie. The matter was argued in the Albany legislature with little result. When Federal funds were sought, President Jefferson declared the idea was presented a hundred years too soon. "Build a canal 350 miles long, through the wilderness? It is little short of madness to think of it!" he said.

Through the following years, the Erie Canal was a bone of contention from one end of the state of New York to the other. Sectional jealousies, partisanship, petty politics, and selfish interest held the canal project back until July 4, 1817. Then, at Rome, New York, the first shovel of earth was lifted in a ceremony beginning one of America's biggest jobs, the digging of the Erie Canal.

It took courage for New York to assume the burden of paying for a canal that finally cost nearly 8 million dollars. At the time there was not even a stage line between Albany and Buffalo, so thin was the population in western New York. Only the vital force and thorough conviction of Governor De Witt Clinton of New York brought the project into reality. The canal was scorned from one end of the state to the other as "Clinton's Folly!"

But the building of the canal went forward, in drama and triumph. In June, 1825, the gates of Black Rock Lock near Buffalo were opened and the waters of Lake Erie flowed eastward. The Erie Canal was now an accomplishment, no longer a dream.

Not only did "Clinton's Ditch" open traffic with the Middle West, but it changed New York from a relatively unimportant town to one of the richest cities in the New World. No other man-made waterway ever exerted the influence on a nation that was the direct result of the Erie Canal. It fixed the destiny of villages, towns, cities, and states; it directed and regulated the movements of entire populations.

Before the advent of the Erie Canal, it cost $100 to move a ton of goods from Buffalo to New York, and required 20 days in transport. On the canal the cost was $10, with time in transit cut to 8 days. This was a boon to urban and rural dweller alike. The consumer paid less; the producer sold more. Everybody benefited. Freight boats soon accommodated passengers. From mixed cargoes of men and merchandise it was but a step to express Packet Boats, with passenger fares fixed at 3½ cents per mile, meals at 2 shillings each. Keen rivalry cut these prices later, with "elegance" the keynote in advertising.

Measured by present-day standards, the elegance of a canal barge some 80 feet long and only 11 feet wide, with only the most primitive concessions made for comfort, would be open to question. A tall man could not stand in the cabin without bumping his head. The typical packet was built like the Ark, with but one deck, which happened to be the roof. The main cabin was saloon and dining room by day, and dormitory by night. When bedtime came, all passengers had to climb to the upper deck and wait there while the bunks were made up for night, each bunk being a narrow wood and metal frame with a strip of canvas fastened over it, in three-high tiers. Choice locations were often drawn by lot, or perhaps assigned in alphabetical order.

Urged on by the success of the Erie, canal companies sprang up all over the country. So many man-made waterways were proposed that it seemed as if the continent would be cut up by canals.

Even before the canal boom reached its peak in the Erie Canal, many forward-looking citizens were discussing a "contraption" invented over in England by a man named Stephenson. This man, so it was reported, had put a sort of "teakettle on wheels" with enough power to pull a "wagon on rails." Man's impatience, his desire for speed and yet more speed, made promoters turn to Stephenson's idea. They wanted to give the "railroad" a trial.

The first railways in America were drawn by horses and they were used to haul heavy construction material. One of the earliest of these was built in 1826 to carry stone for the Bunker Hill monument from quarries at Quincy, Massachusetts. The Baltimore and Ohio Railroad, chartered in 1827, was the first steam railroad to start operation in the United States. In 1830, a race was staged between Peter Cooper's famous *Tom Thumb* locomotive and a horse-drawn train. The course was over 6 miles of parallel track, and although *Tom Thumb* developed a speed of $\frac{1}{8}$ mile an hour, the horse-drawn vehicle won. But the steam railroad advocates were not discouraged. In 1830, locomotive factories were built and the laying of rails began in earnest. Chartered in 1828, the South Carolina Railroad put into service the first successful American-constructive locomotive, the *Best Friend*. It ran between Charleston and Hamburg, South Carolina, a distance of 135½ miles, the longest railroad in the world at the time.

The coaches of the early railroads were built like stagecoaches. The engines burned wood. The heavy smoke and constant showers of sparks and cinders made travel in an open railroad carriage a trying experience. There were no telegraph or automatic signals to control traffic. As there were no brakes, the train crew would jump to the ground on coming into a station and slow the train down with main strength until it came to a stop. Since almost every railroad line had a different width track, there could be no transfer of rolling stock from one line to another, even when they did meet. Goods had to be transferred by hand. But despite obstacles and setbacks, the railroads expanded. From 13 miles of railroad track in operation in 1827, there were 2,818 miles in 1840, and 9,021 in 1850. But all this was in the East. As late as 1840, there was not a single mile of rail west of Detroit.

Pioneers who ventured into the West beyond the ends of rail and road had learned to build a vehicle suited to their needs, the so-called prairie schooner. It took its name from the fact that it was shaped like a boat, and made watertight so that the immigrant could ford streams without getting his poor belongings wet. There were neither bridges nor ferries in those days, and journeys to the West were undertaken only by men and women of stout hearts, able to combat the elements. Mud, sand, rain, the scorching sun, high water, deserts, mountains, and snow, all seemed to defy western colonization. But determined pioneers guided their ox-drawn covered wagons over the Oregon and other trails to the West.

As the openhanded bounty of the vast sunset country revealed itself to the pioneers, they realized that they had found a realm of unlimited opportunity. They selected their lands, built homes, and planned for the future. Slowly towns and villages sprang up, and with the development of agriculture and cattle raising, commerce expanded. Being 2,000 or 3,000 miles from the centers of trade was a handicap, although not too serious a one for the homesteaders. They were self-reliant. They raised what food they needed to eat. They were their own carpenters, bricklayers, and blacksmiths. The demands of the women for manufactured goods were few. It was a leisurely settling and opening up of a new country. There was no rush about it. A horse and wagon could take a man and his family as fast and as far as he wanted to go, to the nearest town or to visit a neighbor.

Then, out of the blue, came the California gold strike. The forty-niners began their rush to the Pacific coast, and they could not get there fast enough. While the wagon trails were all right for settlers, they were too long and slow for eager gold seekers. To get to California more quickly the prospectors headed south and crossed from east to west across Nicaragua or the Isthmus of Panama. Heavy merchandise had to be taken by boat the long, slow, and dangerous way around Cape Horn. Transportation, fast transportation across the continent suddenly became an urgent need.

Gold poured from California in a steady yellow stream eastward, affecting the economic structure of the whole nation. From an ancient but unimportant agricultural Mexican province, California suddenly became a young but important commercial state in the Union. But it still remained a remote land toward the sunset.

While it is true that railroads by this time had made forward strides in the Middle West, the common carrier in the Far West was still the stagecoach—slow, clumsy, and bone shaking. Traveling day and night, the stagecoach trip from Saint Louis to San Francisco could be made in 23 uncomfortable days. While a transcontinental railroad had been discussed before the Civil War, it was a tremendous project that took time and money.

The growing population and the growing business activity in California and along the Pacific coast began to demand better communication, especially better mail service.

In the world of transportation mail always travels fastest. To bring the mail through in record time came the pony express. Although short-lived, this service speeded up the mail between California and Saint Louis and points east.

The pony express was devised by W. H. Russel in 1860 to carry mail between the Mississippi River and California. Pony-express riders had 72-mile runs over which they rode at breakneck speed. Every 24 miles, a rider would reach a relay station, jump from his exhausted horse, clutch his precious mailbags, and jump into the saddle of a fresh horse held ready for him. A pony rider who took more than forty or fifty seconds to dismount, transfer himself and the mail from winded horse to remount, was wasting time. It cost $5 a half ounce to send mail by pony express and it took ten days for a letter to get from Saint Louis to California. The need for fast communication with the West brought the pony express into being and the advent of even faster communication sounded its death knell in November, 1861, when the telegraph reached the west coast. Almost instantly, the clicking of dots and dashes replaced galloping hoofs.

But swift communication was not enough of a link between the East and the rapidly growing West. Only speedy transportation could satisfy man's urge to get where he wanted to go in a hurry. The isolation of California had to be ended with bands of steel between the west coast and the east. The pioneer in that effort was Theodore D. Judah.

As early as 1854, Judah went to San Francisco from New York to help build the Sacramento Valley Railroad. While surveying, Judah found a pass in the Sierra Nevadas suitable for a railroad across the mountain barrier. He went to Washington in 1859, where his plan for a transcontinental railroad met with approval. Returning to California, he tried to inter-est local capitalists, but without success. It was not until 1861 that he gained the support of four men who joined him in organizing the Central Pacific Railroad Company. These men were from varied walks of life: Charles Crocker, a miner and trader; Mark Hopkins and C. P. Huntington, merchants; and Leland Stanford, a New York lawyer who had migrated west.

As the moving spirit behind the venture, Judah again went to Washington, where he secured financial help for the rail-road. The government would pay $16,000 a mile for level track, $32,000 a mile for upgrades, and $48,000 a mile for mountain construction. He also obtained a government grant for the company of twenty sections of public land for each mile of rails laid down.

The Central Pacific Railroad Company began actual work of construction on January 8, 1863, in California on the western end of a railway line that was to be joined with an-other railroad project, the Union Pacific, running west from Omaha, Nebraska.

Railroad construction slowed down during the Civil War, but the war did serve the purpose of showing the vital need for a transcontinental railroad. The gold rush had started things, but as the years passed the realization came that transporta-tion and communication with every part of the United States was essential to national unity. When peace came to the coun-try, railroad construction in the West speeded up, and it was a race in which brain and brawn, picks and rifles, all had their share.

As the singing rails pushed across the land, the problem of feeding the army of big-muscled men who handled the iron and steel and swung the sledges became more acute. Much fresh meat was needed, for men who work hard cannot live on salted or dried meat. This need brought into prominence a character who has become almost legendary: William F. Cody, better known as Buffalo Bill.

Cody, a former pony-express rider, knew the plains as few men knew them when he undertook to supply fresh meat for the workers on the Union Pacific. The buffalo was to be his source of supply. At this time, when the railroad was well under way, about 50 million buffalo roamed the western plains. They had been seen in herds so large that they could not be counted, herds that were 10 miles wide and 10 miles long.

The habits of the buffalo, or North American bison, were fixed. In summer, the buffalo browsed on the northern prairies, but in winter, the herds moved southward by the millions. Herd migrations were usually headed by wise old cows, while the bulls moved on the outer edges of the herd to protect the cows and calves from wolves, coyotes, and bears.

As the railroad extended into buffalo country, it passed through Indian territory, for the Plains Indian had built his entire existence around the buffalo; the meat was his food, and the buffalo hide furnished his tent home and robes to keep him warm in winter. It is no wonder that the Plains Indian greatly resented the coming of the white man, who took his lands; and the railroad workers, who killed his buffalo. The Indian regarded the lands and the buffalo as his own, for he had held sway over these plains for centuries. As long as the whites had kept moving westward, the Indian was merely annoyed. But with the advent of the railroad and the springing up of permanent settlements along the tracks, the Indian's anger over the destruction of his lands and source of food became so great that he demanded revenge. Thus episodes of western history were written in blood.

Bill Cody killed buffalo for food, but never wantonly. With many professional and amateur hunters, however, buffalo killing assumed the proportions of unrestrained slaughter. As the length of the Union Pacific increased, the number of buffalo decreased and the anger of the Indian rose.

Buffalo Bill estimated that in the first 18 months of his meat contract, he killed approximately 5,000 animals. This earned him a small fixed salary and the name that stuck for life to thrill American boys, Buffalo Bill.

He was somewhat discouraged with his job; he had a secret sympathy with the Indians, for he understood the Indian viewpoint. Cody believed that killing buffalo beef for food was entirely justified, but he deplored the destruction of the great herds in the name of sport. The other side of the story was that the buffalo tended to deprive domestic cattle of range grass. The bison herd also presented a serious problem for the railroad, in that moving herds actually pushed pioneer trains off the tracks. Furthermore, buffalo herds were constantly knocking down telegraph poles and breaking telegraph lines. In short, anything in the way of a buffalo herd, be it man, wagon, engine, train, or telegraph pole, was pushed aside or trampled down. Even when buffalo decided to swim a stream, disaster was ahead for any boat in their way. Lewis and Clark tell how they barely escaped with their lives when their boats happened to be in the path of two buffalo herds swimming across a river.

But neither their threat as a nuisance on the railroad right of way nor their destruction of grasslands needed by domestic cattle can justify the ruthless slaughter of the buffalo. Hundreds of thousands were killed for the mere sport by hunters making a game of seeing how many each man could shoot in a day. The time came when professional hunters killed buffalo weighing from 1,500 to 2,000 pounds merely to cut out the animal's tongue that would net 25 cents in the market. When buffalo hides brought as little as 85 cents, skinning the animals was no longer worth the effort.

This wanton destruction ceased only after Congress became interested in the salvation of the buffalo, whose herds once counted by the millions, had been reduced to fewer than 500 animals in about 30 years.

As the buffalo passed, wheels rolled across the land. Pounding! Thundering! Jubilant! The Union Pacific raced westward with its tracklaying and met the rails of the Central Pacific at Promontory, Utah. Where the rails went and the wheels rolled, men followed, staking out homes, ranches, towns. The great West was being settled. The completion of the Union Pacific was a prelude to the building of the Northern Pacific from Saint Paul to Portland. A year later wheels rolled westward over the Southern Pacific, linking New Orleans with San Francisco.

The alluring song of the singing rails was heard clear across the Atlantic in Europe. Millions of European immigrants came to the United States, "the land of opportunity," and headed westward. Waves of Irish, Danes, Swedes, Norwegians, Germans, French, Italians, and English headed for farms in Minnesota, Wisconsin, South Dakota, and on westward. It was the railroad that opened these lands to homesteaders on a large scale.

Railroads extending their rails westward also came to the rescue of one of America's great industries, cattle raising. After the Civil War, Texas found itself cattle poor. There were millions of head of Texas longhorns, but no market. Texas cattlemen, with neither money nor credit, faced bankruptcy unless they could find some way of bringing their cattle north, where beef brought good prices. The problem was solved when the Kansas-Pacific Railroad reached Abilene, Kansas, and the McCoy stockyards absorbed tens of thousands of head of Texas cattle for the eastern markets. By 1870, enormous herds of Texas cattle were being driven over the Chisholm and other famous trails to Abilene, Dodge City, and many other famous cattle towns along the railroads.

Cattle must necessarily be raised in sparsely settled country to give the animals sufficient range, but without a means of transportation to get the beef animals to thickly populated centers where there is a market for meat, the rapid growth of the cattle country would have been impossible. The grass-lands of Wyoming and Montana and adjoining states were ideal for cattle. With the coming of the railroad to that part of the West, came the day of the great cattle ranchers and one of the most exciting chapters in the growth of the West. What improved rail transportation did for the cattlemen, it also did for the farmers, fruitgrowers, and others who turned to the soil for a livelihood.

The year 1859 is one of the most important in the history of transportation. That was the year oil was brought in at Titus-ville, Pennsylvania, an event that had an epochal influence on the turning of wheels in every part of the civilized world. The presence of petroleum in the earth had been known for many years. The Indians of Pennsylvania had scooped crude oil from the surface of streams and used it to cure various ills long before the coming of the whites. Learning of these ancient Indian remedies, Medicine Show men gathered oil from de-pressions in the ground and sold it as a cure-all remedy for man and beast. But it remained for Edwin L. Drake to prove that it was possible to drill wells and tap the vast subterranean reservoirs of oil by the barrel, instead of by the bucket.

Like all pathfinders, Drake faced scorn and ridicule before a gusher of oil shot over his crude derrick on an April day in 1859 at Titusville. The subsequent Pennsylvania oil boom rivaled the California gold rush of 10 years before. It was of even greater world-wide importance. Previous to the discovery of petroleum, animal fats and vegetable oils greased the wheels of the commercial world.

With the coming of petroleum came a new era in commerce and transportation. This oil, so cheap and plentiful, literally lighted the road of commercial progress. During the Civil War that followed its discovery so closely, oil created a trade balance for America abroad that actually meant economic salvation for the Union government. With this liquid gold to give them new power and speed, wheels rolled faster and faster. Wilderness country became settled almost overnight. So great was the land rush that free land, the magnet that drew pioneers toward the setting sun, soon became a thing of the past.

One of the most dramatic and colorful land rushes was the Federal land grant in the Red River country. The territory north of the Red River, as far as the Ozarks and taking in the Cimarron region, was known as Oklahoma, meaning the Land of the Red Man. All but a small part of it was closed to white settlers. But the Indians had lost out before in the face of the white man's migration westward. On April 22, 1889, Oklahoma ceased to be an Indian domain. On that day, at the invitation of Congress, homesteaders from all over the country crowded close behind a starting line, impatiently awaiting the signal gun that was to open the territory to settlers.

All were to have an equal chance, but for weeks thousands of eager men and women had been waiting, each figuring how to beat his rival, in the great race to stake claims to the choicest locations. It was to be first come, first served. Soldiers of the United States Army were on hand to see that everyone got fair play and to prevent the more unscrupulous from jumping the starting gun.

Every type was represented in the mass of humanity that thronged the border, straining their ears for the crack of the gun on that April day. The halt, the lame, the blind, the city sharper with his hired sprinter, the bride and groom whose last dollar had been invested in a horse they hoped would run them to a good section, and whole families with all their worldly possessions stowed in prairie schooners.

As the moment neared, they were all in place, keyed up to the tensity of a line-up of race horses. Then came the long-awaited signal. They were off in a thundering cloud of dust, racing madly, shouting and yelling and urging their animals on. Ahead were the sleek horses with riders; then the mules and burros and light carriages. Next, rumbling and rattling and swaying from side to side, rolled the cumbersome covered wagons. Straggling in the rear, came those on foot, hoping against hope that they would not be too late.

The Oklahoma run is one of the human epics in American history. Before dark on that April 22, 1889, hundreds of home sites had been staked out. Towns sprang up, two of them, Guthrie and Oklahoma City, before the dawn of a new day. And as these first settlers found the land good and rich, others came flocking in. Within a year the Oklahoma of the Indians, a wild expanse of prairie and woodlands, had become the settled Oklahoma Territory of the white man.

At first only the western half of the region was included in the new Oklahoma Territory, but as the years passed, the government bought more and more land from the Indians, opening it up to homesteaders. Later the whole territory was united, and on November 16, 1907, Oklahoma was admitted to the Union as the forty-sixth State.

Before that time, however, in 1890, oil was discovered in the eastern half of Oklahoma, which was still Indian Territory. When the real oil boom came eleven years later, it made many of the Oklahoma Indians rich. Even today, the property owned by some 90,000 Oklahoma Indians, mostly members of the Five Tribes, is said to be worth more than a quarter of a billion dollars.

As transportation and communication became adequate, the bountiful wealth of the West enriched the life of the entire nation. In the hundred-odd years since America had only a few hundred miles of railroad, it has increased its rail mileage to more than 245,000 miles of track on continental North America. Canada has over 42,000 miles of railroad, and the rest of the Americas boast some 80,000 miles.

The building of canals suffered by the success of the "iron horse." But transportation, like other things, moves in cycles. Canals are more in demand today than ever before. It has always remained true that water transportation for both man and his goods is cheaper, dollar for dollar, pound for pound, than any other method.

Today there are plans to cut a canal across Nicaragua in Central America. A ship canal is proposed to cross the state of Florida. The Saint Lawrence-Great Lakes waterway project is again a lively issue.

Man, who began on foot, has speeded up his many forms of travel. Yet he is still demanding more speed and yet more speed. His surface transportation would seem highly adequate at the moment, with wheels spinning in every direction on his myriad networks of iron rails and his countless thousands of concrete highways where millions of motor vehicles serve him, thanks to the by-products of Drake's well, and their like the world over.

But having won the West by means of quickly turning wheels, man looks for new worlds to conquer for the benefit of his fellows. Americans believed that they had conquered the West. But quite recently, pioneer-minded men glanced toward the Columbia River, up in the northwest corner of the United States. There they saw a challenge to the claim that nothing was left to be conquered. Centuries upon centuries ago, the mighty Columbia River had been dammed by a gigantic glacier which forced the river to cut a new channel at right angles to the present course. The glacier then receded toward the Arctic, leaving behind a deep and arid valley.

Why not replace the ancient ice barrier, asked engineers, with a man-made barrier of concrete? The waters so dammed up could be used for irrigation, making fertile the dry and useless lands of the valley. A survey was made in the face of opposition from men who said that the very idea of man trying to harness the Columbia River was impossible and fantastic. But the growth of the west is one long saga of men with vision and determination bringing to reality the impossible and fantastic. And so the Grand Coulee Dam project was born.

To tame the roaring Columbia a huge wall of concrete, larger than anything built by men before, was needed. When it was finished, it was the width of two city blocks at its base. Eleven million cubic yards of concrete went into it, enough concrete to cover a motor highway from Jersey City to Seattle and back again by way of Los Angeles.

As the work progressed, wheels rolled toward Grand Coulee. Thousands of trucks loaded with beans, beef, ham, pork, fruits, and vegetables went in an endless stream to the great kitchens. On one Sunday morning, 3,000 pancakes were served to the workmen in the huge mess hall. And while the men who were building a new monument to progress ate, a ton of turkey was being prepared for the roasting ovens. Day after day, month after month, year after year, food and materials rolled westward as the men kept building. When they were finished, a dam 560 feet high, 400 feet long, and 500 feet thick was ready to test its strength against the might of the Columbia's torrent. And to turn the force of water into power to turn wheels of industry and to put into the operation the wheels of tractors and farm machinery, eight huge generators were installed at Grand Coulee, each requiring a fifty-car freight train to haul its unassembled parts. And behind this monster of concrete can be held a reserve of water to supply 2,000 gallons of water for every human being on earth.

But more than the pouring of concrete went into the making of the Grand Coulee Dam. Whole towns had to be moved. Railroads had to be rerouted. As far as 100 miles away bridges had to be elevated above the rising waters. A big job, but well worth it. In years to come, Grande Coulee will furnish water enough to reclaim some 50,000 acres of unproductive land each year, until a grand total of 1,200,000 acres of arid land have been made to grow green with the magic touch of irrigation. When this latest of the western frontiers has been conquered, an area of 1,965 square miles, or an equivalent of the area of the state of Delaware, will have been added to the nation's productive land. Thus, the wheels of transportation and industry will virtually have added another star to our flag.

In 1903, there was only one airplane in the world, and it flew only 120 feet. Today huge transport air lines cross the continent in a dozen hours and fly in steady service among the Americas. They have enabled man to make a new conquest— the conquest of distance with the shining sword of speed.

But speed is relative. The fastest thing man has at the moment is the fastest thing there is.

What could be faster than an airplane? Another airplane! Dream planes on blueprints today are the swifter planes in the blue air tomorrow. Coming up behind those swifter planes, there may be even swifter rockets: mail rockets, freight rockets, passenger rockets, flashing with the speed of a wish from north to south and east and west linking every part of the Americas.

To summarize: the swift development, expansion, and growth of North America, Central America, and South America was made possible by and will continue through increasingly rapid means of transportation and quick communication as well as through other products of human industry and ingenuity. In the automobiles and trucks and busses that travel the highways in every New World country, in the shining rails that spread their network over the Western Hemisphere, in the steamers and barges that move up and down rivers and canals and over ocean lanes, and in the planes that roar over thousands of miles of intercontinental skyways, is the keystone to the unity, prosperity, and community of interest of the people of the Western World.

Four hundred and fifty years ago, Columbus sailed to find the westward water route to the Indies. The New World was first revealed to the great discoverer on the night of October 11, 1492, when through the darkness he saw a flickering light that could mean only one thing: Land! Cannons boomed! Men cheered! And well they might. For that now long-extinguished light of an Indian fire was a signal beacon that led many generations of many men from many lands to a rich and fertile New World, where their descendants, the Americans, have found contentment and security.

General Reading References

AHL, FRANCIS NORENE: *Wings over South America*, Christopher Publishing House, Boston.

BAKER, J. N. L.: *History of Geographical Discovery and Exploration*, Houghton Mifflin Company, Boston.

BROWN, F. MARTIN: *America's Yesterday*, J. B. Lippincott Company, Philadelphia.

Compton's Pictured Encyclopedia, F. E. Compton & Co., Chicago.

COTTERILL, R. S.: *Short History of the Americas*, Prentice-Hall, Inc., New York.

CROWTHERS, SAMUEL: *Romance and Rise of the American Tropics*, Doubleday, Doran & Company, Inc., New York.

EARLY, ELEANOR: *Lands of Delight*, Houghton Mifflin Company, Boston.

FISKE, JOHN: *Discovery of America*, Houghton Mifflin Company, Boston.

GREENBIE, MARJORIE BARSTOW: *American Saga*, Whittlesey House, McGraw-Hill Book Company, Inc., New York.

HARTLEY, LIVINGSTON: *Our Maginot Line*, J. B. Lippincott Company, Philadelphia.

HATHAWAY, ESSE V.: *Romance of the American Map*, Whittlesey House, McGraw-Hill Book Company, Inc., New York.

HERRING, HUBERT: *Good Neighbors, Argentina, Brazil, Chile*, Yale University Press, New Haven.

KIRKPATRICK, F. A.: *Latin America*, The Macmillan Company, New York.

———: *Spanish Conquistadores*, The Macmillan Company, New York.

LATTIMORE, OWEN: *Mongol Journeys*, Doubleday, Doran & Company, Inc., New York.

MASON, GREGORY: *South of Yesterday*, Henry Holt and Company, Inc., New York.

OUTHWAITE, LEONARD: *Unrolling the Map*, The John Day Company, New York.

PERKINS, DEXTER: *Hands Off: A History of the Monroe Doctrine*, Little, Brown & Company, Boston.

ROBERTSON, WILLIAM SPENCE: *Liberators*, D. Appleton-Century Company, Inc., New York.

———: *Rise of the Spanish-American Republics as Told in the Lives of Their Liberators*, D. Appleton-Century Company, Inc., New York.

SANCHEZ, NELLIE V.: *Stories of the Latin American States*, The Thomas Y. Crowell Company, New York.

———: *Stories of the States*, The Thomas Y. Crowell Company, New York.

STEPHENSON, G. M.: *American History to* 1865, Harper & Brothers, New York.

THOMPSON, R. W.: *Land of Tomorrow*, D. Appleton-Century Company, Inc., New York.

TOMLINSON, EDWARD: *New Roads to Riches in the Other Americas*, Charles Scribner's Sons, New York.

UTTING, MATTIE JOHNS: *Day by Day in South America*, Christopher House, Boston.

VERRILL, A. HYATT: *Great Conquerors of South and Central America*, D. Appleton-Century Company, Inc., New York.

WHITAKER, JOHN: *Americas to the South*, The Macmillan Company, New York.

WILGUS, A. CURTIS: *Development of Hispanic America*, Farrar & Rinehart, Inc., New York.

Chapter 1.   Dawn of a New World

ANDREWS, ROY CHAPMAN: *On the Trail of Ancient Man*, Doubleday, Doran & Company, Inc., New York.

———: *This Amazing Planet*, G. P. Putnam's Sons, New York.

CORNPLANTER, JESSE L.: *Legends of the Longhouse*, J. B. Lippincott Company, Philadelphia.

ELLSWORTH, LINCOLN: *Exploring Today*, Dodd, Mead & Company, Inc., New York.

FISKE, JOHN: *Discovery of America*, Houghton Mifflin Company, Boston.

FORESTER, C. S.: *To the Indies*, Little, Brown & Company, Boston.

LOCKWOOD, FRANK C.: *The Apache Indians*, The Macmillan Company, New York.

MADARIAGA, SALVADOR DE: *Christopher Columbus*, The Macmillan Company, New York.

MARSH, R. O.: *The White Indians of Darien*, G. P. Putnam's Sons, New York.

MASON, GREGORY: *Columbus Came Late*, D. Appleton-Century Company, Inc., New York.

MORRIS, ANN AXTELL: *Digging in the Southwest*, Doubleday, Doran & Company, Inc., New York.

VERRILL, A. HYATT: *The American Indians*, D. Appleton-Century Company, Inc., New York.

WISSLER, CLARK: *Indian Calvacade*, Sheridan House, New York.

Chapter 2.   Queen of the Caribbean

BURBANK, LUTHER: *The Harvest of the Years*, Houghton Mifflin Company, Boston.

CLARK, SYDNEY A.: *Cuban Tapestry*, Robert M. McBride & Company, New York.

GIBSON, O. G.: *Isle of a Hundred Harbors*, Bruce Humphries, Inc., Boston.

HOWARD, SIDNEY: *Yellow Jack*, Harcourt, Brace and Company, Inc., New York.

STRODE, HUDSON: *Pageant of Cuba*, Random House, Inc., New York.

VERRILL, A. HYATT: *Foods America Gave the World*, L. C. Page & Co., Boston.

Chapter 3.   *Land of Golden Empires*

BURBANK, ADDISON: *Mexican Frieze*, Coward-McCann, Inc., New York.

FISHER, LILLIAN E.: *Mexico: Beginning of Mexican Independence*, Christopher House, Boston.

GANN, THOMAS: *Glories of the Maya*, Charles Scribner's Sons, New York.

PARKES, HENRY B.: *History of Mexico*, Houghton Mifflin Company, Boston.

PRESCOTT, W. H.: *Conquest of Mexico*, E. P. Dutton & Company, Inc., New York.

SCHURZ, WILLIAM L.: *Manila Galleon*, E. P. Dutton & Company, Inc., New York.

VAILLANT, GEORGE C.: *Aztecs of Mexico*, Doubleday Doran & Company, Inc., New York.

Chapter 4.   *Lands of the Spanish Main*

BLOM, FRANS: *Conquest of Yucatan*, Houghton Mifflin Company, Boston.

BURBANK, ADDISON: *Guatemala Profile*, Coward-McCann, Inc., New York.

GANN, THOMAS: *Discoveries and Adventures in Central America*, Charles Scribner's Sons, New York.

GREENE, LAWRENCE: *The Filibuster: The Career of William Walker*, Bobbs-Merrill Company, Indianapolis.

HALLE, L. J.: *Transcaribbean*, Longmans, Green & Company, New York.

KELLY, JOHN E.: *Pedro de Alvarado, Conquistador*, Princeton University Press, Princeton, N. J.

KELSEY, VERA, and LILLY DE JONGH OSBORNE: *Four Keys to Guatemala*, Funk & Wagnalls Company, New York.

MORRIS, ANN AXTELL: *Digging in Yucatan*, Doubleday, Doran & Company, Inc., New York.

MUNRO, D. G.: *Five Republics of Central America*, Oxford University Press, New York.

ROTHERY, AGNES: *Central America and Spanish Main*, Houghton Mifflin Company, Boston.

WILSON, CHARLES: *Central America*, Henry Holt and Company, Inc., New York.

Chapter 5. Island of Romantic History

DAVIS, H. P.: *Black Democracy*, Dodge Publishing Company, New York.

GRISMER, RAYMOND L.: *Sailing the Spanish Main*, The Macmillan Company, New York.

HURSTON, Z. N.: *Tell My Horse*, J. B. Lippincott Company, Philadelphia.

KNIGHT, MELWIN: *Americans in Santo Domingo*, Vanguard Press, Inc., New York.

NILES, BLAIR: *Black Haiti*, G. P. Putnam's Sons, New York.

STODDARD, T. L.: *French Revolution in San Domingo*, Houghton Mifflin Company, Boston.

VANDERCOOK, J. W.: *Black Majesty: The Life of Christopher, King of Haiti*, Harper & Brothers, New York.

Chapter 6. Stronghold of the Buccaneers

EARLY, ELEANOR: *Ports of the Sun*, Houghton Mifflin Company, Boston.

ESQUEMELING, A. O.: *Buccaneers of America*, E. P. Dutton & Company, Inc., New York.

GARDNER, W. J.: *History of Jamaica*, D. Appleton-Century Company, Inc., New York.

VANDERCOOK, J. W.: *Caribbee Cruise*, Reynal & Hitchcock, Inc., New York.

VERRILL, A. HYATT: *In the Wake of the Buccaneers*, D. Appleton-Century Company, Inc., New York.

Chapter 7. Where East Meets West

BISHOP, F.: *Panama, Past and Present*, D. Appleton-Century Company, Inc., New York.

LEEUW, HENDRIK DE: *Crossroads of the Buccaneers*, J. B. Lippincott Company, Philadelphia.

MICCELDYK, R. A. VAN: *History of Puerto Rico*, D. Appleton-Century Company, Inc., New York.

SIBERT, WILLIAM L., and JOHN F. STEVENS: *Construction of the Panama Canal*, D. Appleton-Century Company, Inc., New York.

WELLS, CARVETH: *Panamexico*, Robert M. McBride & Company, New York.

WHITE, TRUMBULL: *Puerto Rico and Its People*, Frederick A. Stokes Company, New York.

Chapter 8. Land of the Conquistadors

EARLY, ELEANOR: *Ports of the Sun*, Houghton Mifflin Company, Boston.

GRAHAM, CUNNINGHAME: *Conquest of New Granada*, Houghton Mifflin Company, Boston.

HENAO, JESÚS MARÍA: *History of Colombia*, University of North Carolina Press, Chapel Hill.

McFEE, WILLIAM: *Sunlight in New Granada*, Doubleday, Doran & Company, Inc., New York.

MOZANS, H. J.: *Up the Orinoco and Down the Magdalena*, D. Appleton-Century Company, Inc., New York.

NILES, BLAIR: *Land of Miracles*, Grosset & Dunlap, Inc., New York.

Chapter 9.   Cradle of New World Freedom

ALLEN, H. J.: *Venezuela, A. Democracy*, Doubleday, Doran & Company, Inc., New York.

CRANE, JOHN, and PHYLLIS MARSCHALL: *Dauntless Liberator: Simon Bolivar*, D. Appleton-Century Company, Inc., New York.

FERGUSSON, ERNA: *Venezuela*, Alfred A. Knopf, Inc., New York.

KAHN, MORTON C.: *Djuka, The Bush Negroes of Dutch Guiana*, Viking Press, Inc., New York.

MANINGTON, G.: *West Indies, with British Guiana and British Honduras*, Charles Scribner's Sons, New York.

Chapter 10.   Land of Vast Horizons

CALOGERAS, J. P.: *A History of Brazil*, University of North Carolina Press, Chapel Hill.

FLEMING, P.: *Brazilian Adventure*, Charles Scribner's Sons, New York.

HANSON, EARL PARKER: *Journey to Manaos*, Reynal & Hitchock, Inc., New York.

KELSEY, VERA: *Seven Keys to Brazil*, Funk & Wagnalls Company, New York.

WILLIAMS, MARY W.: *Dom Pedro the Magnanimous. Second Emperor of Brazil*, University of North Carolina Press, Chapel Hill.

Chapter 11.   Liberators of the South

BARRETT, W. E.: *Woman on Horseback*, Frederick A. Stokes Company, New York.

DOMBROWSKI, BARONESS KATHARINA: *Land of Women*, Little, Brown & Company, Boston.

GRAHAM, CUNNINGHAME: *Conquest of the River Plate*, Doubleday, Doran & Company, Inc., New York.

HERNANDEZ, J.: *The Gaucho Martin Fierro*, Farrar & Rinehart, Inc., New York.

HUDSON, W. H.: *Purple Land, Uruguay*, E. P. Dutton & Company, Inc., New York.

LEVENE, RICARDO (Translated and edited by W. S. Robertson): *A History of Argentina*, The Greystone Press, Inc., New York.

RONDE, P. DE: *Paraguay, A Gallant Little Nation*, G. P. Putnam's Sons, New York.

SIMPSON, G. G.: *Attending Marvels: A Patagonian Journal*, The Macmillan Company, New York.

WEDDELL, A. W.: *Introduction to Argentina*, The Greystone Press, Inc., New York.

Chapter 12.   Waters of Storm and Stress

COX, ISAAC J.: *A History of Chile*, University of North Carolina Press, Chapel Hill.

ELLIOTT, L. E.: *Chile Today and Tomorrow*, The Macmillan Company, New York.

RIESENBERG, FELIX: *Cape Horn*, Dodd, Mead & Company, Inc., New York.

SCHOELLKOPF, ANNA: *Don Jose de San Martin*, Liveright Publishing Corporation, New York.

ZWEIG, STEPHEN: *Conqueror of the Seas*, Viking Press, Inc., New York.

Chapter 13.   The Realm of the Inca

MEANS, PHILIP A.: *Fall of the Inca Empire*, Charles Scribner's Sons, New York.

MURPHY, R. C.: *Bird Islands of Peru*, G. P. Putnam's Sons, New York.

NILES, BLAIR: *Peruvian Pageant*, Bobbs-Merrill Company, Indianapolis.

POINDEXTER, M.: *Peruvian Pharaohs*, Christopher House, Boston.

PRESCOTT, W. H.: *Conquest of Peru*, E. P. Dutton & Company, Inc., New York.

Chapter 14.   Land on the Roof of America

DUGUID, J.: *Green Hell*, D. Appleton-Century Company, Inc., New York.

HEWETT, E. L.: *Ancient Andean Life*, Bobbs-Merrill Company, Indianapolis.

MEANS, PHILIP A.: *Ancient Civilizations of the Andes*, Charles Scribner's Sons, New York.

OVERBECK, A. O.: *Living High*, D. Appleton-Century Company, Inc., New York.

WALLE, PAUL: *Bolivia*, T. Fisher Unwin, London.

Chapter 15.   Land on the Equator

BEEBE, W.: *Arcturus Adventure*, G. P. Putnam's Sons, New York.

GILL, RICHARD C.: *Volcano of Gold*, Frederick A. Stokes Company, New York.

————: *White Water and Black Magic*, Henry Holt and Company, Inc., New York.

ROBINSON, WILLIAM ALBERT: *Voyage ot Galápagos*, Harcourt, Brace and Company, Inc., New York.

VON HAGEN, VICTOR W.: *Ecuador, the Unknown*, Oxford University Press, New York.

————: *Off with Their Heads*, The Macmillan Company, New York.

Chapter 16. Paradise of the Pacific

CALL, M. P.: *Hawaiian Caprice*, Fortuny's, New York.

GESSLER, CLIFFORD: *Hawaii, Isles of Enchantment*, D. Appleton-Century Company, Inc., New York.

RIESENBERG, FELIX: *The Pacific Ocean*, Whittlesey House, McGraw-Hill Book Company, Inc., New York.

TEMPSKI, ARMINE, VON: *Born in Paradise*, Duell, Sloan & Pearce, Inc., New York.

WALKER, ELIZABETH, and JEANNETTE SPIESS: *Hawaii and the South Seas*, Coward-McCann, Inc., New York.

WITHINGTON, ANTOINETTE: *Hawaiian Tapestry*, Harper & Brothers, New York.

Chapter 17. Alaska, Land of Tomorrow

ALBEE, WILLIAM: *Kanguk, A Boy of Bering Strait*, Little, Brown & Company, Boston.

CLARK, HENRY W.: *History of Alaska*, The Macmillan Company, New York.

FRANCK, HARRY A.: *Lure of Alaska*, Frederick A. Stokes Company, New York.

GARBER, CLARK M.: *Stories and Legends of the Bering Strait Eskimos*, Christopher House, Boston.

LAYTHA, EDGAR: *North Again for Gold*, Frederick A. Stokes Company, New York.

QUIETT, GLENN C.: *Pay Dirt: A Panorama of American Gold Rushes*, D. Appleton-Century Company, Inc., New York.

STEFANSSON, VILHJALMUR: *My Life with the Eskimos*, The Macmillan Company, New York.

WEYER, EDWARD M., JR.: *Eskimos*, Yale University Press, New Haven.

Chapter 18. Quest for the Northwest Passage

AMERICAN GEOGRAPHICAL SOCIETY: *Leif Ericson's Voyages in the Year* 1000, American Geographical Society, Research Series.

AMUNDSEN, ROALD: *The Northwest Passage*, Constable & Company, Ltd., London.

BRONTMAN, LAZAR: *On Top of the World*, Covici, Friede, Inc., New York.

BURPEE, LAWRENCE J.: *Search for the Western Sea*, Rivers, Ltd., London, England.

ELLSWORTH, LINCOLN: *Beyond Horizons*, Doubleday, Doran & Company, Inc., New York.

MIRSKY, JEANNETTE: *To the North, The Story of Arctic Exploration*, Viking Press, Inc., New York.

OWEN, RUTH BRYAN: *Leaves from a Greenland Diary*, Dodd, Mead & Company, Inc., New York.

SEIDENFADEN, GUNNAR: *Modern Arctic Exploration*, Hale, Cushman & Flint, Inc., Boston.

TRAILL, H. D.: *Life of Sir John Franklin*, Frederick A. Stokes Company, New York.

Chapter 19.   Castles of Dreams in New France

AVERILL, ESTHER: *Voyage of Jacques Cartier*, Viking Press, Inc., New York.

GRANT, W. L.: *Voyages of Samuel de Champlain*, Charles Scribner's Sons, New York.

JACKS, L. V.: *La Salle*, Charles Scribner's Sons, New York.

JAMES, MARQUIS: *Andrew Jackson: The Border Captain*, Bobbs-Merrill Company, Indianapolis.

SAXON, LYLE: *Father Mississippi*, D. Appleton-Century Company, Inc., New York.

THWAITES, REUBEN S.: *Jesuit Relations*, Albert & Charles Boni, Inc., New York.

Chapter 20.   Wealth in the Wilderness

ALTER, J. C.: *James Bridger*, Charles Scribner's Sons, New York.

DALGLIESH, ALICE, and LOIS MALOY: *James Bridger*, Charles Scribner's Sons, New York.

FURLONG, PHILIP J.: *Our Pioneers and Patriots*, W. H. Sadlier, New York.

LARPENTEUR, CHARLES: *Forty Years a Fur Trader*, The Lakeside Press Chicago.

MACKAY, DOUGLAS: *Honourable Company*, Tudor Publishing Co., New York.

NUTE, GRACE LEE: *The Voyageur*, D. Appleton-Century Company, Inc., New York.

PORTER, K. W.: *John Jacob Astor*, Harvard University Press, Cambridge, Mass.

SETON, ERNEST THOMPSON: *Wild Animals at Home*, Grosset & Dunlap, Inc., New York.

Chapter 21. People of the Morning Light

ASHLEY, CLIFFORD W.: *The Yankee Whaler*, Houghton Mifflin Company, Boston.

CHATTERTON, E. K.: *Whalers and Whaling*, J. B. Lippincott Company, Philadelphia.

DALGLIESH, ALICE, and LOIS MALOY: *America Begins*, Charles Scribner's Sons, New York.

FURLONG, PHILIP J.: *Our Pioneers and Patriots*, W. H. Sadlier, New York.

HARTMAN, GERTRUDE: *These United States*, The Macmillan Company, New York.

HOLBROOK, STEWART H.: *Ethan Allen*, The Macmillan Company, New York.

———: *Holy Old Mackinaw*, The Macmillan Company, New York.

INNIS, HAROLD A.: *Cod Fisheries*, Yale University Press, New Haven.

LODGE, HENRY CABOT: *George Washington* (Vols. 1 and 2), Houghton Mifflin Company, Boston.

MELVILLE, HERMAN: *Moby Dick*, Garden City Publishing Company, Inc., New York.

MITCHELL, LUCY SPRAGUE: *North America*, The Macmillan Company, New York.

RIGGS, DIONIS COFFIN: *From Off Island*, Whittlesey House, McGraw-Hill Book Company, Inc., New York.

Chapter 22. Settlers of the Southern Seaboard

DRAKE, SAMUEL ADAMS: *Making of Virginia and the Middle Colonies*, Charles Scribner's Sons, New York.

DWIGHT, ALLAN: *The First Virginians*, Thomas Nelson & Sons, New York.

FORBES-LINDSAY, C. H.: *Captain John Smith*, J. B. Lippincott Company, Philadelphia.

KELLY, MARGARET D.: *Story of Sir Walter Raleigh*, E. P. Dutton & Company, Inc., New York.

NILES, BLAIR: *The James*, Farrar & Rinehart, Inc., New York.

VAN DYKE, PAUL: *George Washington: The Son of His Country*, (1732–1775), Charles Scribner's Sons, New York.

Chapter 23. Red Men and Blue Grass

BARSTOW, CHARLES L.: *Explorers and Settlers*, D. Appleton-Century Company, Inc., New York.

BRUCE, H. ADDINGTON: *Daniel Boone and the Wilderness Road*, The Macmillan Company, New York.

CROUSE, D. E.: *The Ohio Gateway*, Charles Scribner's Sons, New York.

DORRANCE, WARD ALLISON: *Where the Rivers Meet*, Charles Scribner's Sons, New York.

KNOOP, FAITH YINGLING: *Quest of the Cavaliers*, Longmans, Green & Company, New York.

LENDER, CHARLES F.: *Down the Ohio with Clark*, The Thomas Y. Crowell Company, New York.

SAXON, LYLE: *Father Mississippi*, D. Appleton-Century Company, Inc., New York.

TWAIN, MARK: *Life on the Mississippi*, Harper & Brothers, New York.

Chapter 24.   *The Lone Star Rises*

BARRETT, S. M.: *Geronimo's Story of His Life*, Duffield & Co., New York.

BENSON, ALLEN L.: *The Story of Geology*, Farrar & Rinehart, Inc., New York.

DRIGGS, HOWARD R., and SARAH S. KING: *Rise of the Lone Star*, Frederick A. Stokes Company, New York.

FERGUSSON, ERNA: *Our Southwest*, Alfred A. Knopf, Inc., New York.

HANIGHEN, F. C.: *Santa Anna, the Napoleon of the West*, Coward-McCann, Inc., New York.

HOUGH, EMERSON: *Story of the Cowboy*, D. Appleton-Century Company, Inc., New York.

POWELL, JOHN WESLEY: *Through the Grand Canyon*, The Macmillan Company, New York.

WISSLER, CLARK: *Indians of the United States*, Doubleday, Doran & Company, Inc., New York.

Chapter 25.   *Gateway to the Setting Sun*

ATHERTON, GERTRUDE: *Story of California*, Blue Ribbon Books, Inc., New York.

BANCROFT, H. H.: *History of the Pacific States*, Bancroft, Whitney Co., San Francisco.

CLARK, DAN E.: *The West in American History*, The Thomas Y. Crowell Company, New York.

FISHER, VARDIS: *City of Illusion*, Harper & Brothers, New York.

HEBARD, GRACE A. R.: *Sacajawea*, Arthur H. Clark Company, Glendale, Calif.

HOLBROOK, STEWART H.: *Holy Old Mackinaw*, The Macmillan Company, New York.

METCALF, C. L., and W. P. FLINT: *Destructive and Useful Insects*, McGraw-Hill Book Company, Inc., New York.

NEVINS, ALLAN: *Fremont, Pathmarker of the West*, D. Appleton-Century, Company, Inc., New York.

PARKMAN, FRANCIS: *The Oregon Trail*, Little, Brown & Company, Boston.

VESTAL, STANLEY: *Kit Carson*, Houghton Mifflin Company, Boston.

Chapter 26. Wheels Roll Westward

BRANCH, E. DOUGLAS: *The Cowboy and His Interpreters*, D. Appleton-Century Company, Inc., New York.

BRIDGES, ALEXANDER W.: *Great Canals*, Thomas Nelson & Sons, New York.

BURT, STRUTHERS: *Powder River*, Farrar & Rinehart, Inc., New York.

CLARK, WILLIAM H.: *Railroads and Rivers*, L. C. Page & Co., Boston.

COLLINS, FRANCIS A.: *Our Harbors and Inland Waterways*, D. Appleton-Century Company, Inc., New York.

CROWTHERS, J. G.: *Famous American Men of Science*, W. W. Norton & Company, Inc., New York.

DRIGGS, HOWARD R.: *The Pony Express Goes Through*, Frederick A. Stokes Company, New York.

EDMONDS, W. D.: *Chad Hanna*, Little, Brown & Company, Boston.

GIDDENS, PAUL H.: *The Birth of the Oil Industry*, The Macmillan Company, New York.

HALL, CHARLES GILBERT: *Through by Rail*, The Macmillan Company, New York.

HARLOW, ALVIN F.: *Old Towpaths*, D. Appleton-Century Company, Inc., New York.

———: *When Horses Pulled Boats*, Thomas Nelson & Sons, New York.

QUIETT, GLENN C.: *They Built the West*, D. Appleton-Century Company, Inc., New York.

RECK, FRANKLIN M.: *Romance of American Transportation*, The Thomas Y. Crowell Company, New York.

THOMPSON, SLASON: *Short History of American Railways*, D. Appleton-Century Company, Inc., New York.

TYLER, DAVID BUDLONG: *Steam Conquers the Atlantic*, D. Appleton-Century Company, Inc., New York.

Index

~~~